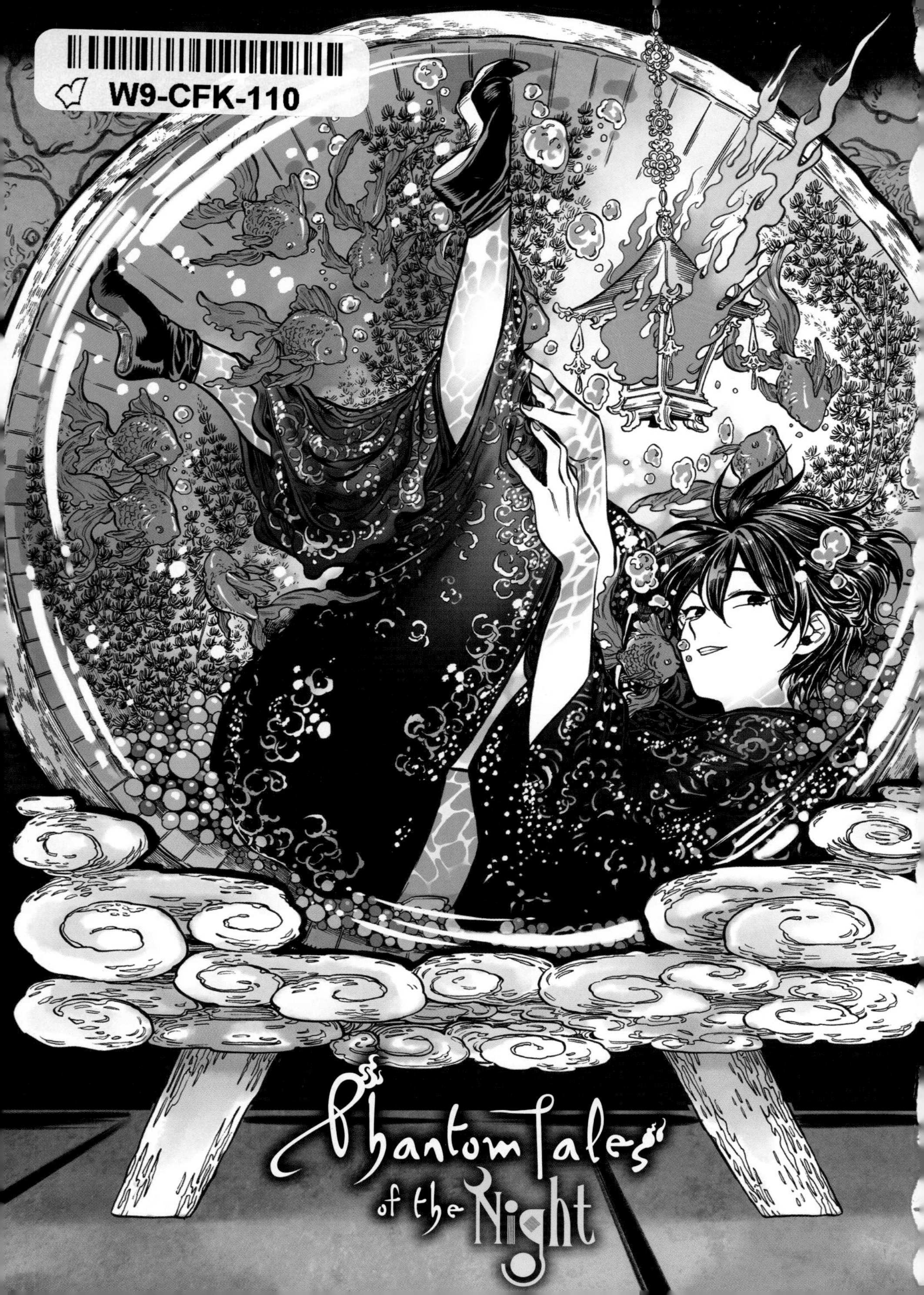
Phantom Tales
of the Night

CONTENTS

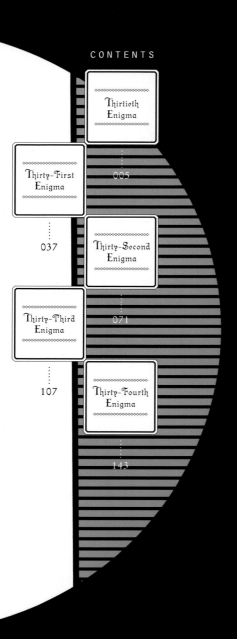

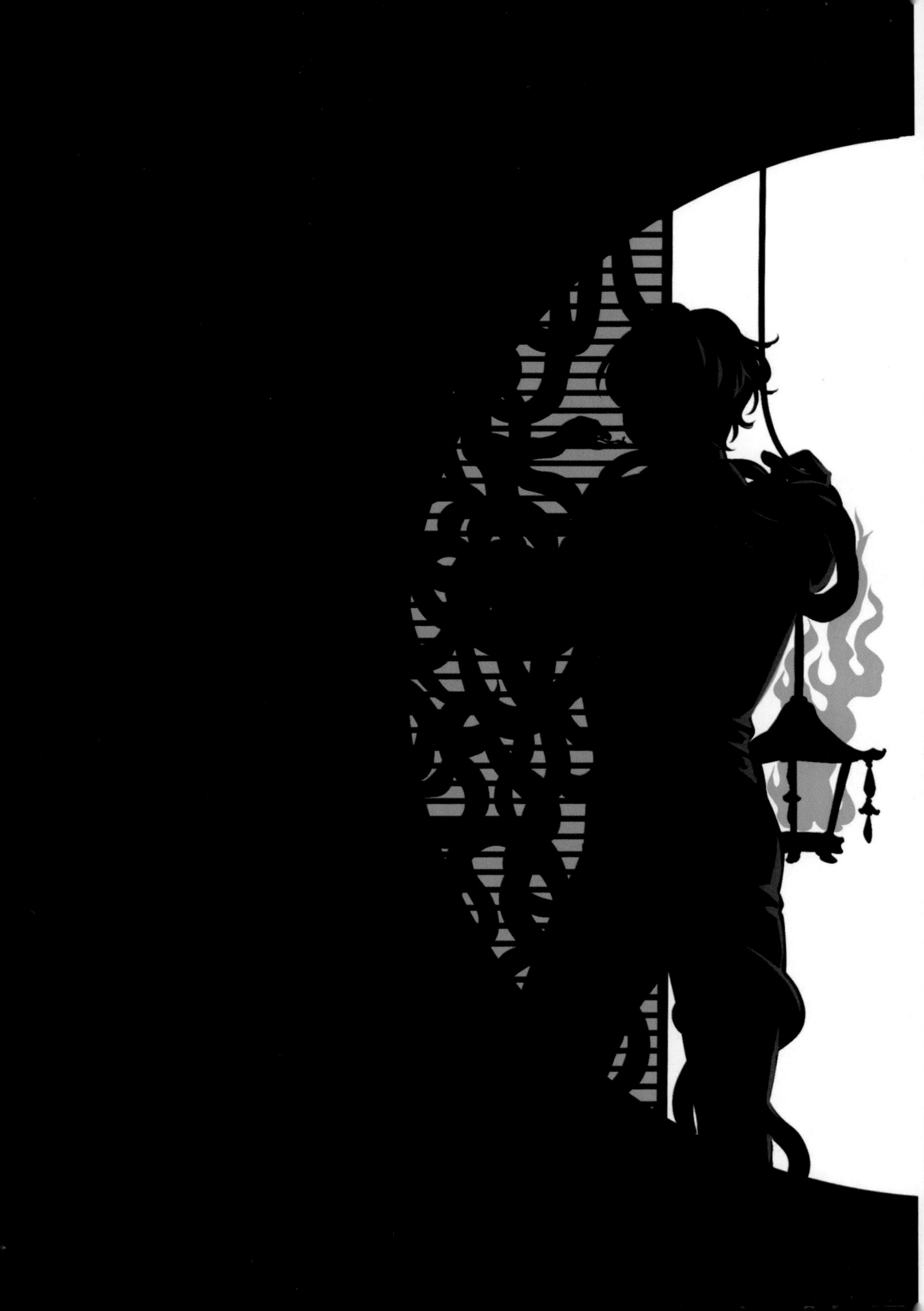

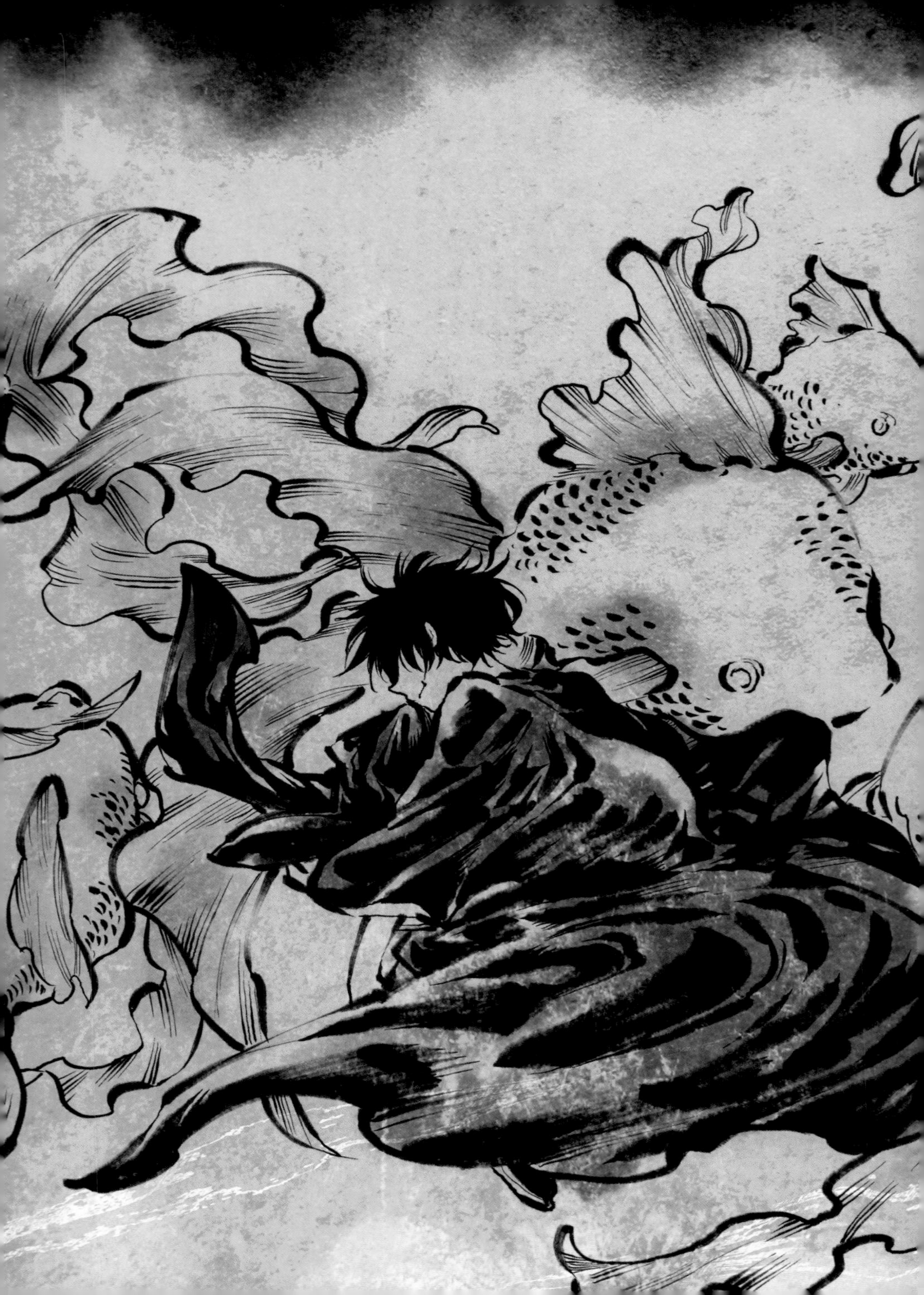

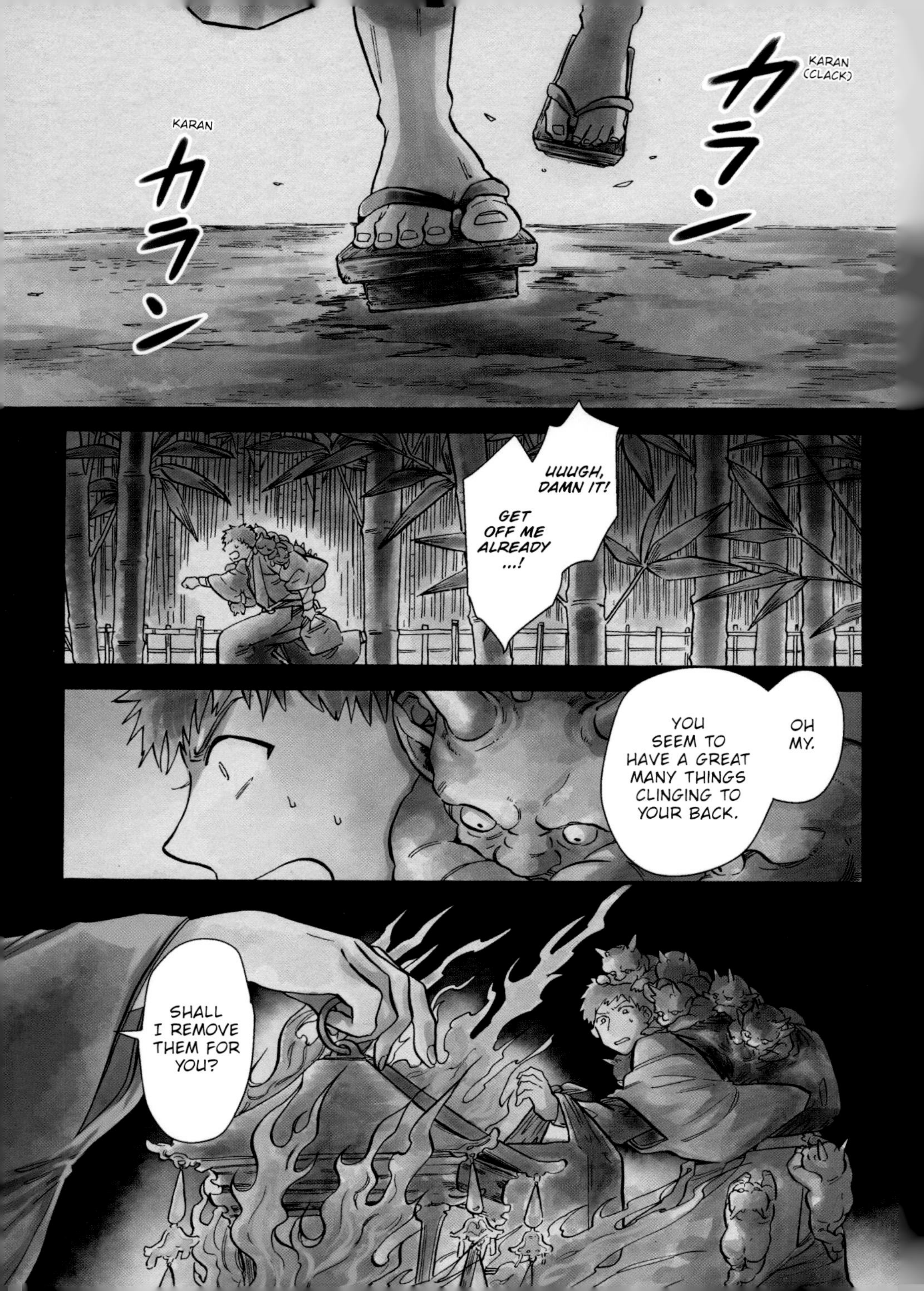

カラン
KARAN (CLACK)
カラン
KARAN
UUUGH, DAMN IT!
GET OFF ME ALREADY ...!
OH MY.
YOU SEEM TO HAVE A GREAT MANY THINGS CLINGING TO YOUR BACK.
SHALL I REMOVE THEM FOR YOU?

7

Phantom Tales of the Night

MATSURI

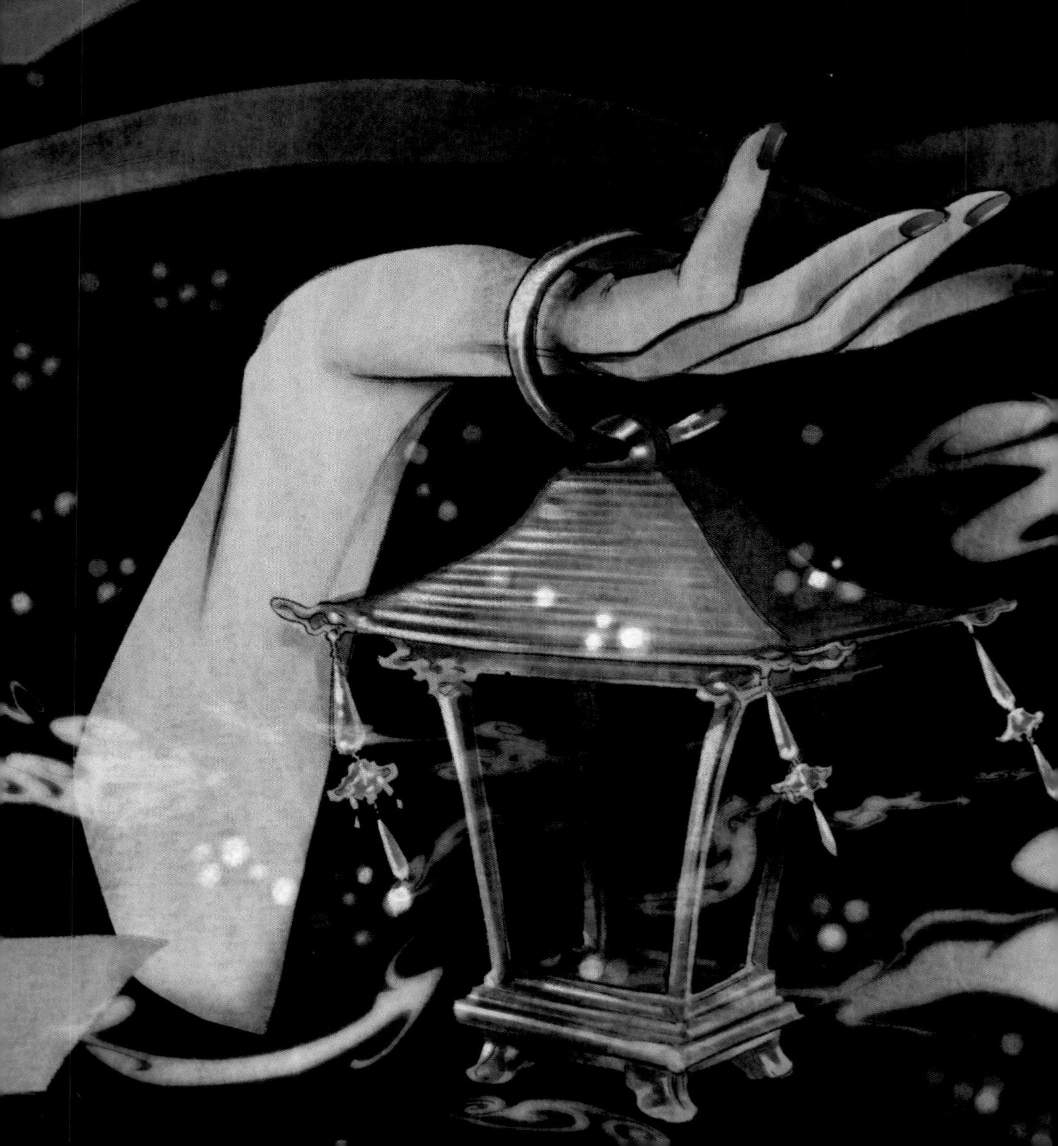

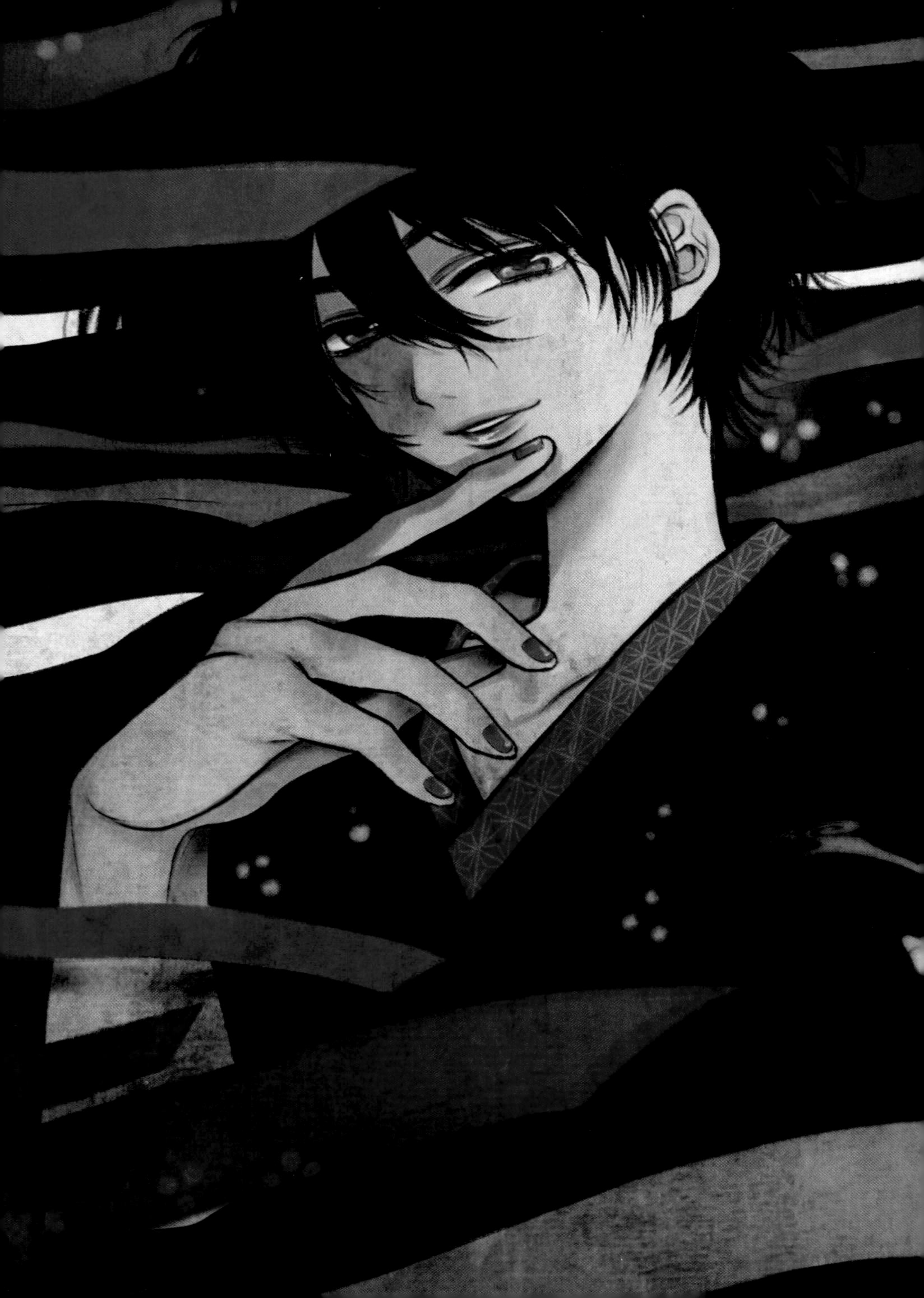

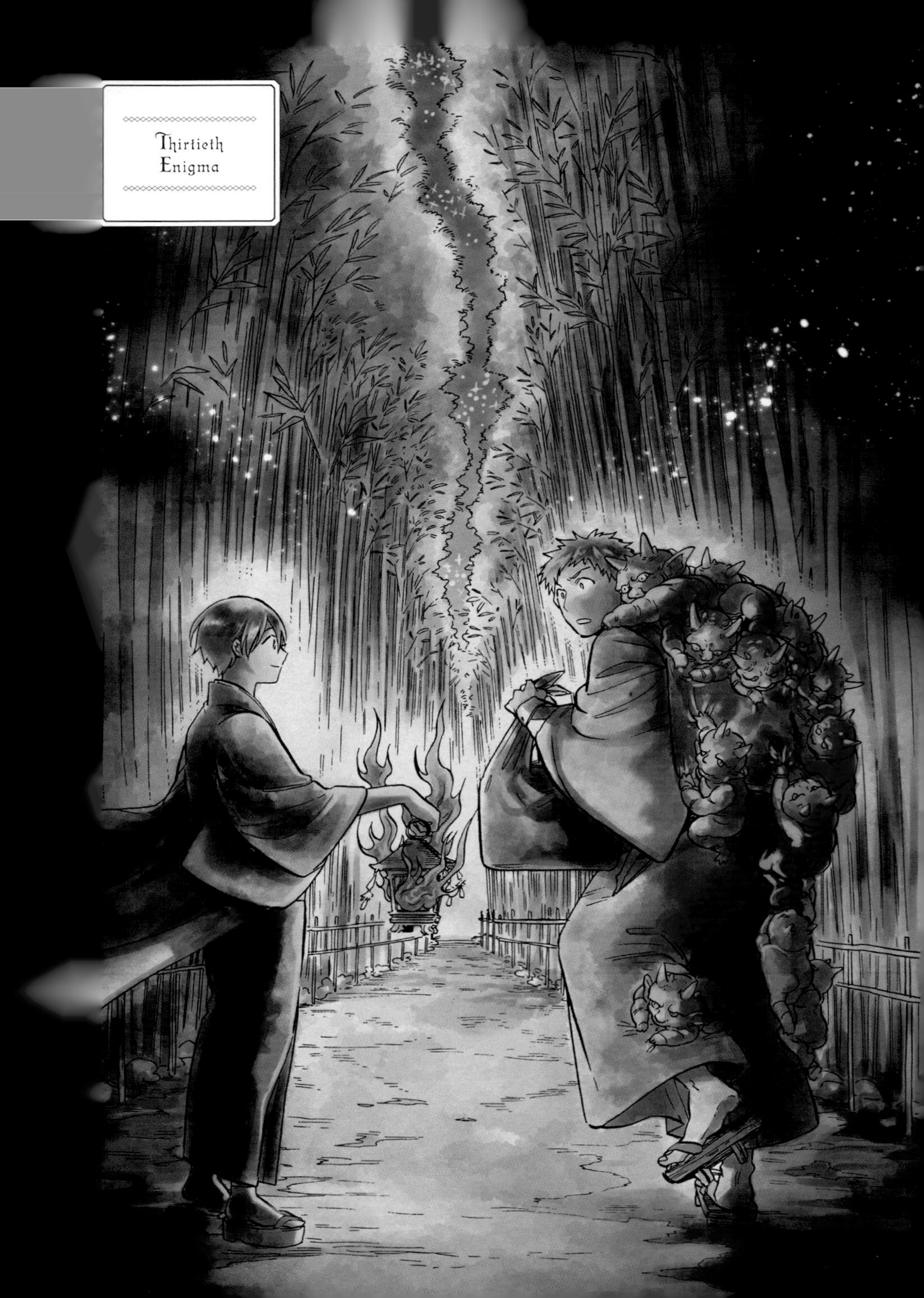
Thirtieth
Enigma

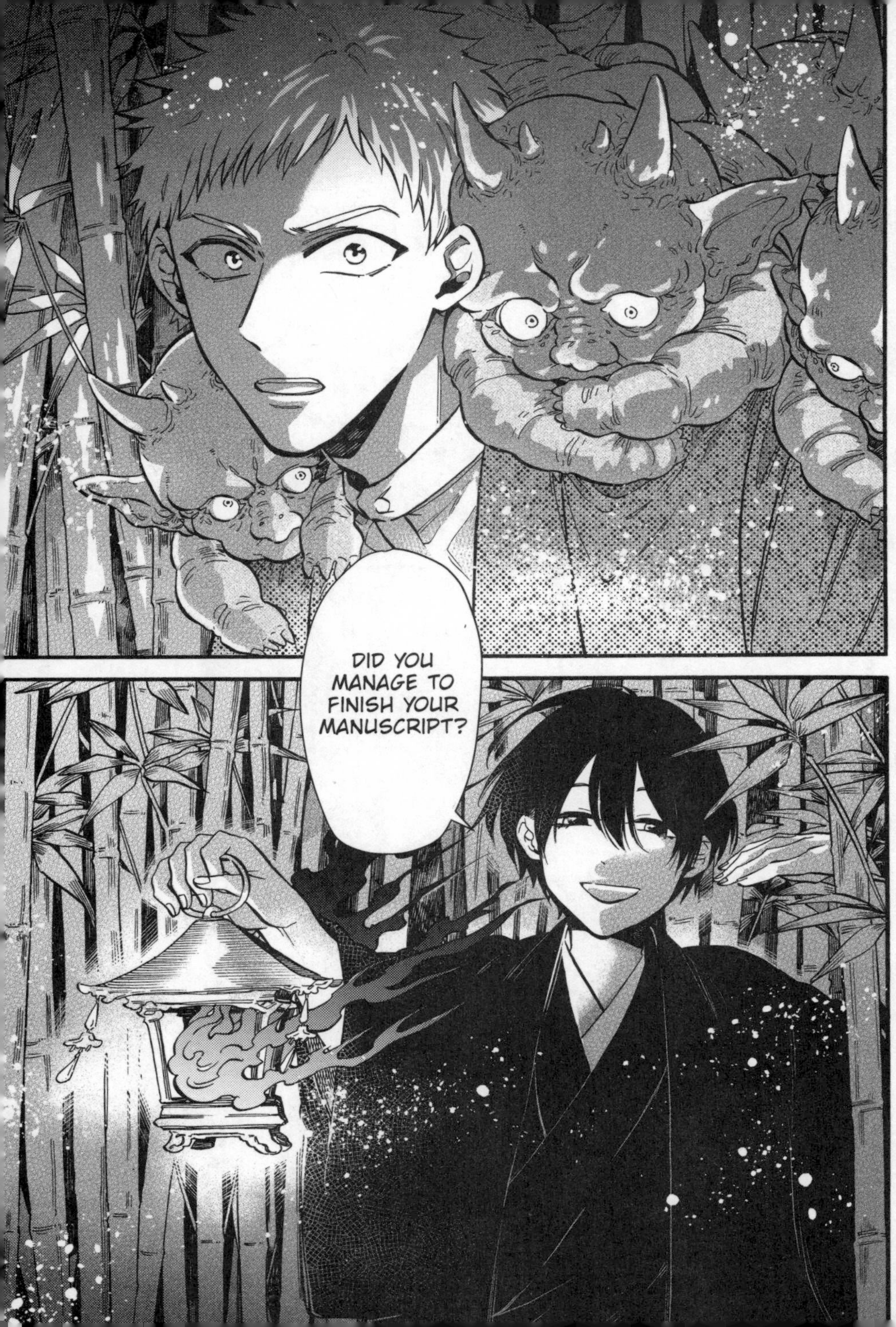
DID YOU MANAGE TO FINISH YOUR MANUSCRIPT?

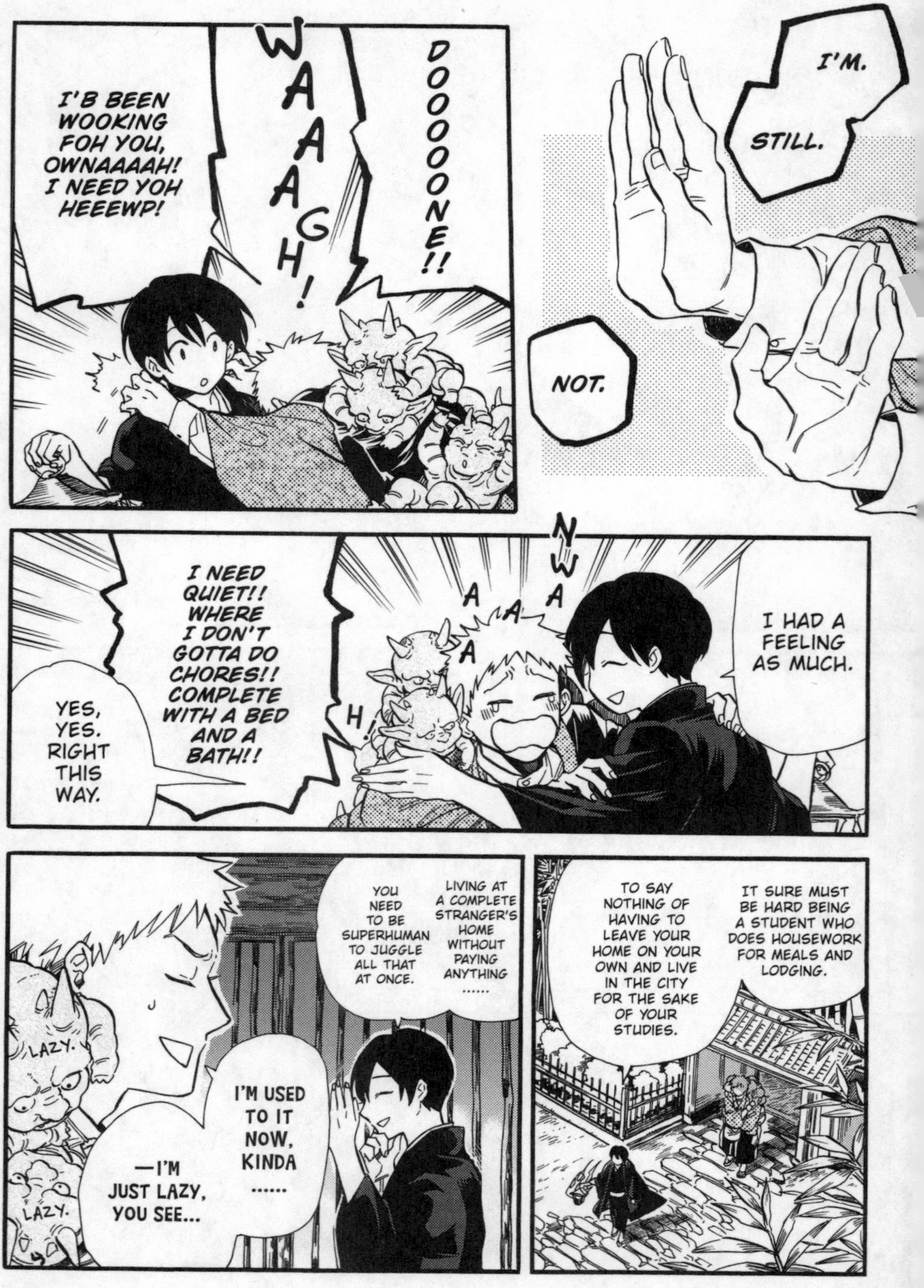
I'M.
STILL.
NOT.
DOOOOOOONE!!
WAAAAGH!
I'B BEEN WOOKING FOH YOU, OWNAAAAH! I NEED YOH HEEEWP!
I HAD A FEELING AS MUCH.
NWAAAAH!
I NEED QUIET!! WHERE I DON'T GOTTA DO CHORES!! COMPLETE WITH A BED AND A BATH!!
YES, YES. RIGHT THIS WAY.
IT SURE MUST BE HARD BEING A STUDENT WHO DOES HOUSEWORK FOR MEALS AND LODGING.
TO SAY NOTHING OF HAVING TO LEAVE YOUR HOME ON YOUR OWN AND LIVE IN THE CITY FOR THE SAKE OF YOUR STUDIES.
LIVING AT A COMPLETE STRANGER'S HOME WITHOUT PAYING ANYTHING ......
YOU NEED TO BE SUPERHUMAN TO JUGGLE ALL THAT AT ONCE.
I'M USED TO IT NOW, KINDA ......
—I'M JUST LAZY, YOU SEE...
LAZY.
LAZY.

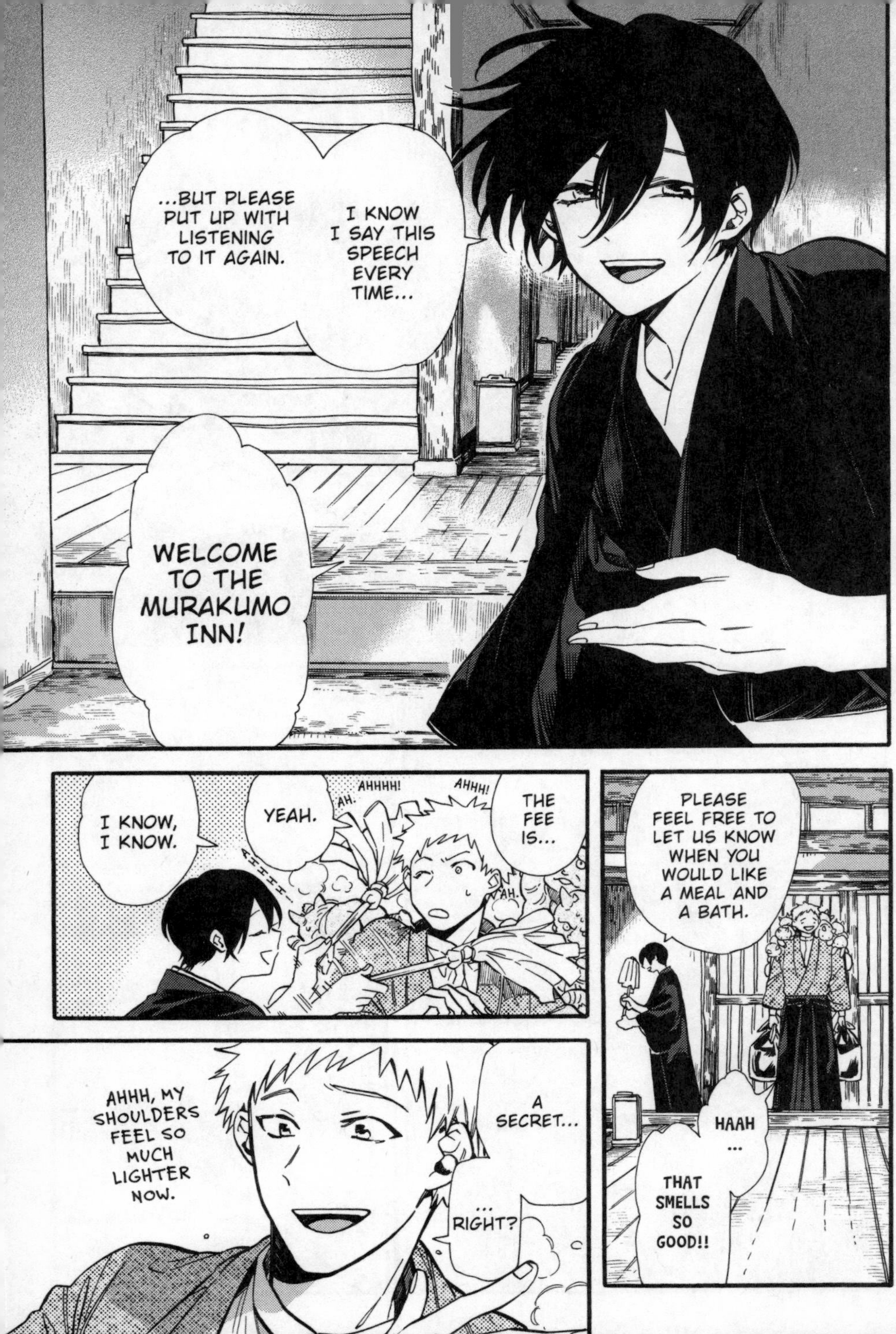
I KNOW I SAY THIS SPEECH EVERY TIME...
...BUT PLEASE PUT UP WITH LISTENING TO IT AGAIN.
WELCOME TO THE MURAKUMO INN!
PLEASE FEEL FREE TO LET US KNOW WHEN YOU WOULD LIKE A MEAL AND A BATH.
HAAH ...
THAT SMELLS SO GOOD!!
THE FEE IS...
AHHH!
AH.
AHHHH!
AH.
YEAH.
I KNOW, I KNOW.
A SECRET...
... RIGHT?
AHHH, MY SHOULDERS FEEL SO MUCH LIGHTER NOW.

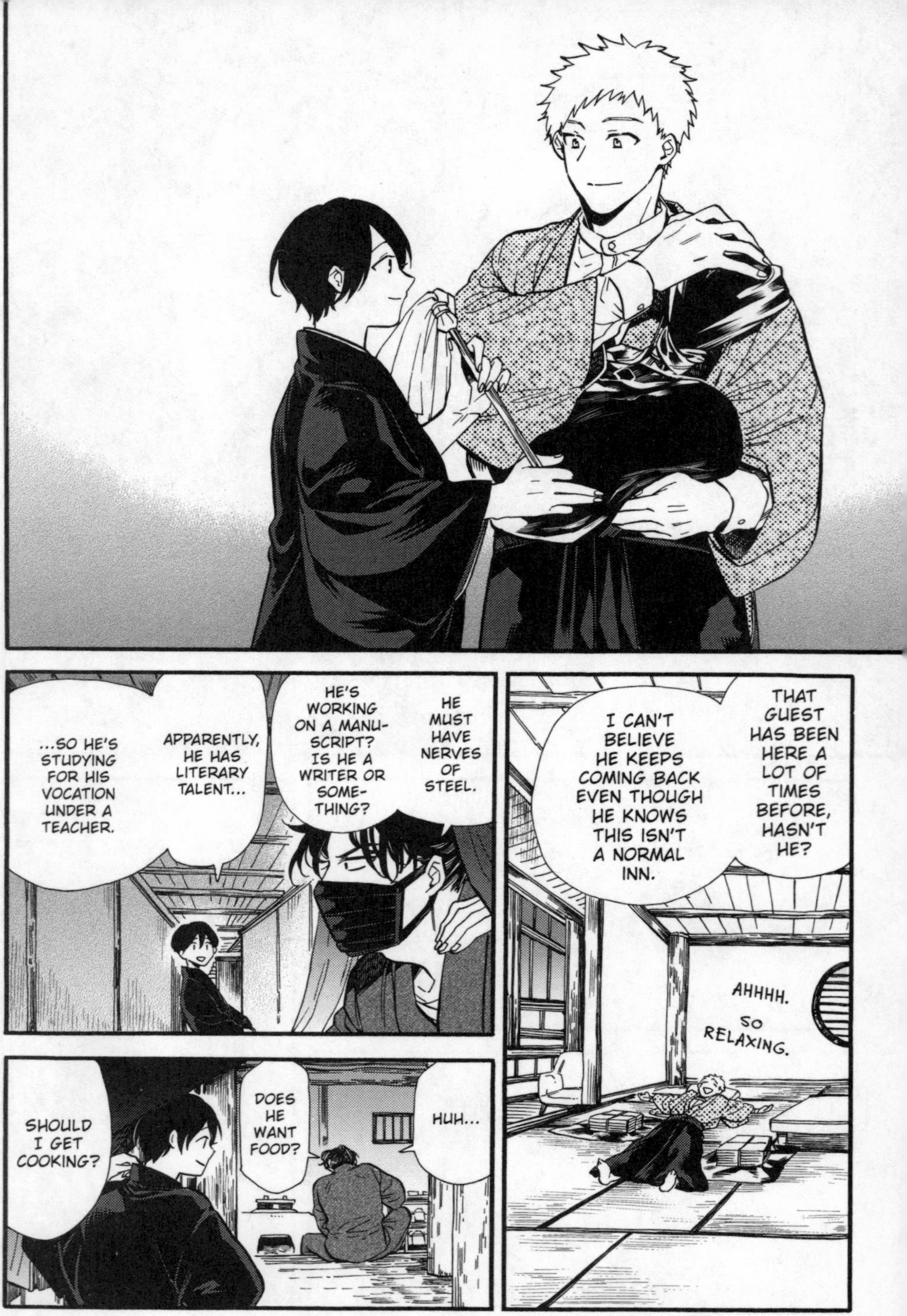
THAT GUEST HAS BEEN HERE A LOT OF TIMES BEFORE, HASN'T HE?
I CAN'T BELIEVE HE KEEPS COMING BACK EVEN THOUGH HE KNOWS THIS ISN'T A NORMAL INN.
AHHHH.
SO RELAXING.
HE MUST HAVE NERVES OF STEEL.
HE'S WORKING ON A MANU-SCRIPT? IS HE A WRITER OR SOME-THING?
APPARENTLY, HE HAS LITERARY TALENT...
...SO HE'S STUDYING FOR HIS VOCATION UNDER A TEACHER.
HUH...
DOES HE WANT FOOD?
SHOULD I GET COOKING?

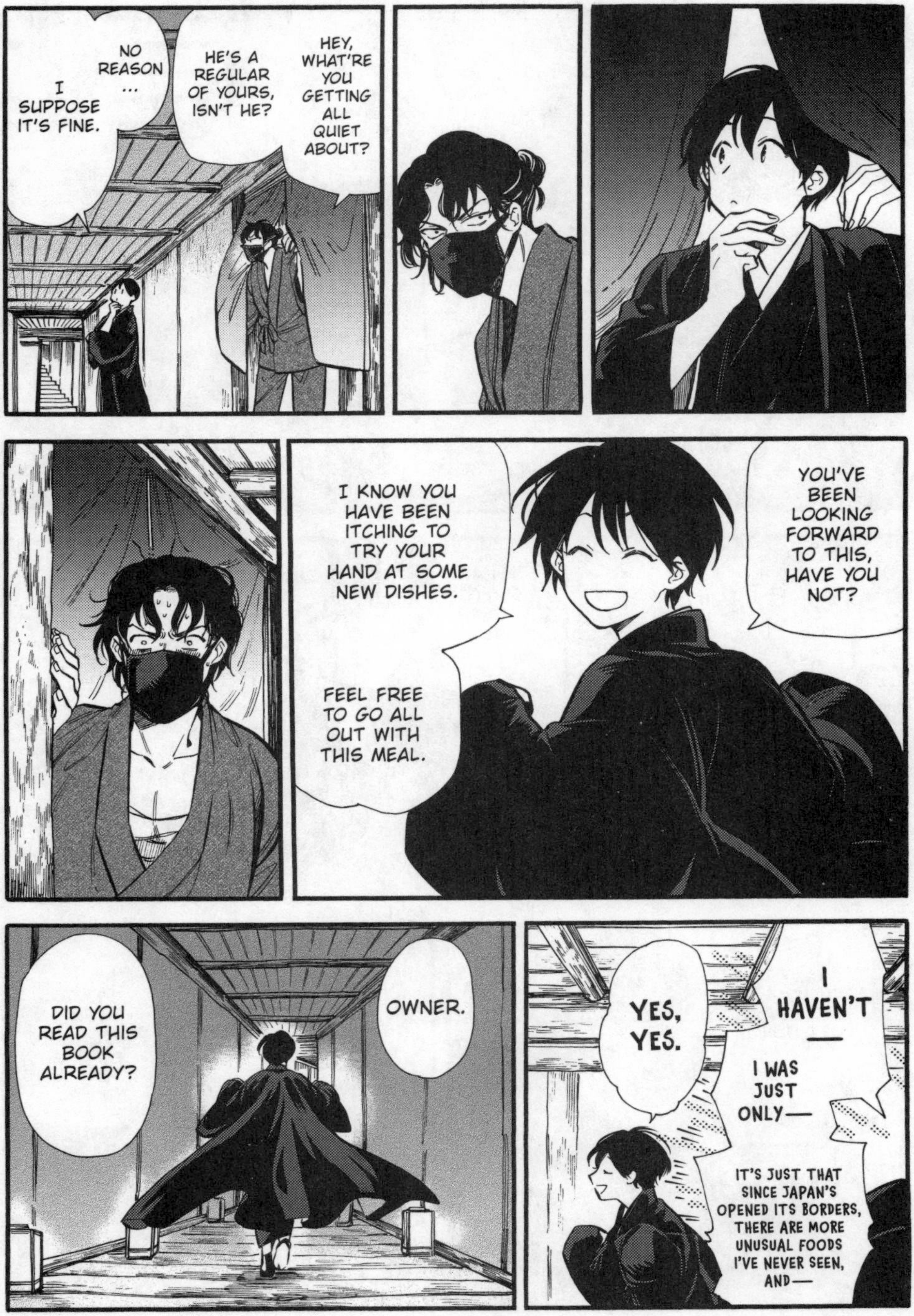
HEY, WHAT'RE YOU GETTING ALL QUIET ABOUT?
HE'S A REGULAR OF YOURS, ISN'T HE?
NO REASON ...
I SUPPOSE IT'S FINE.
YOU'VE BEEN LOOKING FORWARD TO THIS, HAVE YOU NOT?
I KNOW YOU HAVE BEEN ITCHING TO TRY YOUR HAND AT SOME NEW DISHES.
FEEL FREE TO GO ALL OUT WITH THIS MEAL.
I HAVEN'T —
YES, YES.
I WAS JUST ONLY—
IT'S JUST THAT SINCE JAPAN'S OPENED ITS BORDERS, THERE ARE MORE UNUSUAL FOODS I'VE NEVER SEEN, AND—
OWNER.
DID YOU READ THIS BOOK ALREADY?

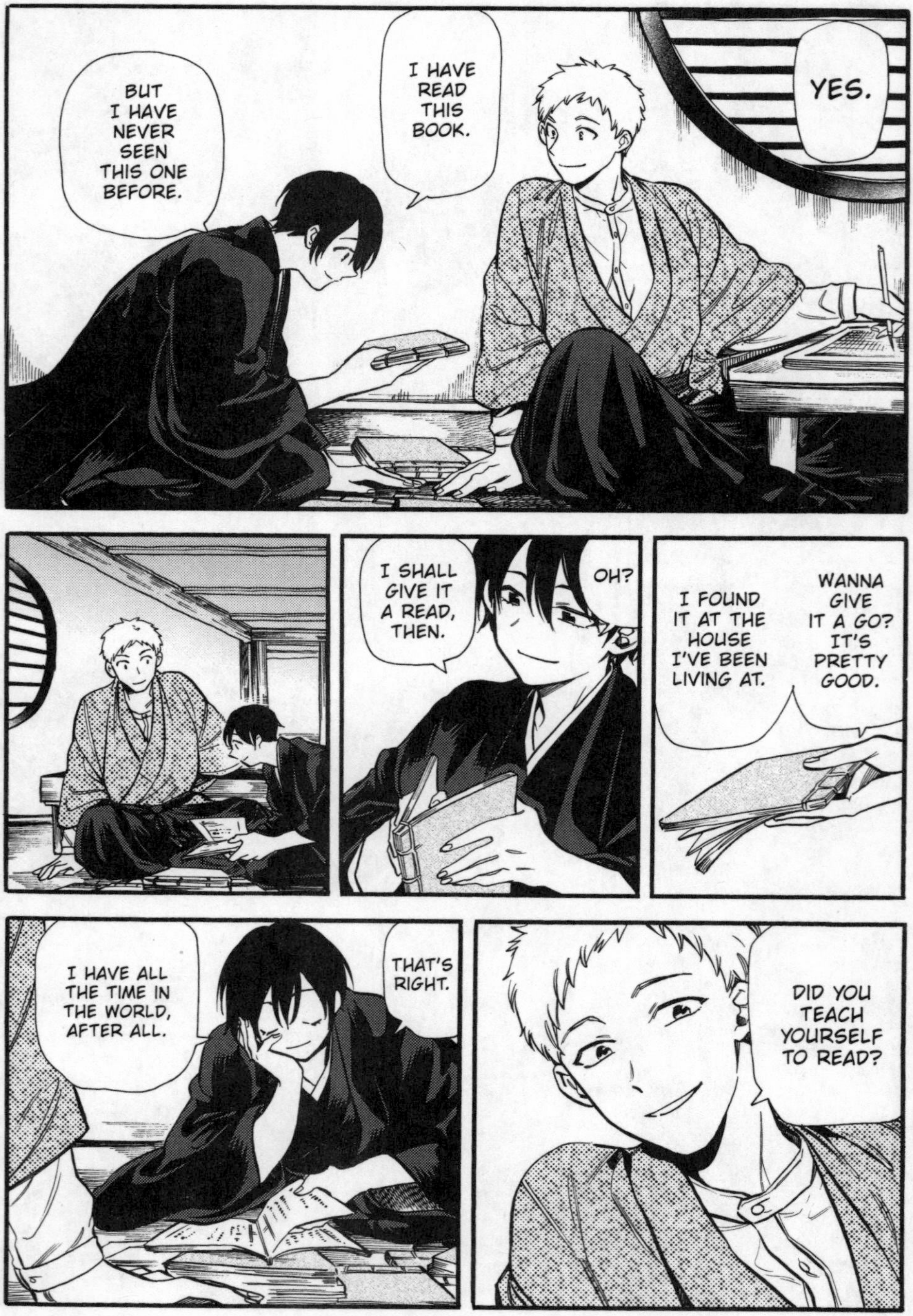
YES.
I HAVE READ THIS BOOK.
BUT I HAVE NEVER SEEN THIS ONE BEFORE.
WANNA GIVE IT A GO? IT'S PRETTY GOOD.
I FOUND IT AT THE HOUSE I'VE BEEN LIVING AT.
OH?
I SHALL GIVE IT A READ, THEN.
DID YOU TEACH YOURSELF TO READ?
THAT'S RIGHT.
I HAVE ALL THE TIME IN THE WORLD, AFTER ALL.

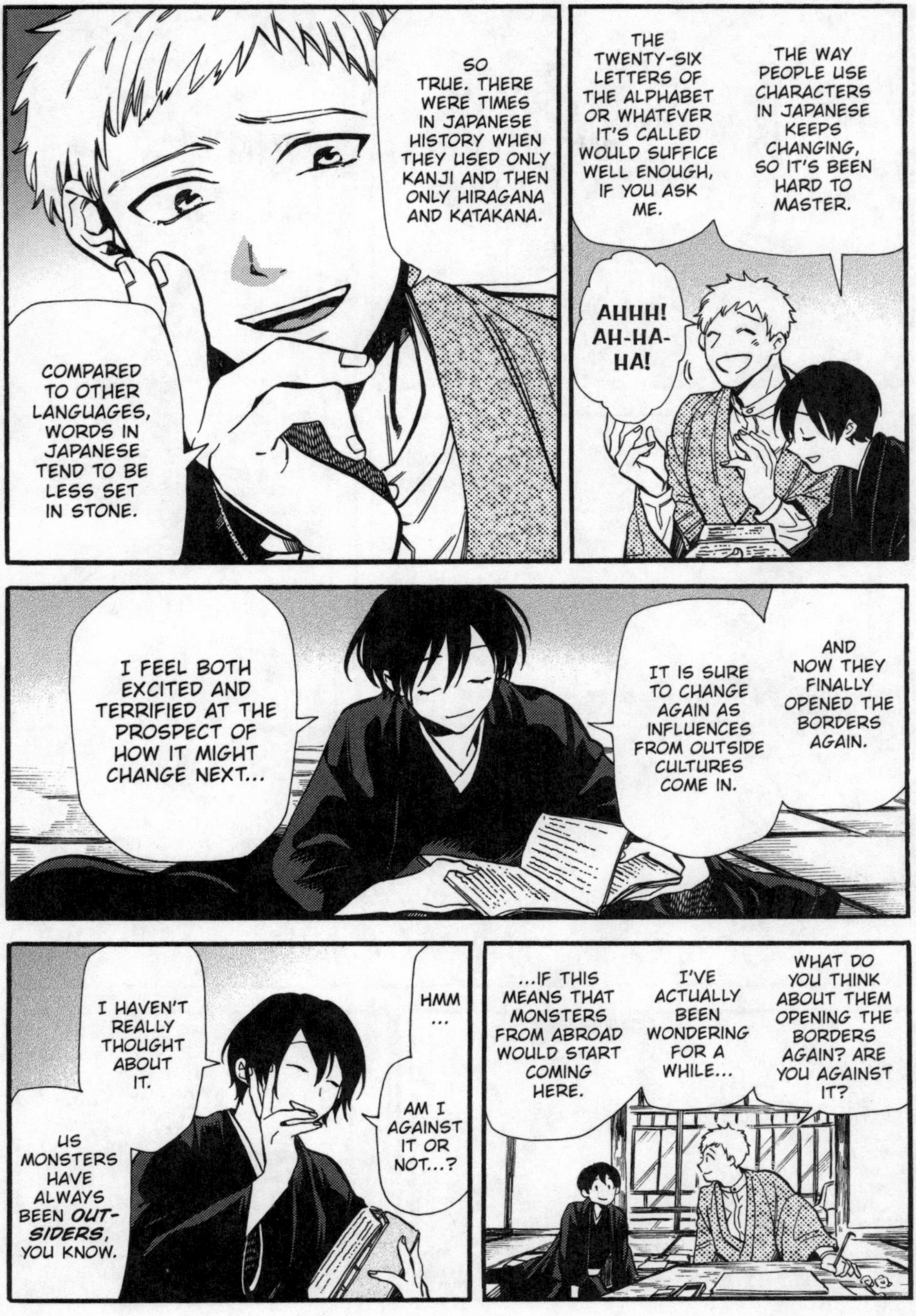
THE WAY PEOPLE USE CHARACTERS IN JAPANESE KEEPS CHANGING, SO IT'S BEEN HARD TO MASTER.
THE TWENTY-SIX LETTERS OF THE ALPHABET OR WHATEVER IT'S CALLED WOULD SUFFICE WELL ENOUGH, IF YOU ASK ME.
AHHH! AH-HA-HA!
SO TRUE. THERE WERE TIMES IN JAPANESE HISTORY WHEN THEY USED ONLY KANJI AND THEN ONLY HIRAGANA AND KATAKANA.
COMPARED TO OTHER LANGUAGES, WORDS IN JAPANESE TEND TO BE LESS SET IN STONE.
AND NOW THEY FINALLY OPENED THE BORDERS AGAIN.
IT IS SURE TO CHANGE AGAIN AS INFLUENCES FROM OUTSIDE CULTURES COME IN.
I FEEL BOTH EXCITED AND TERRIFIED AT THE PROSPECT OF HOW IT MIGHT CHANGE NEXT...
WHAT DO YOU THINK ABOUT THEM OPENING THE BORDERS AGAIN? ARE YOU AGAINST IT?
I'VE ACTUALLY BEEN WONDERING FOR A WHILE...
...IF THIS MEANS THAT MONSTERS FROM ABROAD WOULD START COMING HERE.
HMM ...
AM I AGAINST IT OR NOT...?
I HAVEN'T REALLY THOUGHT ABOUT IT.
US MONSTERS HAVE ALWAYS BEEN ***OUT-SIDERS***, YOU KNOW.

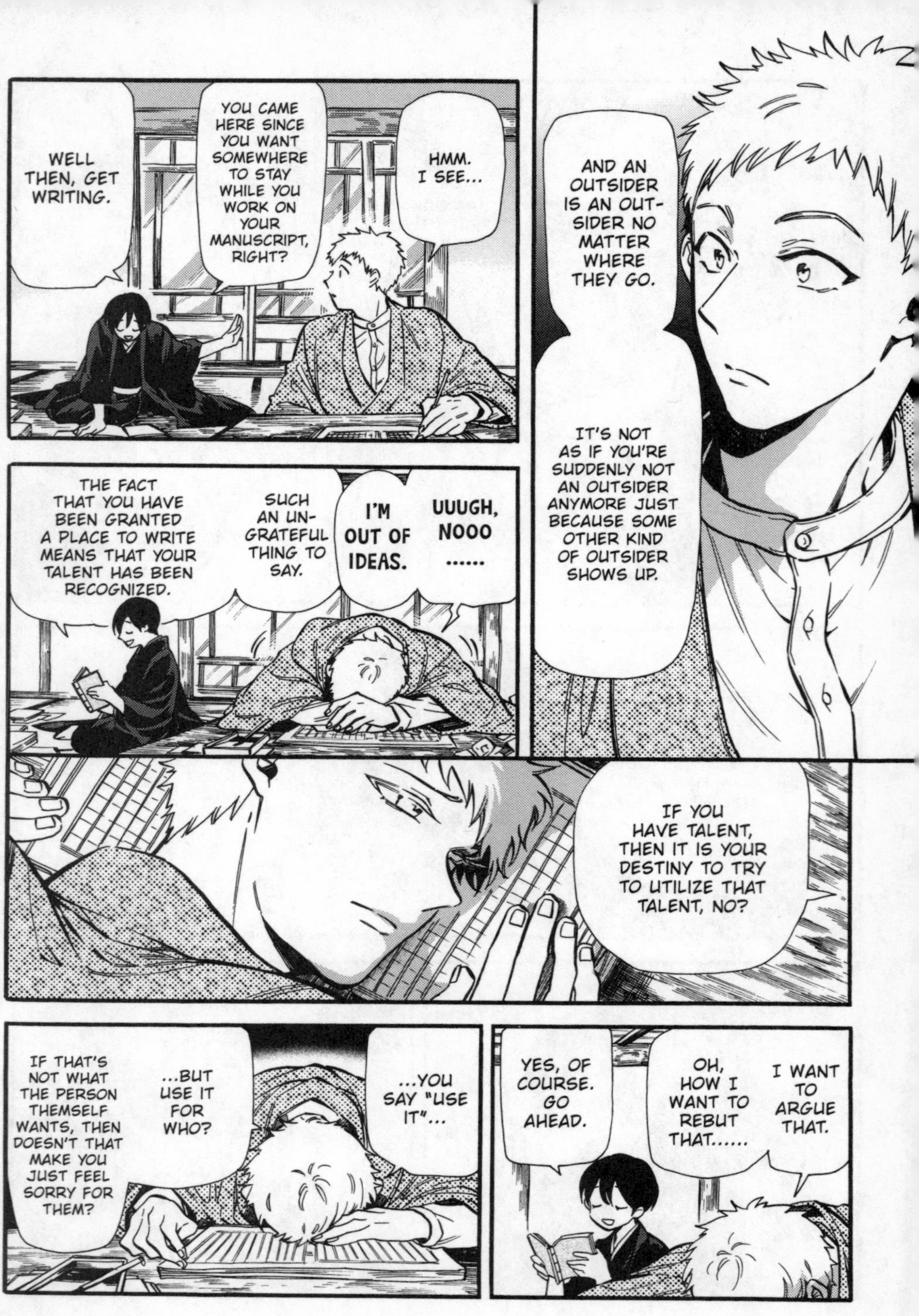
AND AN OUTSIDER IS AN OUTSIDER NO MATTER WHERE THEY GO.
IT'S NOT AS IF YOU'RE SUDDENLY NOT AN OUTSIDER ANYMORE JUST BECAUSE SOME OTHER KIND OF OUTSIDER SHOWS UP.
HMM. I SEE...
YOU CAME HERE SINCE YOU WANT SOMEWHERE TO STAY WHILE YOU WORK ON YOUR MANUSCRIPT, RIGHT?
WELL THEN, GET WRITING.
UUUGH, NOOO ......
I'M OUT OF IDEAS.
SUCH AN UNGRATEFUL THING TO SAY.
THE FACT THAT YOU HAVE BEEN GRANTED A PLACE TO WRITE MEANS THAT YOUR TALENT HAS BEEN RECOGNIZED.
IF YOU HAVE TALENT, THEN IT IS YOUR DESTINY TO TRY TO UTILIZE THAT TALENT, NO?
I WANT TO ARGUE THAT.
OH, HOW I WANT TO REBUT THAT......
YES, OF COURSE. GO AHEAD.
...YOU SAY "USE IT"...
...BUT USE IT FOR WHO?
IF THAT'S NOT WHAT THE PERSON THEMSELF WANTS, THEN DOESN'T THAT MAKE YOU JUST FEEL SORRY FOR THEM?

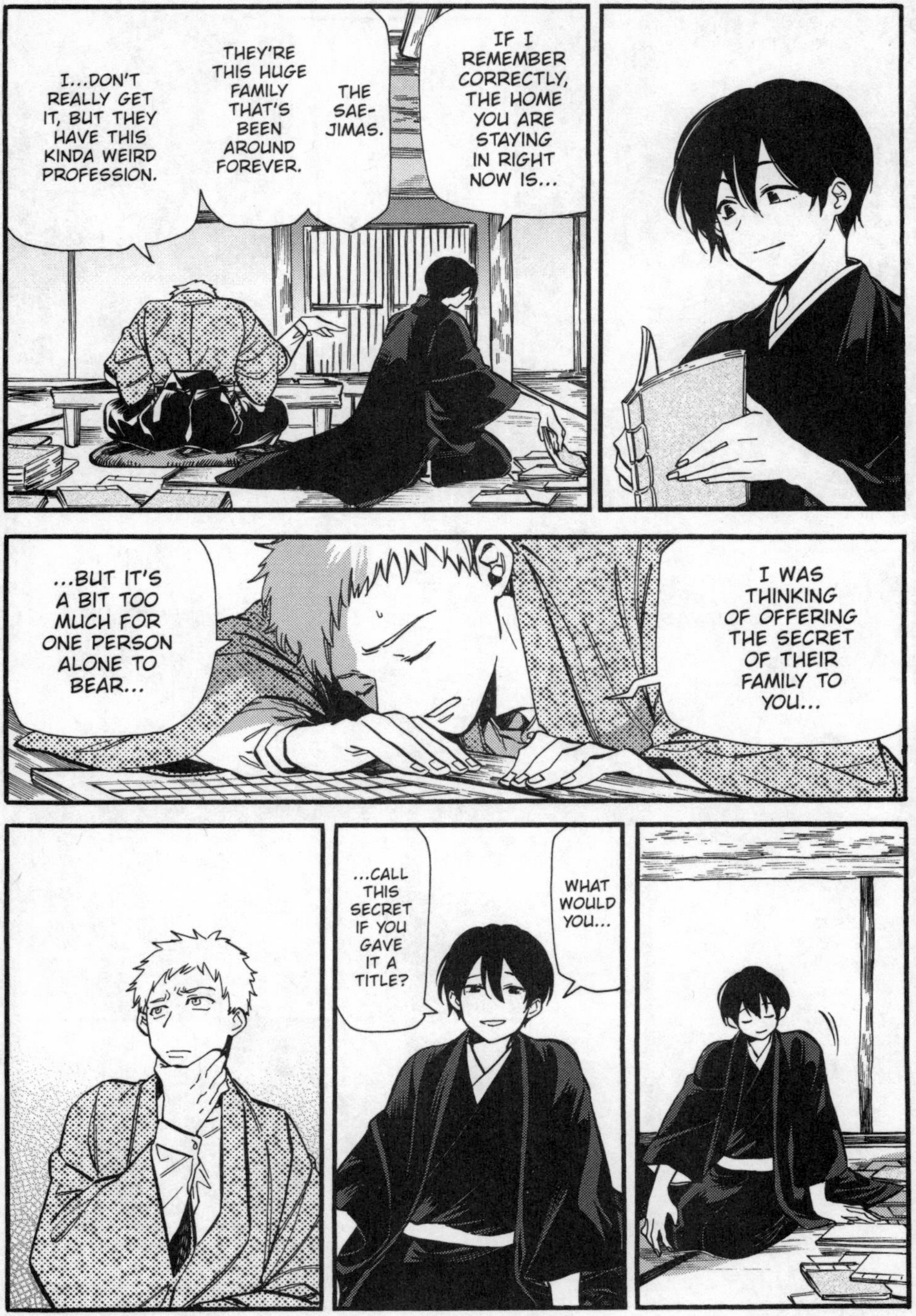
IF I REMEMBER CORRECTLY, THE HOME YOU ARE STAYING IN RIGHT NOW IS...
THE SAE-JIMAS.
THEY'RE THIS HUGE FAMILY THAT'S BEEN AROUND FOREVER.
I...DON'T REALLY GET IT, BUT THEY HAVE THIS KINDA WEIRD PROFESSION.
I WAS THINKING OF OFFERING THE SECRET OF THEIR FAMILY TO YOU...
...BUT IT'S A BIT TOO MUCH FOR ONE PERSON ALONE TO BEAR...
WHAT WOULD YOU...
...CALL THIS SECRET IF YOU GAVE IT A TITLE?

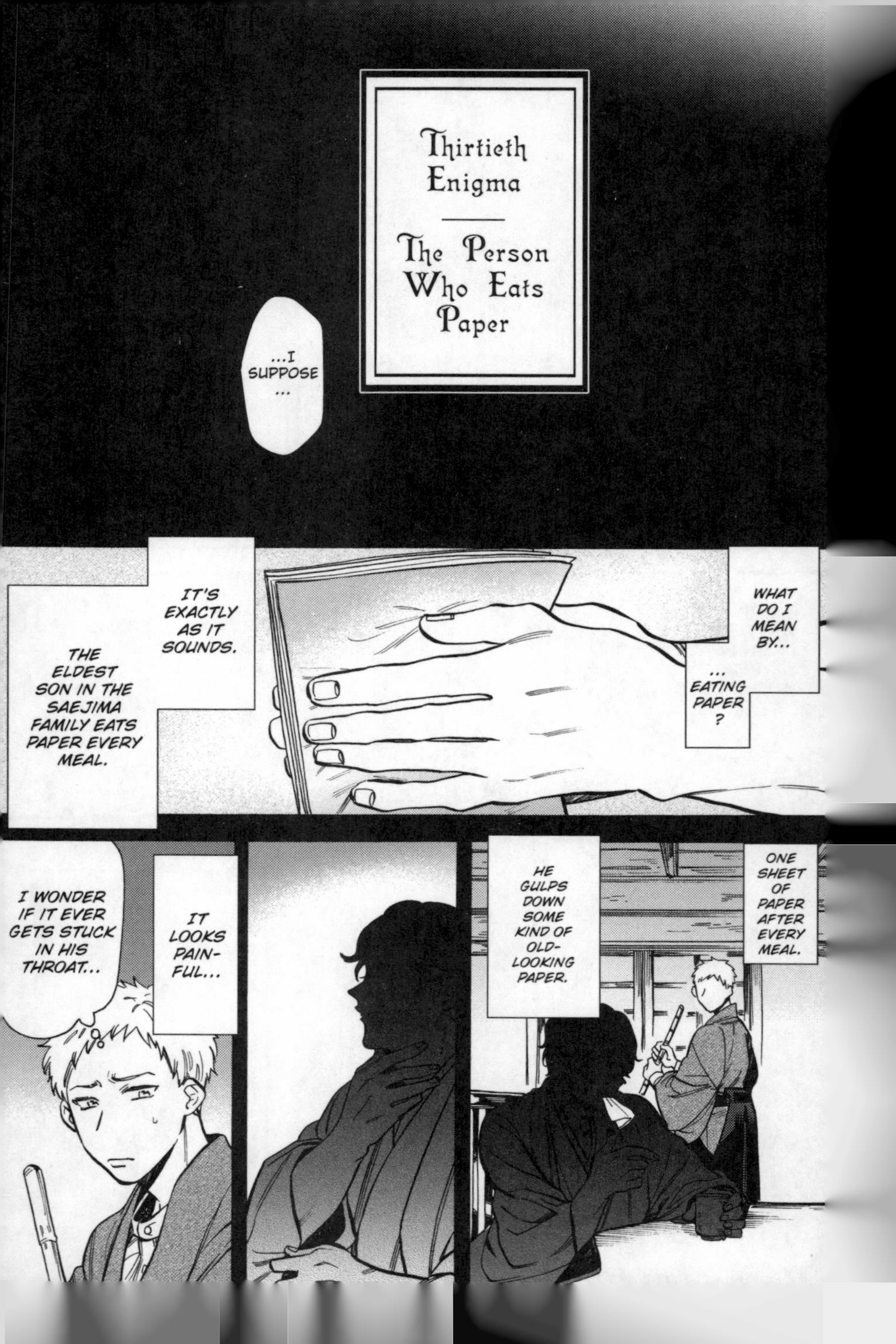
Thirtieth Enigma
The Person Who Eats Paper
...I SUPPOSE...
WHAT DO I MEAN BY...
...EATING PAPER?
IT'S EXACTLY AS IT SOUNDS.
THE ELDEST SON IN THE SAEJIMA FAMILY EATS PAPER EVERY MEAL.
ONE SHEET OF PAPER AFTER EVERY MEAL.
HE GULPS DOWN SOME KIND OF OLD-LOOKING PAPER.
IT LOOKS PAIN-FUL...
I WONDER IF IT EVER GETS STUCK IN HIS THROAT...

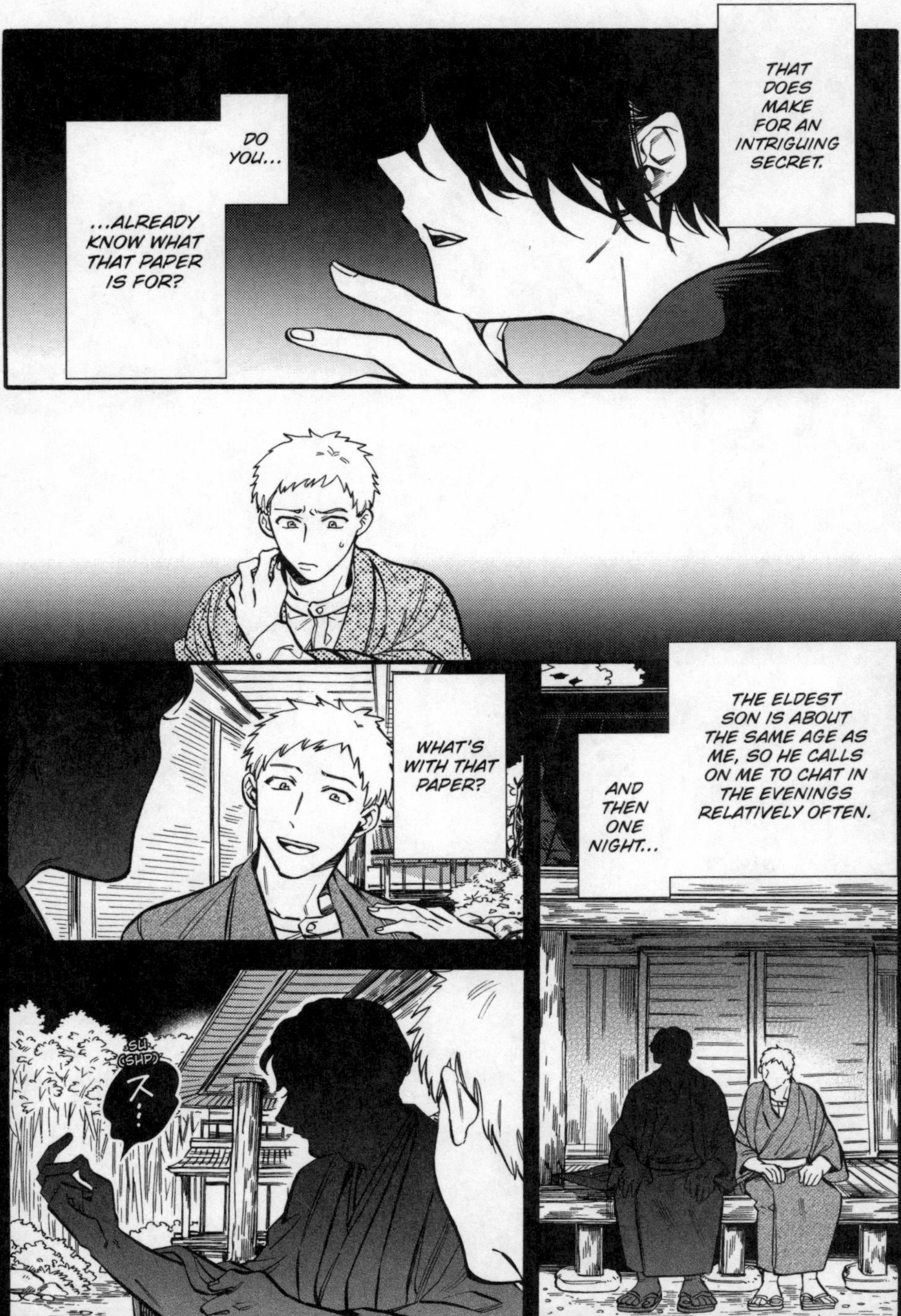
THAT DOES MAKE FOR AN INTRIGUING SECRET.
DO YOU...
...ALREADY KNOW WHAT THAT PAPER IS FOR?
THE ELDEST SON IS ABOUT THE SAME AGE AS ME, SO HE CALLS ON ME TO CHAT IN THE EVENINGS RELATIVELY OFTEN.
AND THEN ONE NIGHT...
WHAT'S WITH THAT PAPER?
SU (SHP)
ス...

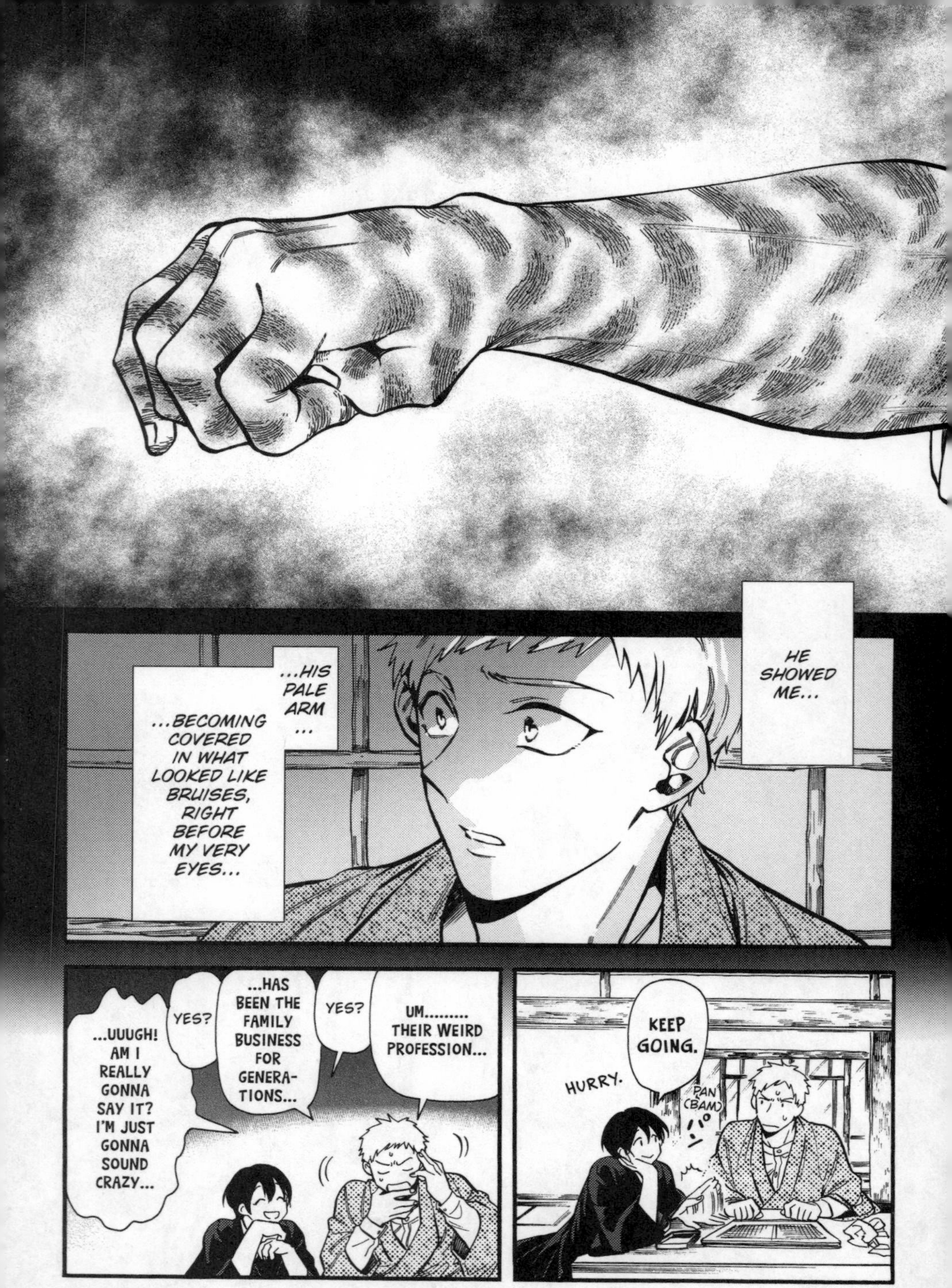
HE SHOWED ME...
...HIS PALE ARM...
...BECOMING COVERED IN WHAT LOOKED LIKE BRUISES, RIGHT BEFORE MY VERY EYES...
KEEP GOING.
HURRY.
PAN (BAM)
UM......... THEIR WEIRD PROFESSION...
YES?
...HAS BEEN THE FAMILY BUSINESS FOR GENERA-TIONS...
YES?
...UUUGH! AM I REALLY GONNA SAY IT? I'M JUST GONNA SOUND CRAZY...

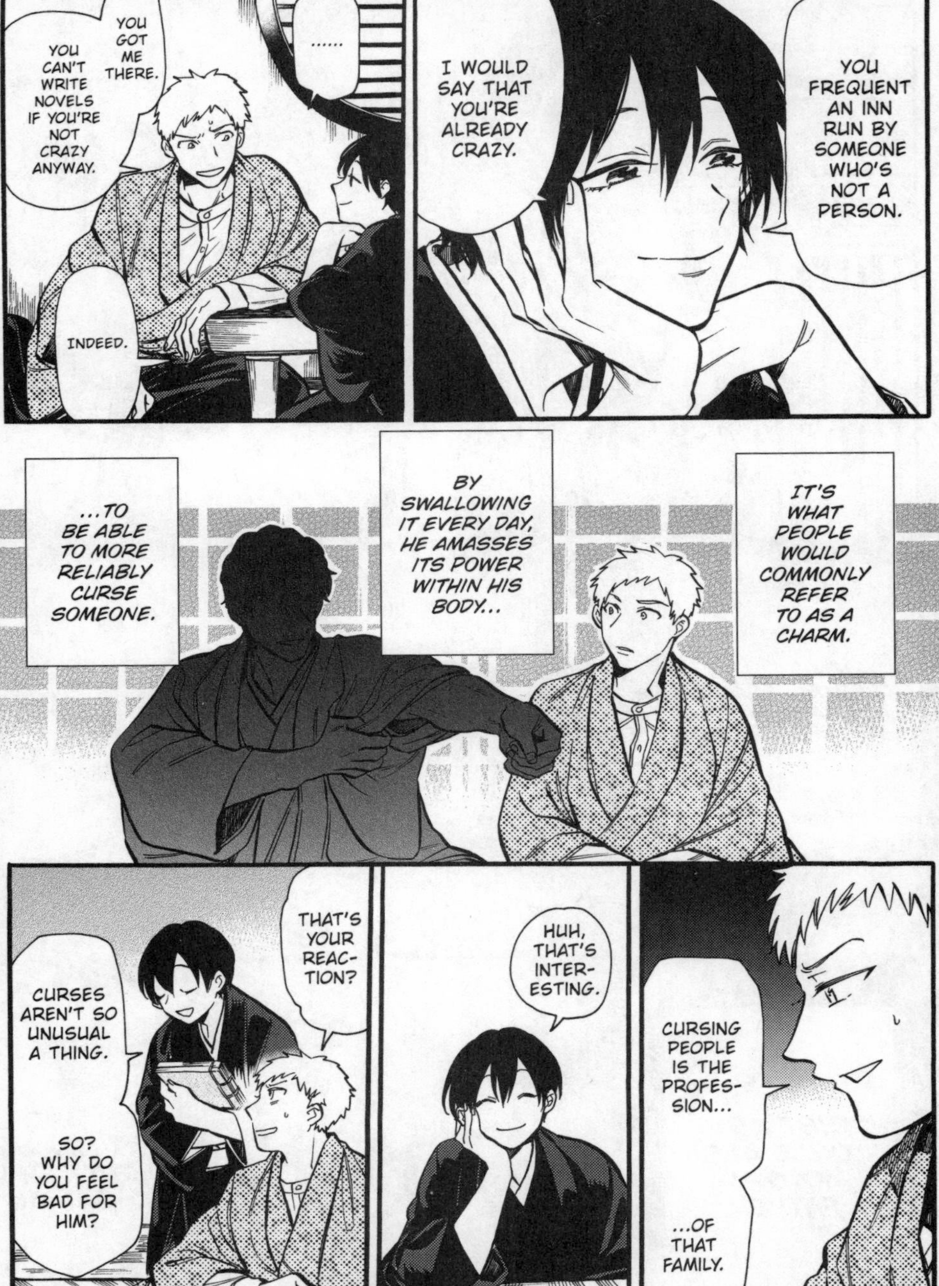
YOU FREQUENT AN INN RUN BY SOMEONE WHO'S NOT A PERSON.
I WOULD SAY THAT YOU'RE ALREADY CRAZY.
......
YOU GOT ME THERE.
YOU CAN'T WRITE NOVELS IF YOU'RE NOT CRAZY ANYWAY.
INDEED.
IT'S WHAT PEOPLE WOULD COMMONLY REFER TO AS A CHARM.
BY SWALLOWING IT EVERY DAY, HE AMASSES ITS POWER WITHIN HIS BODY...
...TO BE ABLE TO MORE RELIABLY CURSE SOMEONE.
CURSING PEOPLE IS THE PROFESSION...
...OF THAT FAMILY.
HUH, THAT'S INTERESTING.
THAT'S YOUR REACTION?
CURSES AREN'T SO UNUSUAL A THING.
SO? WHY DO YOU FEEL BAD FOR HIM?

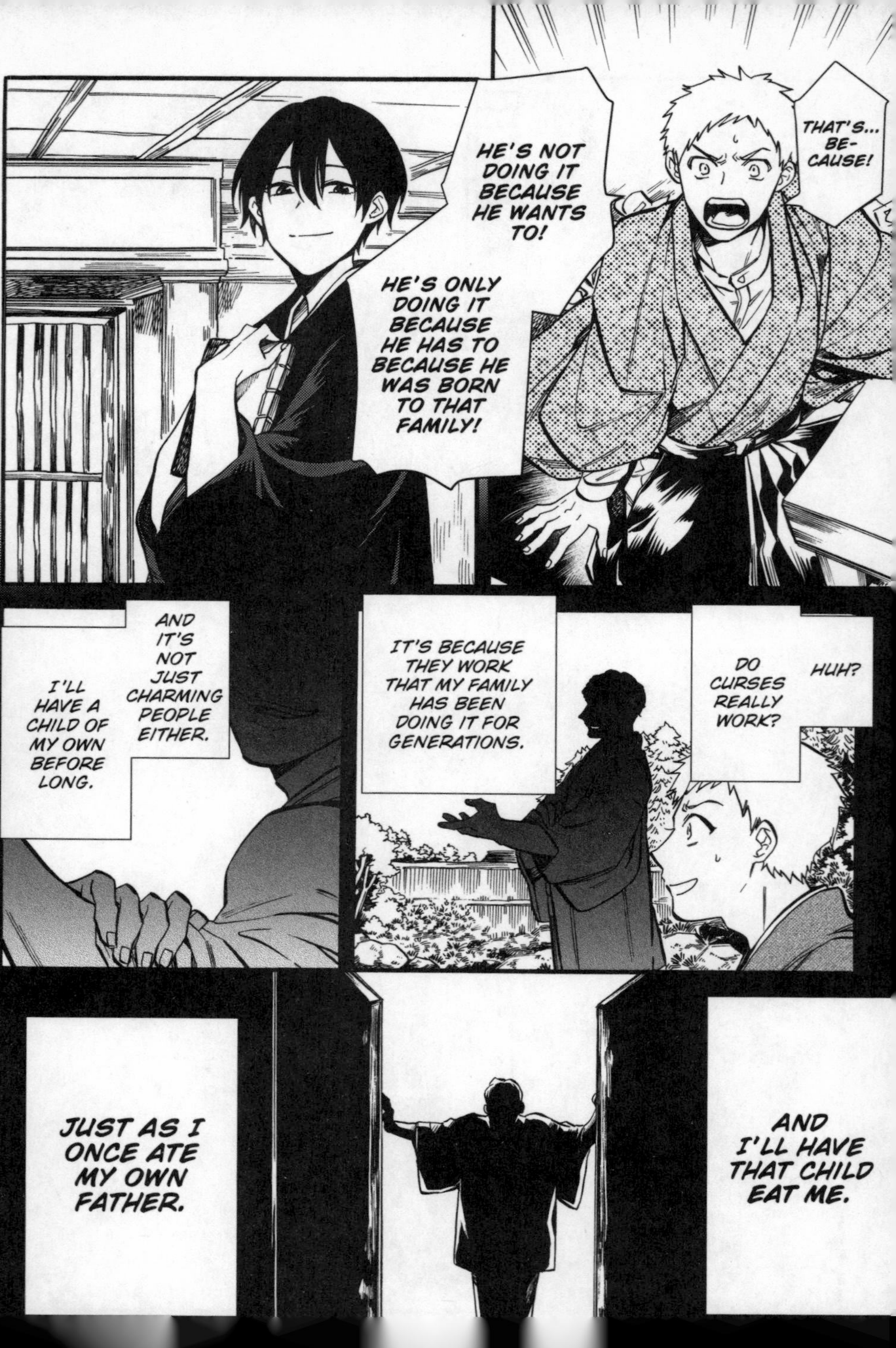
THAT'S... BE-CAUSE!
HE'S NOT DOING IT BECAUSE HE WANTS TO!
HE'S ONLY DOING IT BECAUSE HE HAS TO BECAUSE HE WAS BORN TO THAT FAMILY!
HUH?
DO CURSES REALLY WORK?
IT'S BECAUSE THEY WORK THAT MY FAMILY HAS BEEN DOING IT FOR GENERATIONS.
AND IT'S NOT JUST CHARMING PEOPLE EITHER.
I'LL HAVE A CHILD OF MY OWN BEFORE LONG.
AND I'LL HAVE THAT CHILD EAT ME.
JUST AS I ONCE ATE MY OWN FATHER.

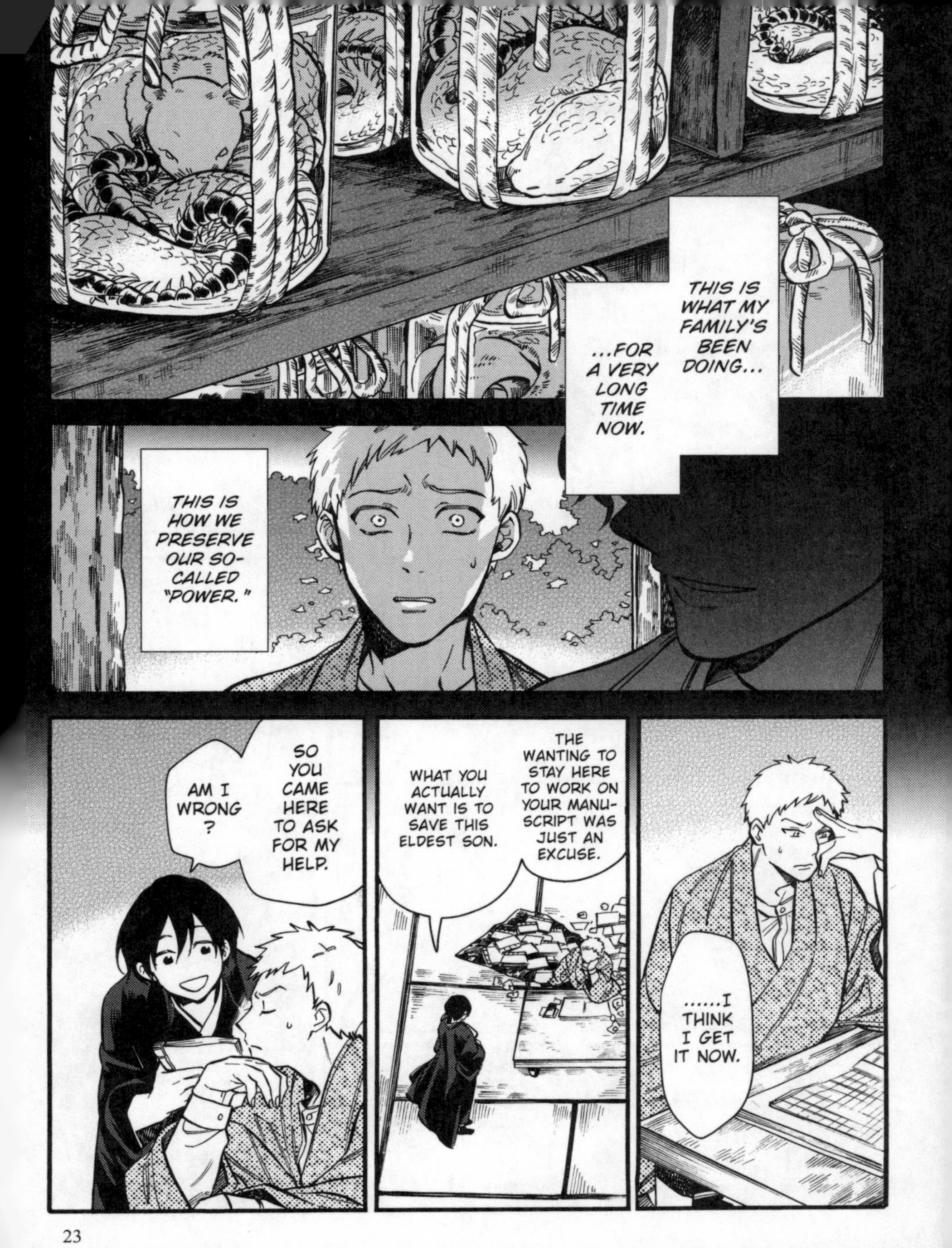
THIS IS WHAT MY FAMILY'S BEEN DOING...
...FOR A VERY LONG TIME NOW.
THIS IS HOW WE PRESERVE OUR SO-CALLED "POWER."
......I THINK I GET IT NOW.
THE WANTING TO STAY HERE TO WORK ON YOUR MANU-SCRIPT WAS JUST AN EXCUSE.
WHAT YOU ACTUALLY WANT IS TO SAVE THIS ELDEST SON.
SO YOU CAME HERE TO ASK FOR MY HELP.
AM I WRONG?

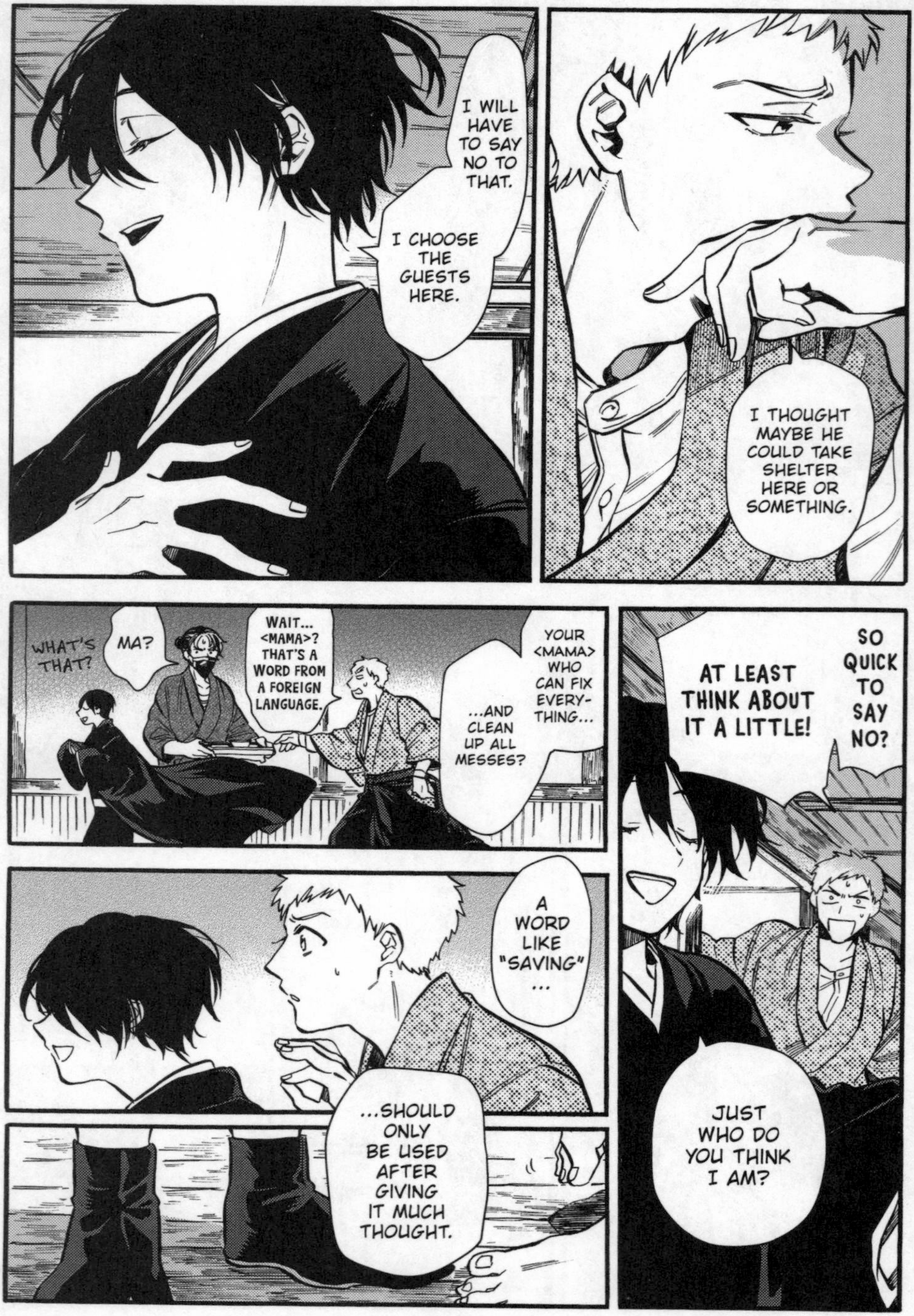
I THOUGHT MAYBE HE COULD TAKE SHELTER HERE OR SOMETHING.
I WILL HAVE TO SAY NO TO THAT.
I CHOOSE THE GUESTS HERE.
SO QUICK TO SAY NO?
AT LEAST THINK ABOUT IT A LITTLE!
JUST WHO DO YOU THINK I AM?
YOUR <MAMA> WHO CAN FIX EVERY-THING...
...AND CLEAN UP ALL MESSES?
WAIT... <MAMA>? THAT'S A WORD FROM A FOREIGN LANGUAGE.
MA?
WHAT'S THAT?
A WORD LIKE "SAVING" ...
...SHOULD ONLY BE USED AFTER GIVING IT MUCH THOUGHT.

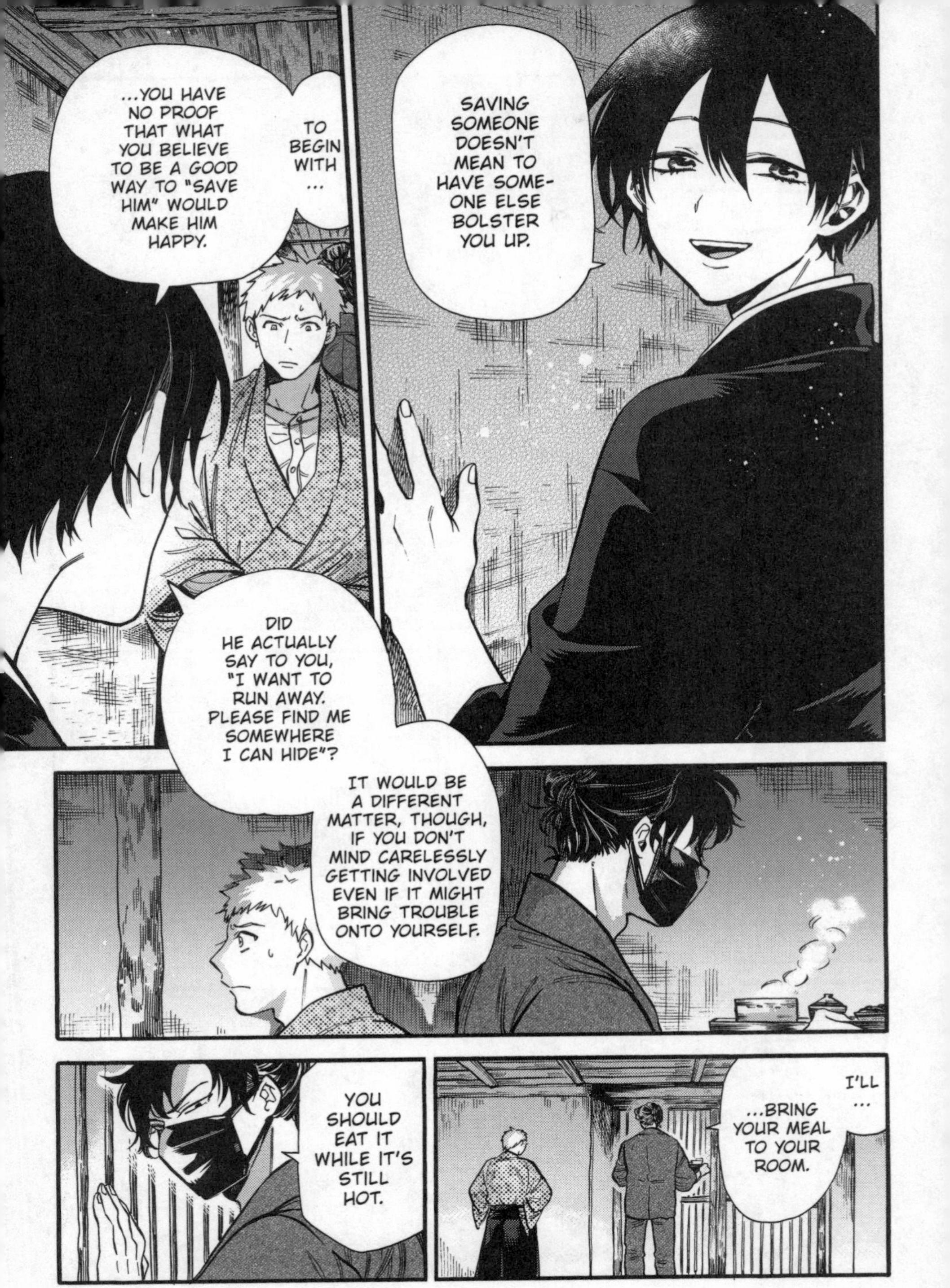
SAVING SOMEONE DOESN'T MEAN TO HAVE SOME-ONE ELSE BOLSTER YOU UP.
TO BEGIN WITH ...
...YOU HAVE NO PROOF THAT WHAT YOU BELIEVE TO BE A GOOD WAY TO "SAVE HIM" WOULD MAKE HIM HAPPY.
DID HE ACTUALLY SAY TO YOU, "I WANT TO RUN AWAY. PLEASE FIND ME SOMEWHERE I CAN HIDE"?
IT WOULD BE A DIFFERENT MATTER, THOUGH, IF YOU DON'T MIND CARELESSLY GETTING INVOLVED EVEN IF IT MIGHT BRING TROUBLE ONTO YOURSELF.
I'LL ...
...BRING YOUR MEAL TO YOUR ROOM.
YOU SHOULD EAT IT WHILE IT'S STILL HOT.

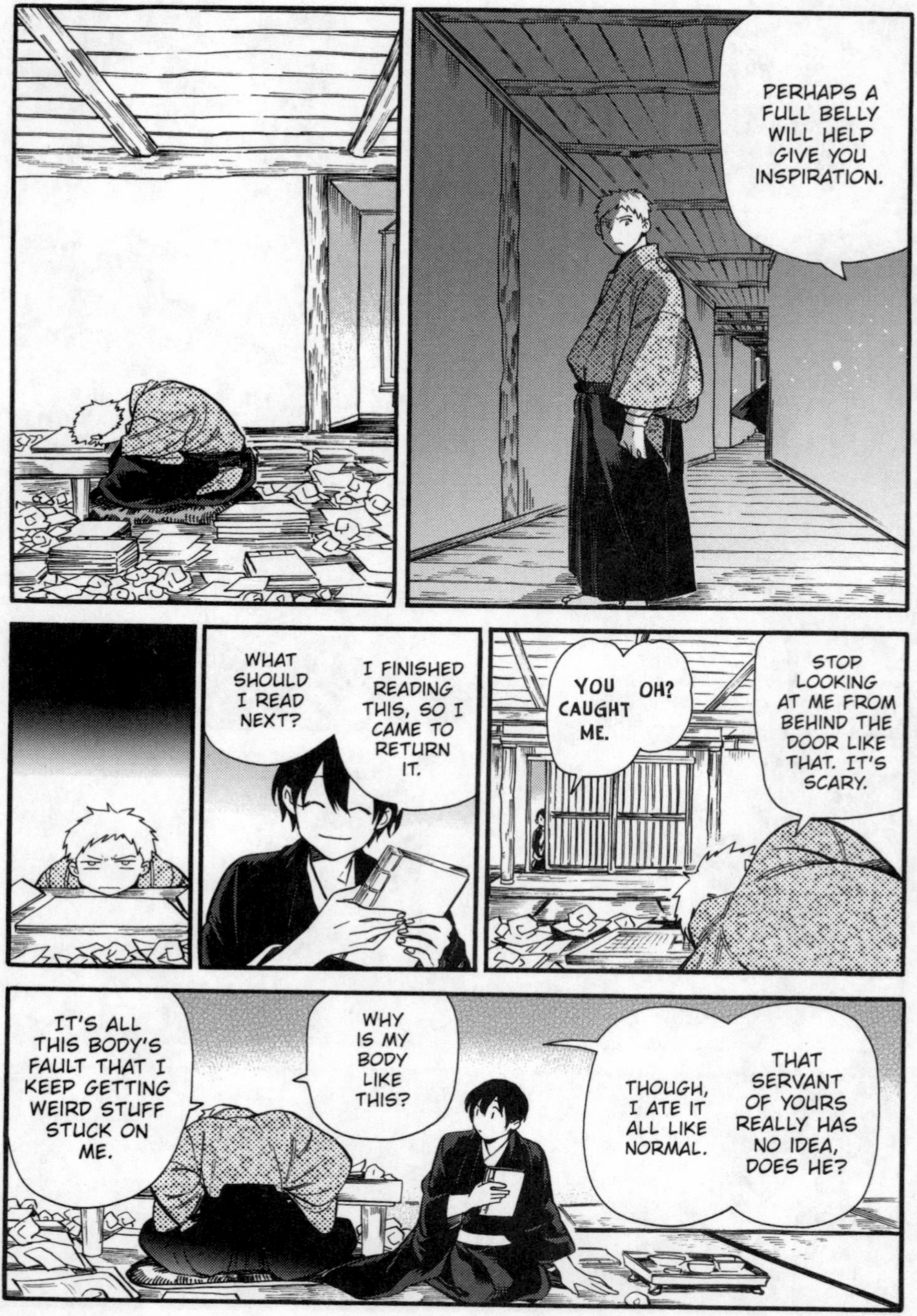
PERHAPS A FULL BELLY WILL HELP GIVE YOU INSPIRATION.
STOP LOOKING AT ME FROM BEHIND THE DOOR LIKE THAT. IT'S SCARY.
OH?
YOU CAUGHT ME.
I FINISHED READING THIS, SO I CAME TO RETURN IT.
WHAT SHOULD I READ NEXT?
THAT SERVANT OF YOURS REALLY HAS NO IDEA, DOES HE?
THOUGH, I ATE IT ALL LIKE NORMAL.
WHY IS MY BODY LIKE THIS?
IT'S ALL THIS BODY'S FAULT THAT I KEEP GETTING WEIRD STUFF STUCK ON ME.

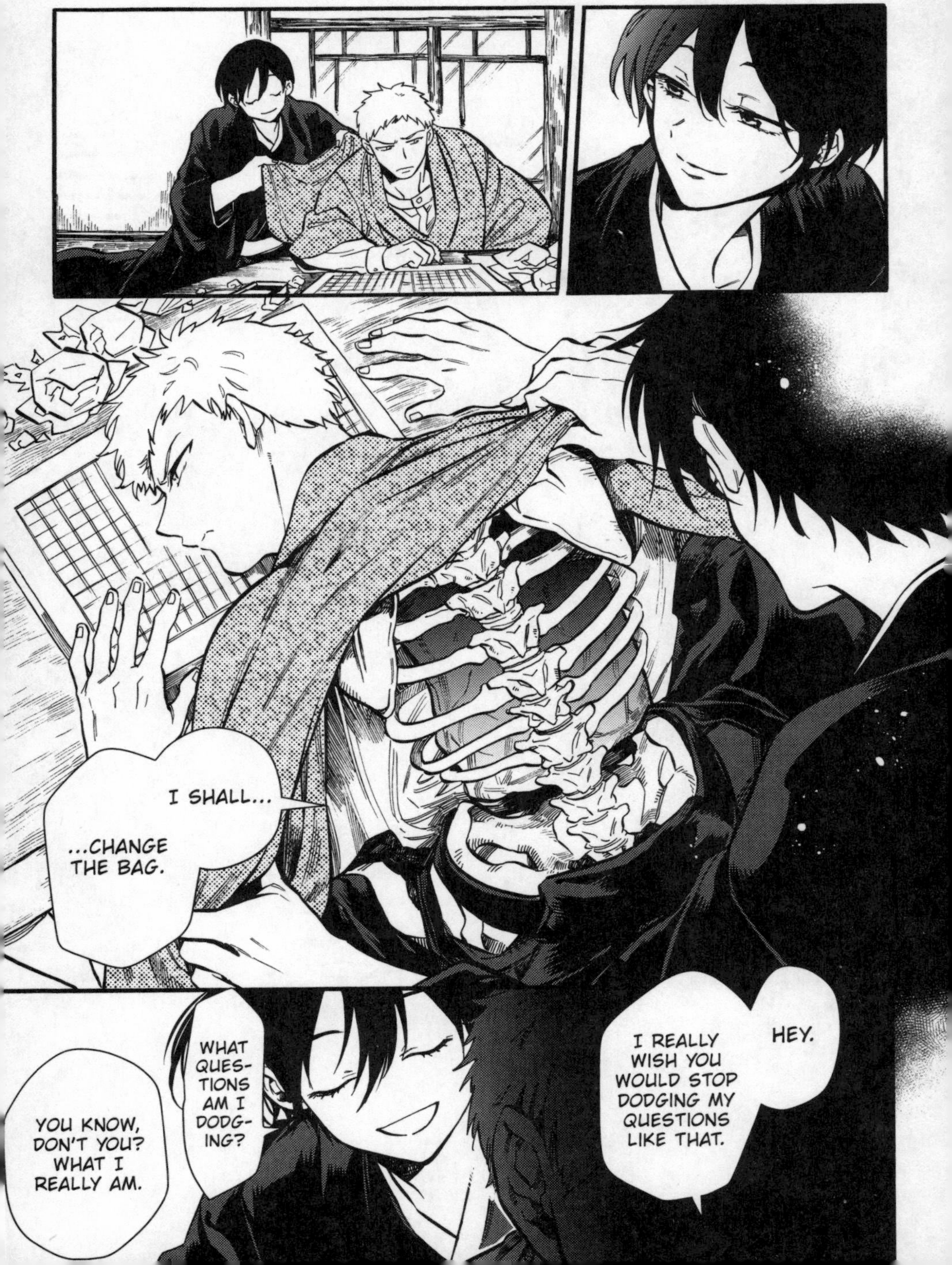
I SHALL...
...CHANGE THE BAG.
HEY.
I REALLY WISH YOU WOULD STOP DODGING MY QUESTIONS LIKE THAT.
WHAT QUES-TIONS AM I DODG-ING?
YOU KNOW, DON'T YOU? WHAT I REALLY AM.

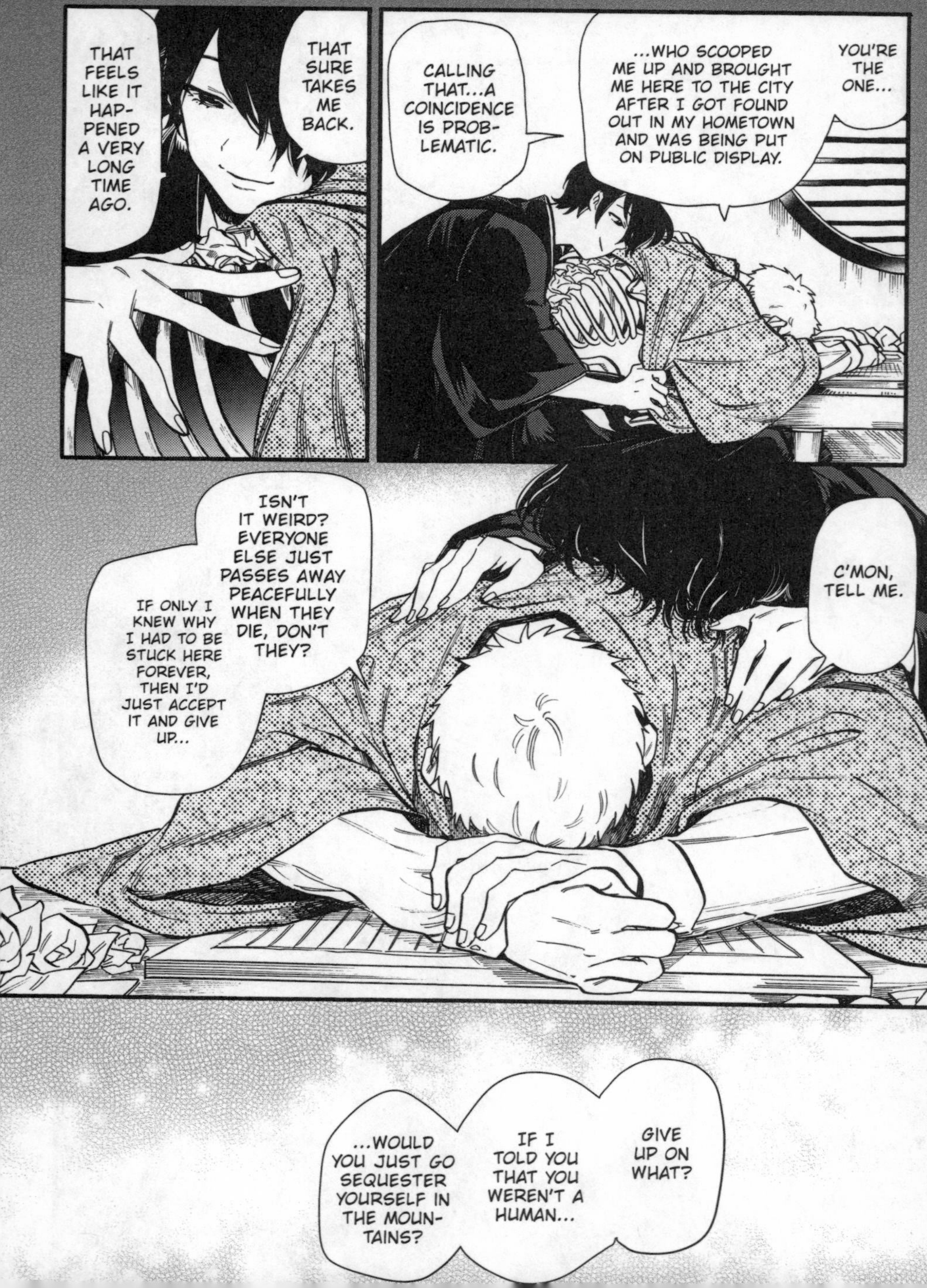
YOU'RE THE ONE...
...WHO SCOOPED ME UP AND BROUGHT ME HERE TO THE CITY AFTER I GOT FOUND OUT IN MY HOMETOWN AND WAS BEING PUT ON PUBLIC DISPLAY.
CALLING THAT...A COINCIDENCE IS PROBLEMATIC.
THAT SURE TAKES ME BACK.
THAT FEELS LIKE IT HAPPENED A VERY LONG TIME AGO.
C'MON, TELL ME.
ISN'T IT WEIRD? EVERYONE ELSE JUST PASSES AWAY PEACEFULLY WHEN THEY DIE, DON'T THEY?
IF ONLY I KNEW WHY I HAD TO BE STUCK HERE FOREVER, THEN I'D JUST ACCEPT IT AND GIVE UP...
GIVE UP ON WHAT?
IF I TOLD YOU THAT YOU WEREN'T A HUMAN...
...WOULD YOU JUST GO SEQUESTER YOURSELF IN THE MOUNTAINS?

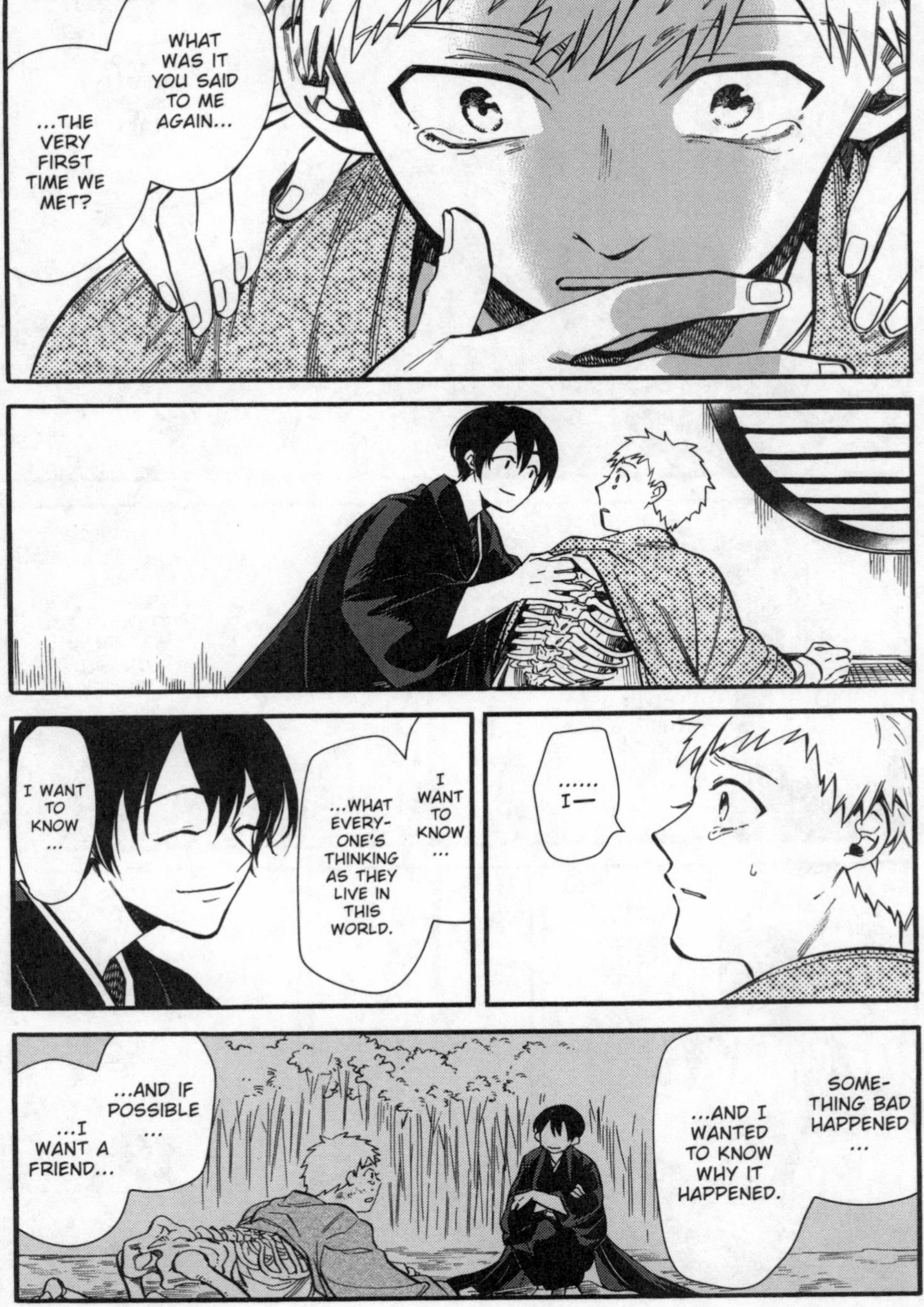
WHAT WAS IT YOU SAID TO ME AGAIN...
...THE VERY FIRST TIME WE MET?
......
I—
I WANT TO KNOW ...
...WHAT EVERYONE'S THINKING AS THEY LIVE IN THIS WORLD.
I WANT TO KNOW ...
SOMETHING BAD HAPPENED ...
...AND I WANTED TO KNOW WHY IT HAPPENED.
...AND IF POSSIBLE ...
...I WANT A FRIEND...

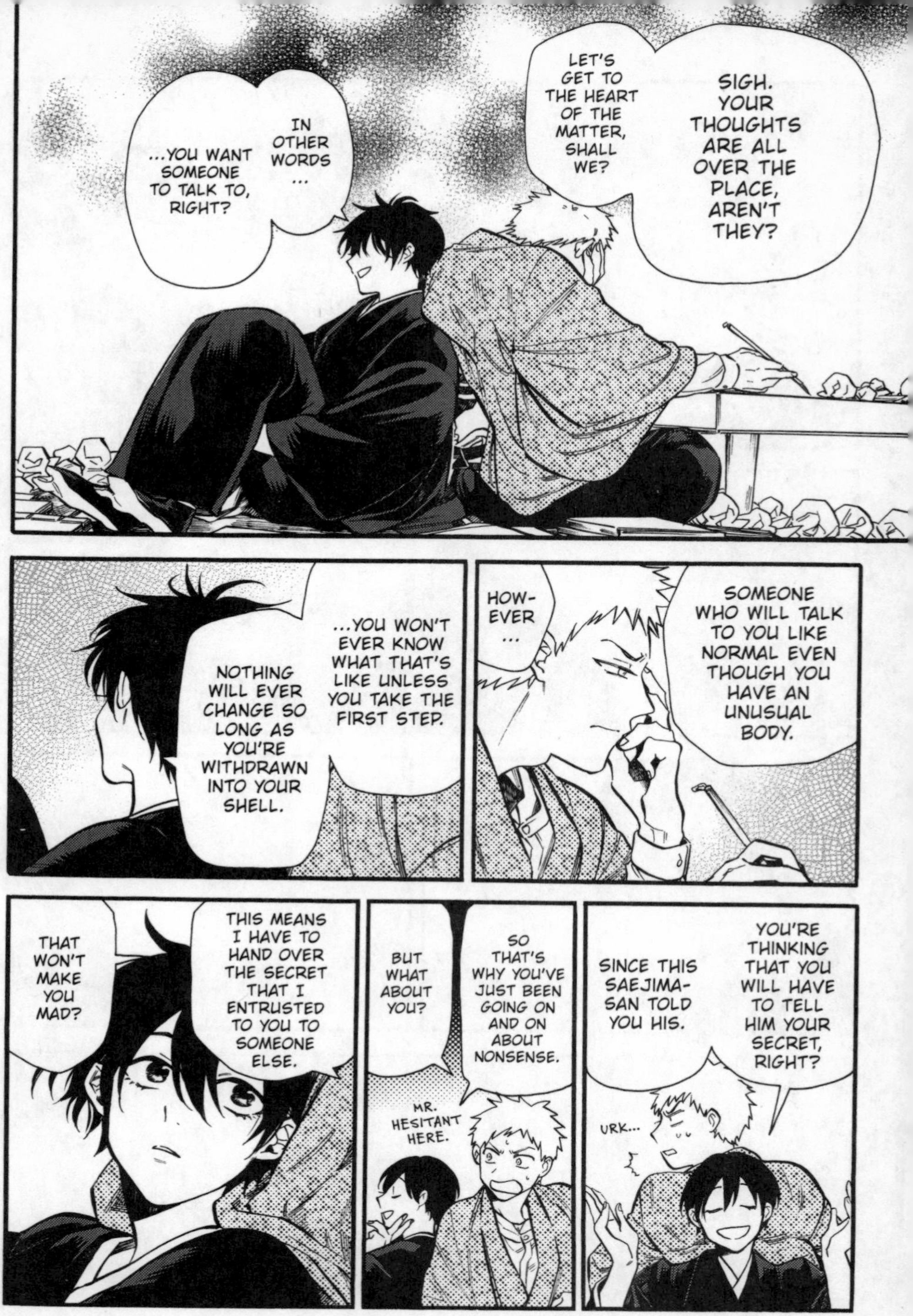
SIGH. YOUR THOUGHTS ARE ALL OVER THE PLACE, AREN'T THEY?
LET'S GET TO THE HEART OF THE MATTER, SHALL WE?
IN OTHER WORDS...
...YOU WANT SOMEONE TO TALK TO, RIGHT?
SOMEONE WHO WILL TALK TO YOU LIKE NORMAL EVEN THOUGH YOU HAVE AN UNUSUAL BODY.
HOW-EVER...
...YOU WON'T EVER KNOW WHAT THAT'S LIKE UNLESS YOU TAKE THE FIRST STEP.
NOTHING WILL EVER CHANGE SO LONG AS YOU'RE WITHDRAWN INTO YOUR SHELL.
YOU'RE THINKING THAT YOU WILL HAVE TO TELL HIM YOUR SECRET, RIGHT?
SINCE THIS SAEJIMA-SAN TOLD YOU HIS.
URK...
SO THAT'S WHY YOU'VE JUST BEEN GOING ON AND ON ABOUT NONSENSE.
BUT WHAT ABOUT YOU?
MR. HESITANT HERE.
THIS MEANS I HAVE TO HAND OVER THE SECRET THAT I ENTRUSTED TO YOU TO SOMEONE ELSE.
THAT WON'T MAKE YOU MAD?

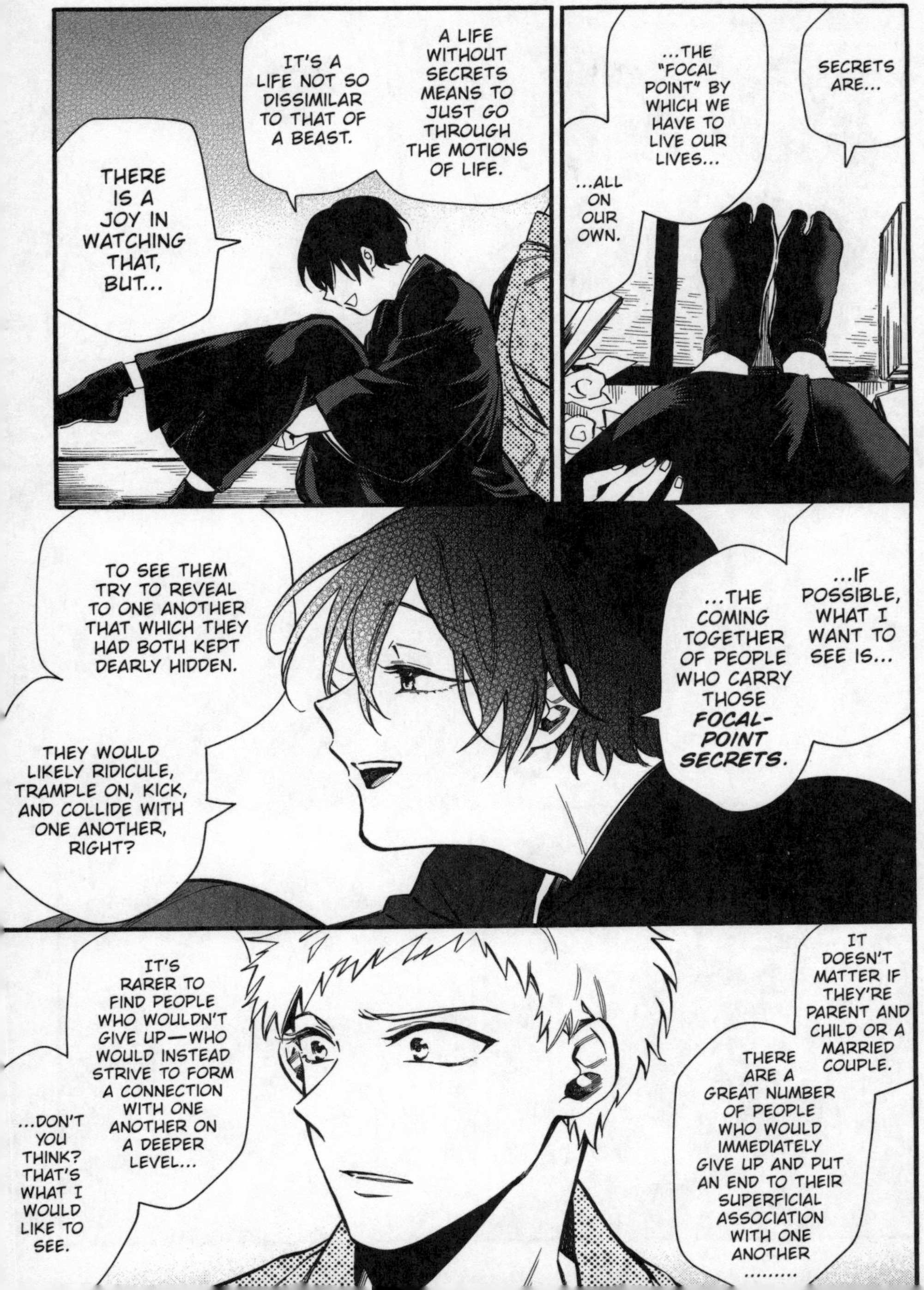
SECRETS ARE...
...THE "FOCAL POINT" BY WHICH WE HAVE TO LIVE OUR LIVES...
...ALL ON OUR OWN.
A LIFE WITHOUT SECRETS MEANS TO JUST GO THROUGH THE MOTIONS OF LIFE.
IT'S A LIFE NOT SO DISSIMILAR TO THAT OF A BEAST.
THERE IS A JOY IN WATCHING THAT, BUT...
...IF POSSIBLE, WHAT I WANT TO SEE IS...
...THE COMING TOGETHER OF PEOPLE WHO CARRY THOSE *FOCAL-POINT SECRETS*.
TO SEE THEM TRY TO REVEAL TO ONE ANOTHER THAT WHICH THEY HAD BOTH KEPT DEARLY HIDDEN.
THEY WOULD LIKELY RIDICULE, TRAMPLE ON, KICK, AND COLLIDE WITH ONE ANOTHER, RIGHT?
IT DOESN'T MATTER IF THEY'RE PARENT AND CHILD OR A MARRIED COUPLE.
THERE ARE A GREAT NUMBER OF PEOPLE WHO WOULD IMMEDIATELY GIVE UP AND PUT AN END TO THEIR SUPERFICIAL ASSOCIATION WITH ONE ANOTHER ....
IT'S RARER TO FIND PEOPLE WHO WOULDN'T GIVE UP—WHO WOULD INSTEAD STRIVE TO FORM A CONNECTION WITH ONE ANOTHER ON A DEEPER LEVEL...
...DON'T YOU THINK? THAT'S WHAT I WOULD LIKE TO SEE.

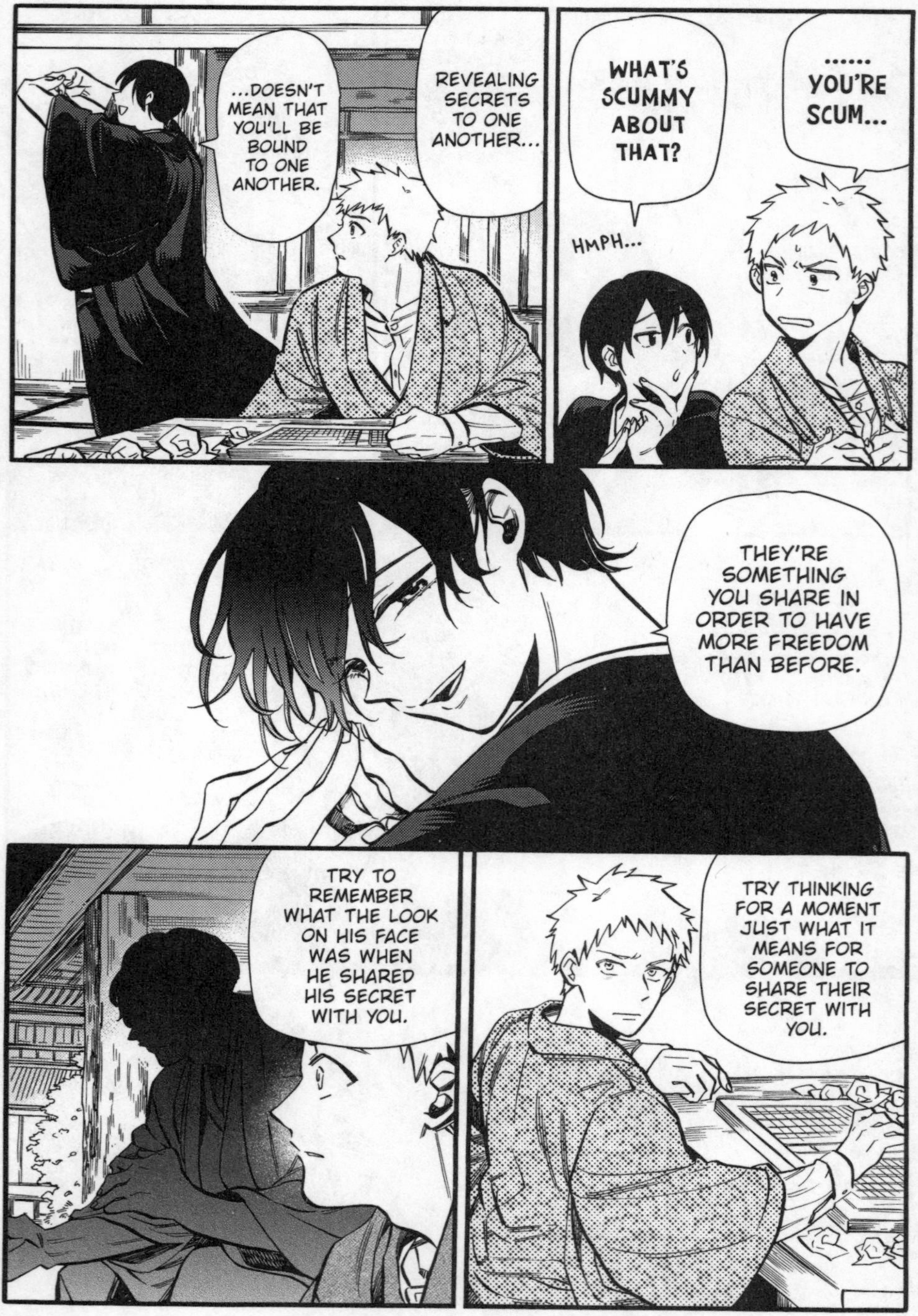
...... YOU'RE SCUM...
WHAT'S SCUMMY ABOUT THAT?
HMPH...
REVEALING SECRETS TO ONE ANOTHER...
...DOESN'T MEAN THAT YOU'LL BE BOUND TO ONE ANOTHER.
THEY'RE SOMETHING YOU SHARE IN ORDER TO HAVE MORE FREEDOM THAN BEFORE.
TRY THINKING FOR A MOMENT JUST WHAT IT MEANS FOR SOMEONE TO SHARE THEIR SECRET WITH YOU.
TRY TO REMEMBER WHAT THE LOOK ON HIS FACE WAS WHEN HE SHARED HIS SECRET WITH YOU.

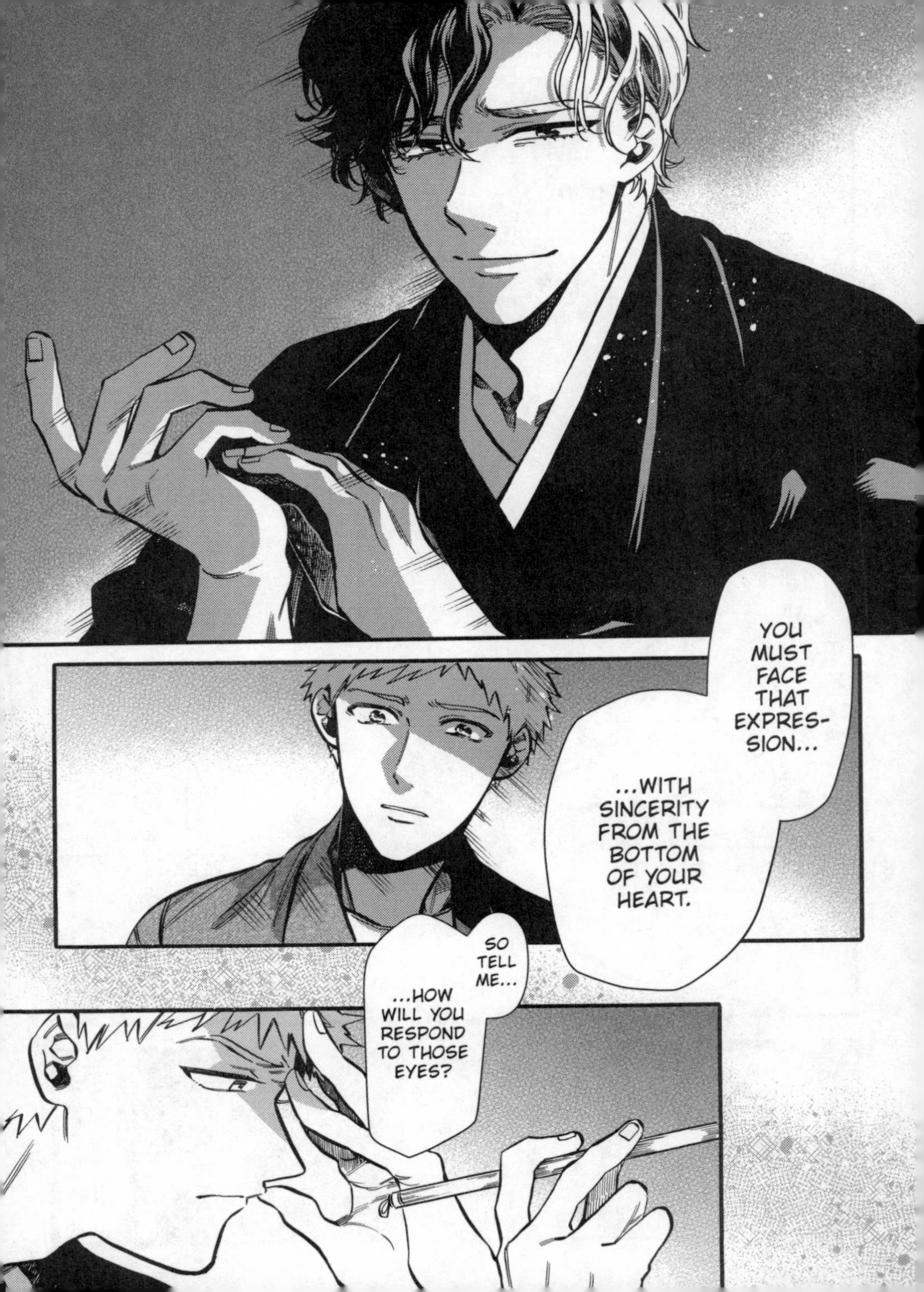
YOU MUST FACE THAT EXPRES-SION...
...WITH SINCERITY FROM THE BOTTOM OF YOUR HEART.
SO TELL ME...
...HOW WILL YOU RESPOND TO THOSE EYES?

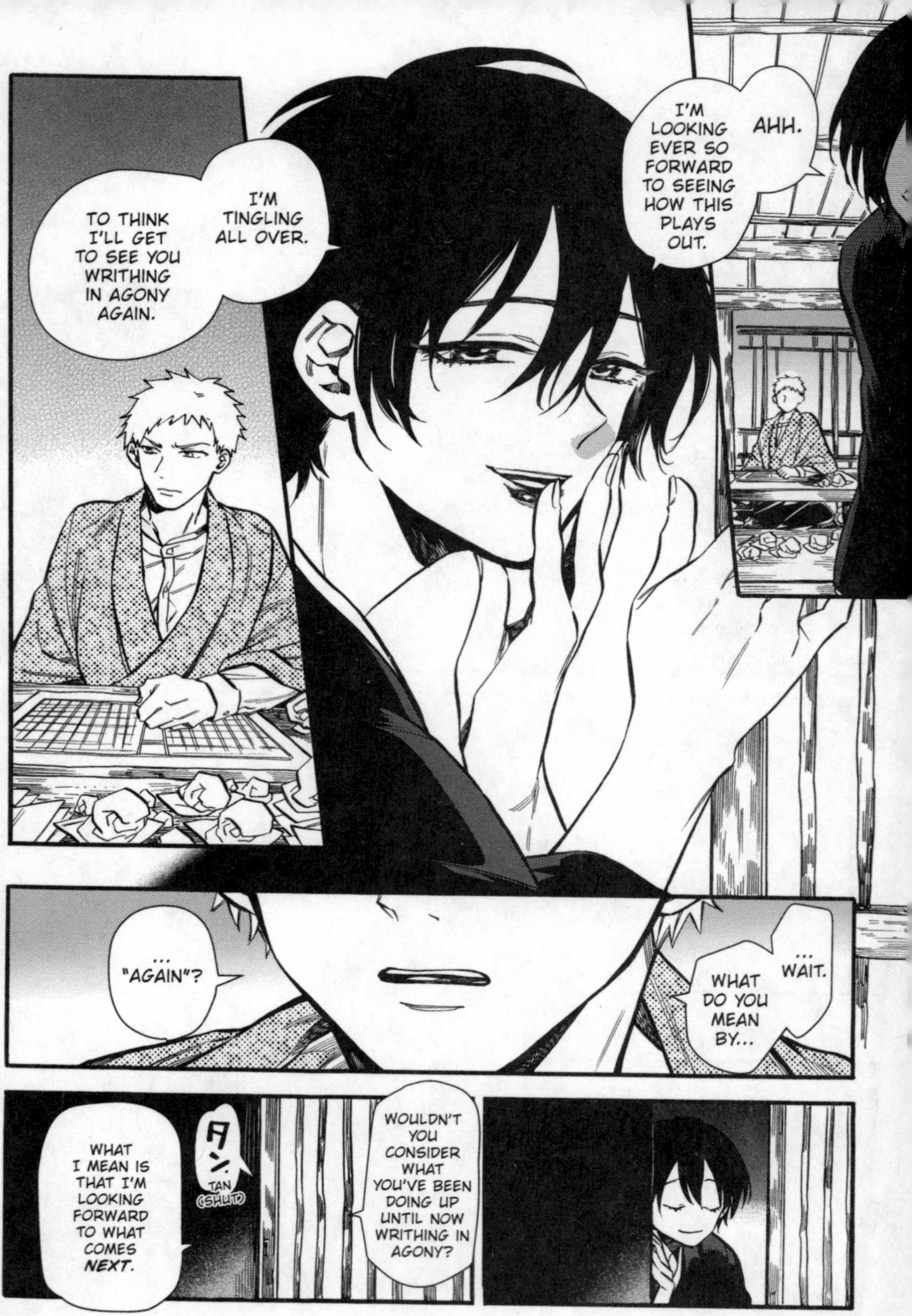
AHH.
I'M LOOKING EVER SO FORWARD TO SEEING HOW THIS PLAYS OUT.
I'M TINGLING ALL OVER.
TO THINK I'LL GET TO SEE YOU WRITHING IN AGONY AGAIN.
... WAIT.
WHAT DO YOU MEAN BY...
... "AGAIN"?
WOULDN'T YOU CONSIDER WHAT YOU'VE BEEN DOING UP UNTIL NOW WRITHING IN AGONY?
タン
TAN (SHUT)
WHAT I MEAN IS THAT I'M LOOKING FORWARD TO WHAT COMES ***NEXT***.

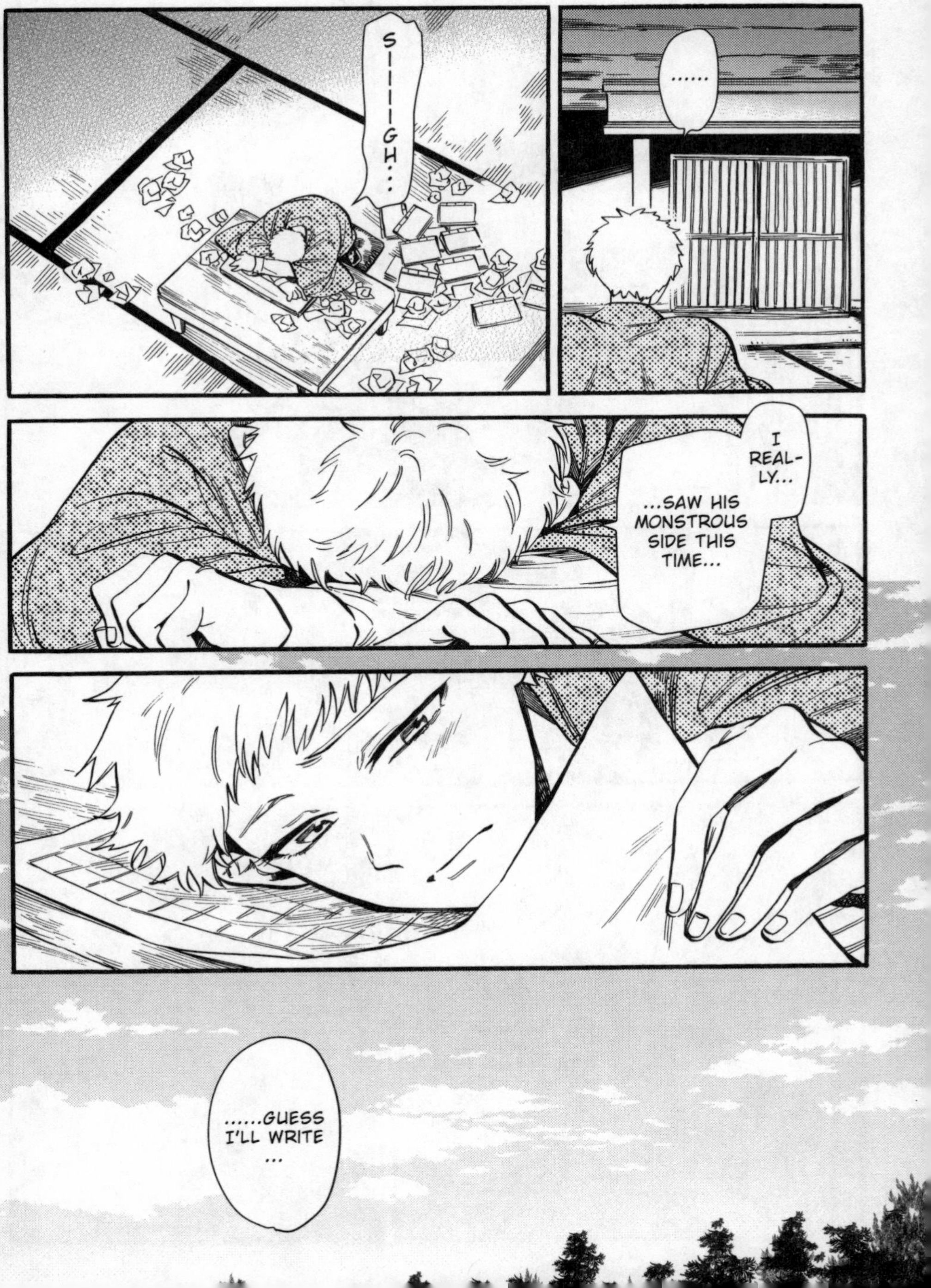
......
S-I-I-I-I-G-H...
I REAL-LY...
...SAW HIS MONSTROUS SIDE THIS TIME...
......GUESS I'LL WRITE ...

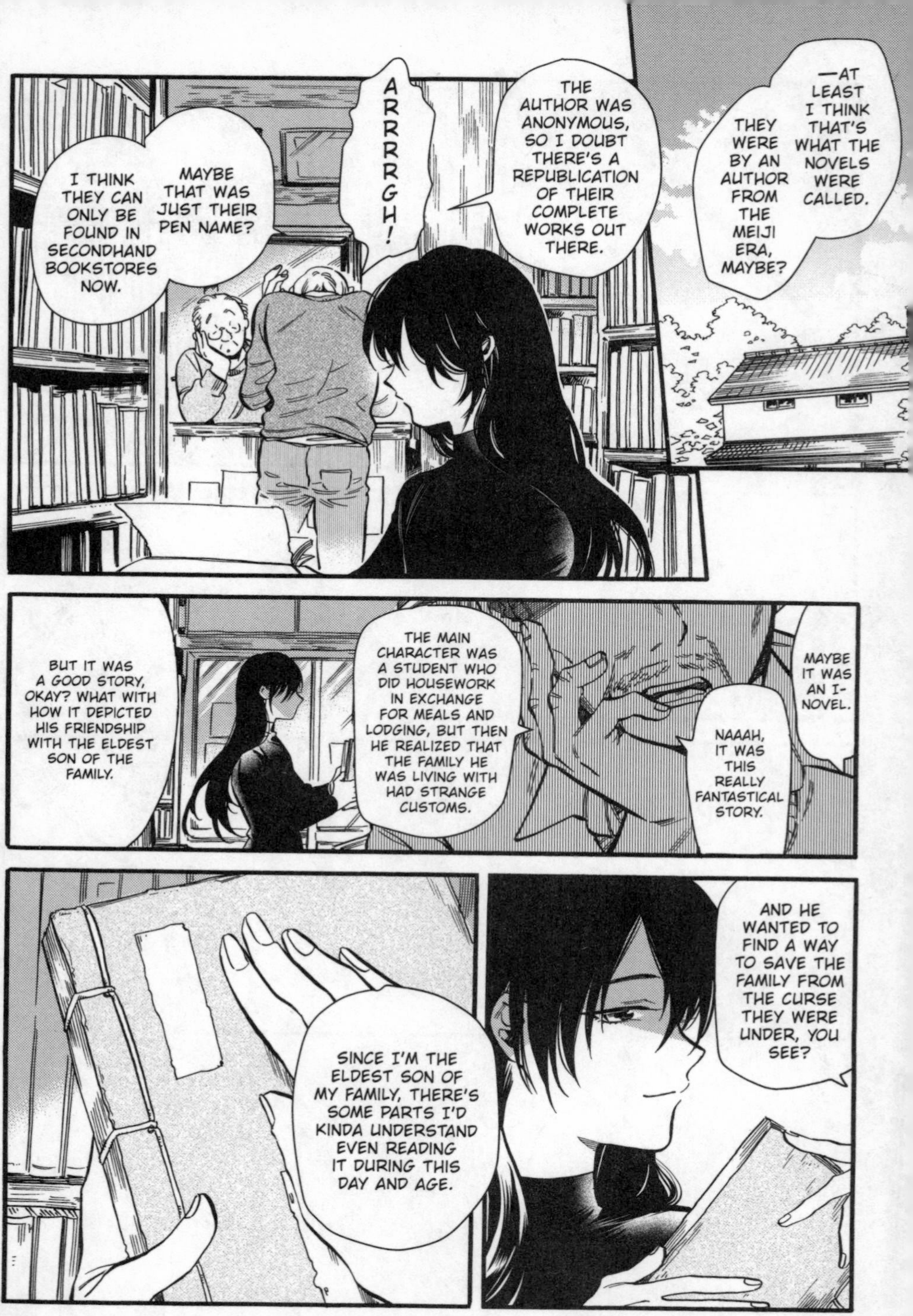
THEY WERE BY AN AUTHOR FROM THE MEIJI ERA, MAYBE?
—AT LEAST I THINK THAT'S WHAT THE NOVELS WERE CALLED.
THE AUTHOR WAS ANONYMOUS, SO I DOUBT THERE'S A REPUBLICATION OF THEIR COMPLETE WORKS OUT THERE.
ARRRRGH!
MAYBE THAT WAS JUST THEIR PEN NAME?
I THINK THEY CAN ONLY BE FOUND IN SECONDHAND BOOKSTORES NOW.
MAYBE IT WAS AN I-NOVEL.
NAAAH, IT WAS THIS REALLY FANTASTICAL STORY.
THE MAIN CHARACTER WAS A STUDENT WHO DID HOUSEWORK IN EXCHANGE FOR MEALS AND LODGING, BUT THEN HE REALIZED THAT THE FAMILY HE WAS LIVING WITH HAD STRANGE CUSTOMS.
BUT IT WAS A GOOD STORY, OKAY? WHAT WITH HOW IT DEPICTED HIS FRIENDSHIP WITH THE ELDEST SON OF THE FAMILY.
AND HE WANTED TO FIND A WAY TO SAVE THE FAMILY FROM THE CURSE THEY WERE UNDER, YOU SEE?
SINCE I'M THE ELDEST SON OF MY FAMILY, THERE'S SOME PARTS I'D KINDA UNDERSTAND EVEN READING IT DURING THIS DAY AND AGE.

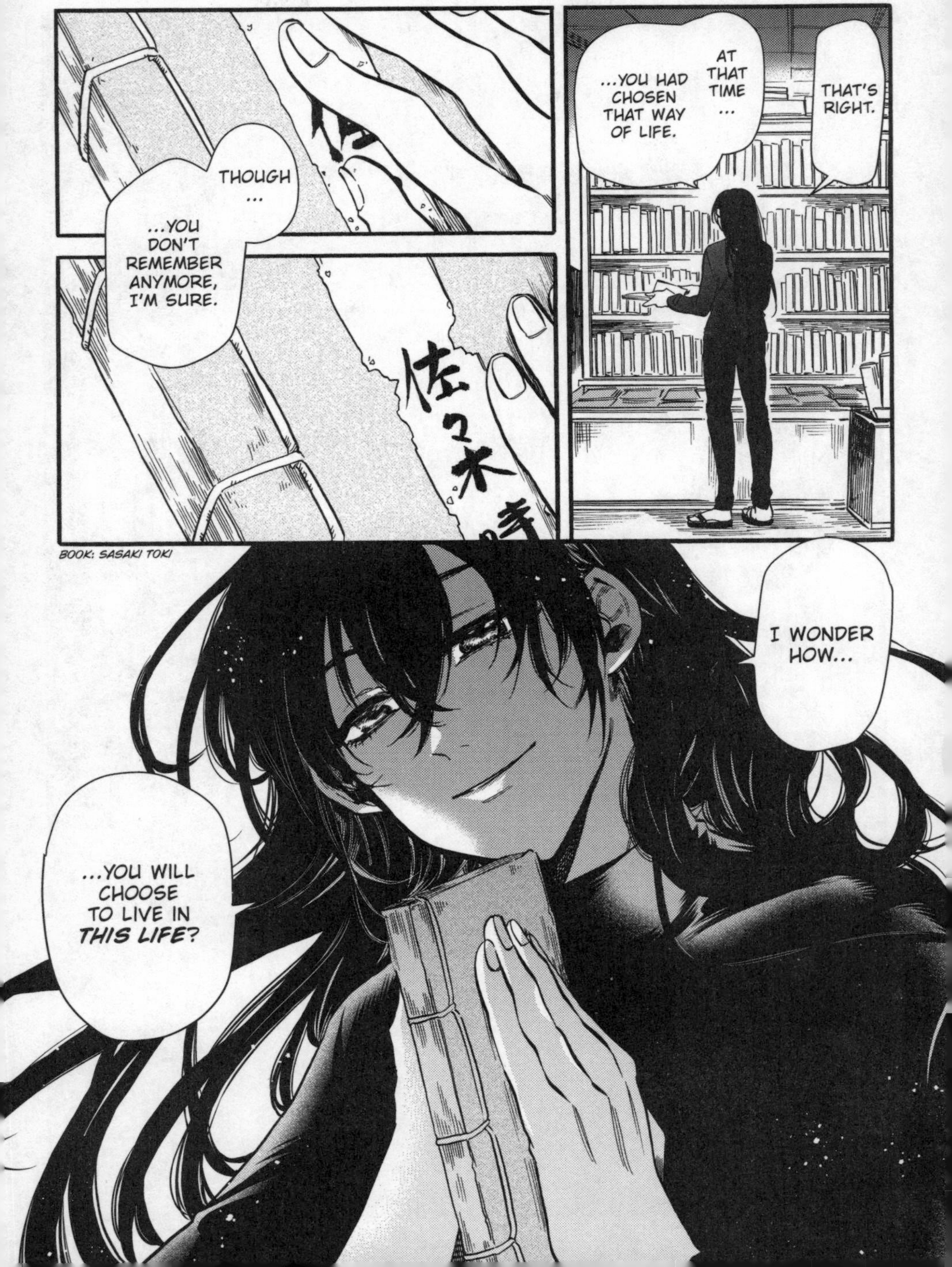
THAT'S RIGHT.
AT THAT TIME...
...YOU HAD CHOSEN THAT WAY OF LIFE.
THOUGH...
...YOU DON'T REMEMBER ANYMORE, I'M SURE.
佐々木時
BOOK: SASAKI TOKI
I WONDER HOW...
...YOU WILL CHOOSE TO LIVE IN *THIS LIFE*?

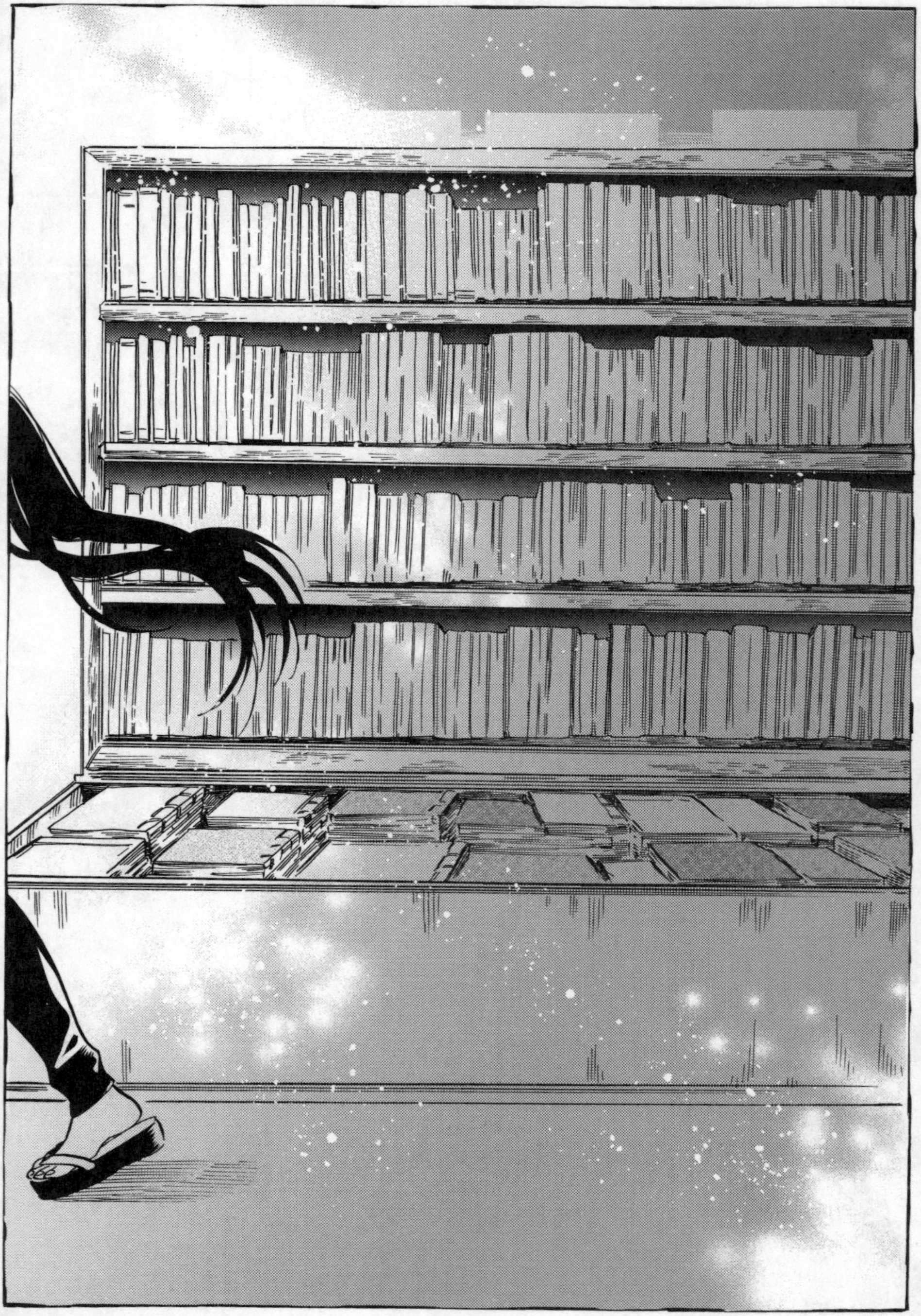

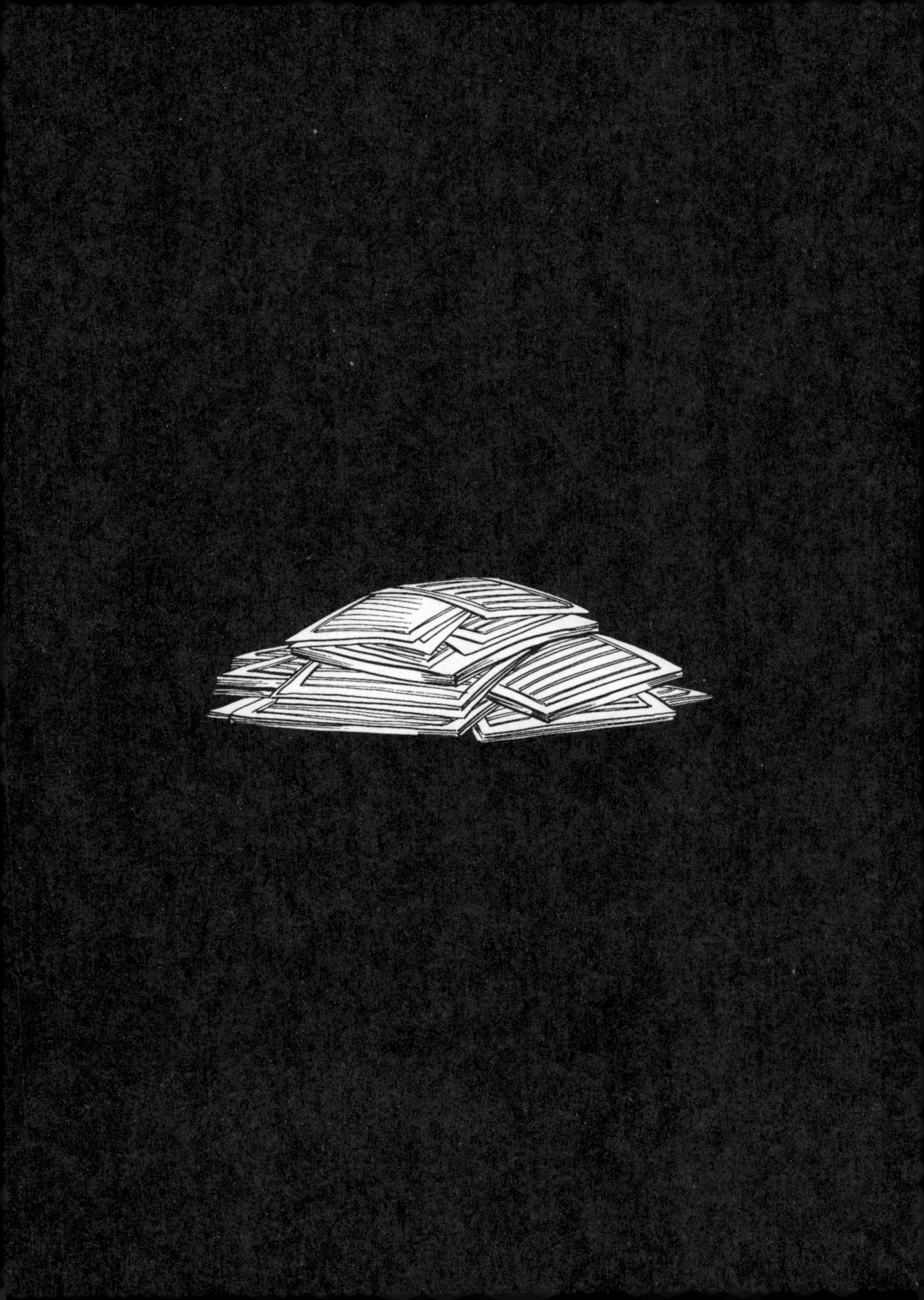

Phantom Tales of the Night

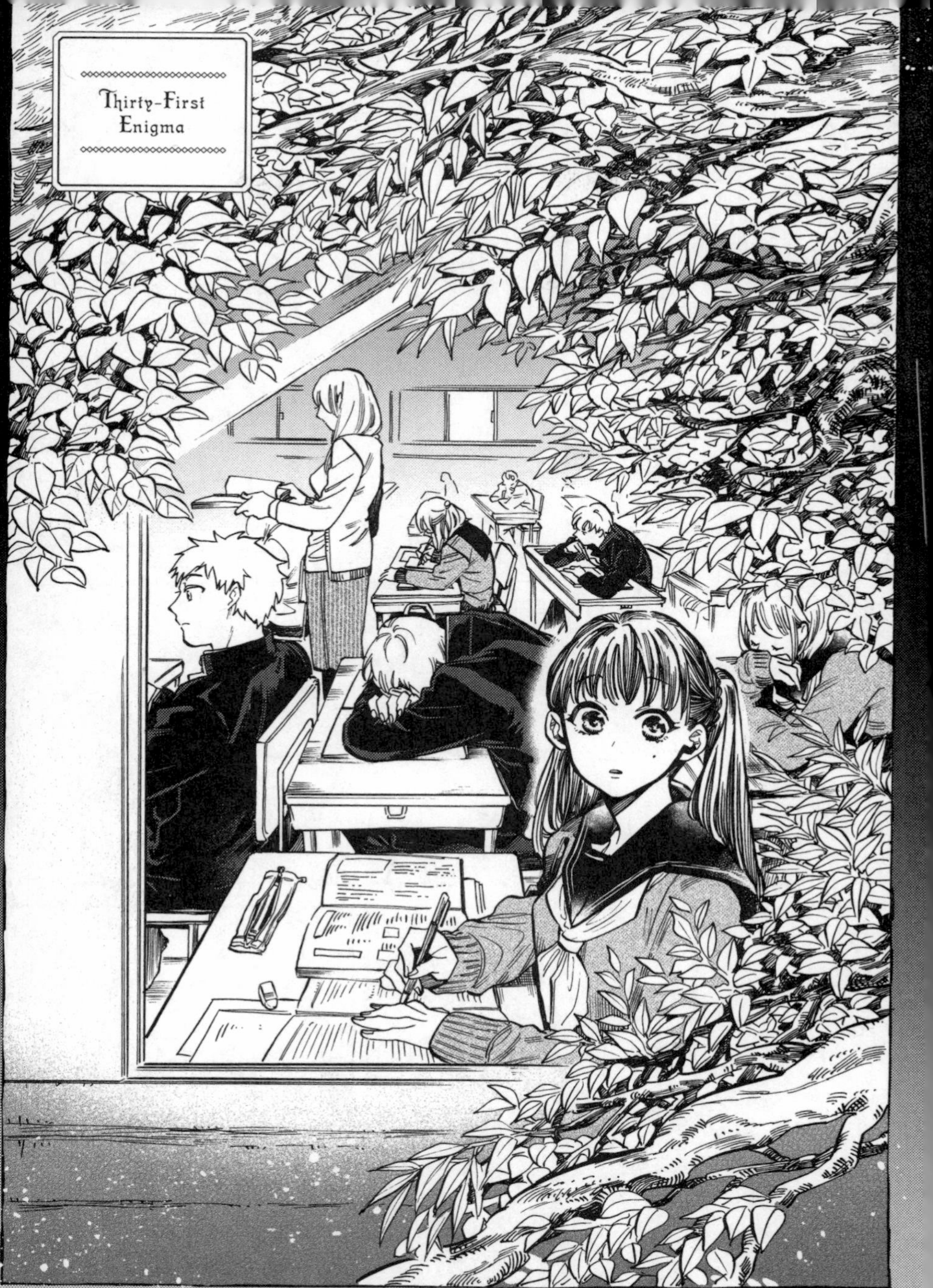
Thirty-First
Enigma

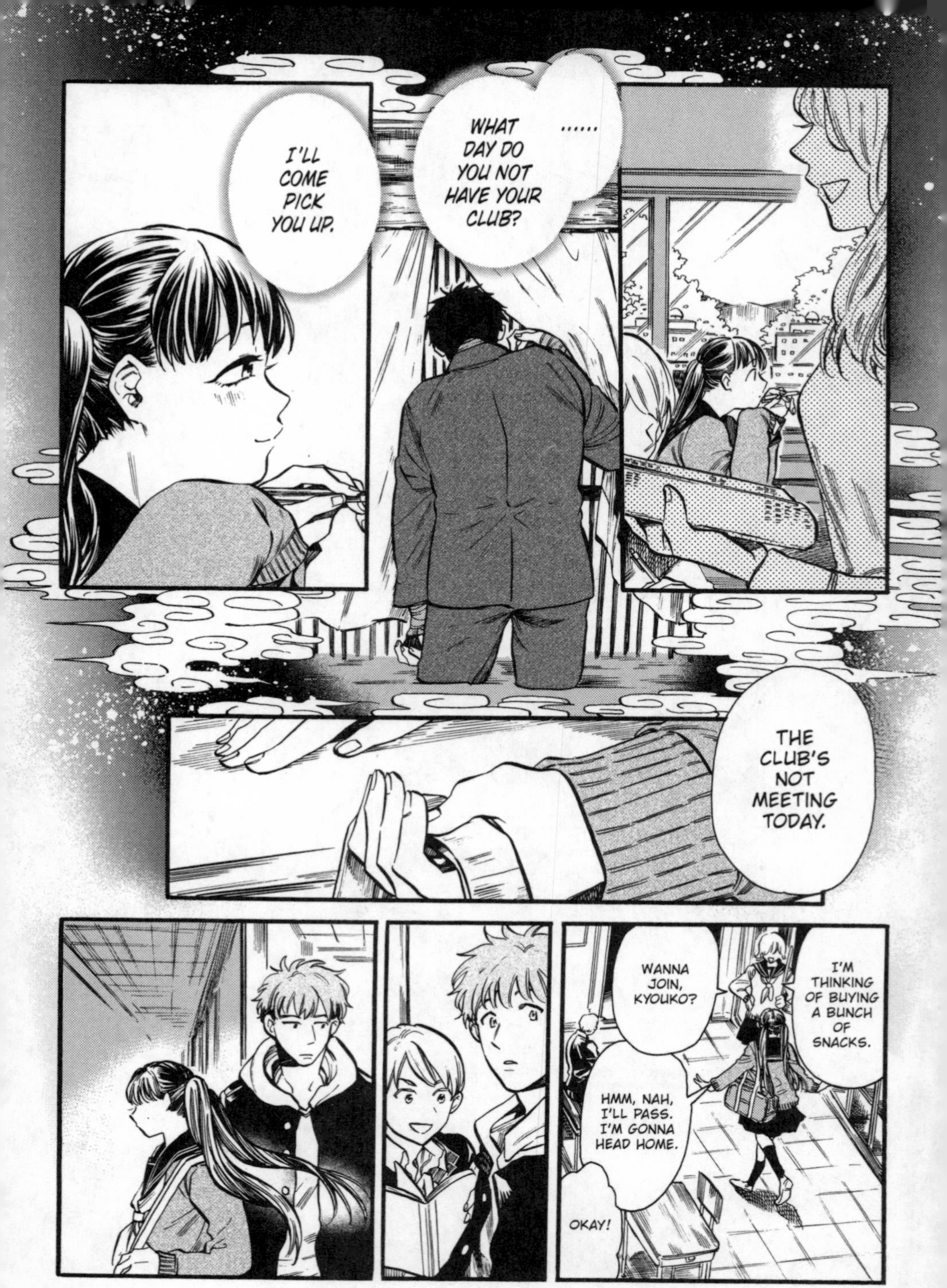
......
WHAT DAY DO YOU NOT HAVE YOUR CLUB?
I'LL COME PICK YOU UP.
THE CLUB'S NOT MEETING TODAY.
I'M THINKING OF BUYING A BUNCH OF SNACKS.
WANNA JOIN, KYOUKO?
HMM, NAH, I'LL PASS. I'M GONNA HEAD HOME.
OKAY!

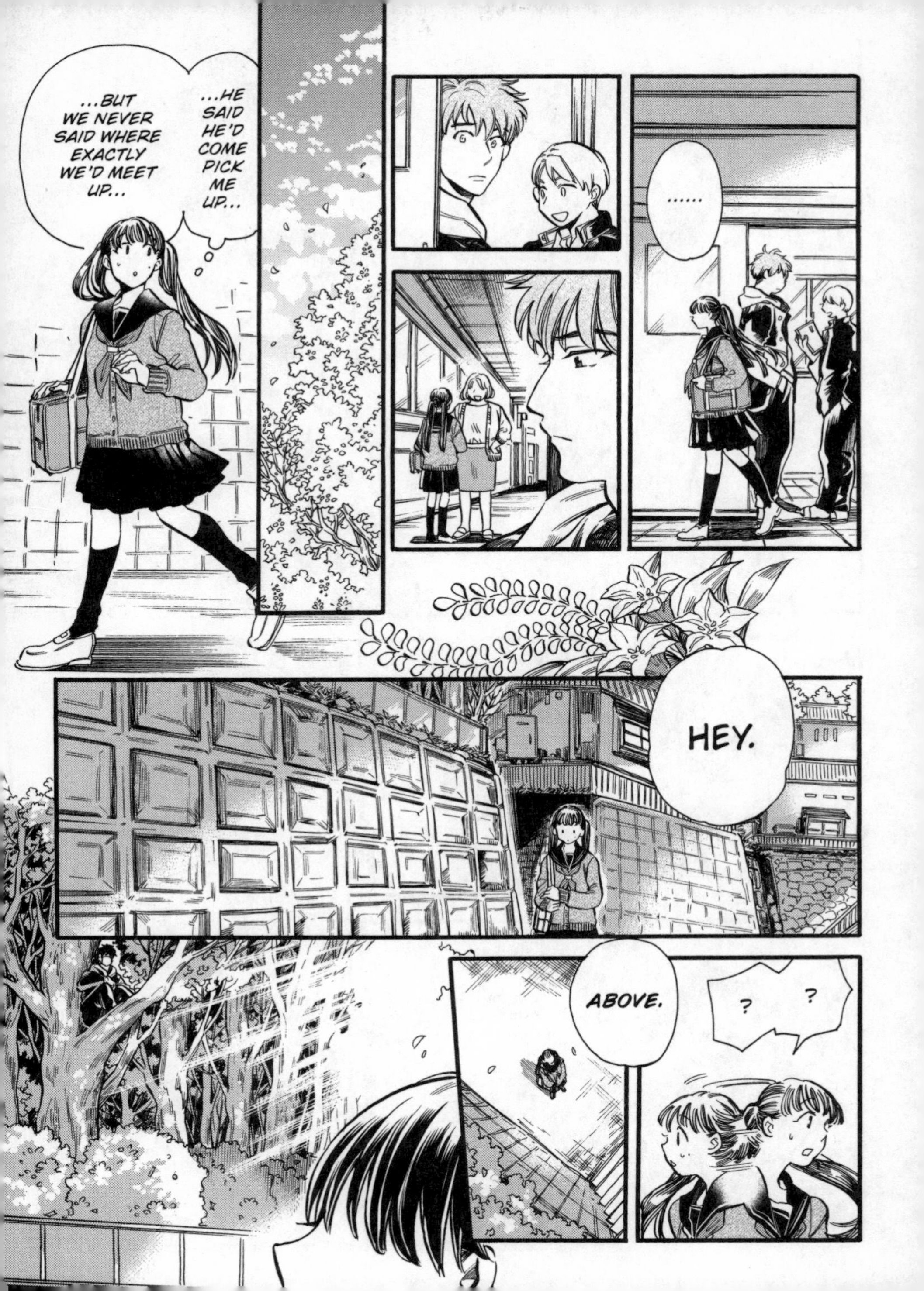
......
...HE SAID HE'D COME PICK ME UP...
...BUT WE NEVER SAID WHERE EXACTLY WE'D MEET UP...
HEY.
? ?
ABOVE.

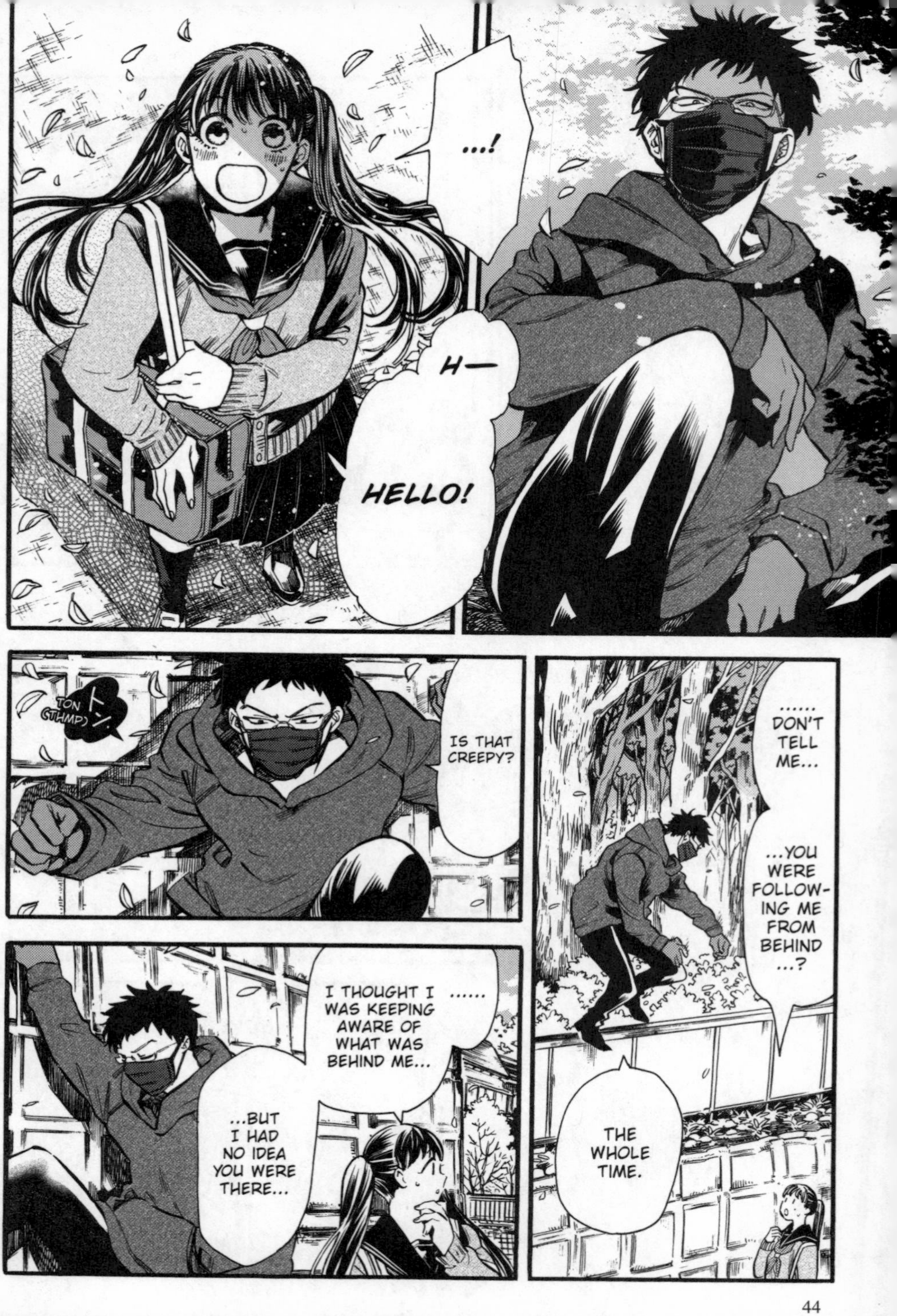
...!
H—
HELLO!
...... DON'T TELL ME...
...YOU WERE FOLLOWING ME FROM BEHIND...?
THE WHOLE TIME.
TON (THMP)
IS THAT CREEPY?
I THOUGHT I WAS KEEPING AWARE OF WHAT WAS BEHIND ME...
......
...BUT I HAD NO IDEA YOU WERE THERE...

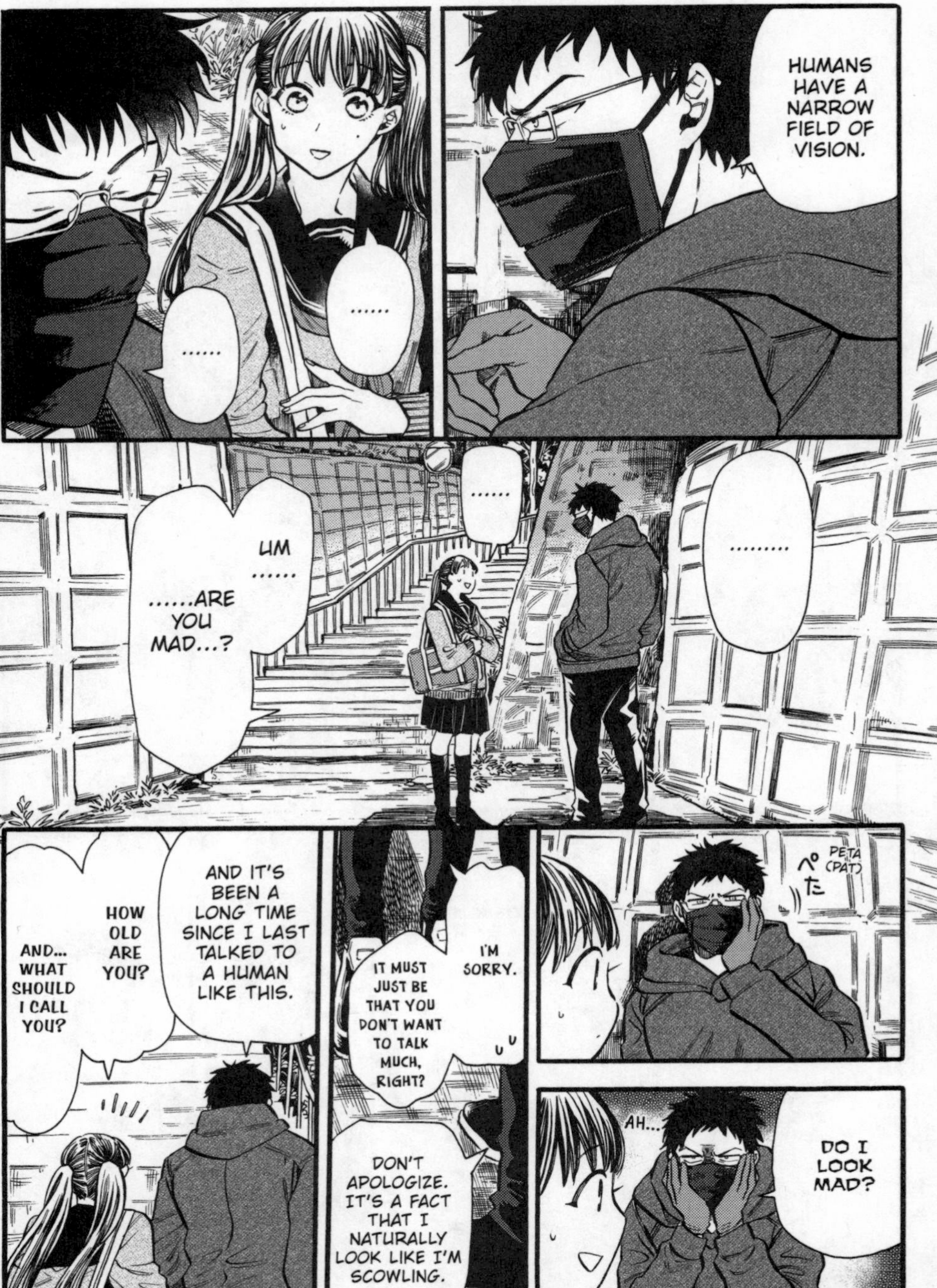
HUMANS HAVE A NARROW FIELD OF VISION.
......
......
....
......
UM ......
......ARE YOU MAD...?
ぺた PETA (PAT)
DO I LOOK MAD?
AH...
I'M SORRY.
IT MUST JUST BE THAT YOU DON'T WANT TO TALK MUCH, RIGHT?
DON'T APOLOGIZE. IT'S A FACT THAT I NATURALLY LOOK LIKE I'M SCOWLING.
AND IT'S BEEN A LONG TIME SINCE I LAST TALKED TO A HUMAN LIKE THIS.
HOW OLD ARE YOU?
AND... WHAT SHOULD I CALL YOU?

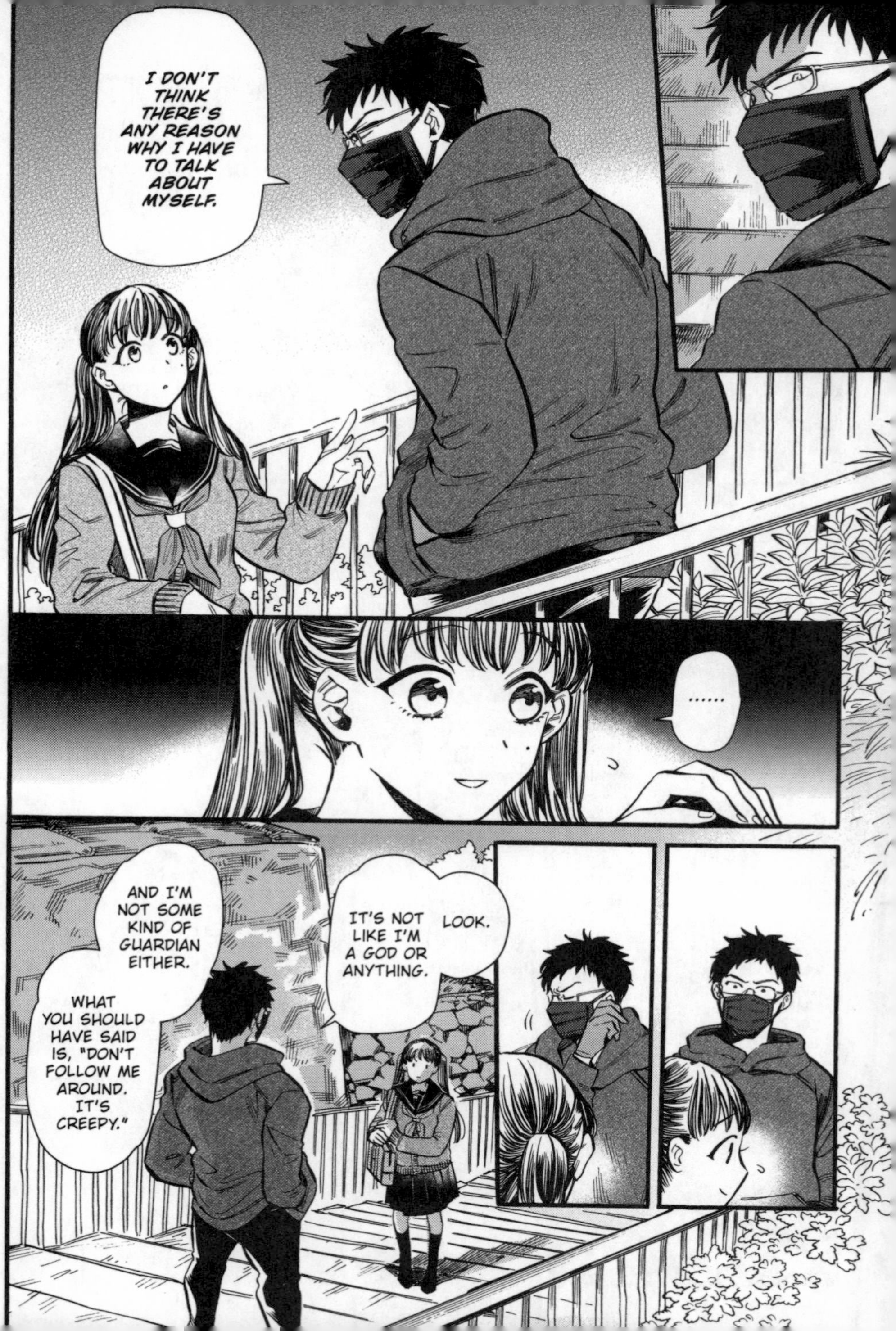
I DON'T THINK THERE'S ANY REASON WHY I HAVE TO TALK ABOUT MYSELF.
......
LOOK.
IT'S NOT LIKE I'M A GOD OR ANYTHING.
AND I'M NOT SOME KIND OF GUARDIAN EITHER.
WHAT YOU SHOULD HAVE SAID IS, "DON'T FOLLOW ME AROUND. IT'S CREEPY."

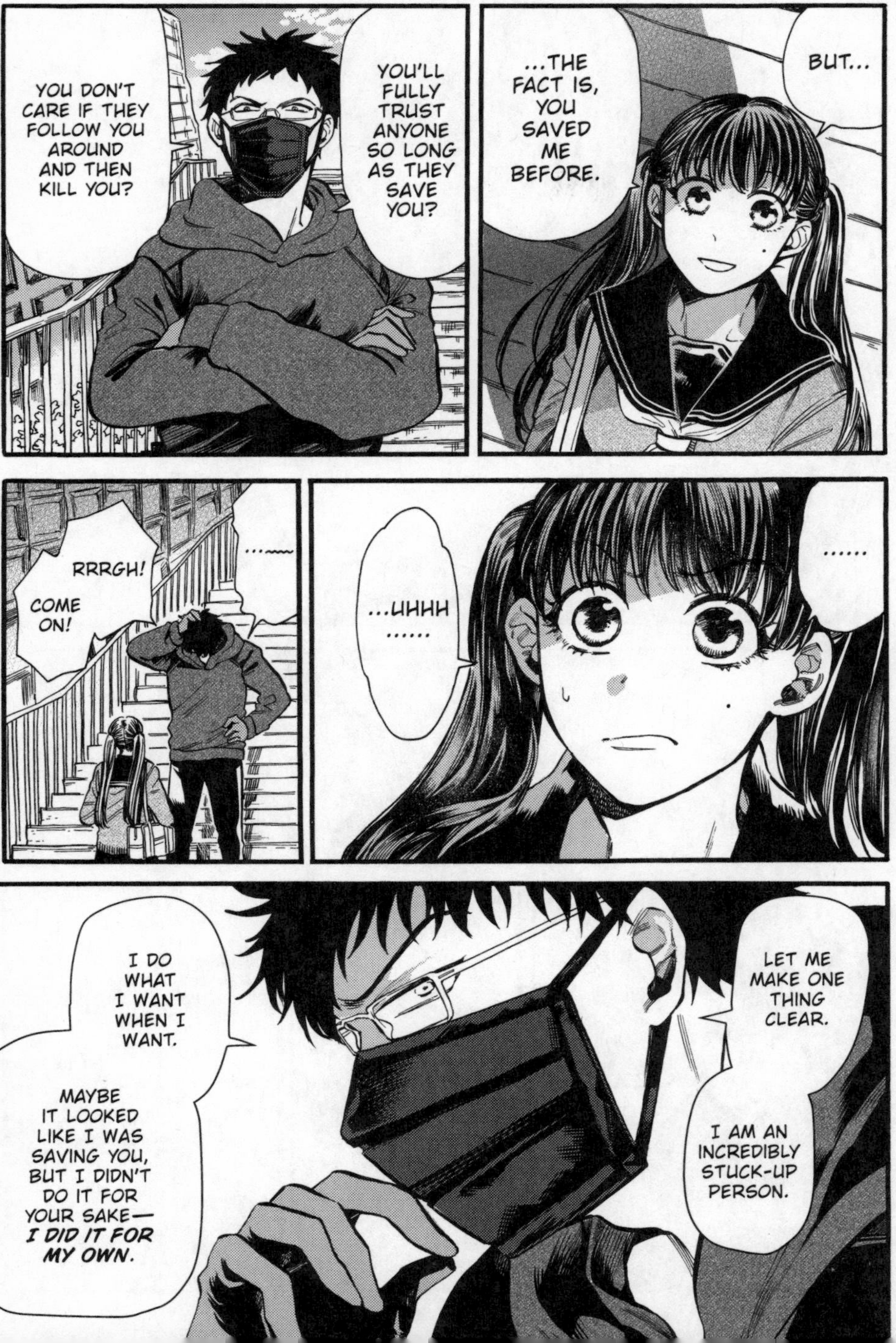
BUT...
...THE FACT IS, YOU SAVED ME BEFORE.
YOU'LL FULLY TRUST ANYONE SO LONG AS THEY SAVE YOU?
YOU DON'T CARE IF THEY FOLLOW YOU AROUND AND THEN KILL YOU?
......
...UHHH ......
...~~
RRRGH!
COME ON!
LET ME MAKE ONE THING CLEAR.
I AM AN INCREDIBLY STUCK-UP PERSON.
I DO WHAT I WANT WHEN I WANT.
MAYBE IT LOOKED LIKE I WAS SAVING YOU, BUT I DIDN'T DO IT FOR YOUR SAKE— *I DID IT FOR MY OWN.*

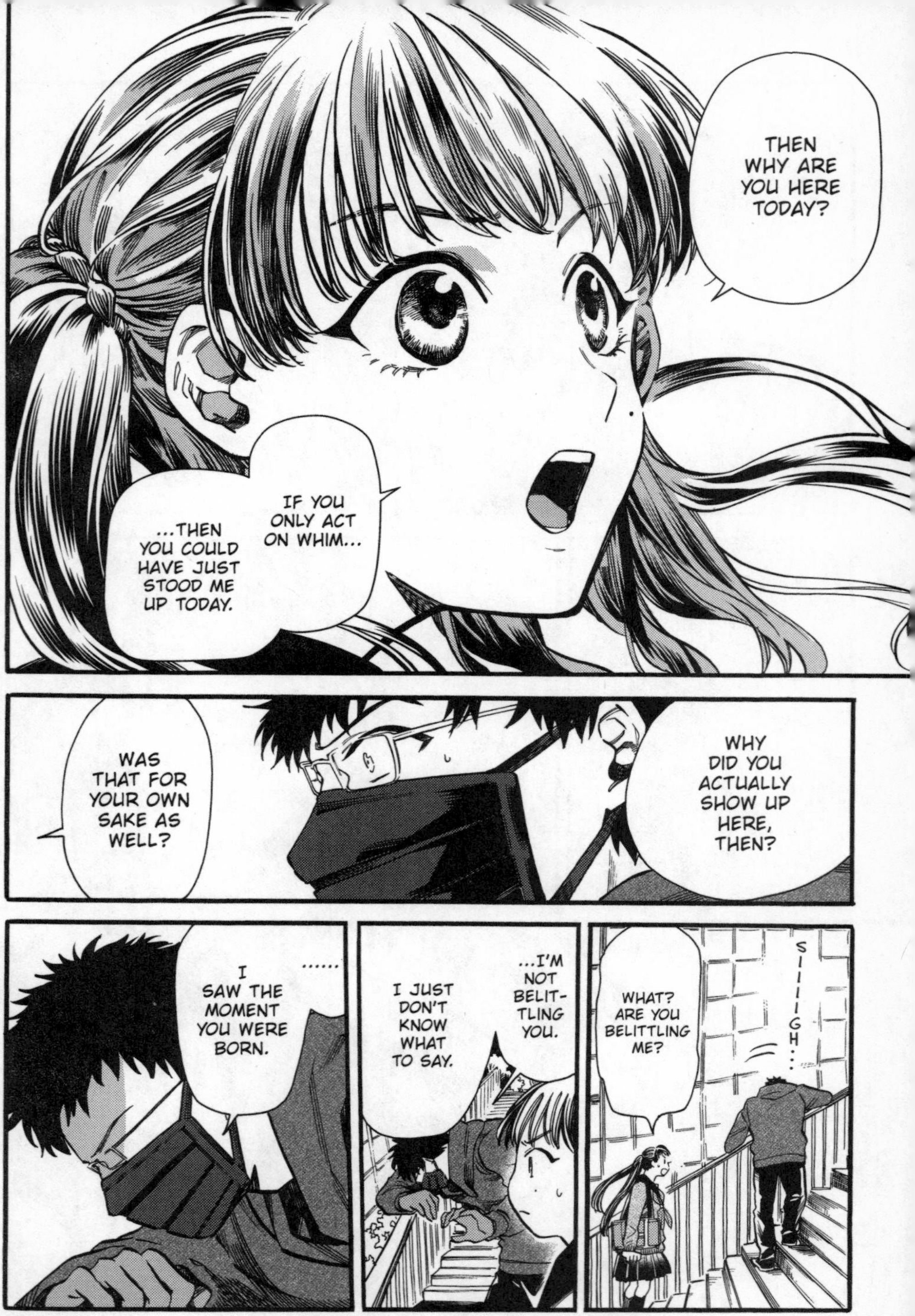
THEN WHY ARE YOU HERE TODAY?
IF YOU ONLY ACT ON WHIM...
...THEN YOU COULD HAVE JUST STOOD ME UP TODAY.
WHY DID YOU ACTUALLY SHOW UP HERE, THEN?
WAS THAT FOR YOUR OWN SAKE AS WELL?
S-I-I-I-G-H...
WHAT? ARE YOU BELITTLING ME?
...I'M NOT BELIT-TLING YOU.
I JUST DON'T KNOW WHAT TO SAY.
......
I SAW THE MOMENT YOU WERE BORN.

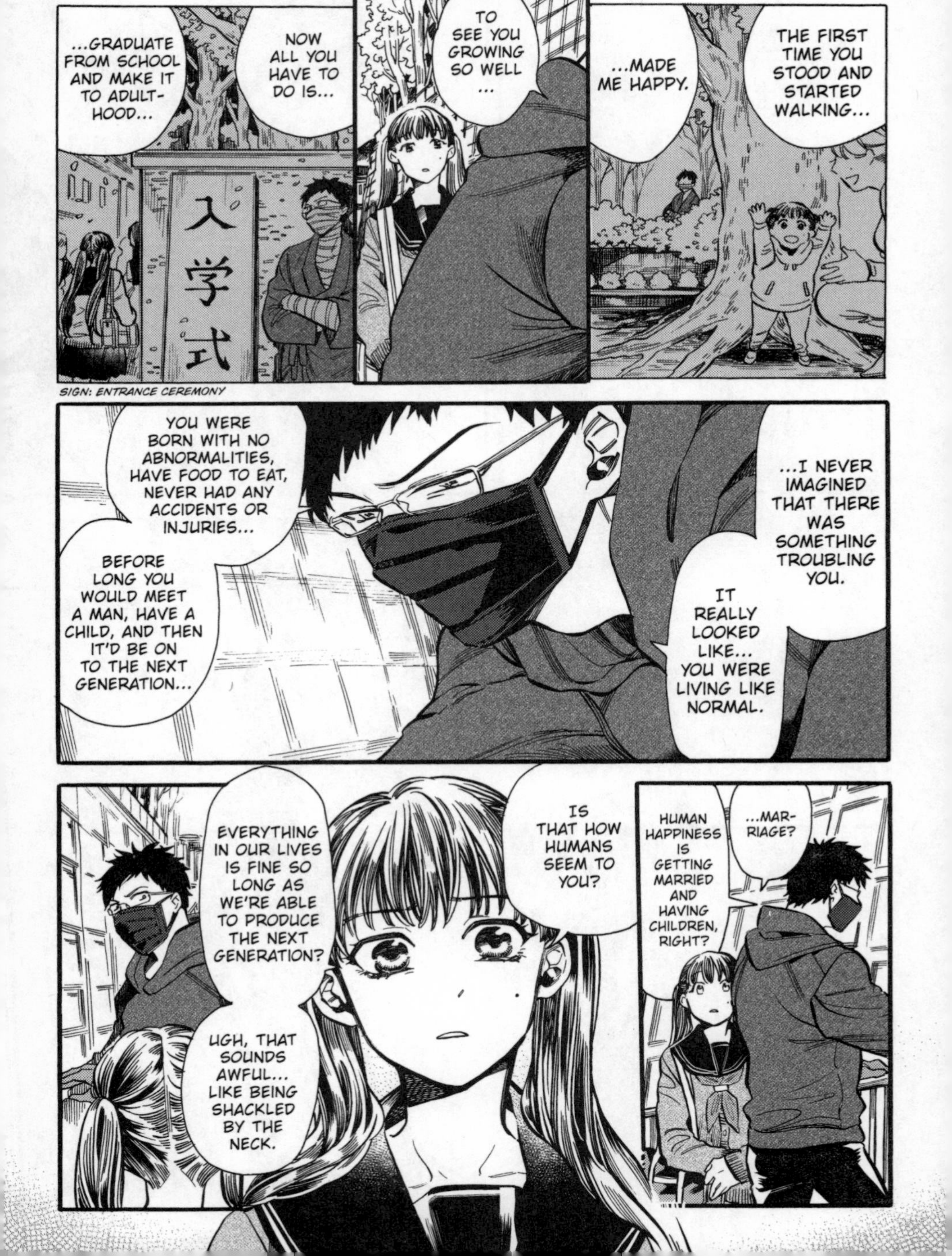

THE FIRST TIME YOU STOOD AND STARTED WALKING...
...MADE ME HAPPY.
TO SEE YOU GROWING SO WELL ...
NOW ALL YOU HAVE TO DO IS...
...GRADUATE FROM SCHOOL AND MAKE IT TO ADULTHOOD...
入学式
SIGN: ENTRANCE CEREMONY
...I NEVER IMAGINED THAT THERE WAS SOMETHING TROUBLING YOU.
IT REALLY LOOKED LIKE... YOU WERE LIVING LIKE NORMAL.
YOU WERE BORN WITH NO ABNORMALITIES, HAVE FOOD TO EAT, NEVER HAD ANY ACCIDENTS OR INJURIES...
BEFORE LONG YOU WOULD MEET A MAN, HAVE A CHILD, AND THEN IT'D BE ON TO THE NEXT GENERATION...
...MARRIAGE?
HUMAN HAPPINESS IS GETTING MARRIED AND HAVING CHILDREN, RIGHT?
IS THAT HOW HUMANS SEEM TO YOU?
EVERYTHING IN OUR LIVES IS FINE SO LONG AS WE'RE ABLE TO PRODUCE THE NEXT GENERATION?
UGH, THAT SOUNDS AWFUL... LIKE BEING SHACKLED BY THE NECK.

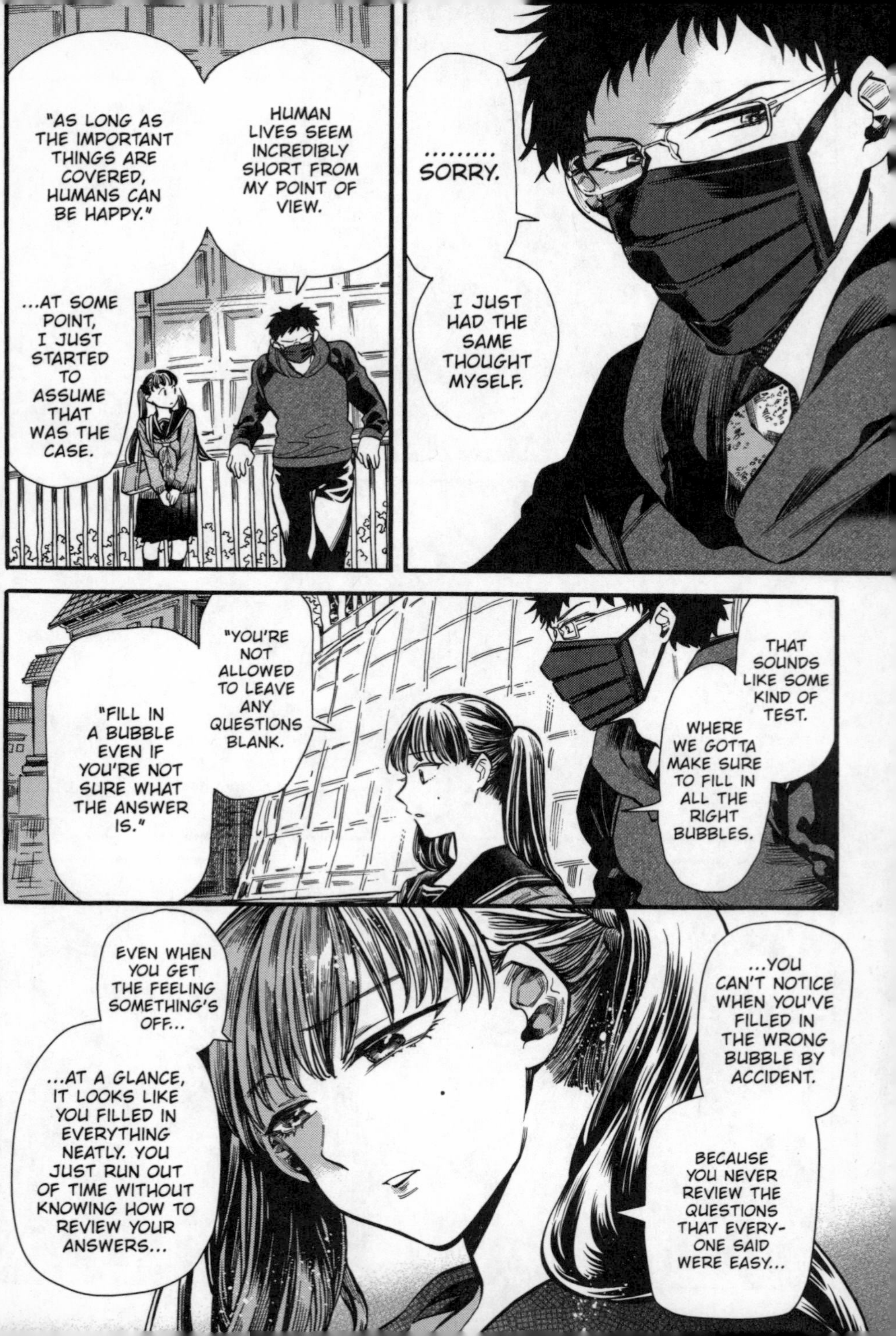
....
SORRY.
I JUST HAD THE SAME THOUGHT MYSELF.
HUMAN LIVES SEEM INCREDIBLY SHORT FROM MY POINT OF VIEW.
"AS LONG AS THE IMPORTANT THINGS ARE COVERED, HUMANS CAN BE HAPPY."
...AT SOME POINT, I JUST STARTED TO ASSUME THAT WAS THE CASE.
THAT SOUNDS LIKE SOME KIND OF TEST.
WHERE WE GOTTA MAKE SURE TO FILL IN ALL THE RIGHT BUBBLES.
"YOU'RE NOT ALLOWED TO LEAVE ANY QUESTIONS BLANK.
"FILL IN A BUBBLE EVEN IF YOU'RE NOT SURE WHAT THE ANSWER IS."
...YOU CAN'T NOTICE WHEN YOU'VE FILLED IN THE WRONG BUBBLE BY ACCIDENT.
BECAUSE YOU NEVER REVIEW THE QUESTIONS THAT EVERY-ONE SAID WERE EASY...
EVEN WHEN YOU GET THE FEELING SOMETHING'S OFF...
...AT A GLANCE, IT LOOKS LIKE YOU FILLED IN EVERYTHING NEATLY. YOU JUST RUN OUT OF TIME WITHOUT KNOWING HOW TO REVIEW YOUR ANSWERS...

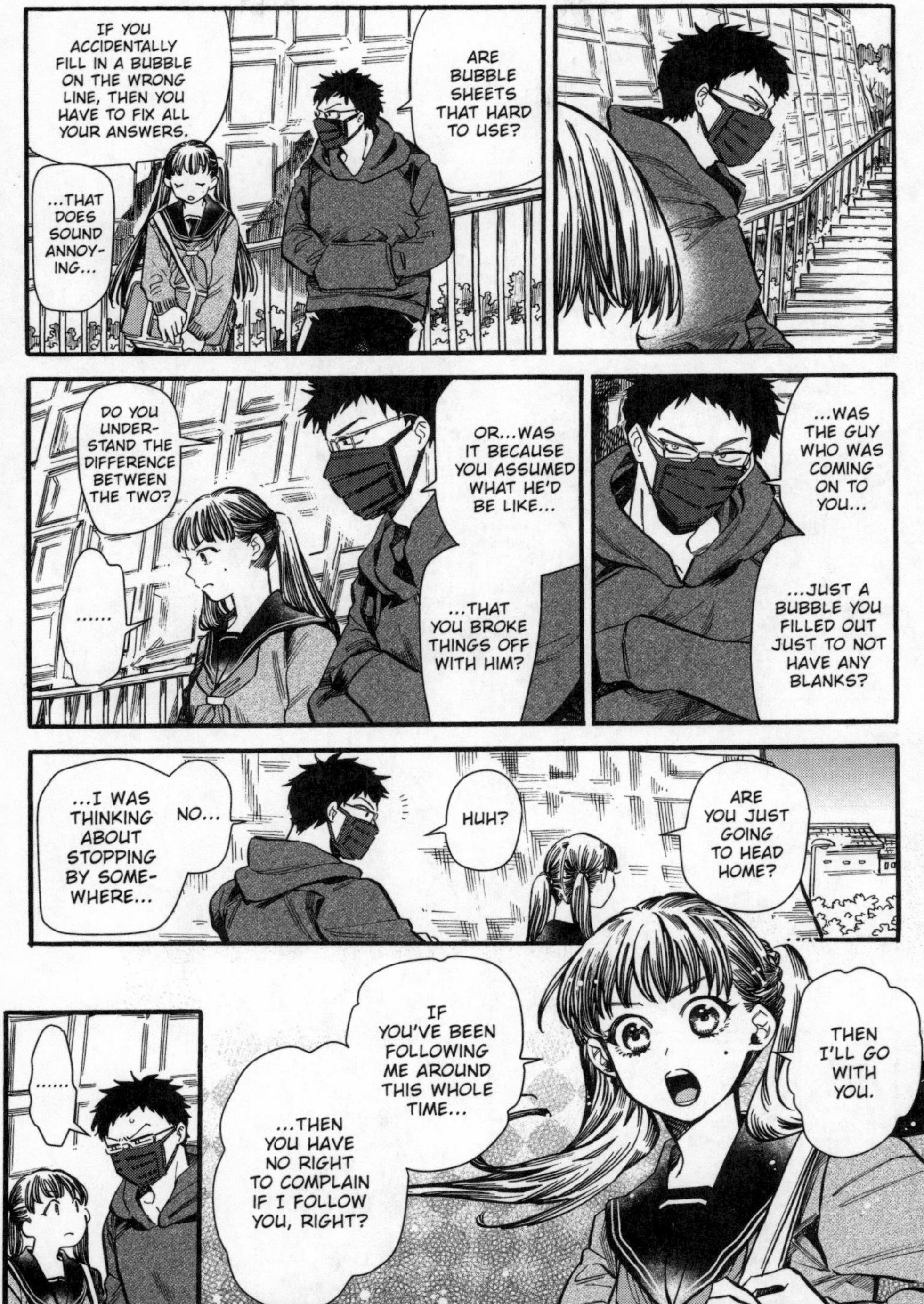
ARE BUBBLE SHEETS THAT HARD TO USE?
IF YOU ACCIDENTALLY FILL IN A BUBBLE ON THE WRONG LINE, THEN YOU HAVE TO FIX ALL YOUR ANSWERS.
...THAT DOES SOUND ANNOY-ING...
...WAS THE GUY WHO WAS COMING ON TO YOU...
...JUST A BUBBLE YOU FILLED OUT JUST TO NOT HAVE ANY BLANKS?
OR...WAS IT BECAUSE YOU ASSUMED WHAT HE'D BE LIKE...
...THAT YOU BROKE THINGS OFF WITH HIM?
DO YOU UNDER-STAND THE DIFFERENCE BETWEEN THE TWO?
......
ARE YOU JUST GOING TO HEAD HOME?
HUH?
NO...
...I WAS THINKING ABOUT STOPPING BY SOME-WHERE...
THEN I'LL GO WITH YOU.
IF YOU'VE BEEN FOLLOWING ME AROUND THIS WHOLE TIME...
...THEN YOU HAVE NO RIGHT TO COMPLAIN IF I FOLLOW YOU, RIGHT?
......

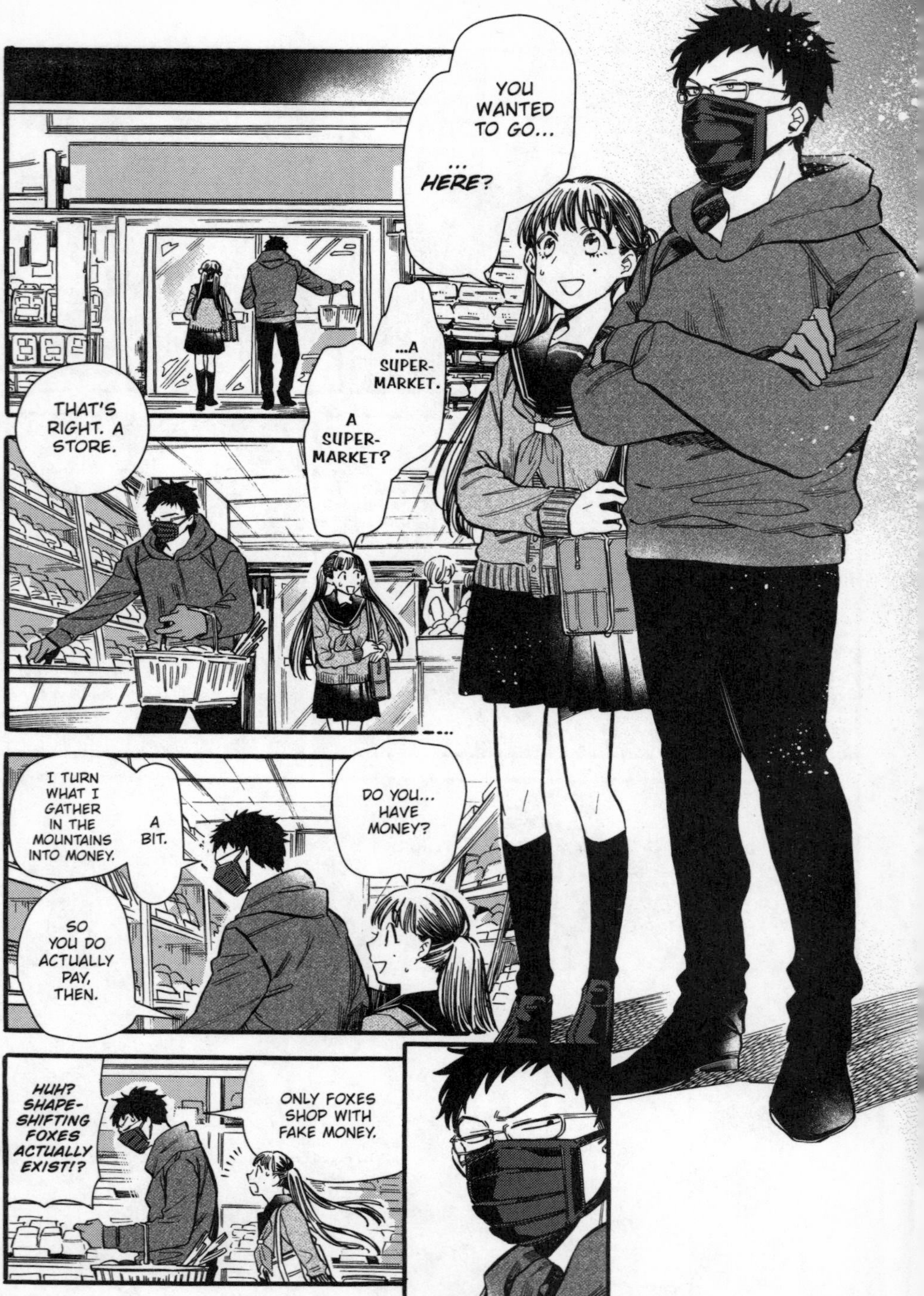
YOU WANTED TO GO...
... HERE?
...A SUPER-MARKET.
A SUPER-MARKET?
THAT'S RIGHT. A STORE.
....
DO YOU... HAVE MONEY?
A BIT.
I TURN WHAT I GATHER IN THE MOUNTAINS INTO MONEY.
SO YOU DO ACTUALLY PAY, THEN.
ONLY FOXES SHOP WITH FAKE MONEY.
HUH? SHAPE-SHIFTING FOXES ACTUALLY EXIST!?

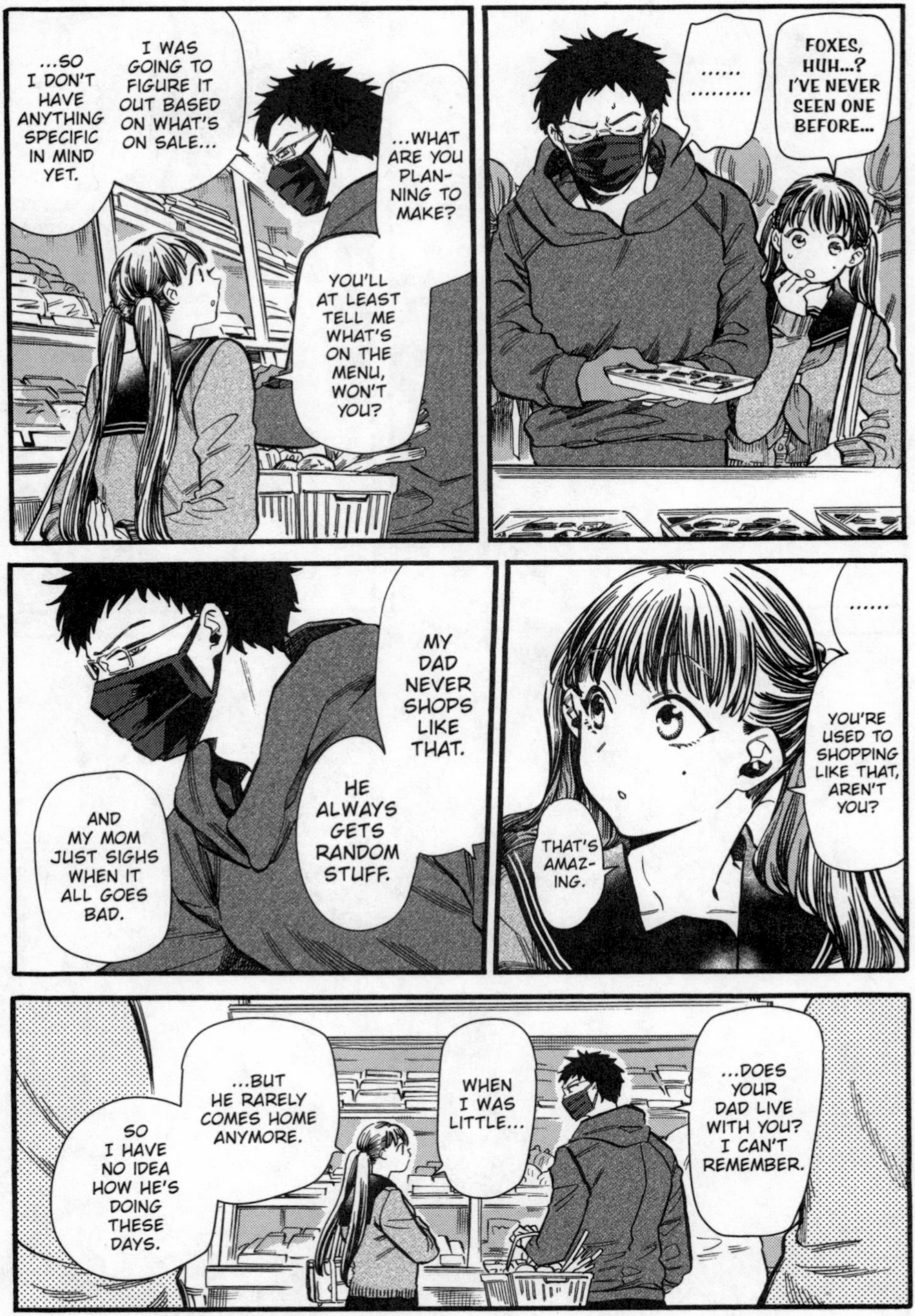
FOXES, HUH...? I'VE NEVER SEEN ONE BEFORE...
....
...WHAT ARE YOU PLAN-NING TO MAKE?
I WAS GOING TO FIGURE IT OUT BASED ON WHAT'S ON SALE...
...SO I DON'T HAVE ANYTHING SPECIFIC IN MIND YET.
YOU'LL AT LEAST TELL ME WHAT'S ON THE MENU, WON'T YOU?
......
YOU'RE USED TO SHOPPING LIKE THAT, AREN'T YOU?
THAT'S AMAZ-ING.
MY DAD NEVER SHOPS LIKE THAT.
HE ALWAYS GETS RANDOM STUFF.
AND MY MOM JUST SIGHS WHEN IT ALL GOES BAD.
...DOES YOUR DAD LIVE WITH YOU? I CAN'T REMEMBER.
WHEN I WAS LITTLE...
...BUT HE RARELY COMES HOME ANYMORE.
SO I HAVE NO IDEA HOW HE'S DOING THESE DAYS.

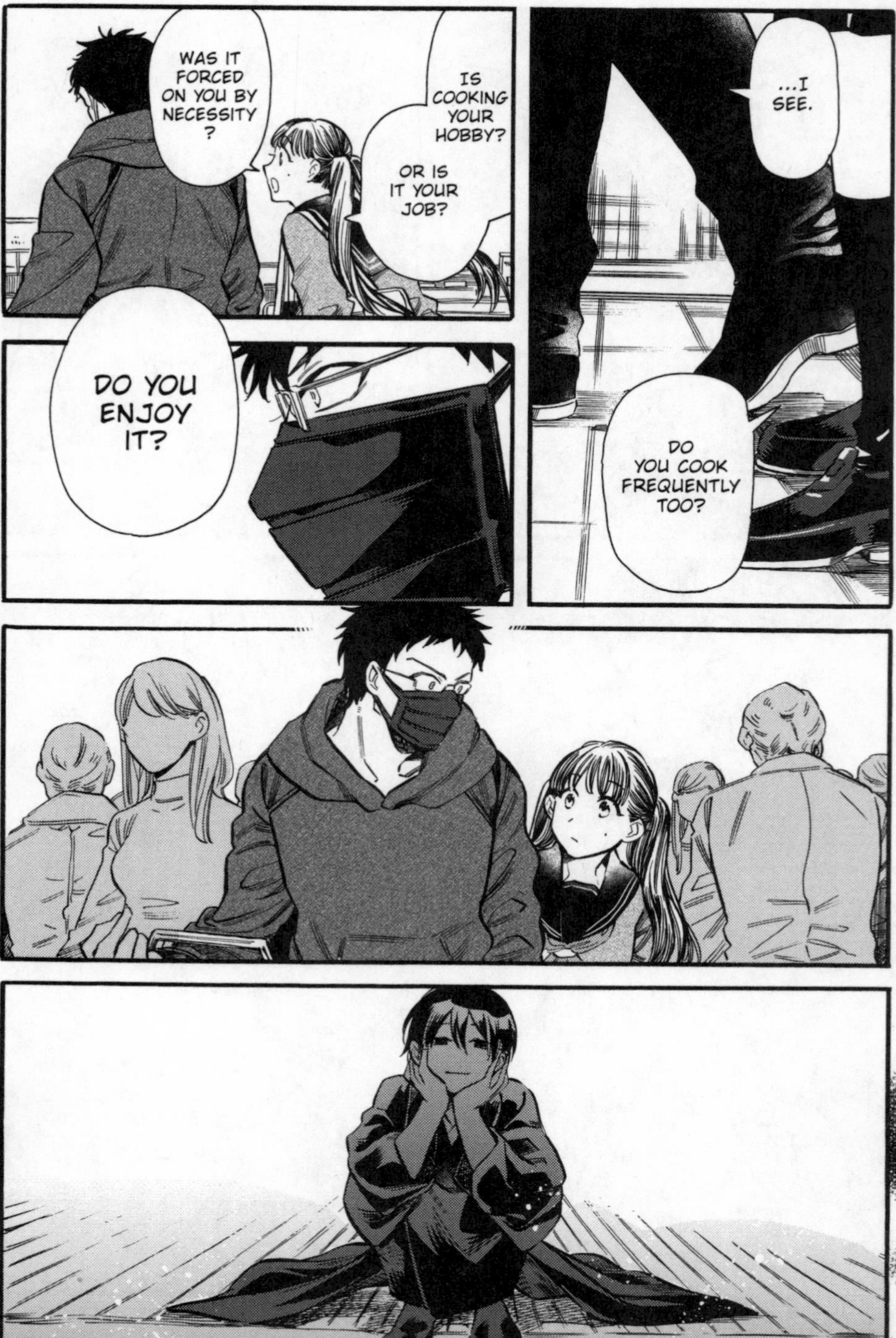
...I SEE.
DO YOU COOK FREQUENTLY TOO?
IS COOKING YOUR HOBBY?
OR IS IT YOUR JOB?
WAS IT FORCED ON YOU BY NECESSITY?
DO YOU ENJOY IT?

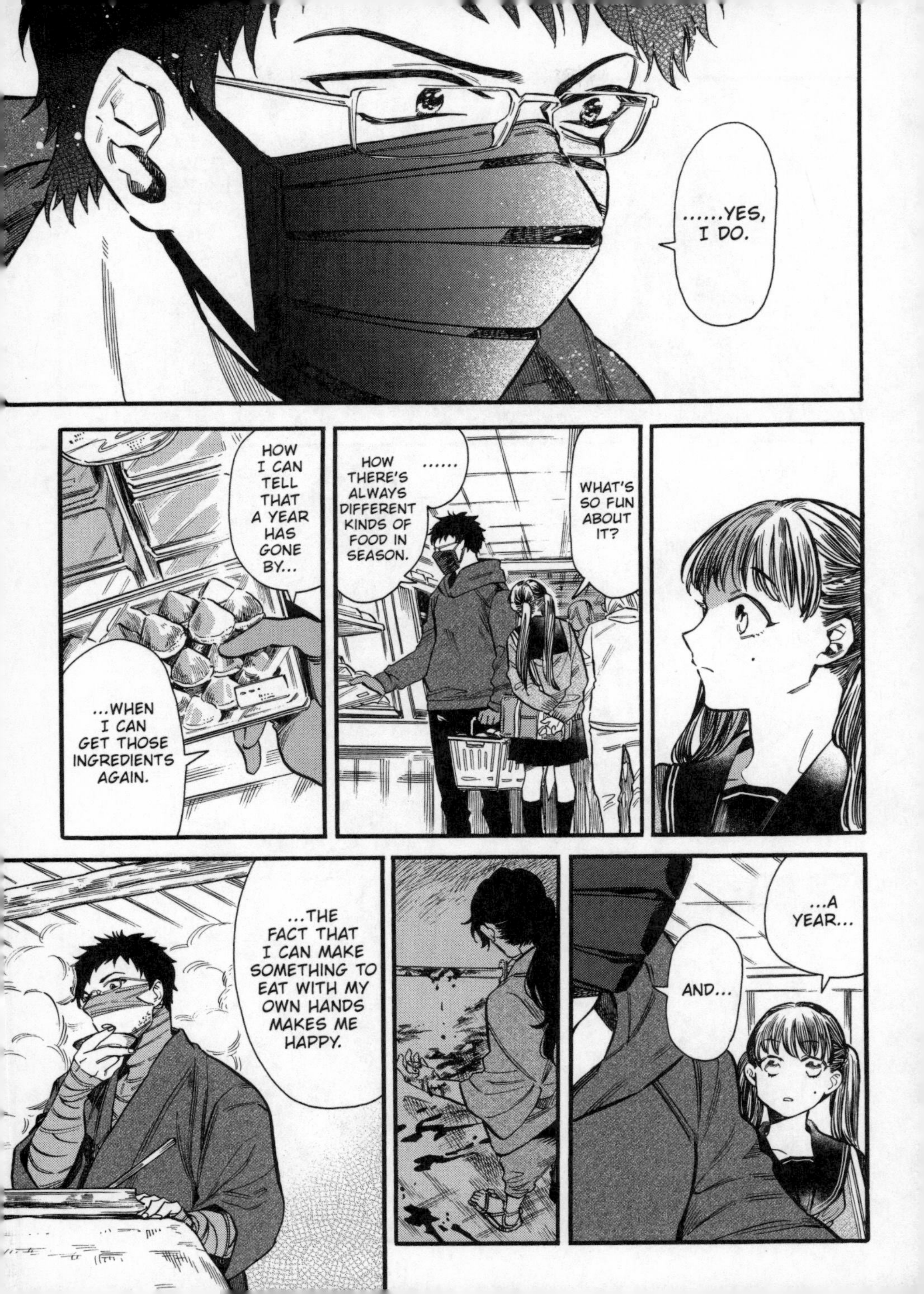

......YES, I DO.
WHAT'S SO FUN ABOUT IT?
......
HOW THERE'S ALWAYS DIFFERENT KINDS OF FOOD IN SEASON.
HOW I CAN TELL THAT A YEAR HAS GONE BY...
...WHEN I CAN GET THOSE INGREDIENTS AGAIN.
...A YEAR...
AND...
...THE FACT THAT I CAN MAKE SOMETHING TO EAT WITH MY OWN HANDS MAKES ME HAPPY.

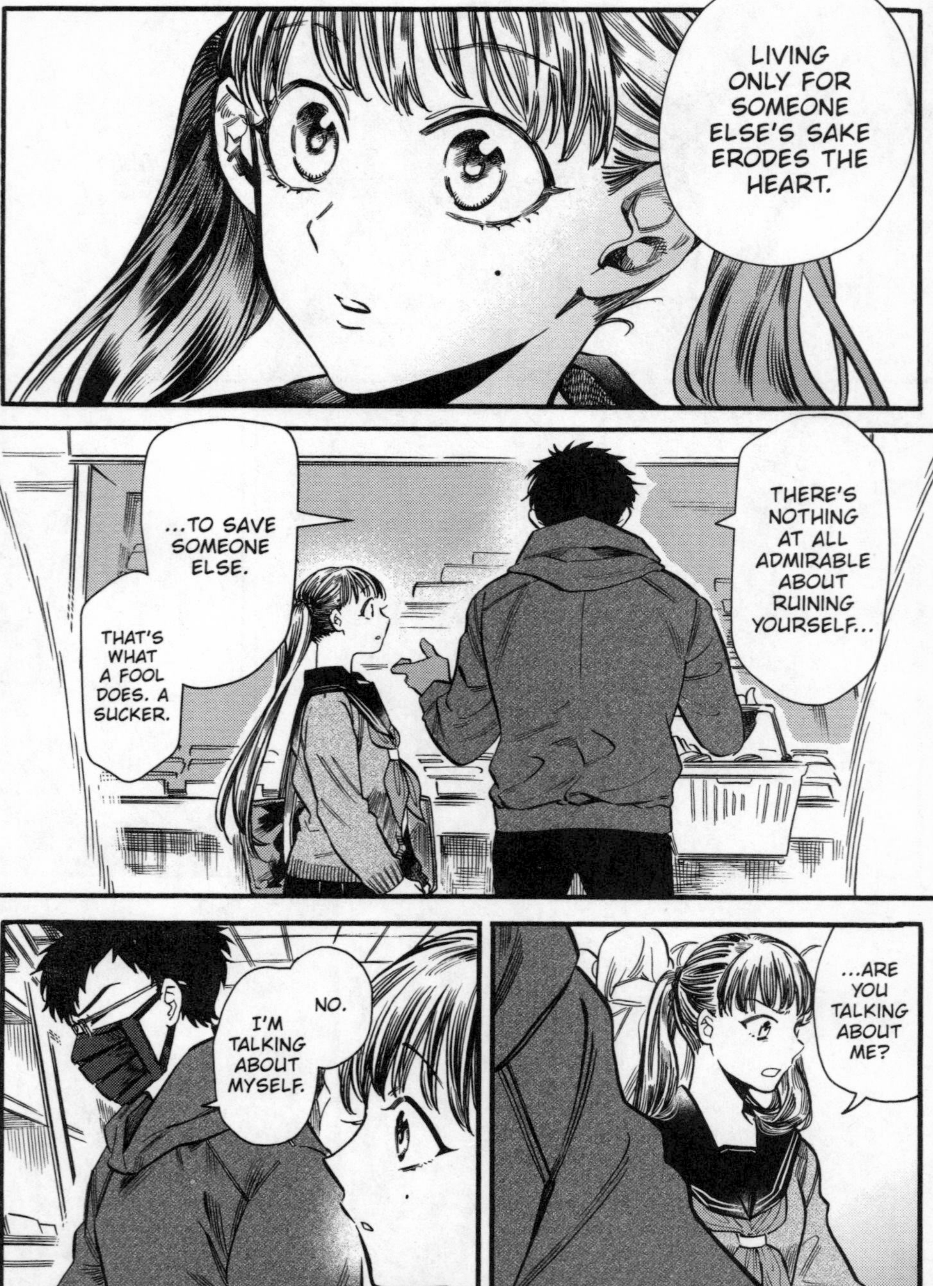
LIVING ONLY FOR SOMEONE ELSE'S SAKE ERODES THE HEART.
THERE'S NOTHING AT ALL ADMIRABLE ABOUT RUINING YOURSELF...
...TO SAVE SOMEONE ELSE.
THAT'S WHAT A FOOL DOES. A SUCKER.
...ARE YOU TALKING ABOUT ME?
NO.
I'M TALKING ABOUT MYSELF.

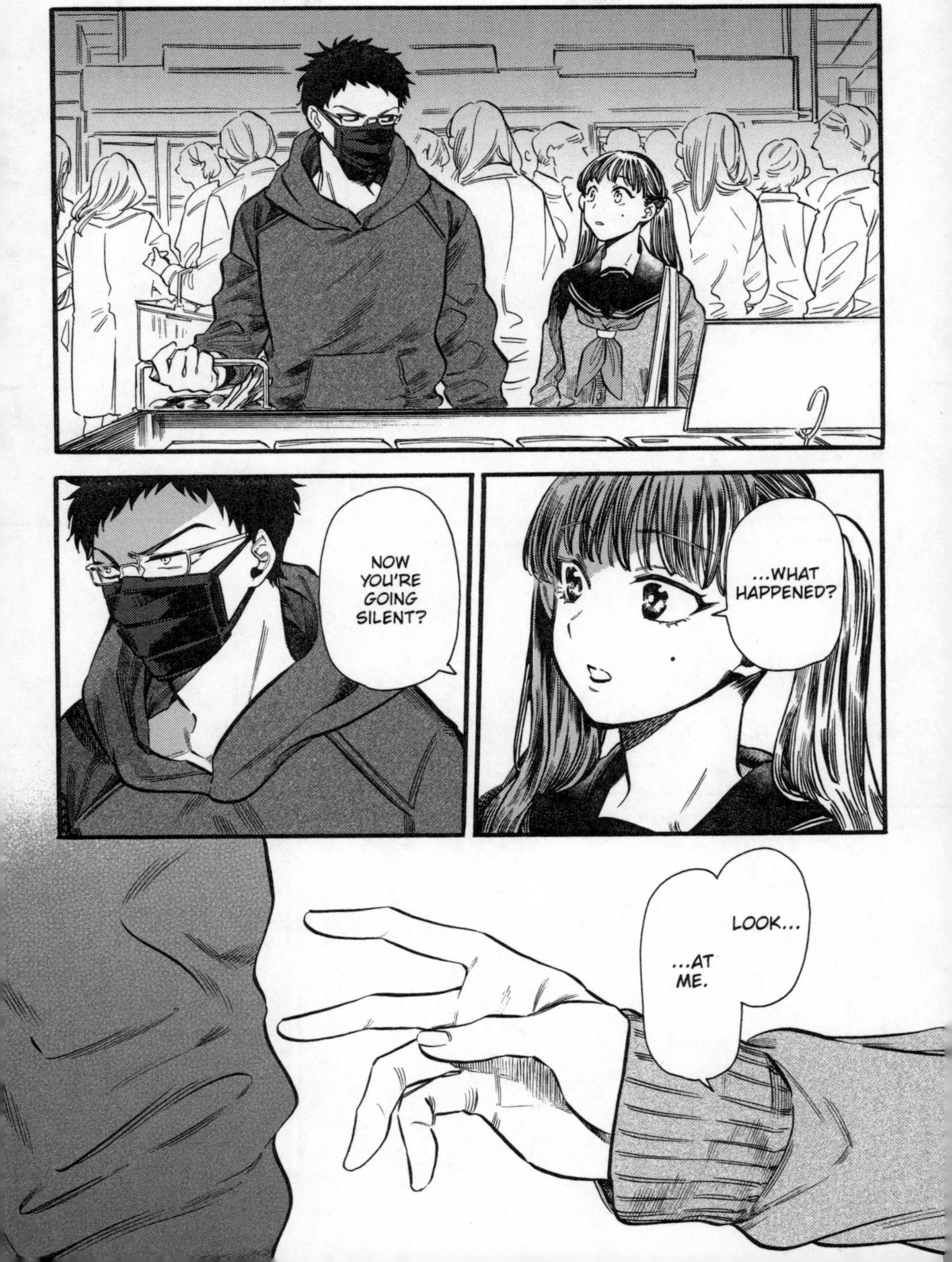
...WHAT HAPPENED?
NOW YOU'RE GOING SILENT?
LOOK...
...AT ME.

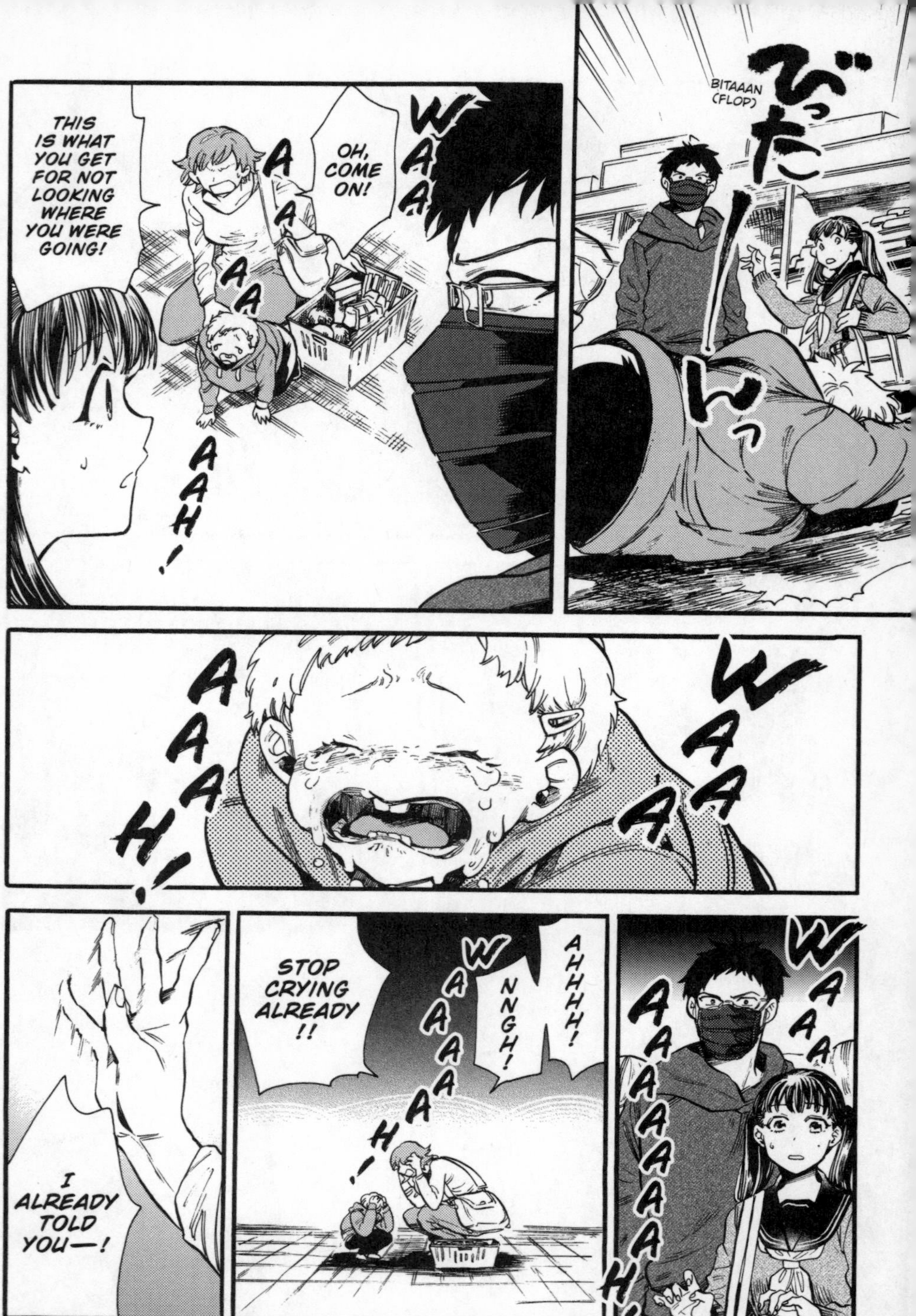

びったーんっ
BITAAAN (FLOP)
WAAA
OH, COME ON!
AAAAAAAH!
THIS IS WHAT YOU GET FOR NOT LOOKING WHERE YOU WERE GOING!
WAAAA
AAAAH!!
WAAAAAAAAAAAAAAAH!
AHHHH!
NNGH!
STOP CRYING ALREADY!!
WAAAAAAH!
I ALREADY TOLD YOU—!

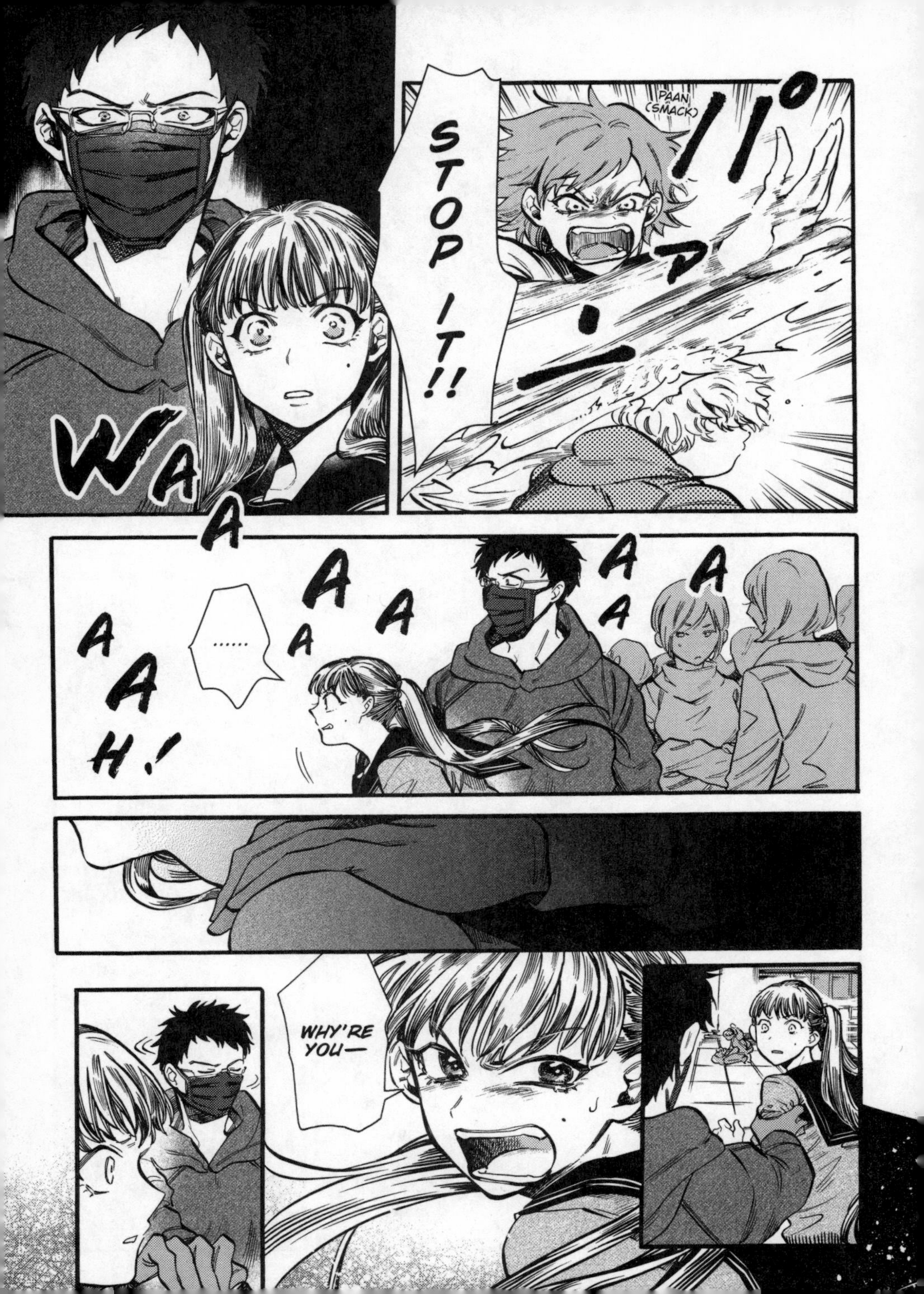

STOP IT!!
PAAN (SMACK)
パ
ー
ン
WAAAAAAAAAAAH!
......
WHY'RE YOU—

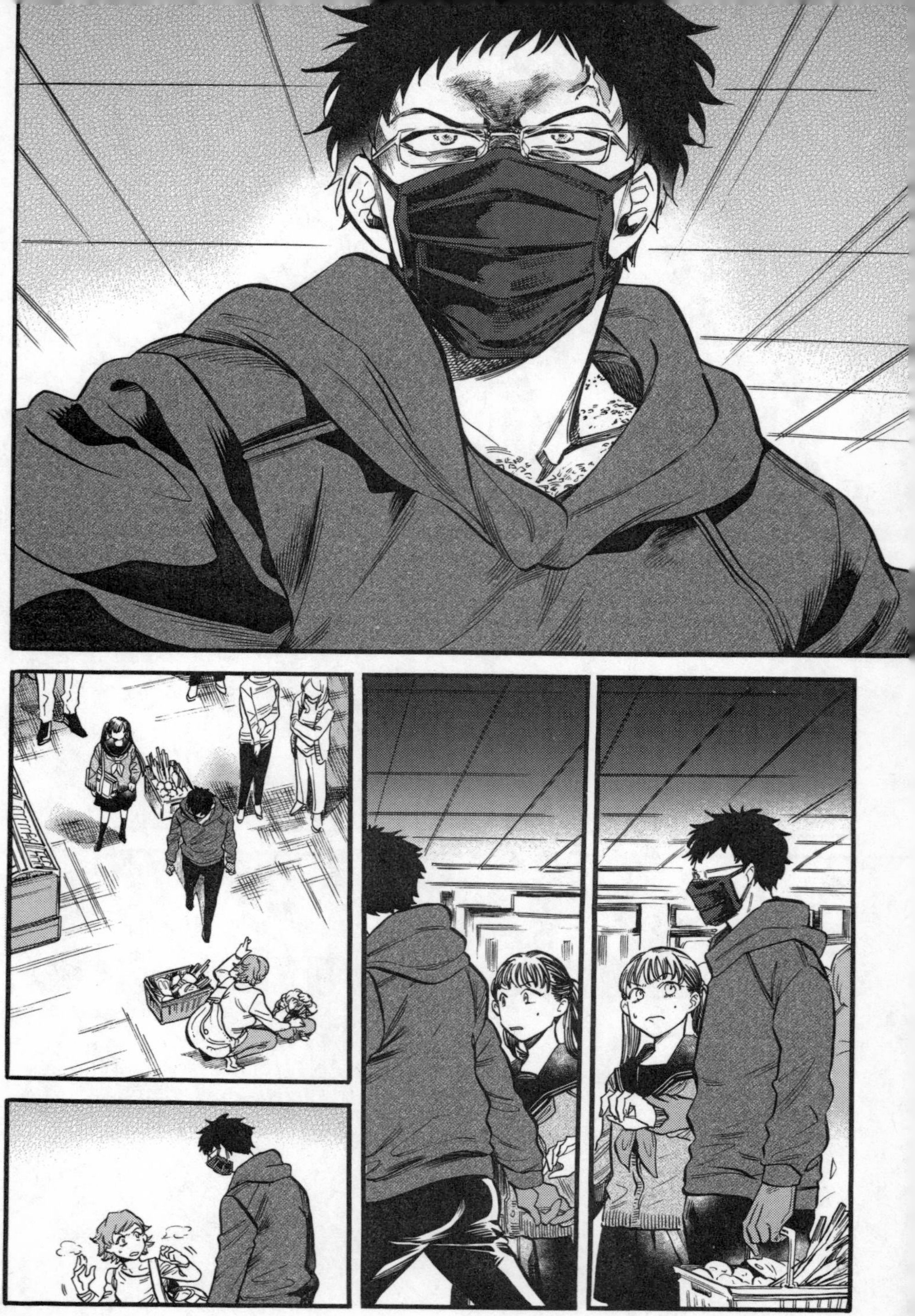

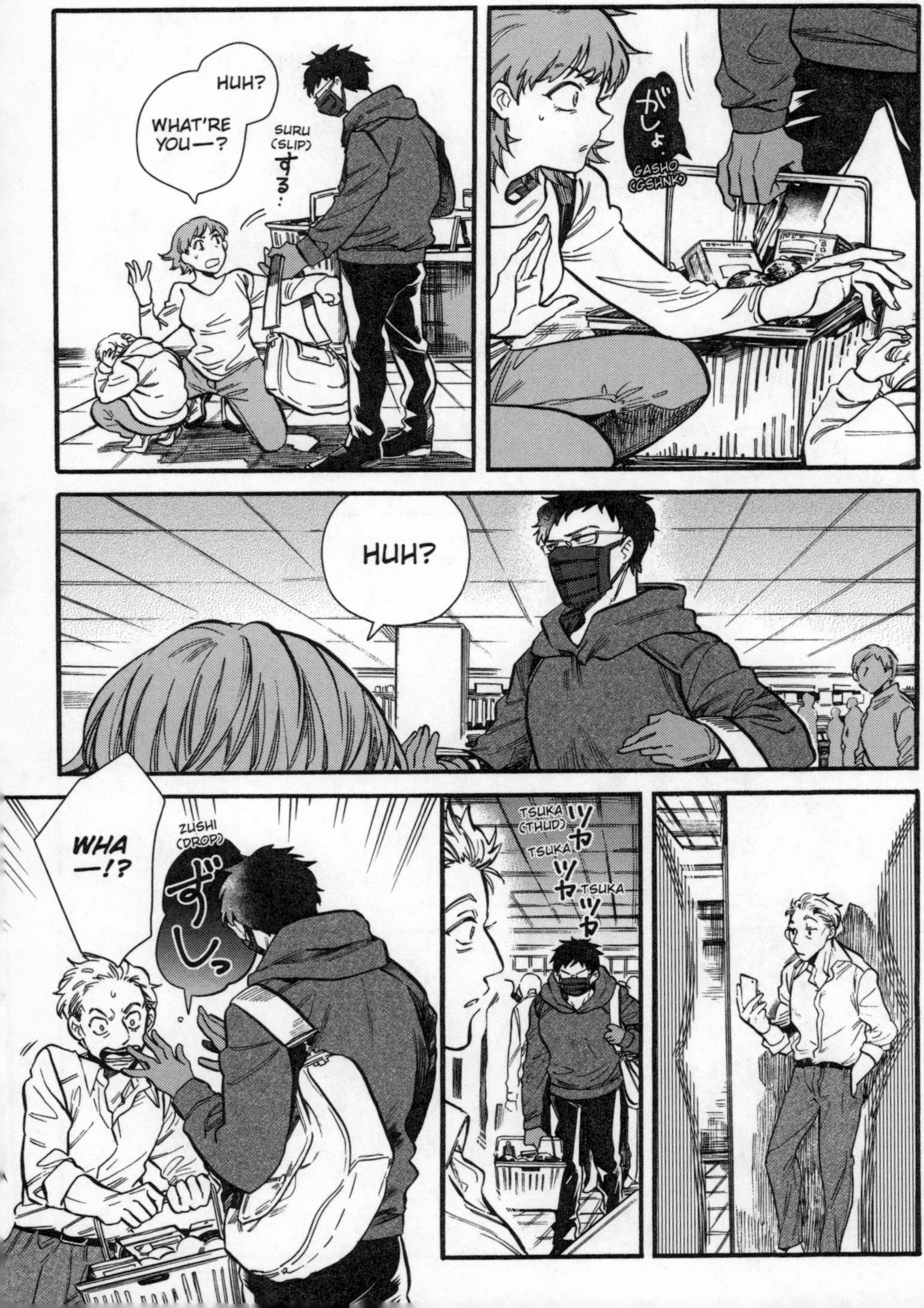
がしょ・
GASHO (GSHNK)
HUH?
WHAT'RE YOU—?
SURU (SLIP)
する…
HUH?
TSUKA (THUD)
ツカ
TSUKA
ツカ
TSUKA
ツカ
WHA—!?
ZUSHI (DROP)
ずしっ

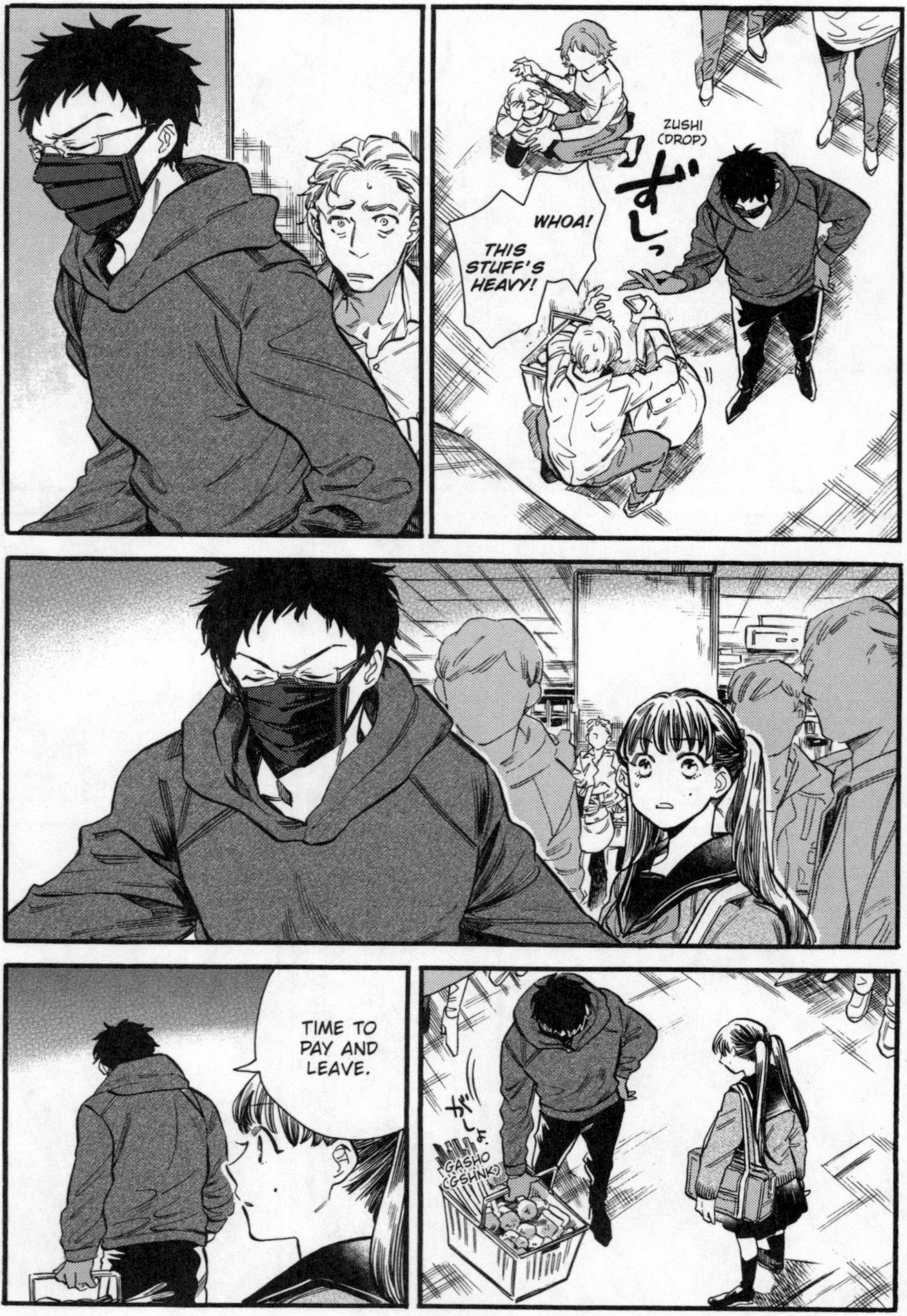
ZUSHI (DROP)
ずしっ
WHOA! THIS STUFF'S HEAVY!
がしょ.
GASHO (GSHNK)
TIME TO PAY AND LEAVE.

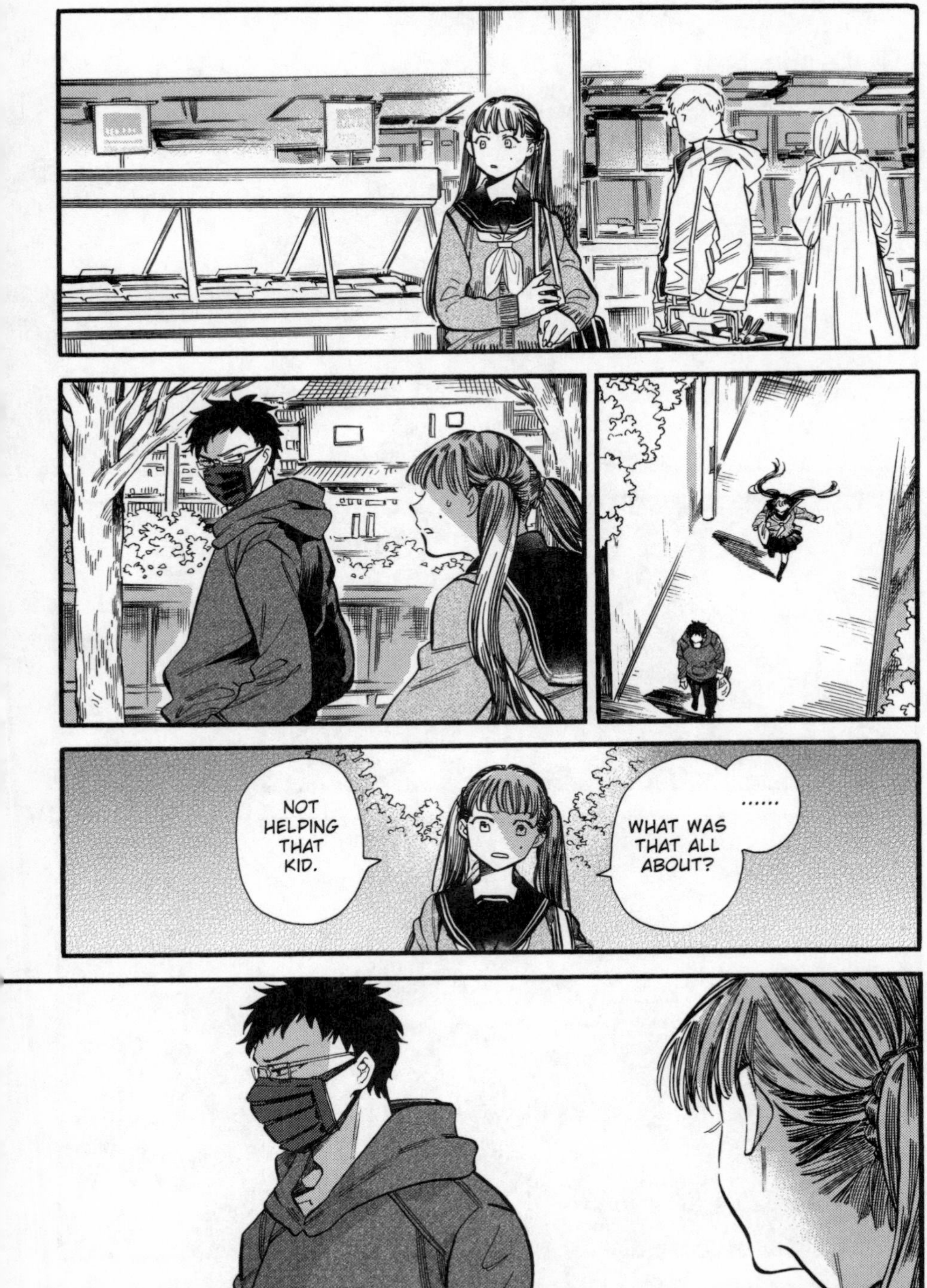
......
WHAT WAS THAT ALL ABOUT?
NOT HELPING THAT KID.

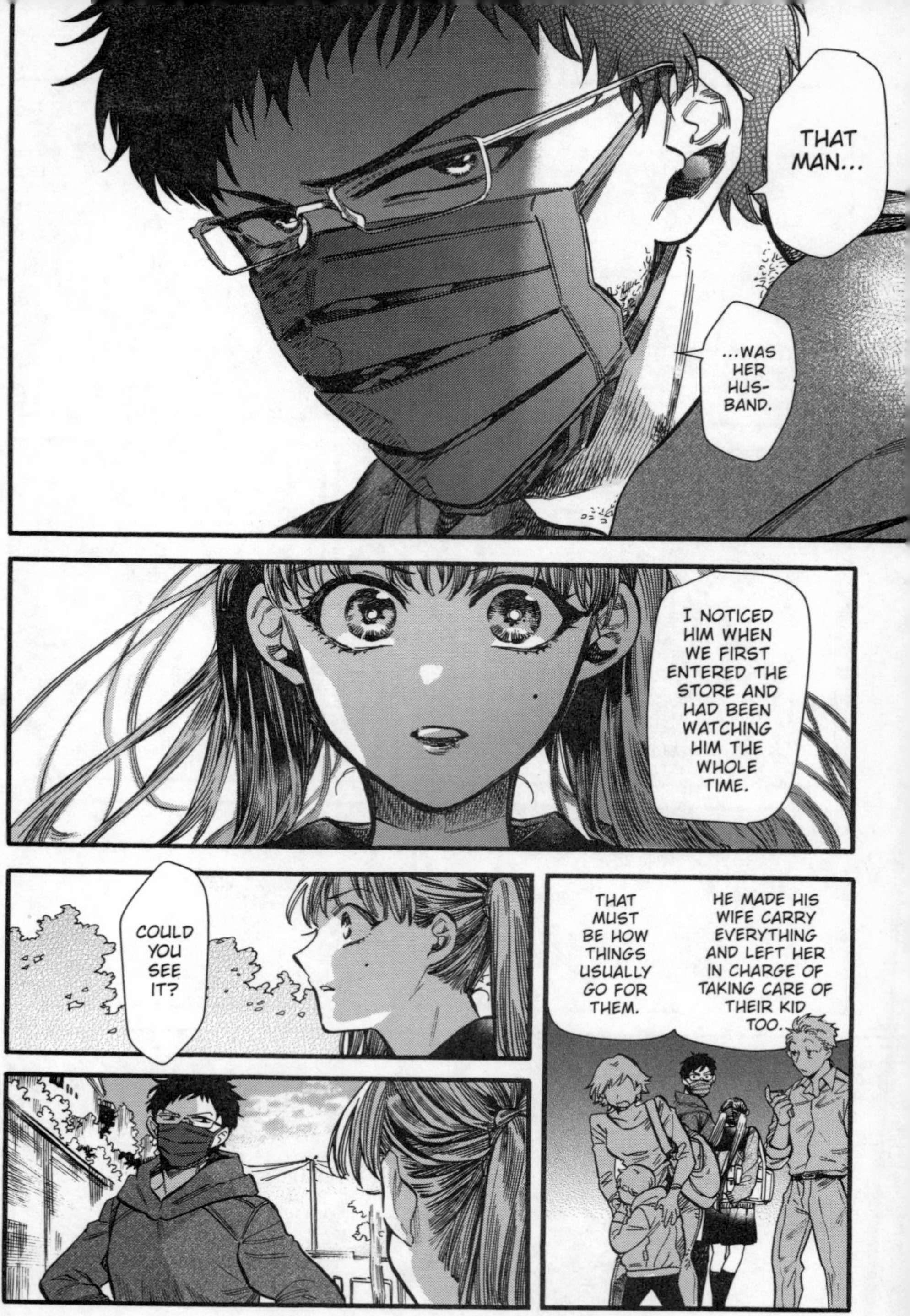
THAT MAN...
...WAS HER HUS-BAND.
I NOTICED HIM WHEN WE FIRST ENTERED THE STORE AND HAD BEEN WATCHING HIM THE WHOLE TIME.
HE MADE HIS WIFE CARRY EVERYTHING AND LEFT HER IN CHARGE OF TAKING CARE OF THEIR KID TOO.
THAT MUST BE HOW THINGS USUALLY GO FOR THEM.
COULD YOU SEE IT?

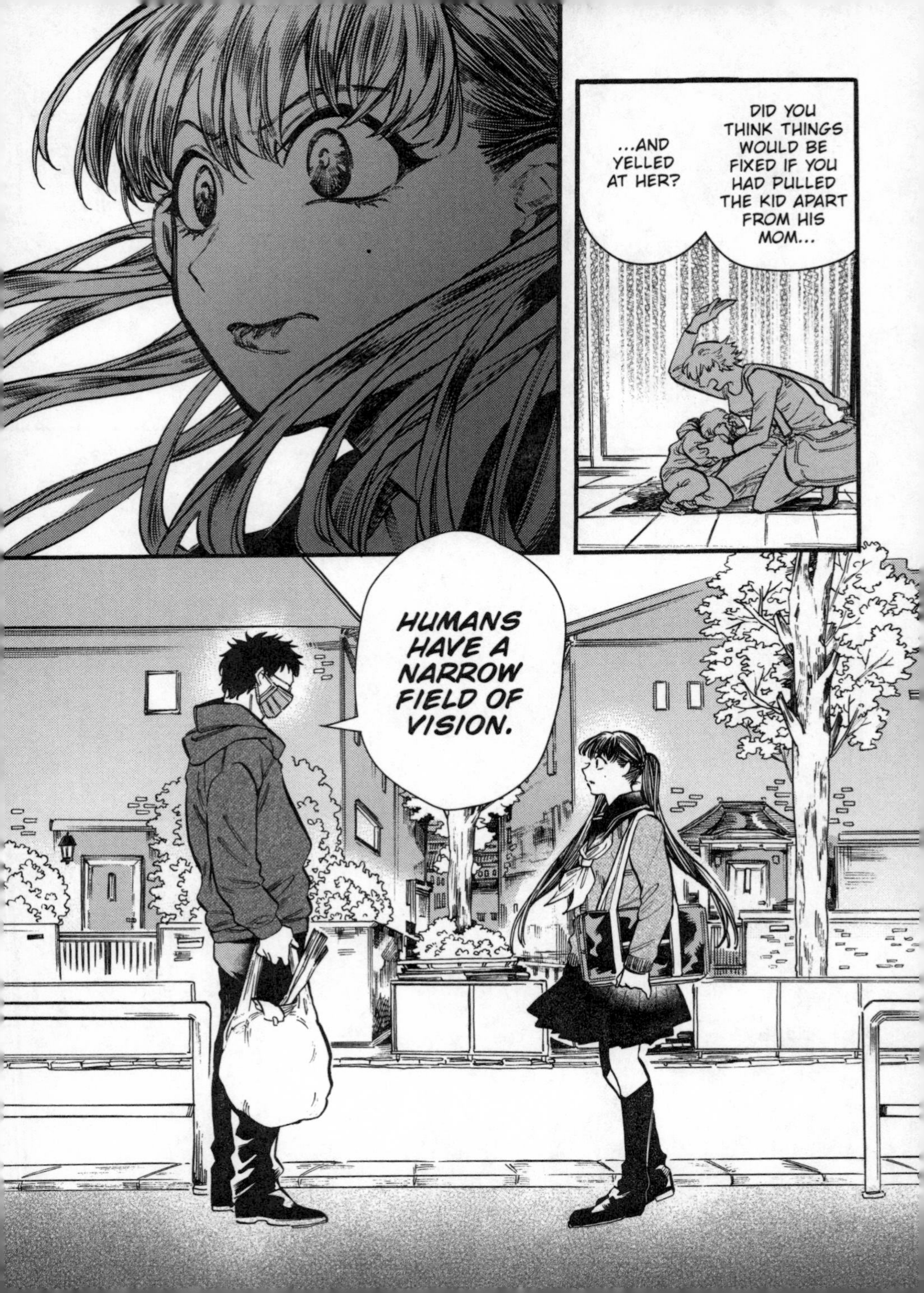
DID YOU THINK THINGS WOULD BE FIXED IF YOU HAD PULLED THE KID APART FROM HIS MOM...
...AND YELLED AT HER?
HUMANS HAVE A NARROW FIELD OF VISION.

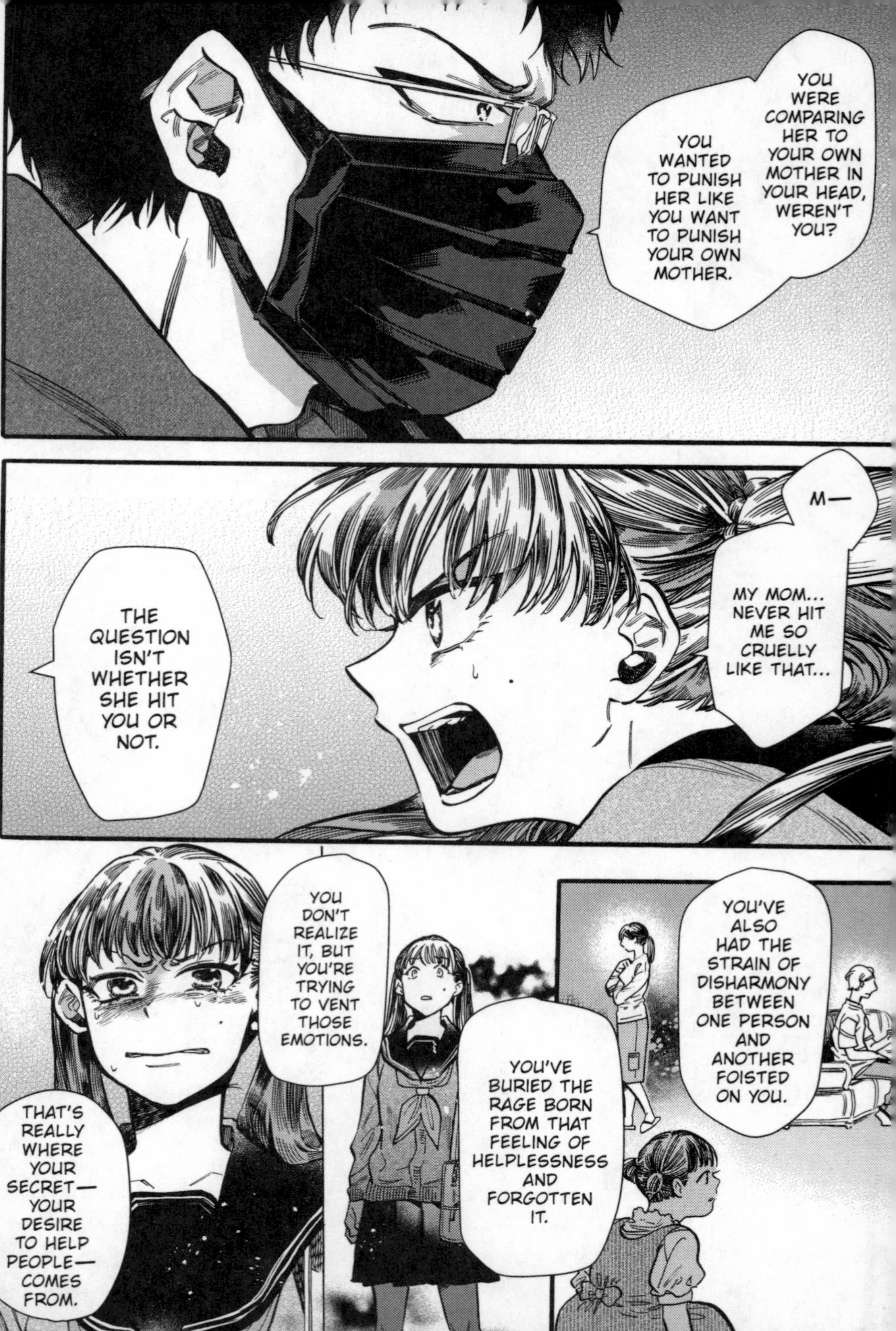
YOU WERE COMPARING HER TO YOUR OWN MOTHER IN YOUR HEAD, WEREN'T YOU?
YOU WANTED TO PUNISH HER LIKE YOU WANT TO PUNISH YOUR OWN MOTHER.
M—
MY MOM... NEVER HIT ME SO CRUELLY LIKE THAT...
THE QUESTION ISN'T WHETHER SHE HIT YOU OR NOT.
YOU'VE ALSO HAD THE STRAIN OF DISHARMONY BETWEEN ONE PERSON AND ANOTHER FOISTED ON YOU.
YOU'VE BURIED THE RAGE BORN FROM THAT FEELING OF HELPLESSNESS AND FORGOTTEN IT.
YOU DON'T REALIZE IT, BUT YOU'RE TRYING TO VENT THOSE EMOTIONS.
THAT'S REALLY WHERE YOUR SECRET—YOUR DESIRE TO HELP PEOPLE—COMES FROM.

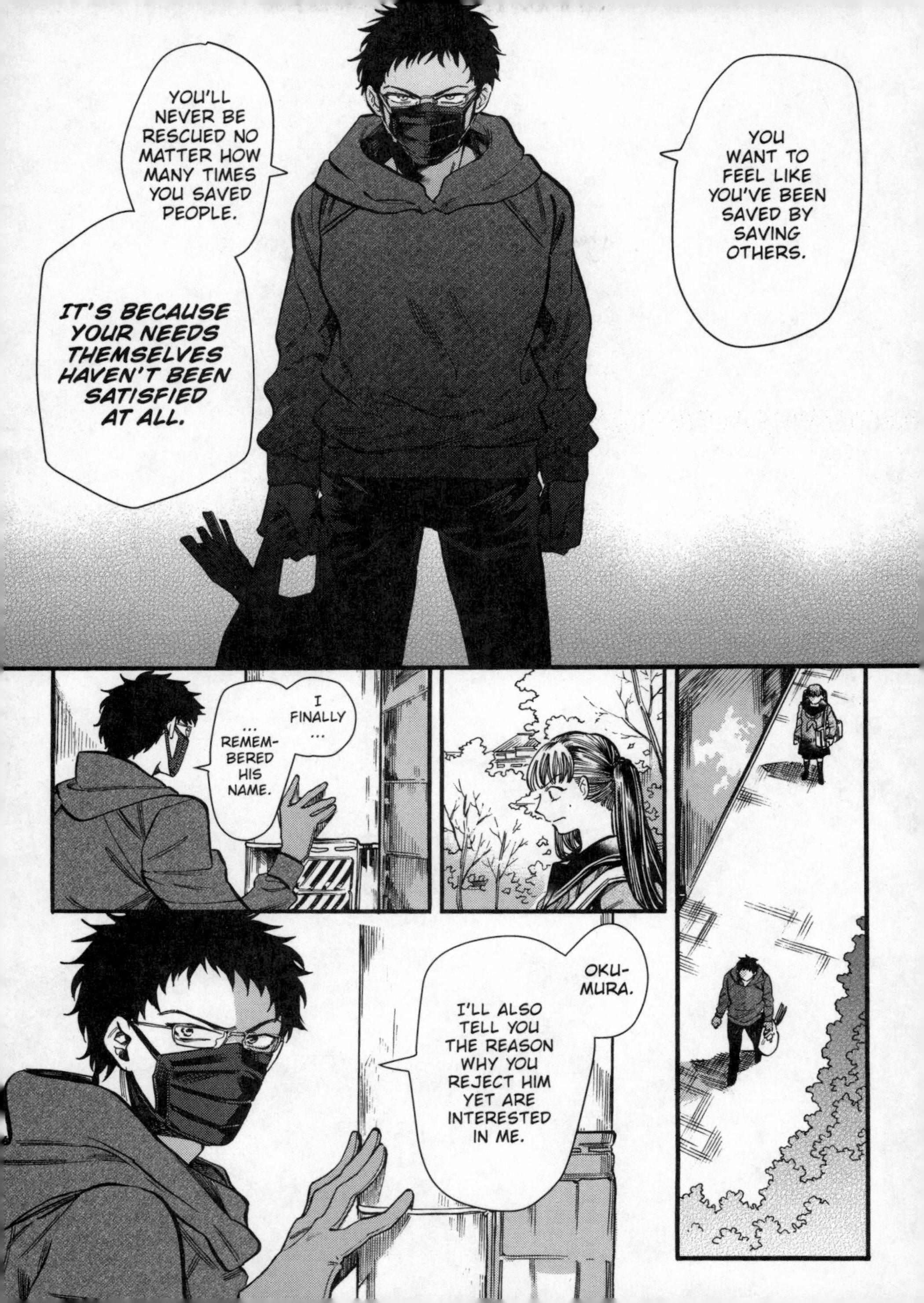
YOU WANT TO FEEL LIKE YOU'VE BEEN SAVED BY SAVING OTHERS.
YOU'LL NEVER BE RESCUED NO MATTER HOW MANY TIMES YOU SAVED PEOPLE.
IT'S BECAUSE YOUR NEEDS THEMSELVES HAVEN'T BEEN SATISFIED AT ALL.
I FINALLY ... ... REMEMBERED HIS NAME.
OKU-MURA.
I'LL ALSO TELL YOU THE REASON WHY YOU REJECT HIM YET ARE INTERESTED IN ME.

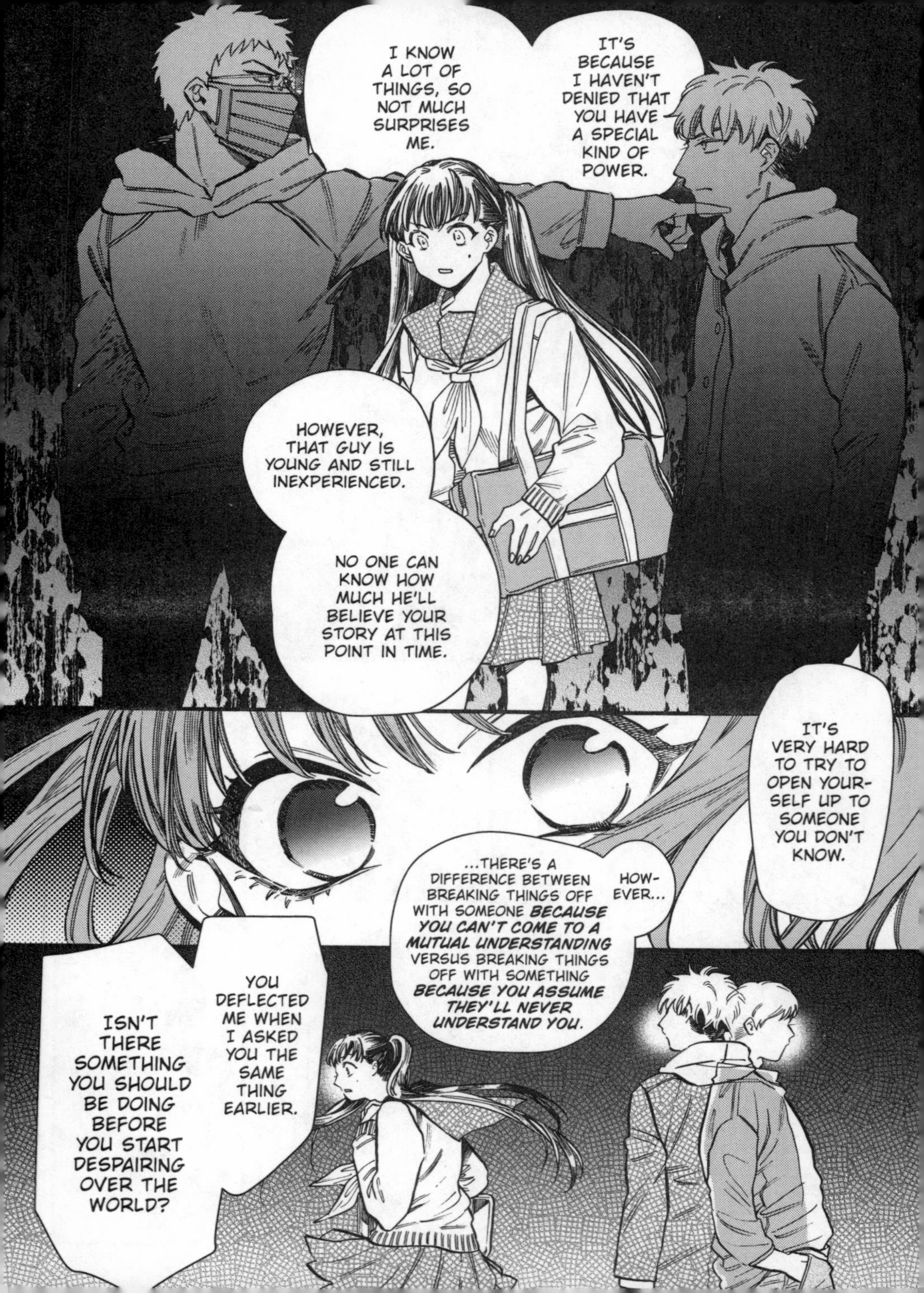
IT'S BECAUSE I HAVEN'T DENIED THAT YOU HAVE A SPECIAL KIND OF POWER.
I KNOW A LOT OF THINGS, SO NOT MUCH SURPRISES ME.
HOWEVER, THAT GUY IS YOUNG AND STILL INEXPERIENCED.
NO ONE CAN KNOW HOW MUCH HE'LL BELIEVE YOUR STORY AT THIS POINT IN TIME.
IT'S VERY HARD TO TRY TO OPEN YOUR-SELF UP TO SOMEONE YOU DON'T KNOW.
HOW-EVER...
...THERE'S A DIFFERENCE BETWEEN BREAKING THINGS OFF WITH SOMEONE ***BECAUSE YOU CAN'T COME TO A MUTUAL UNDERSTANDING*** VERSUS BREAKING THINGS OFF WITH SOMETHING ***BECAUSE YOU ASSUME THEY'LL NEVER UNDERSTAND YOU.***
YOU DEFLECTED ME WHEN I ASKED YOU THE SAME THING EARLIER.
ISN'T THERE SOMETHING YOU SHOULD BE DOING BEFORE YOU START DESPAIRING OVER THE WORLD?

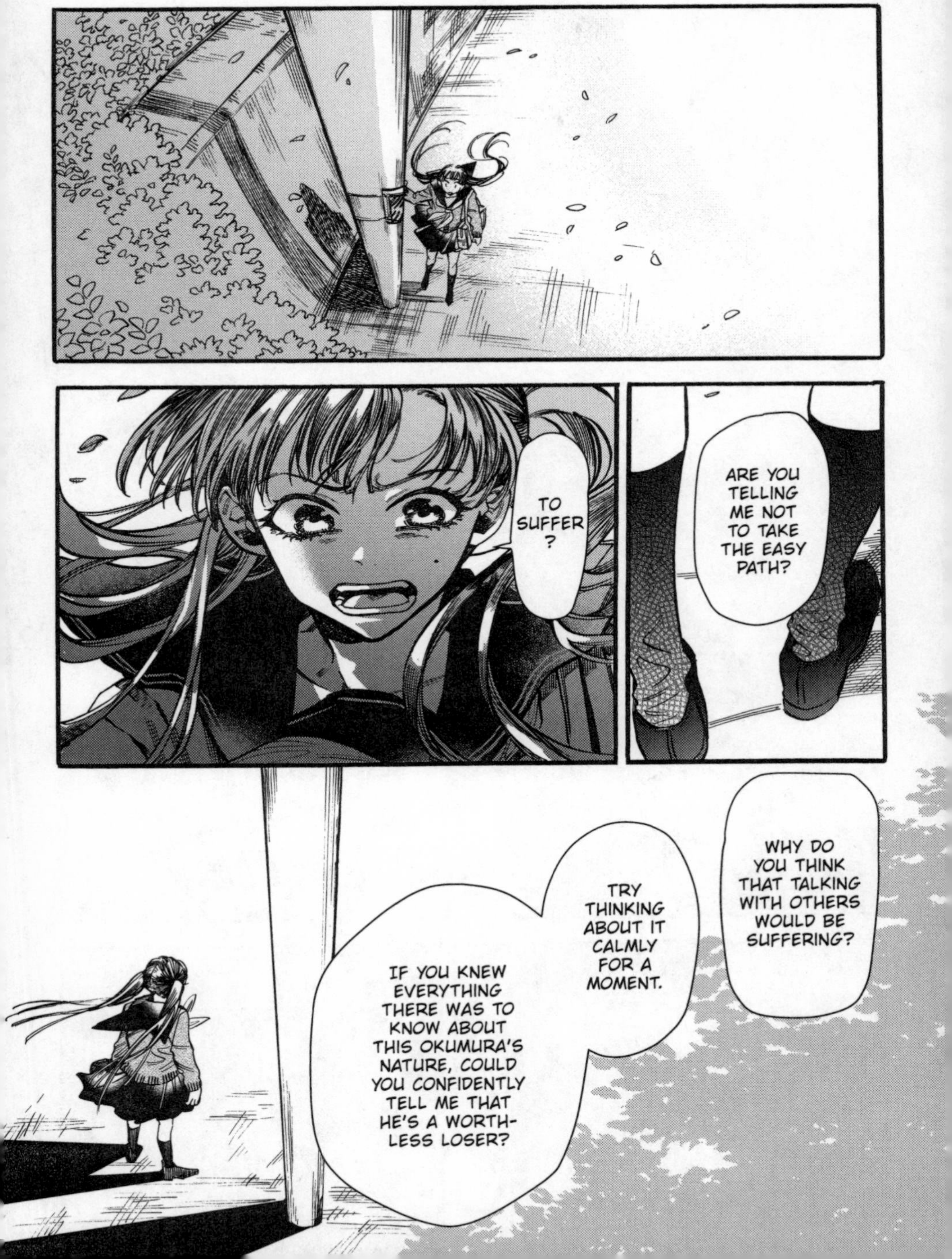
ARE YOU TELLING ME NOT TO TAKE THE EASY PATH?
TO SUFFER?
WHY DO YOU THINK THAT TALKING WITH OTHERS WOULD BE SUFFERING?
TRY THINKING ABOUT IT CALMLY FOR A MOMENT.
IF YOU KNEW EVERYTHING THERE WAS TO KNOW ABOUT THIS OKUMURA'S NATURE, COULD YOU CONFIDENTLY TELL ME THAT HE'S A WORTH-LESS LOSER?

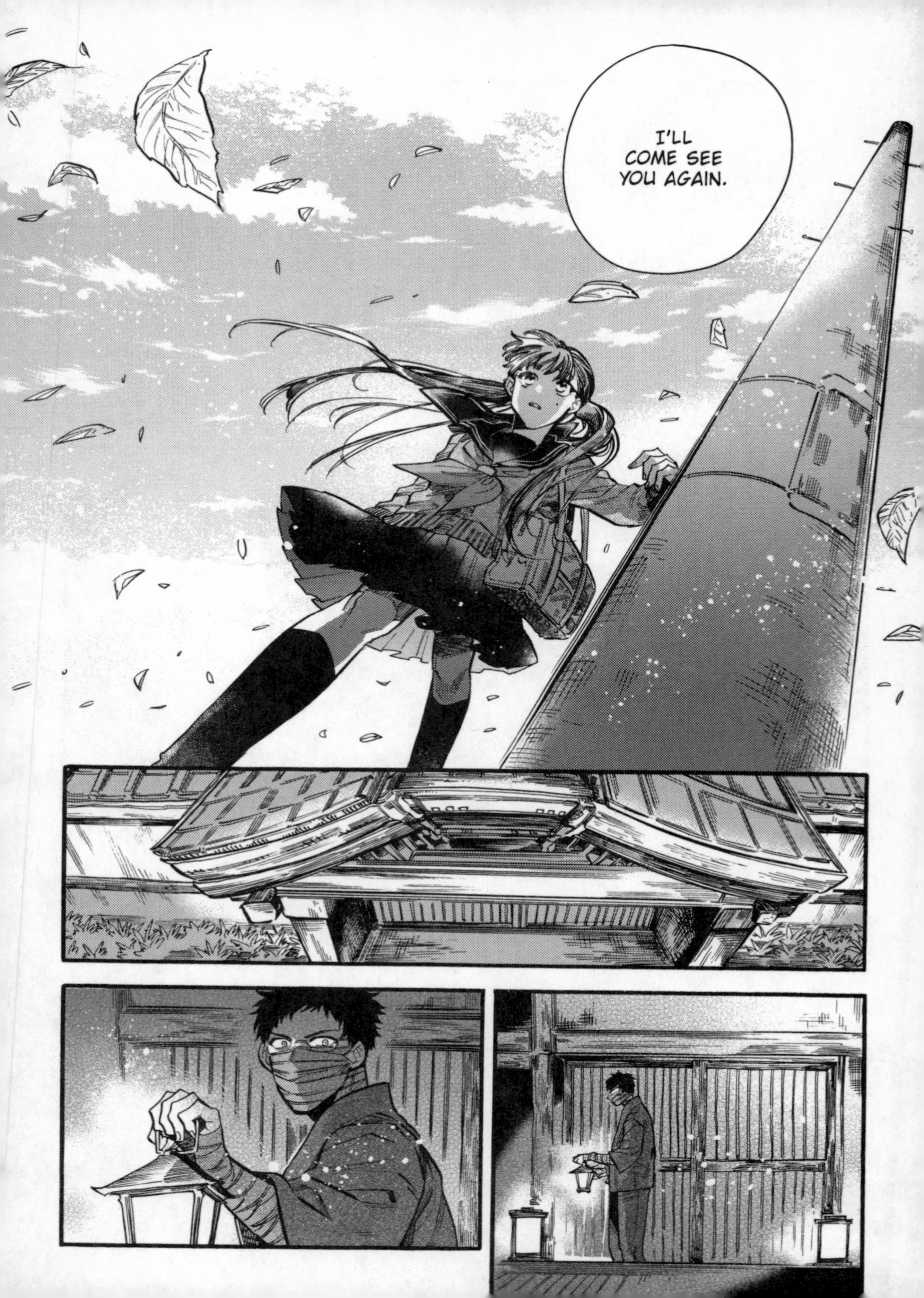
I'LL COME SEE YOU AGAIN.

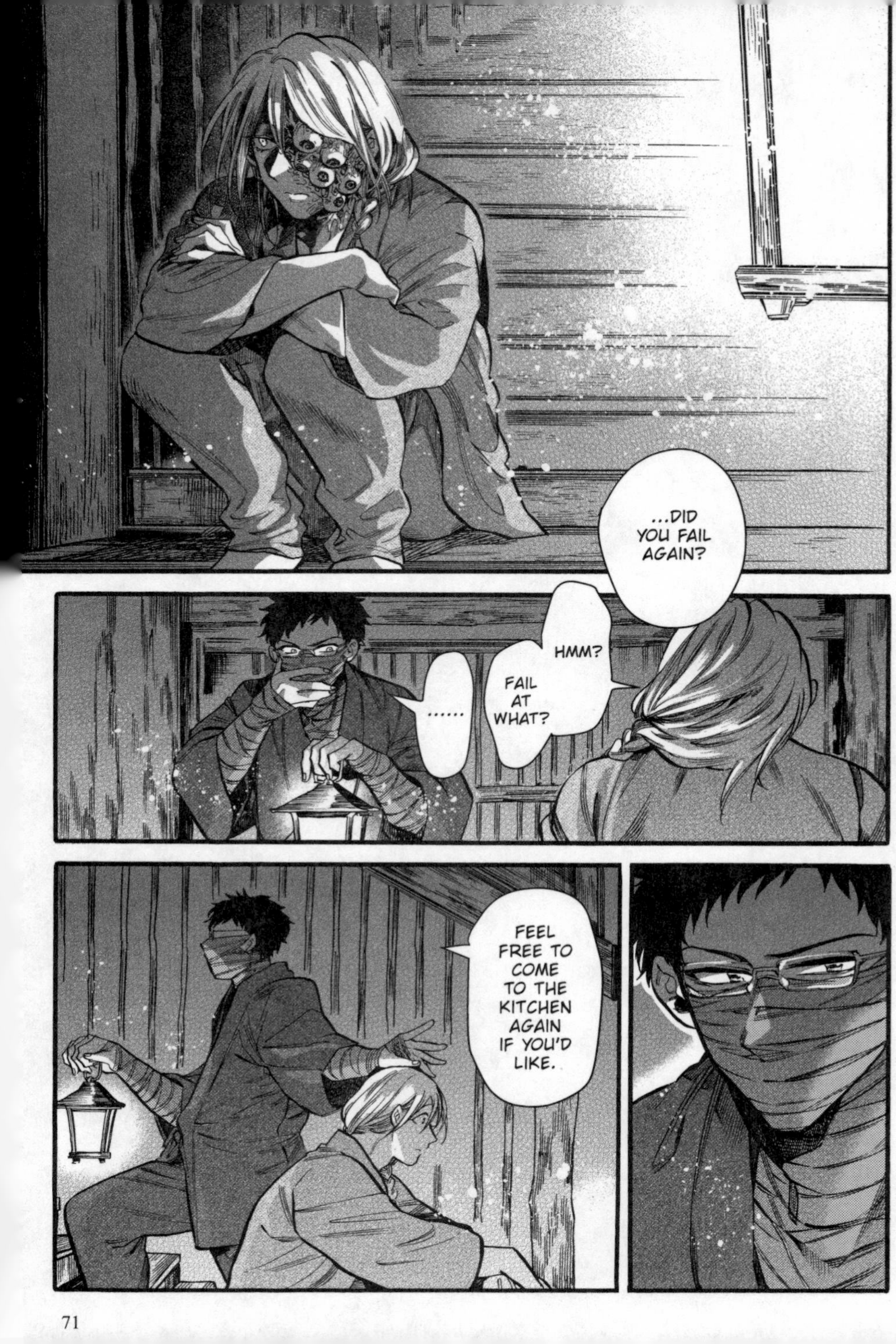
...DID YOU FAIL AGAIN?
HMM? FAIL AT WHAT?
......
FEEL FREE TO COME TO THE KITCHEN AGAIN IF YOU'D LIKE.

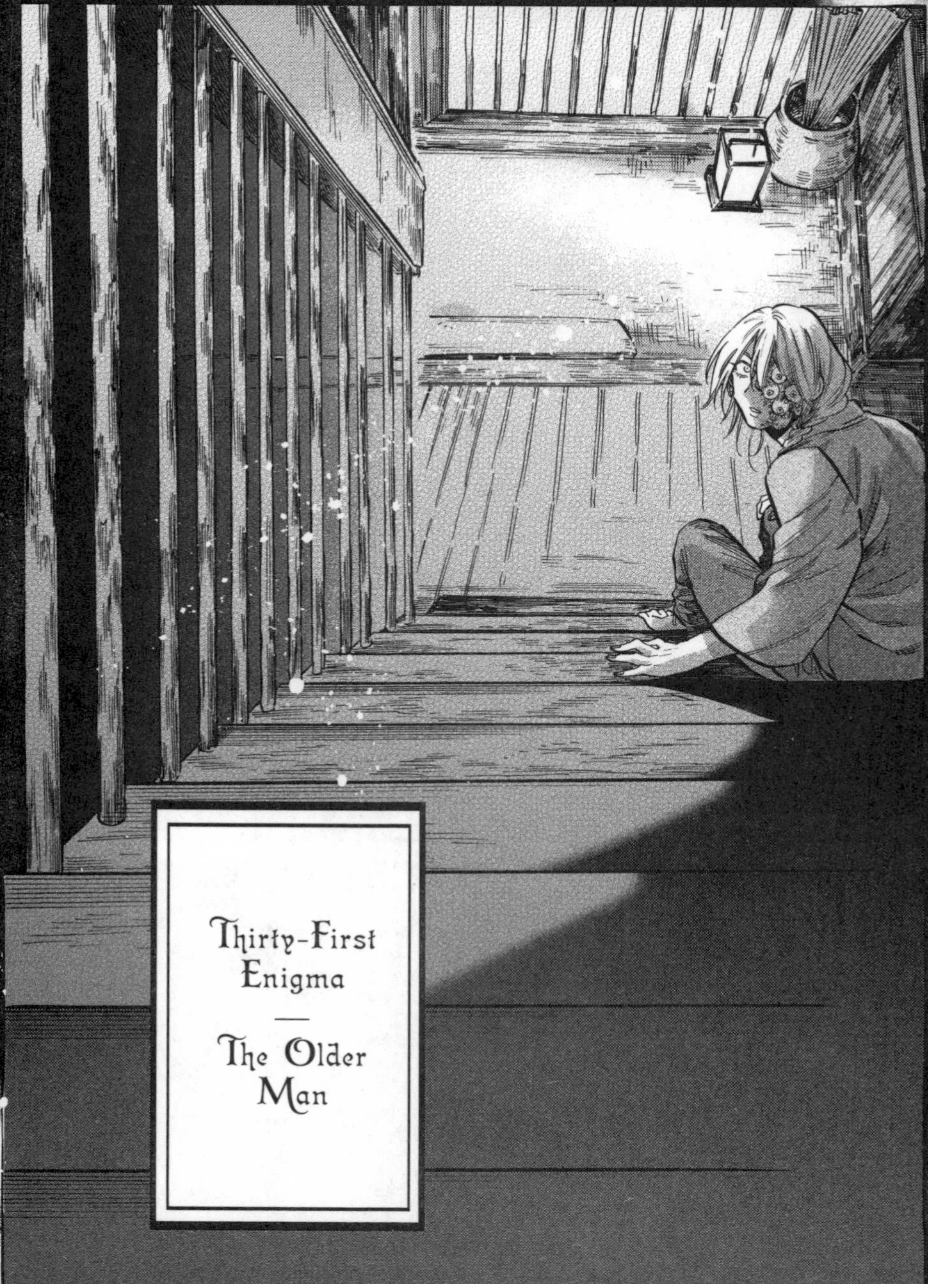
Thirty-First Enigma
—
The Older Man

Phantom Tales of the Night

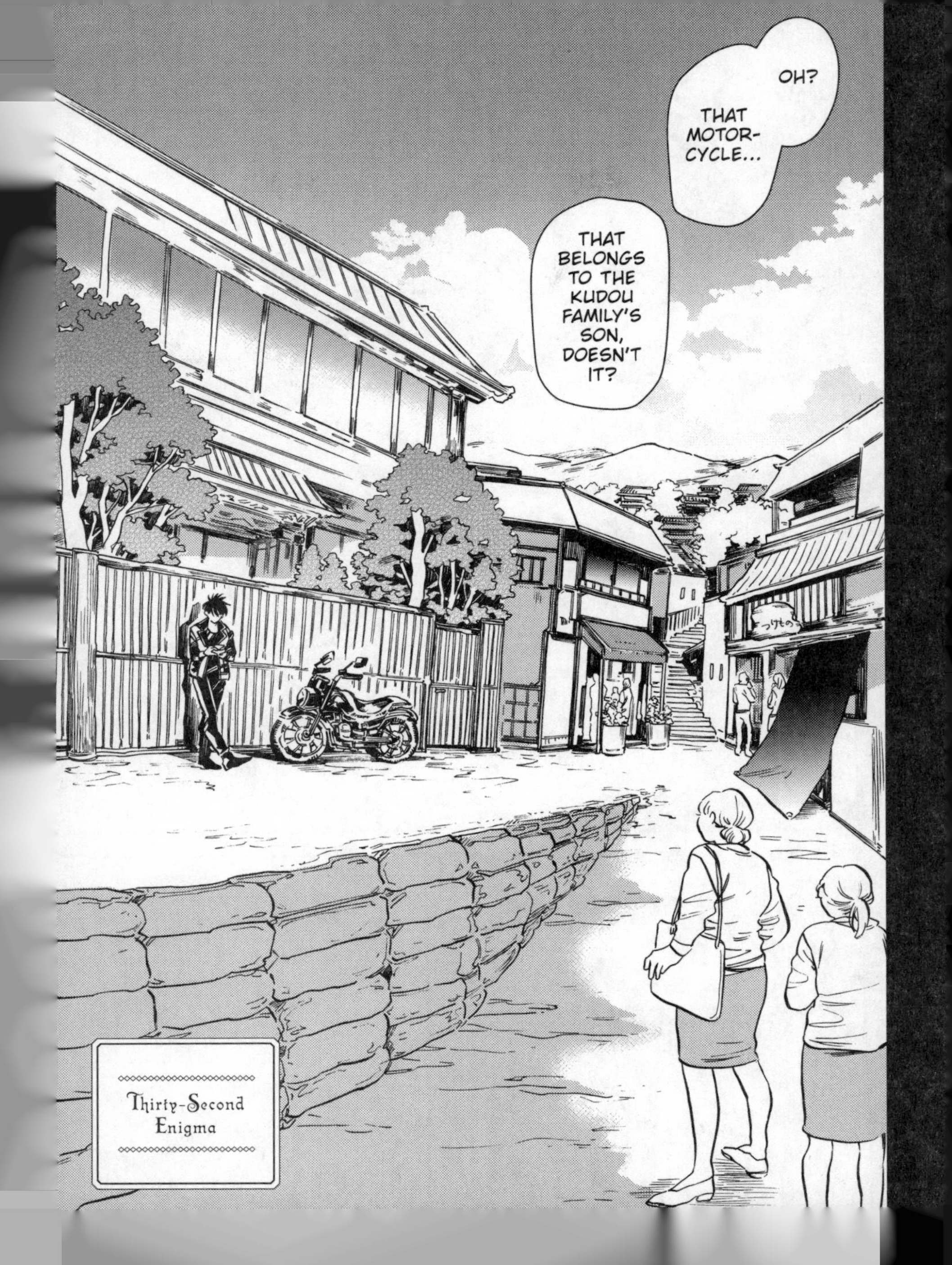
OH?
THAT MOTOR-CYCLE...
THAT BELONGS TO THE KUDOU FAMILY'S SON, DOESN'T IT?
Thirty-Second Enigma

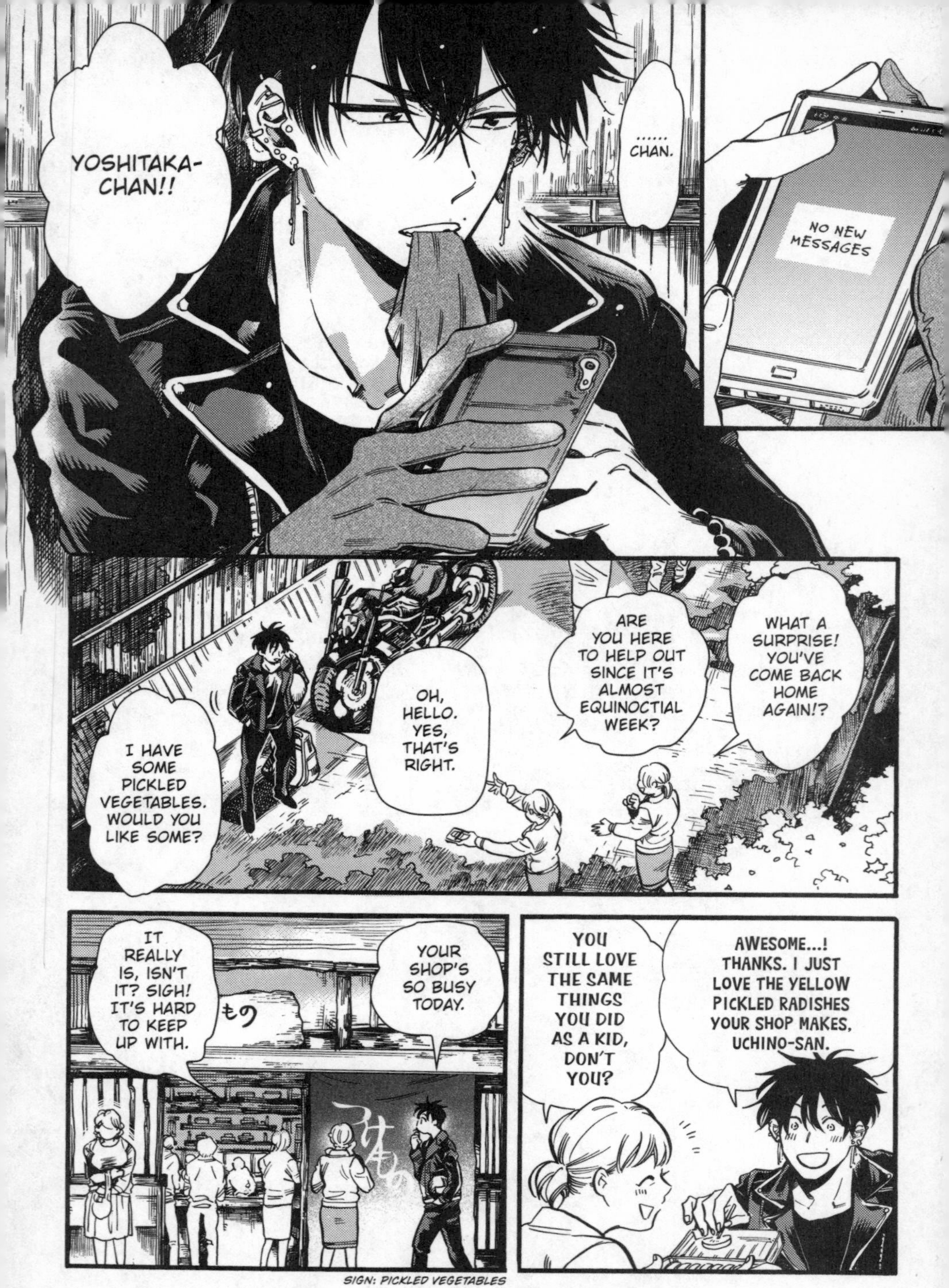

NO NEW MESSAGES
......CHAN.
YOSHITAKA-CHAN!!
WHAT A SURPRISE! YOU'VE COME BACK HOME AGAIN!?
ARE YOU HERE TO HELP OUT SINCE IT'S ALMOST EQUINOCTIAL WEEK?
OH, HELLO. YES, THAT'S RIGHT.
I HAVE SOME PICKLED VEGETABLES. WOULD YOU LIKE SOME?
AWESOME...! THANKS. I JUST LOVE THE YELLOW PICKLED RADISHES YOUR SHOP MAKES, UCHINO-SAN.
YOU STILL LOVE THE SAME THINGS YOU DID AS A KID, DON'T YOU?
YOUR SHOP'S SO BUSY TODAY.
IT REALLY IS, ISN'T IT? SIGH! IT'S HARD TO KEEP UP WITH.
もの
つけもの

SIGN: PICKLED VEGETABLES

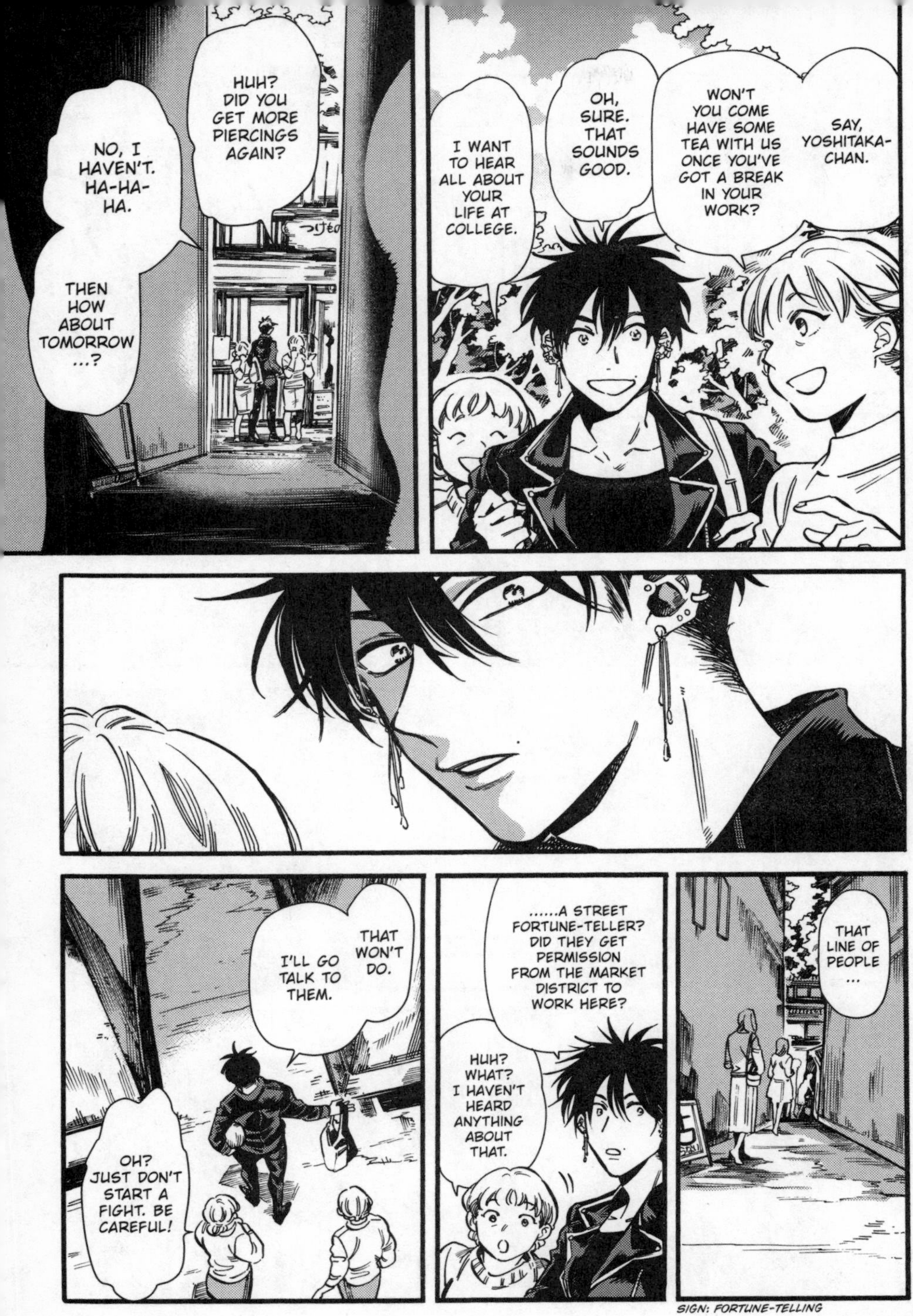
SAY, YOSHITAKA-CHAN.
WON'T YOU COME HAVE SOME TEA WITH US ONCE YOU'VE GOT A BREAK IN YOUR WORK?
OH, SURE. THAT SOUNDS GOOD.
I WANT TO HEAR ALL ABOUT YOUR LIFE AT COLLEGE.
HUH? DID YOU GET MORE PIERCINGS AGAIN?
NO, I HAVEN'T. HA-HA-HA.
THEN HOW ABOUT TOMORROW ...?
THAT LINE OF PEOPLE ...
......A STREET FORTUNE-TELLER? DID THEY GET PERMISSION FROM THE MARKET DISTRICT TO WORK HERE?
HUH? WHAT? I HAVEN'T HEARD ANYTHING ABOUT THAT.
THAT WON'T DO.
I'LL GO TALK TO THEM.
OH? JUST DON'T START A FIGHT. BE CAREFUL!

SIGN: FORTUNE-TELLING

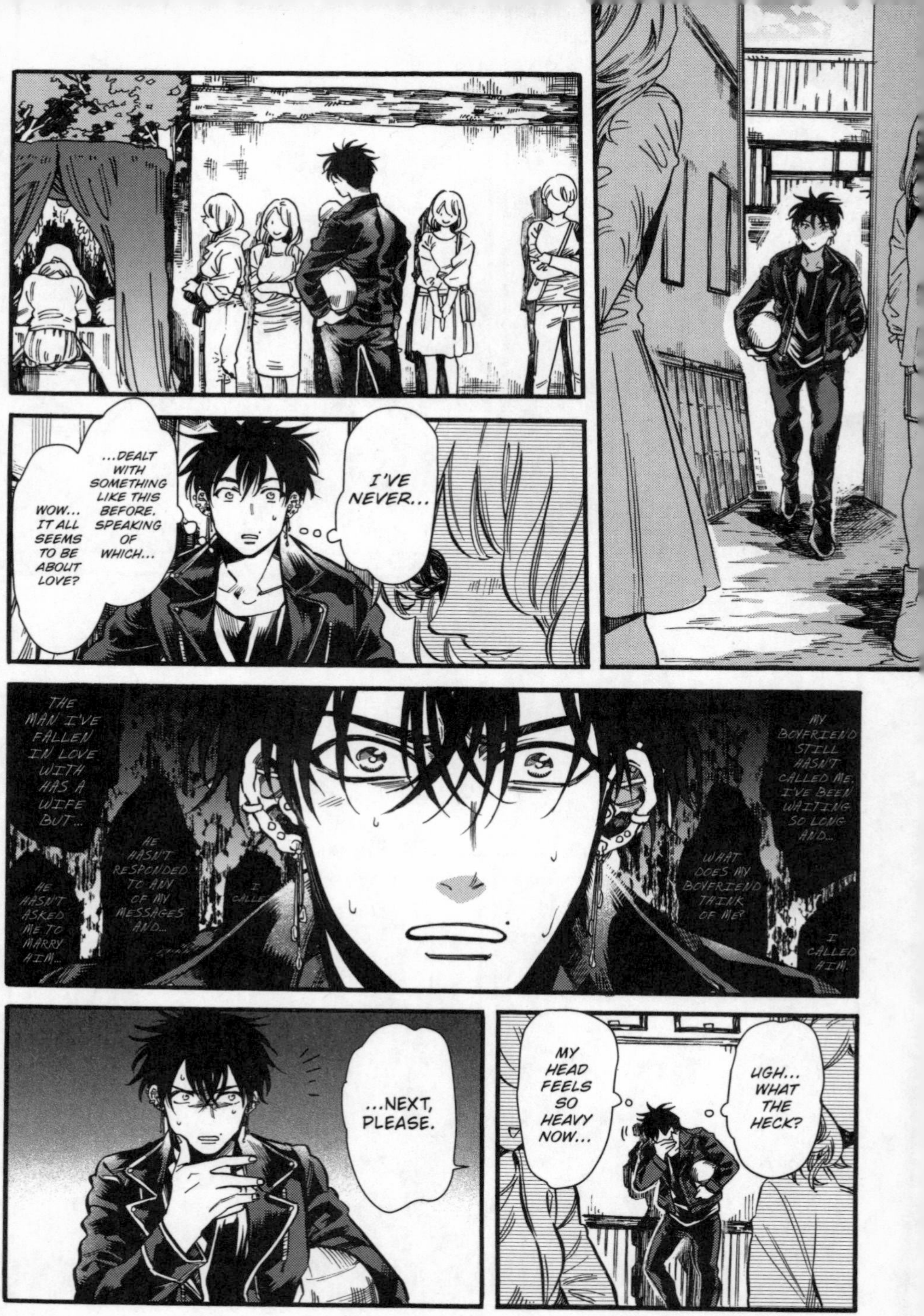
I'VE NEVER...
...DEALT WITH SOMETHING LIKE THIS BEFORE. SPEAKING OF WHICH...
WOW... IT ALL SEEMS TO BE ABOUT LOVE?
MY BOYFRIEND STILL HASN'T CALLED ME. I'VE BEEN WAITING SO LONG AND...
WHAT DOES MY BOYFRIEND THINK OF ME?
I CALLED HIM.
THE MAN I'VE FALLEN IN LOVE WITH HAS A WIFE BUT...
HE HASN'T RESPONDED TO ANY OF MY MESSAGES AND...
HE HASN'T ASKED ME TO MARRY HIM...
UGH... WHAT THE HECK?
MY HEAD FEELS SO HEAVY NOW...
...NEXT, PLEASE.

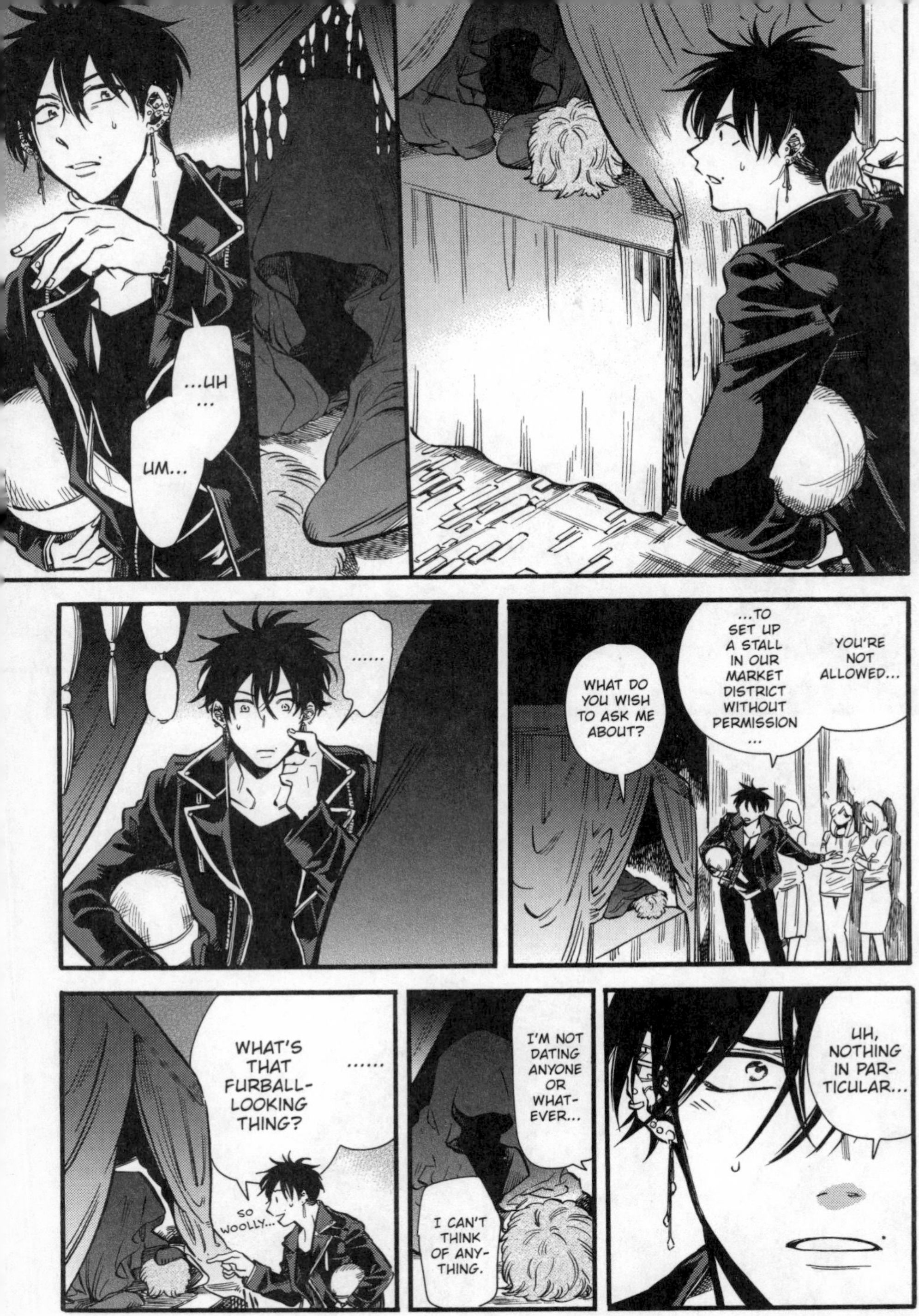
...UH ...
UM...
YOU'RE NOT ALLOWED...
...TO SET UP A STALL IN OUR MARKET DISTRICT WITHOUT PERMISSION ...
WHAT DO YOU WISH TO ASK ME ABOUT?
......
UH, NOTHING IN PAR-TICULAR...
I'M NOT DATING ANYONE OR WHAT-EVER...
I CAN'T THINK OF ANY-THING.
......
WHAT'S THAT FURBALL-LOOKING THING?
SO WOOLLY...

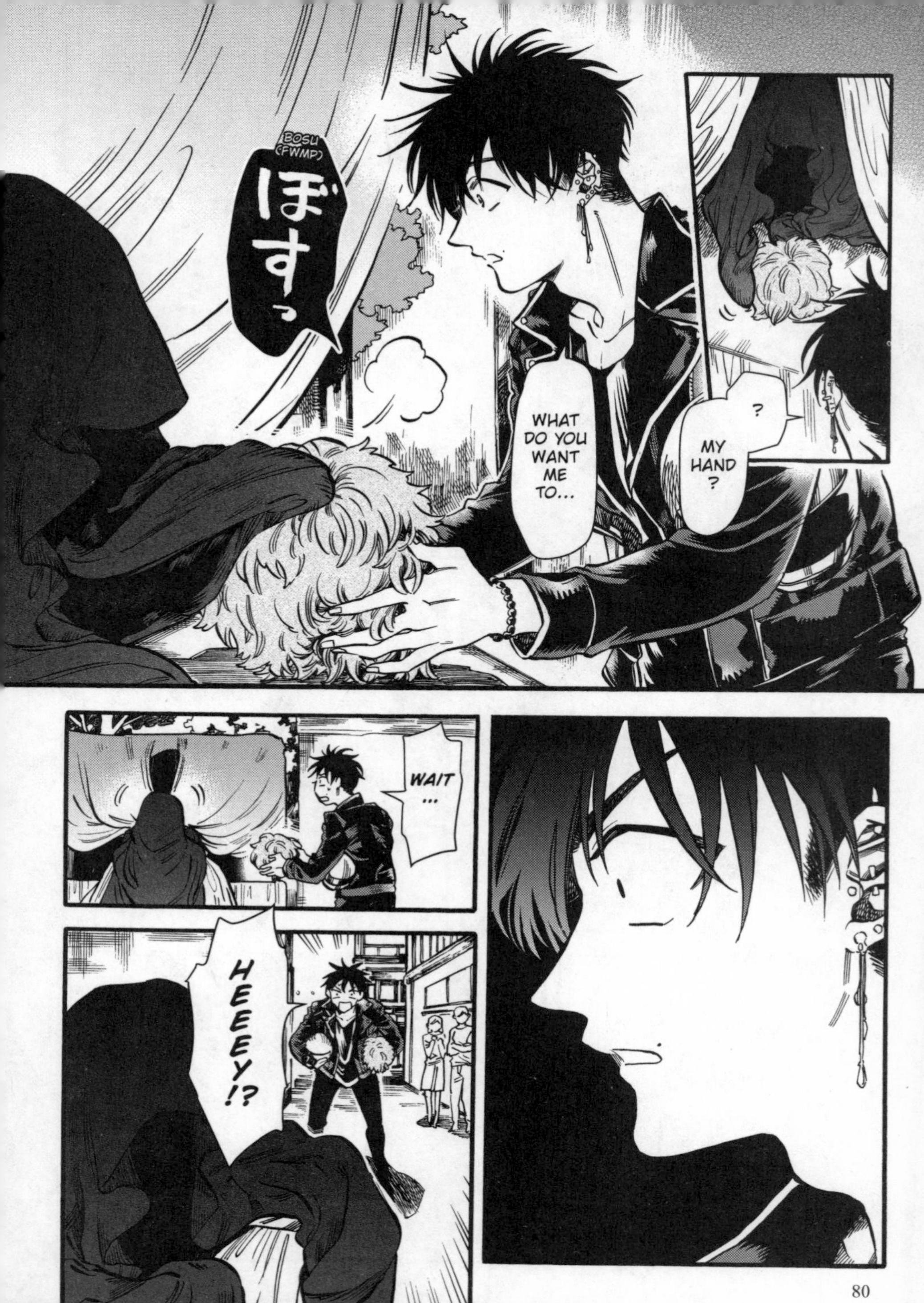
?
MY HAND?
ぼすっ
BOSU (FWMP)
WHAT DO YOU WANT ME TO...
WAIT...
HEEEEY!?

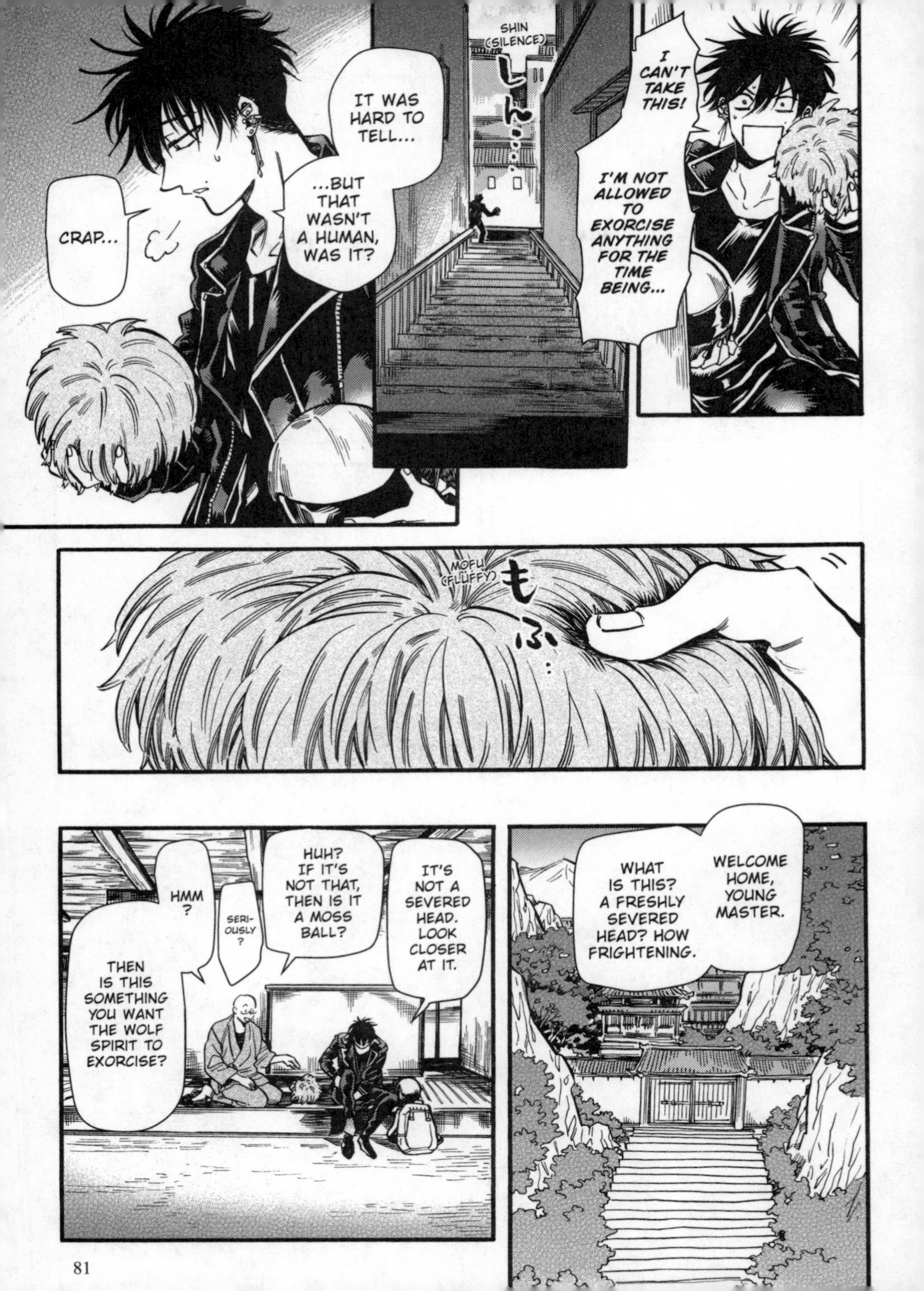
I CAN'T TAKE THIS!
I'M NOT ALLOWED TO EXORCISE ANYTHING FOR THE TIME BEING...
SHIN (SILENCE)
しん......
IT WAS HARD TO TELL...
...BUT THAT WASN'T A HUMAN, WAS IT?
CRAP...
MOFU (FLUFFY)
もふ..
WELCOME HOME, YOUNG MASTER.
WHAT IS THIS? A FRESHLY SEVERED HEAD? HOW FRIGHTENING.
IT'S NOT A SEVERED HEAD. LOOK CLOSER AT IT.
HUH? IF IT'S NOT THAT, THEN IS IT A MOSS BALL?
SERIOUSLY?
HMM?
THEN IS THIS SOMETHING YOU WANT THE WOLF SPIRIT TO EXORCISE?

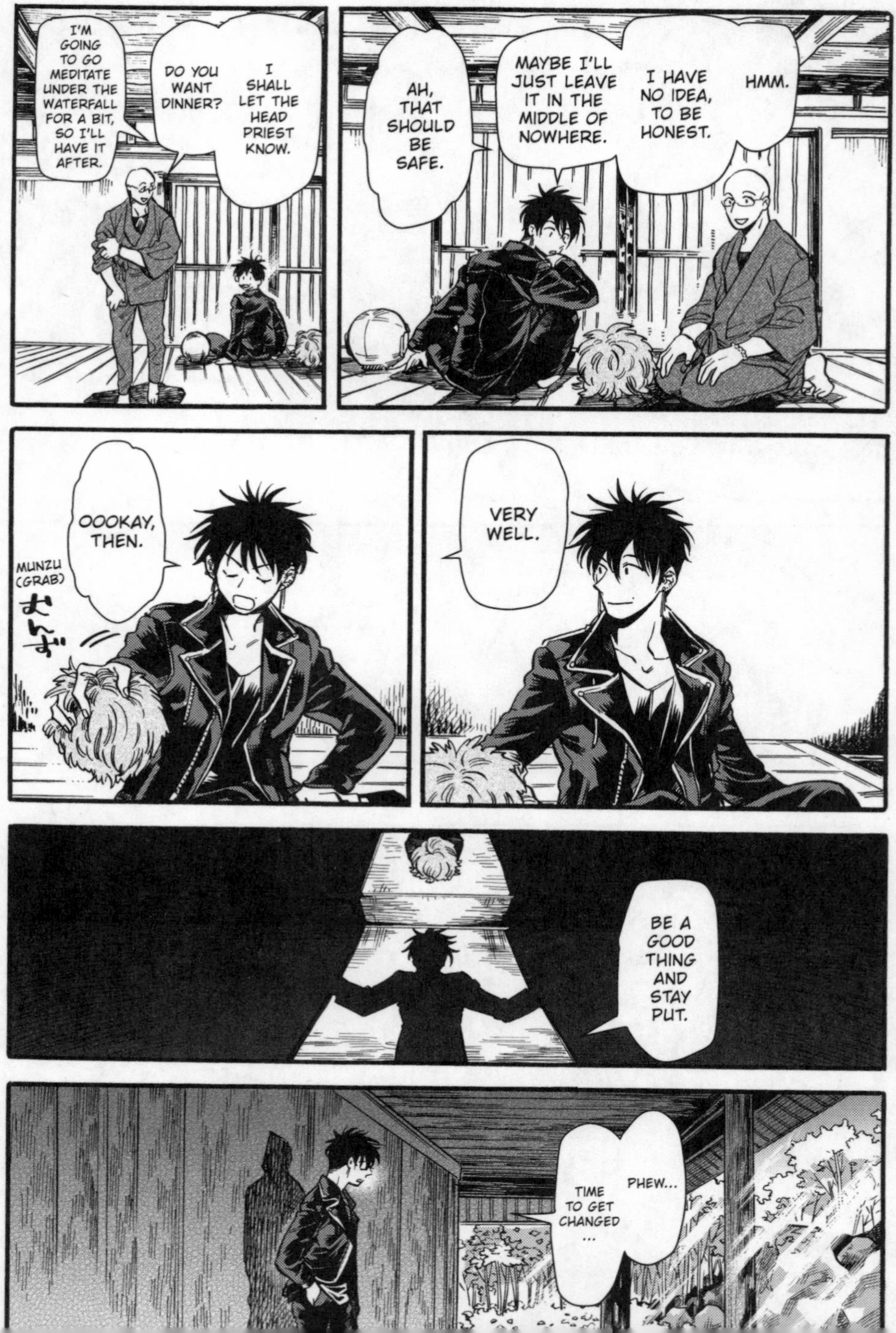
HMM.
I HAVE NO IDEA, TO BE HONEST.
MAYBE I'LL JUST LEAVE IT IN THE MIDDLE OF NOWHERE.
AH, THAT SHOULD BE SAFE.
I SHALL LET THE HEAD PRIEST KNOW.
DO YOU WANT DINNER?
I'M GOING TO GO MEDITATE UNDER THE WATERFALL FOR A BIT, SO I'LL HAVE IT AFTER.
VERY WELL.
OOOKAY, THEN.
MUNZU (GRAB)
むんず
BE A GOOD THING AND STAY PUT.
PHEW...
TIME TO GET CHANGED ...

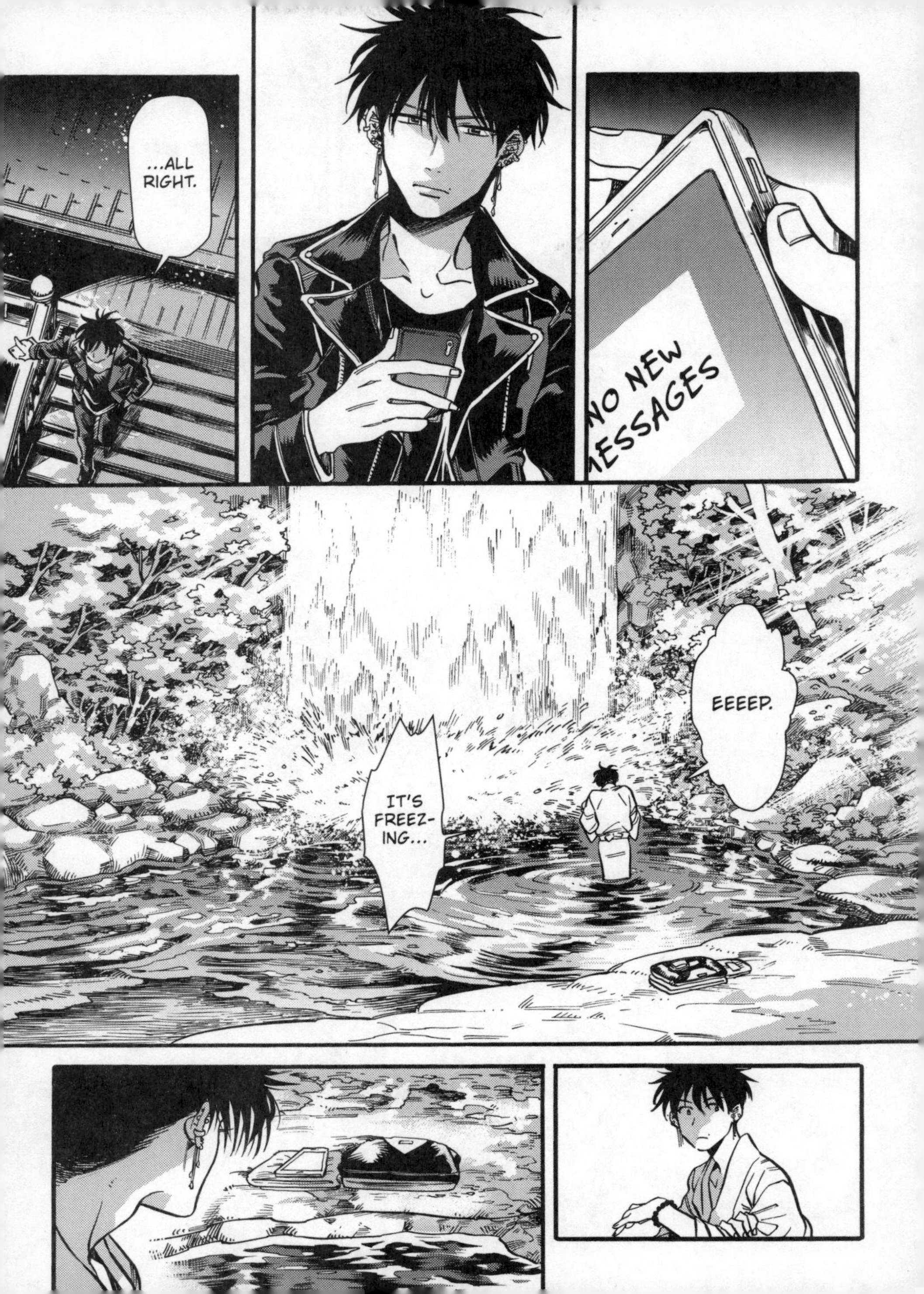
NO NEW MESSAGES
...ALL RIGHT.
EEEEP.
IT'S FREEZ-ING...

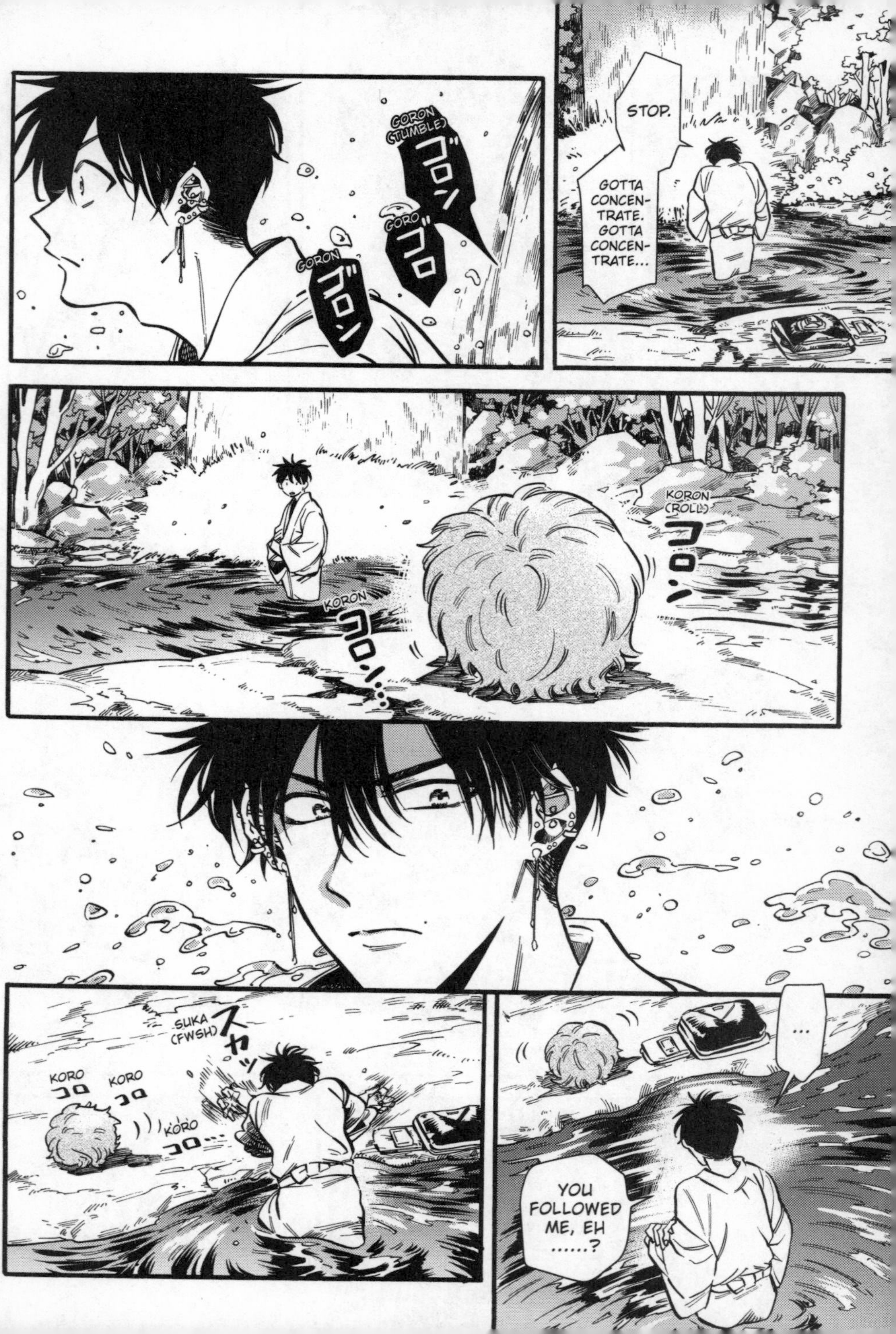
STOP.
GOTTA CONCENTRATE. GOTTA CONCENTRATE...
GORON (TUMBLE) ゴロン
GORO ゴロ
GORON ゴロン
KORON (ROLL) コロン
KORON コロン…
...
YOU FOLLOWED ME, EH ......?
SUKA (FWSH) スカッ
KORO コロ
KORO コロ
KORO コロ…

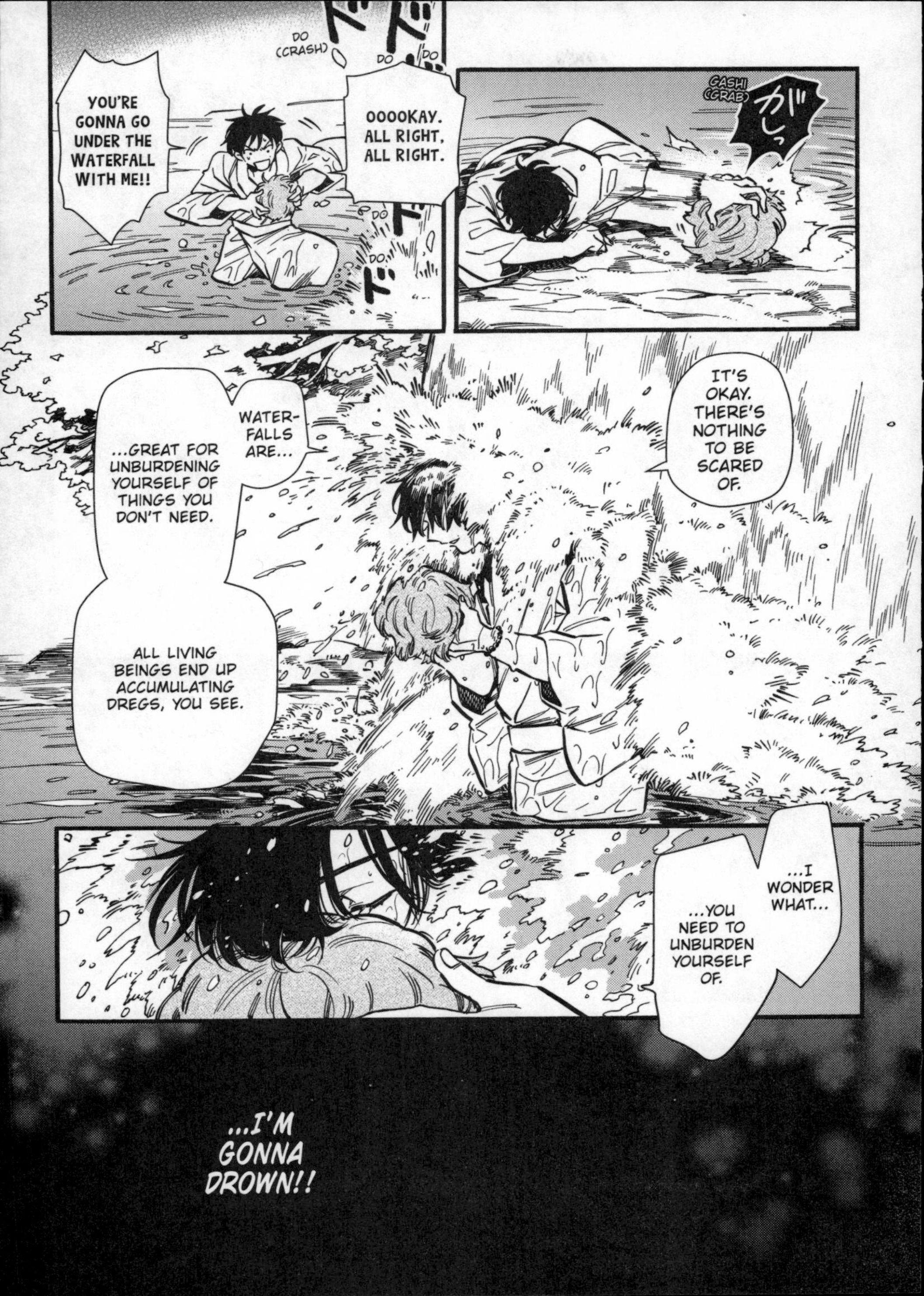
GASHI (GRAB)
がしっ
ドド
DO
DO
DO (CRASH)
OOOOKAY. ALL RIGHT, ALL RIGHT.
YOU'RE GONNA GO UNDER THE WATERFALL WITH ME!!
DO
ド
DO
ド
IT'S OKAY. THERE'S NOTHING TO BE SCARED OF.
WATER-FALLS ARE...
...GREAT FOR UNBURDENING YOURSELF OF THINGS YOU DON'T NEED.
ALL LIVING BEINGS END UP ACCUMULATING DREGS, YOU SEE.
...I WONDER WHAT...
...YOU NEED TO UNBURDEN YOURSELF OF.
...I'M GONNA DROWN!!

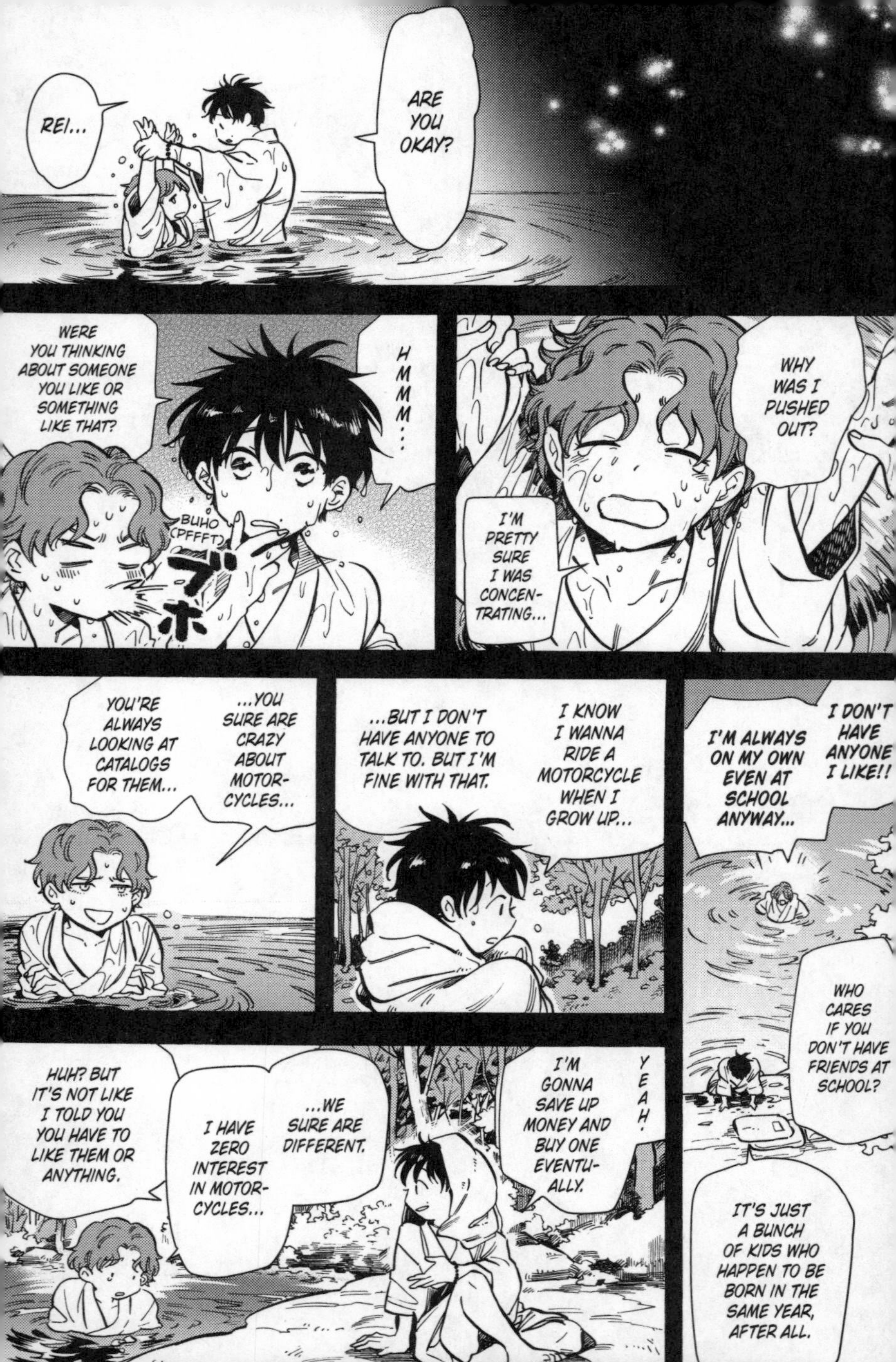
ARE YOU OKAY?
REI...
WHY WAS I PUSHED OUT?
I'M PRETTY SURE I WAS CONCEN-TRATING...
HMMM...
WERE YOU THINKING ABOUT SOMEONE YOU LIKE OR SOMETHING LIKE THAT?
BUHO (PFFFT)
ブホ
I DON'T HAVE ANYONE I LIKE!!
I'M ALWAYS ON MY OWN EVEN AT SCHOOL ANYWAY...
WHO CARES IF YOU DON'T HAVE FRIENDS AT SCHOOL?
IT'S JUST A BUNCH OF KIDS WHO HAPPEN TO BE BORN IN THE SAME YEAR, AFTER ALL.
I KNOW I WANNA RIDE A MOTORCYCLE WHEN I GROW UP...
...BUT I DON'T HAVE ANYONE TO TALK TO. BUT I'M FINE WITH THAT.
...YOU SURE ARE CRAZY ABOUT MOTOR-CYCLES...
YOU'RE ALWAYS LOOKING AT CATALOGS FOR THEM...
YEAH!
I'M GONNA SAVE UP MONEY AND BUY ONE EVENTU-ALLY.
...WE SURE ARE DIFFERENT.
I HAVE ZERO INTEREST IN MOTOR-CYCLES...
HUH? BUT IT'S NOT LIKE I TOLD YOU YOU HAVE TO LIKE THEM OR ANYTHING.

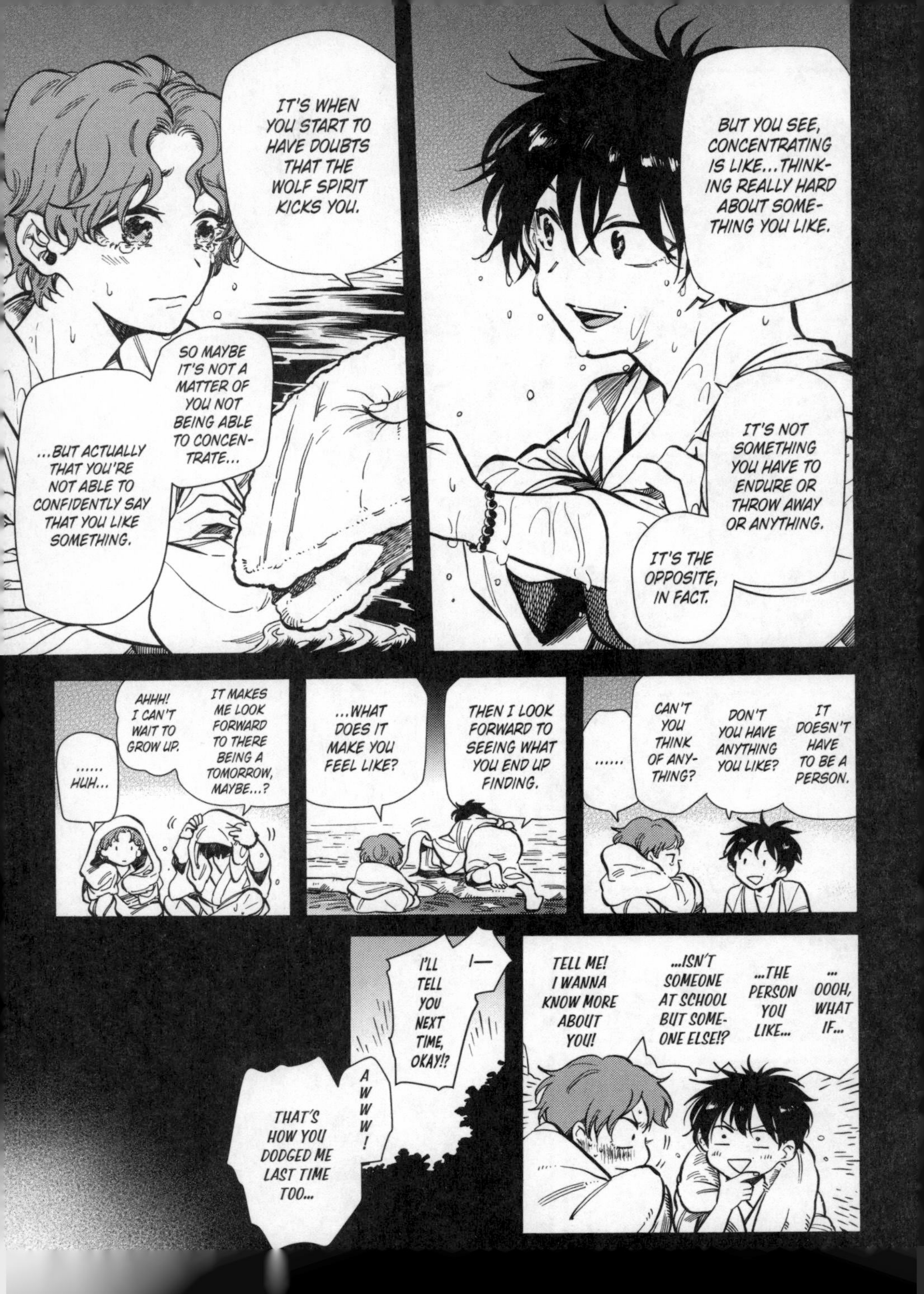
BUT YOU SEE, CONCENTRATING IS LIKE...THINKING REALLY HARD ABOUT SOMETHING YOU LIKE.
IT'S NOT SOMETHING YOU HAVE TO ENDURE OR THROW AWAY OR ANYTHING.
IT'S THE OPPOSITE, IN FACT.
IT'S WHEN YOU START TO HAVE DOUBTS THAT THE WOLF SPIRIT KICKS YOU.
SO MAYBE IT'S NOT A MATTER OF YOU NOT BEING ABLE TO CONCENTRATE...
...BUT ACTUALLY THAT YOU'RE NOT ABLE TO CONFIDENTLY SAY THAT YOU LIKE SOMETHING.
IT DOESN'T HAVE TO BE A PERSON.
DON'T YOU HAVE ANYTHING YOU LIKE?
CAN'T YOU THINK OF ANYTHING?
......
THEN I LOOK FORWARD TO SEEING WHAT YOU END UP FINDING.
...WHAT DOES IT MAKE YOU FEEL LIKE?
IT MAKES ME LOOK FORWARD TO THERE BEING A TOMORROW, MAYBE...?
AHHH! I CAN'T WAIT TO GROW UP.
...... HUH...
... OOOH, WHAT IF...
...THE PERSON YOU LIKE...
...ISN'T SOMEONE AT SCHOOL BUT SOMEONE ELSE!?
TELL ME! I WANNA KNOW MORE ABOUT YOU!
I—
I'LL TELL YOU NEXT TIME, OKAY!?
AWWW!
THAT'S HOW YOU DODGED ME LAST TIME TOO...

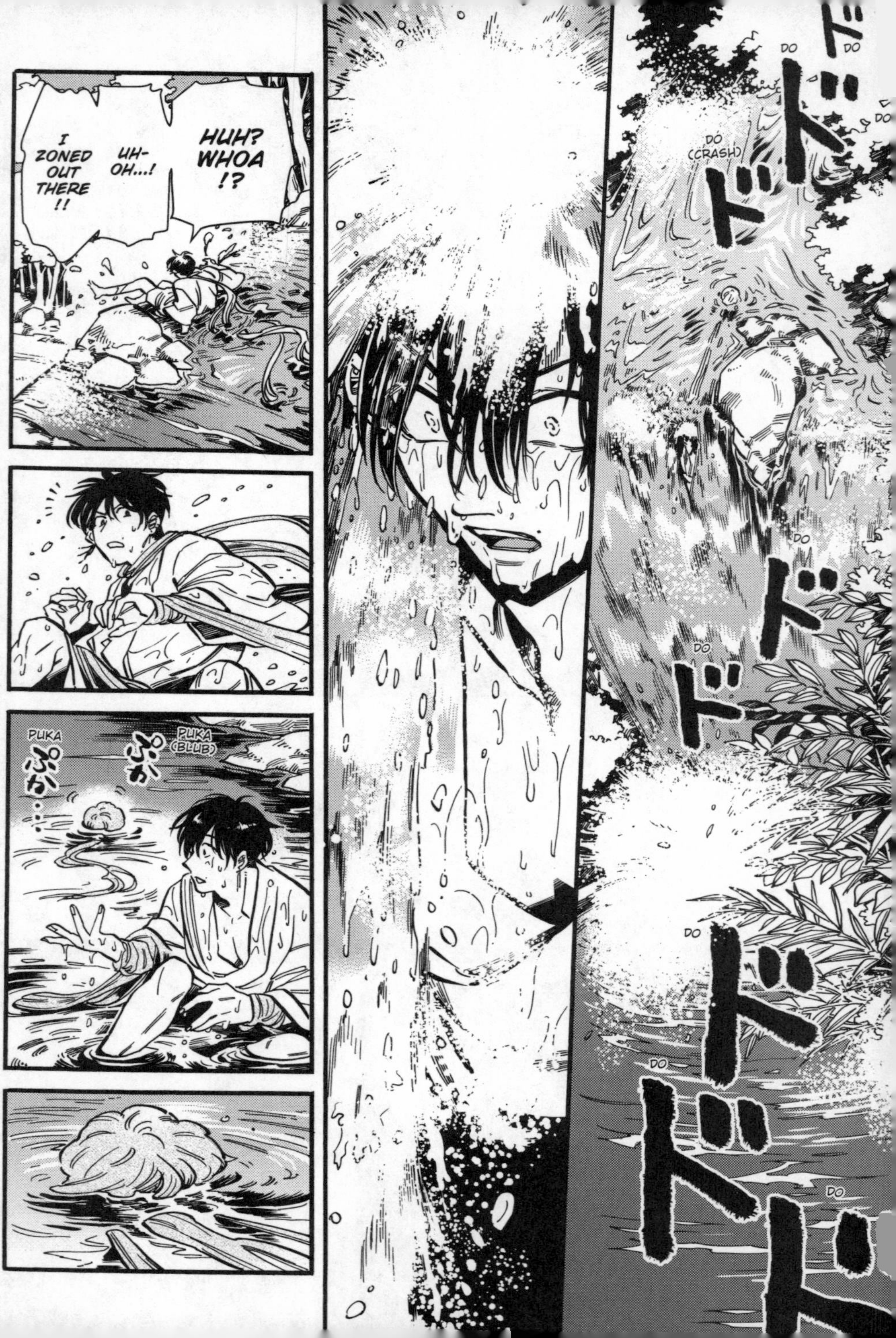
DO
DO
DO
DO (CRASH)
DO
DO
DO
DO
DO
HUH? WHOA !?
UH-OH...!
I ZONED OUT THERE !!
PUKA (BLUB)
PUKA

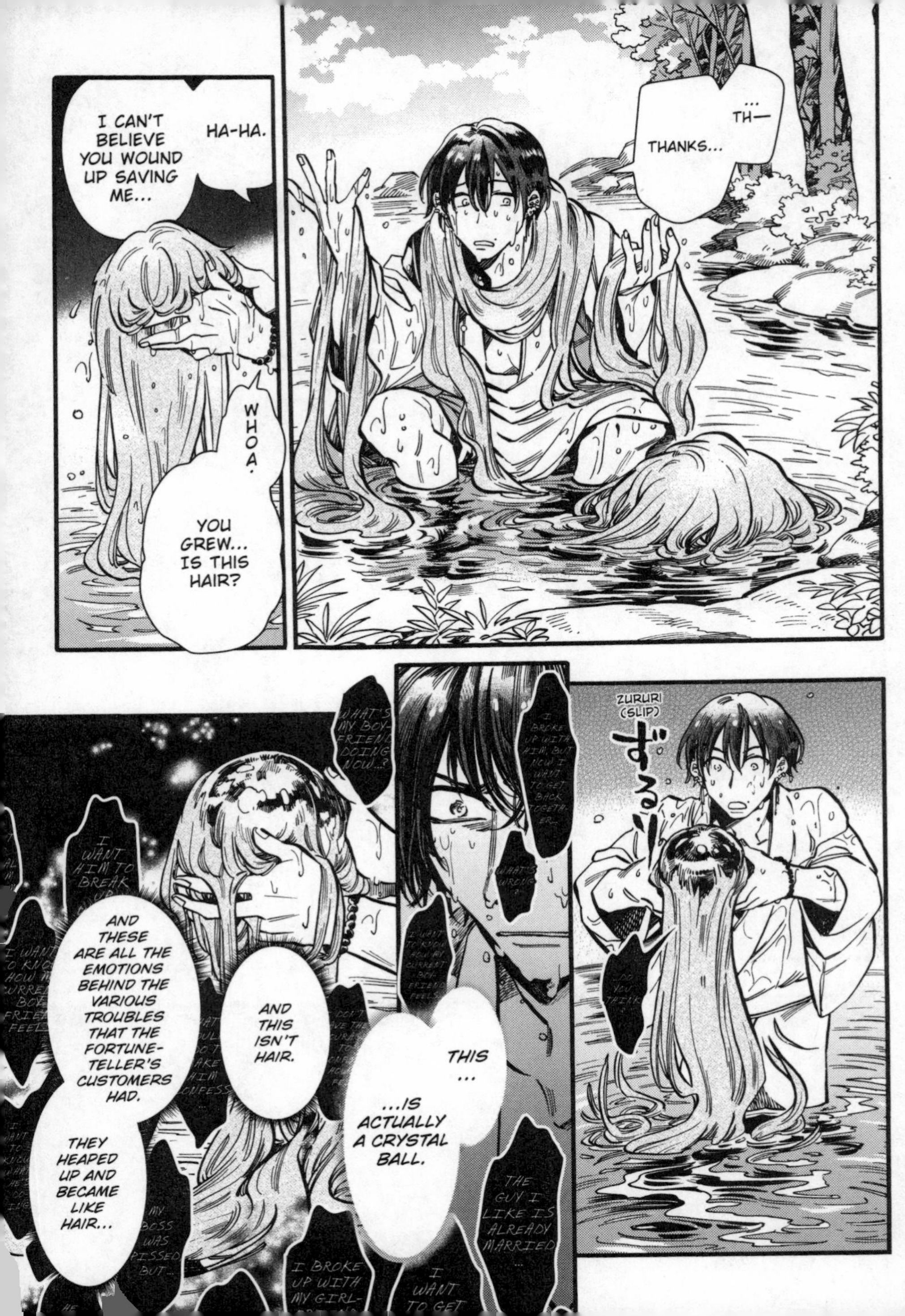
... TH— THANKS...
HA-HA.
I CAN'T BELIEVE YOU WOUND UP SAVING ME...
WHOA.
YOU GREW... IS THIS HAIR?
ZURURI (SLIP)
ずるっ
DO YOU THINK
WHAT'S MY BOYFRIEND DOING NOW...?
I BROKE UP WITH HIM, BUT NOW I WANT TO GET BACK TOGETHER...
WHAT'S WRONG?
THIS ...
...IS ACTUALLY A CRYSTAL BALL.
THE GUY I LIKE IS ALREADY MARRIED...
I WANT TO GET
I BROKE UP WITH MY GIRL-
AND THIS ISN'T HAIR.
AND THESE ARE ALL THE EMOTIONS BEHIND THE VARIOUS TROUBLES THAT THE FORTUNE-TELLER'S CUSTOMERS HAD.
THEY HEAPED UP AND BECAME LIKE HAIR...
MY BOSS WAS PISSED BUT...

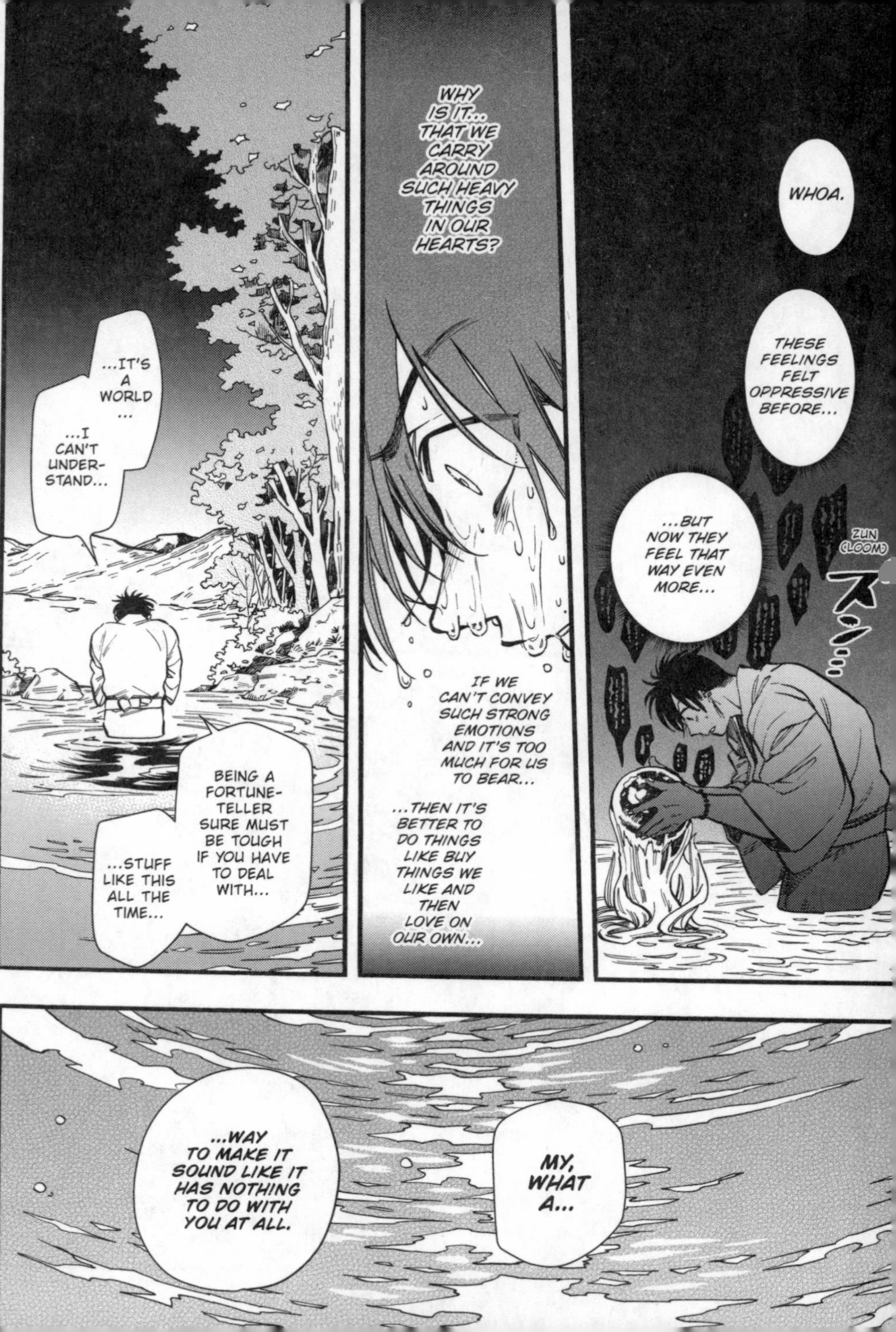
WHOA.
THESE FEELINGS FELT OPPRESSIVE BEFORE...
...BUT NOW THEY FEEL THAT WAY EVEN MORE...
ZUN (LOOM)
WHY IS IT... THAT WE CARRY AROUND SUCH HEAVY THINGS IN OUR HEARTS?
IF WE CAN'T CONVEY SUCH STRONG EMOTIONS AND IT'S TOO MUCH FOR US TO BEAR...
...THEN IT'S BETTER TO DO THINGS LIKE BUY THINGS WE LIKE AND THEN LOVE ON OUR OWN...
...IT'S A WORLD ... ...I CAN'T UNDER-STAND...
BEING A FORTUNE-TELLER SURE MUST BE TOUGH IF YOU HAVE TO DEAL WITH...
...STUFF LIKE THIS ALL THE TIME...
MY, WHAT A...
...WAY TO MAKE IT SOUND LIKE IT HAS NOTHING TO DO WITH YOU AT ALL.

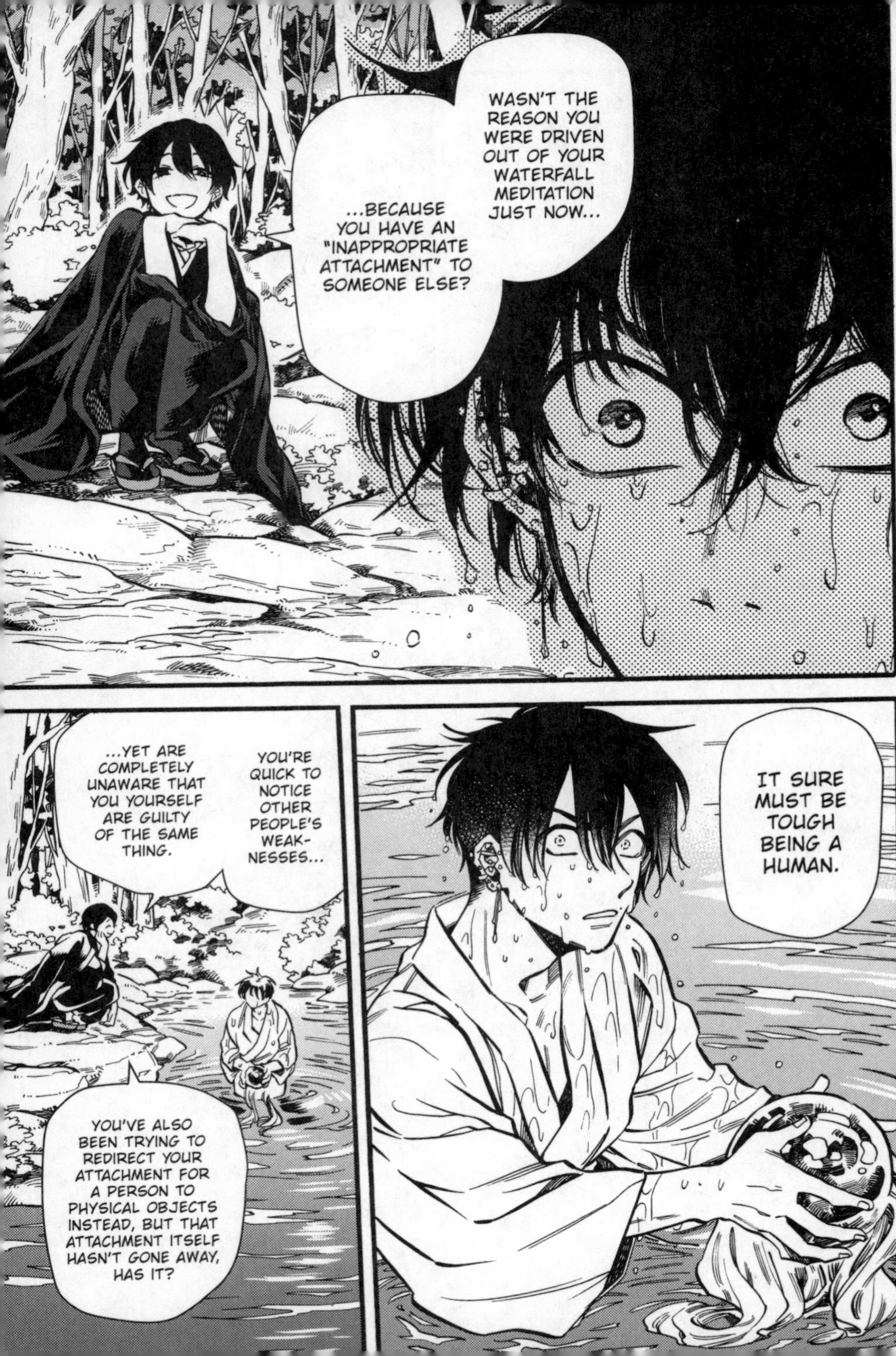
WASN'T THE REASON YOU WERE DRIVEN OUT OF YOUR WATERFALL MEDITATION JUST NOW...
...BECAUSE YOU HAVE AN "INAPPROPRIATE ATTACHMENT" TO SOMEONE ELSE?
IT SURE MUST BE TOUGH BEING A HUMAN.
YOU'RE QUICK TO NOTICE OTHER PEOPLE'S WEAK-NESSES...
...YET ARE COMPLETELY UNAWARE THAT YOU YOURSELF ARE GUILTY OF THE SAME THING.
YOU'VE ALSO BEEN TRYING TO REDIRECT YOUR ATTACHMENT FOR A PERSON TO PHYSICAL OBJECTS INSTEAD, BUT THAT ATTACHMENT ITSELF HASN'T GONE AWAY, HAS IT?

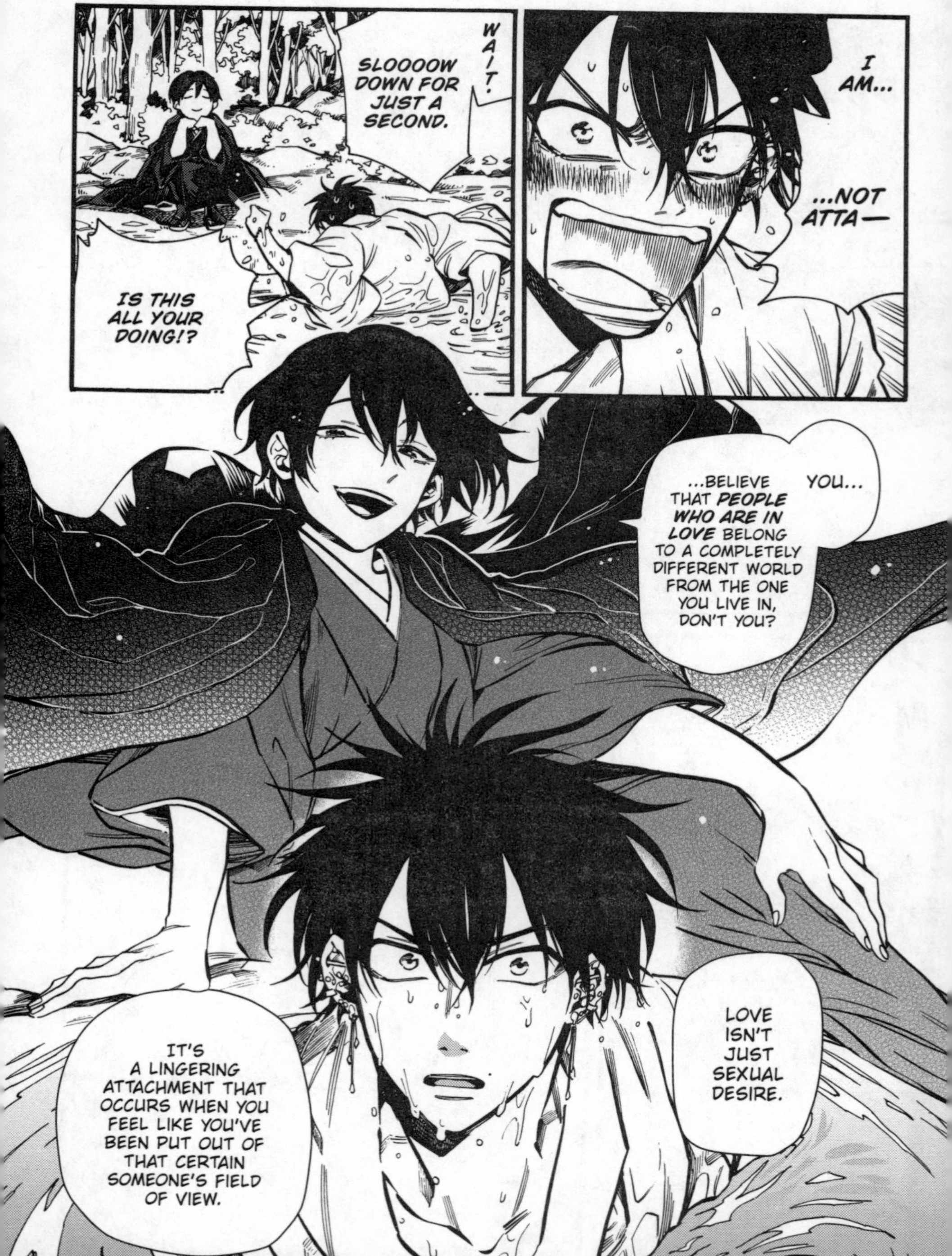
I AM...
...NOT ATTA—
WAIT!
SLOOOOW DOWN FOR JUST A SECOND.
IS THIS ALL YOUR DOING!?
YOU...
...BELIEVE THAT PEOPLE WHO ARE IN LOVE BELONG TO A COMPLETELY DIFFERENT WORLD FROM THE ONE YOU LIVE IN, DON'T YOU?
LOVE ISN'T JUST SEXUAL DESIRE.
IT'S A LINGERING ATTACHMENT THAT OCCURS WHEN YOU FEEL LIKE YOU'VE BEEN PUT OUT OF THAT CERTAIN SOMEONE'S FIELD OF VIEW.

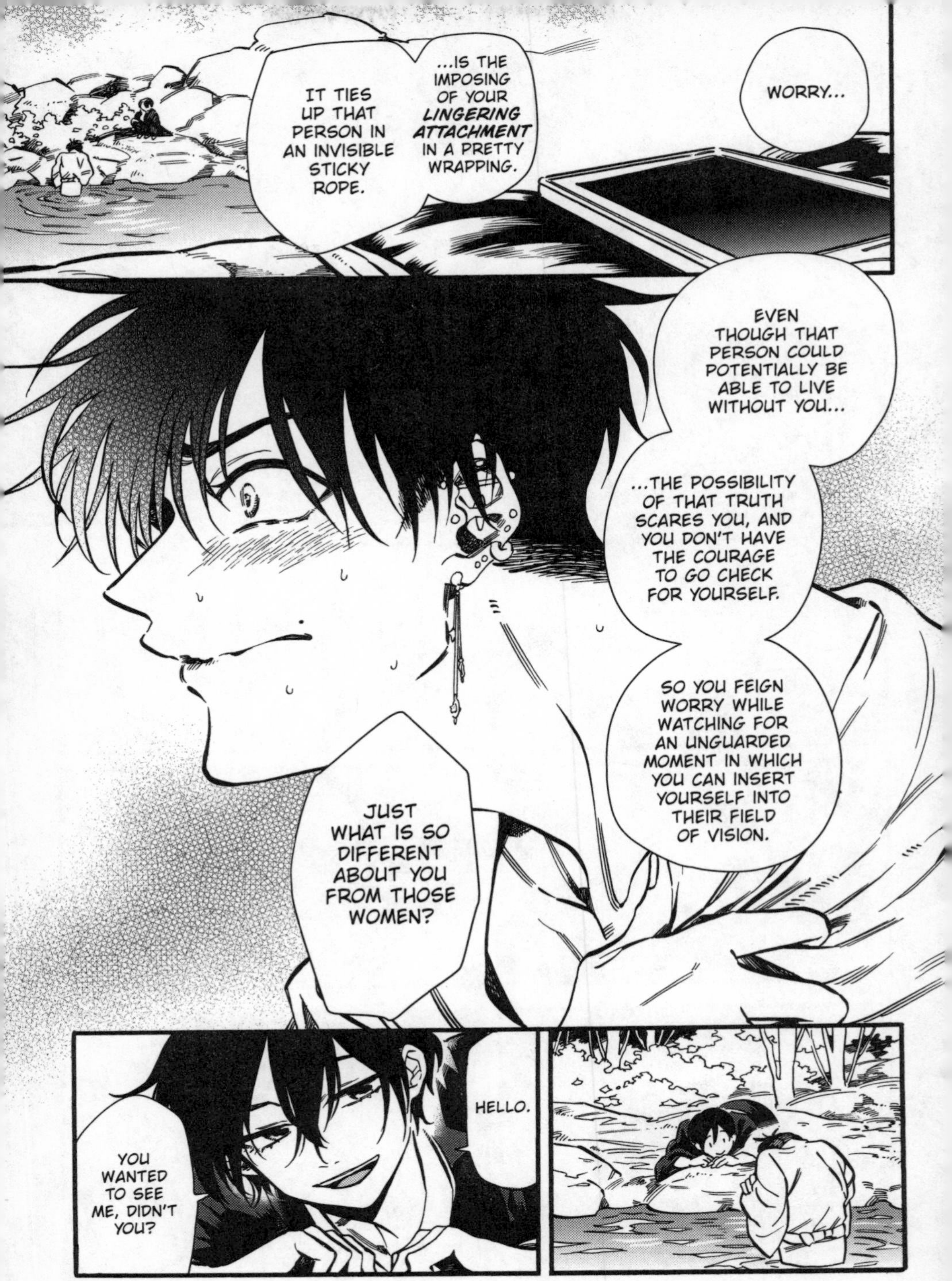
WORRY...
...IS THE IMPOSING OF YOUR LINGERING ATTACHMENT IN A PRETTY WRAPPING.
IT TIES UP THAT PERSON IN AN INVISIBLE STICKY ROPE.
EVEN THOUGH THAT PERSON COULD POTENTIALLY BE ABLE TO LIVE WITHOUT YOU...
...THE POSSIBILITY OF THAT TRUTH SCARES YOU, AND YOU DON'T HAVE THE COURAGE TO GO CHECK FOR YOURSELF.
SO YOU FEIGN WORRY WHILE WATCHING FOR AN UNGUARDED MOMENT IN WHICH YOU CAN INSERT YOURSELF INTO THEIR FIELD OF VISION.
JUST WHAT IS SO DIFFERENT ABOUT YOU FROM THOSE WOMEN?
HELLO.
YOU WANTED TO SEE ME, DIDN'T YOU?

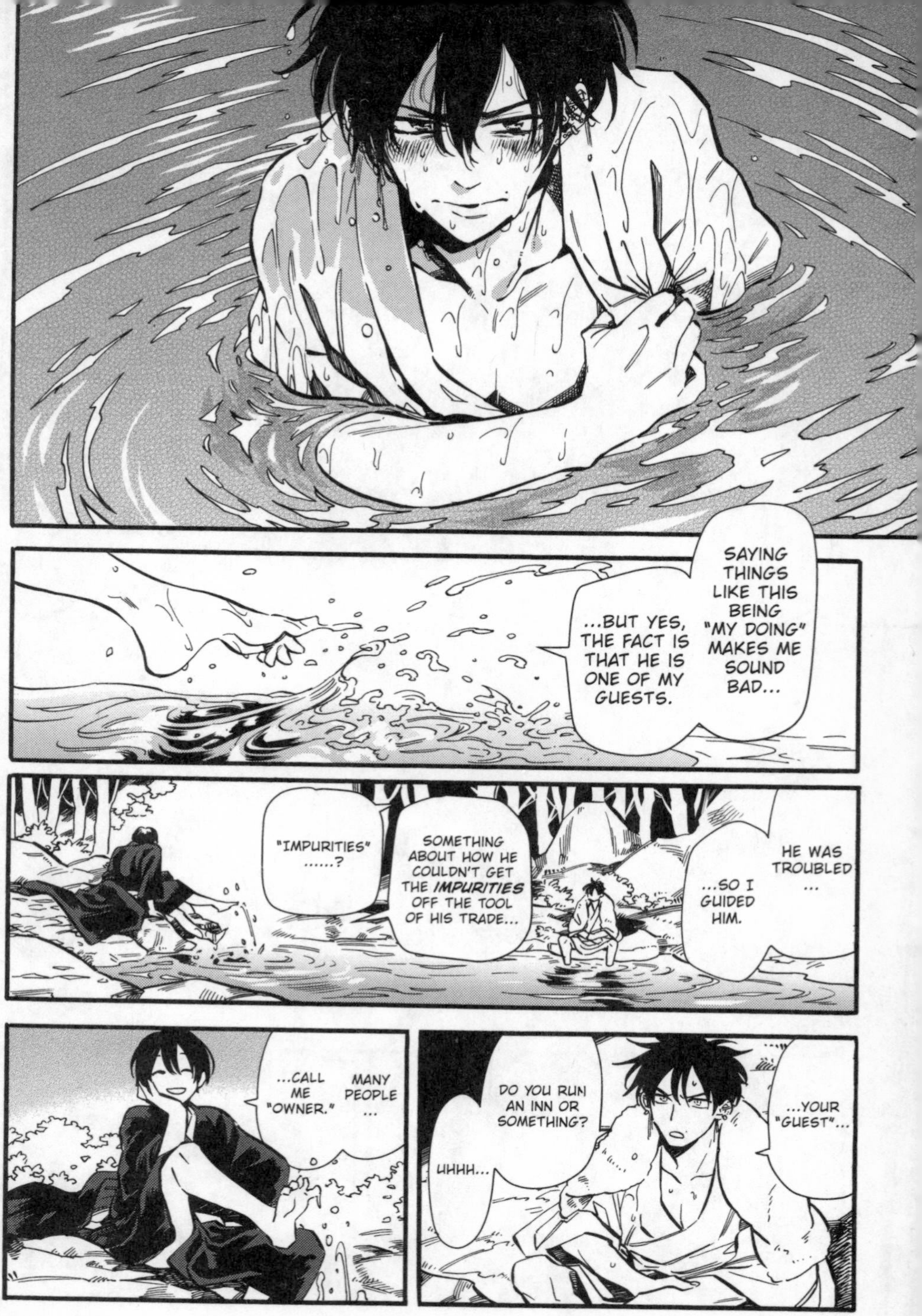
SAYING THINGS LIKE THIS BEING "MY DOING" MAKES ME SOUND BAD...
...BUT YES, THE FACT IS THAT HE IS ONE OF MY GUESTS.
HE WAS TROUBLED...
...SO I GUIDED HIM.
SOMETHING ABOUT HOW HE COULDN'T GET THE *IMPURITIES* OFF THE TOOL OF HIS TRADE...
"IMPURITIES" ......?
...YOUR "GUEST"...
DO YOU RUN AN INN OR SOMETHING?
UHHH...
MANY PEOPLE...
...CALL ME "OWNER."

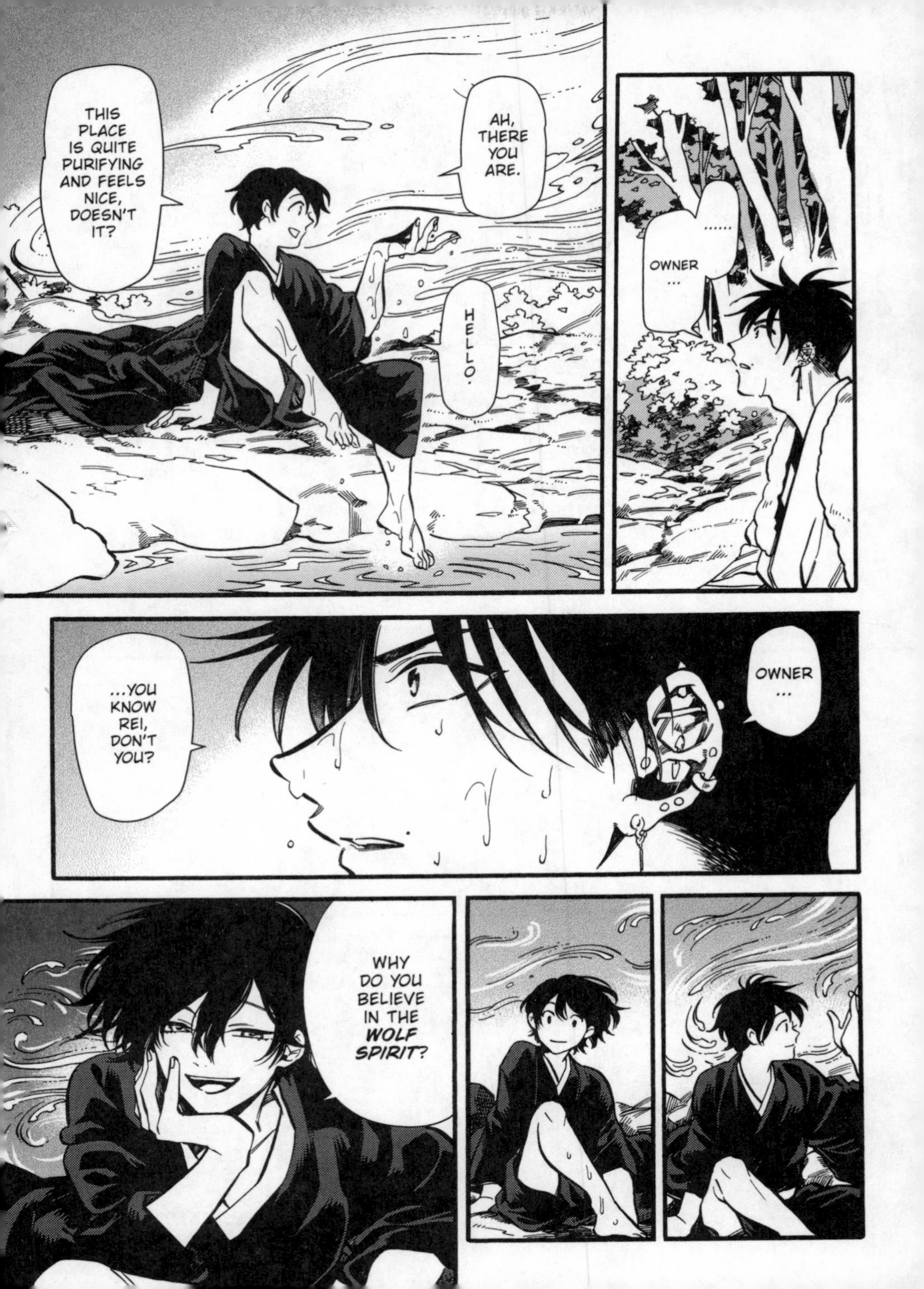
......
OWNER ...
AH, THERE YOU ARE.
HELLO.
THIS PLACE IS QUITE PURIFYING AND FEELS NICE, DOESN'T IT?
OWNER ...
...YOU KNOW REI, DON'T YOU?
WHY DO YOU BELIEVE IN THE *WOLF SPIRIT*?

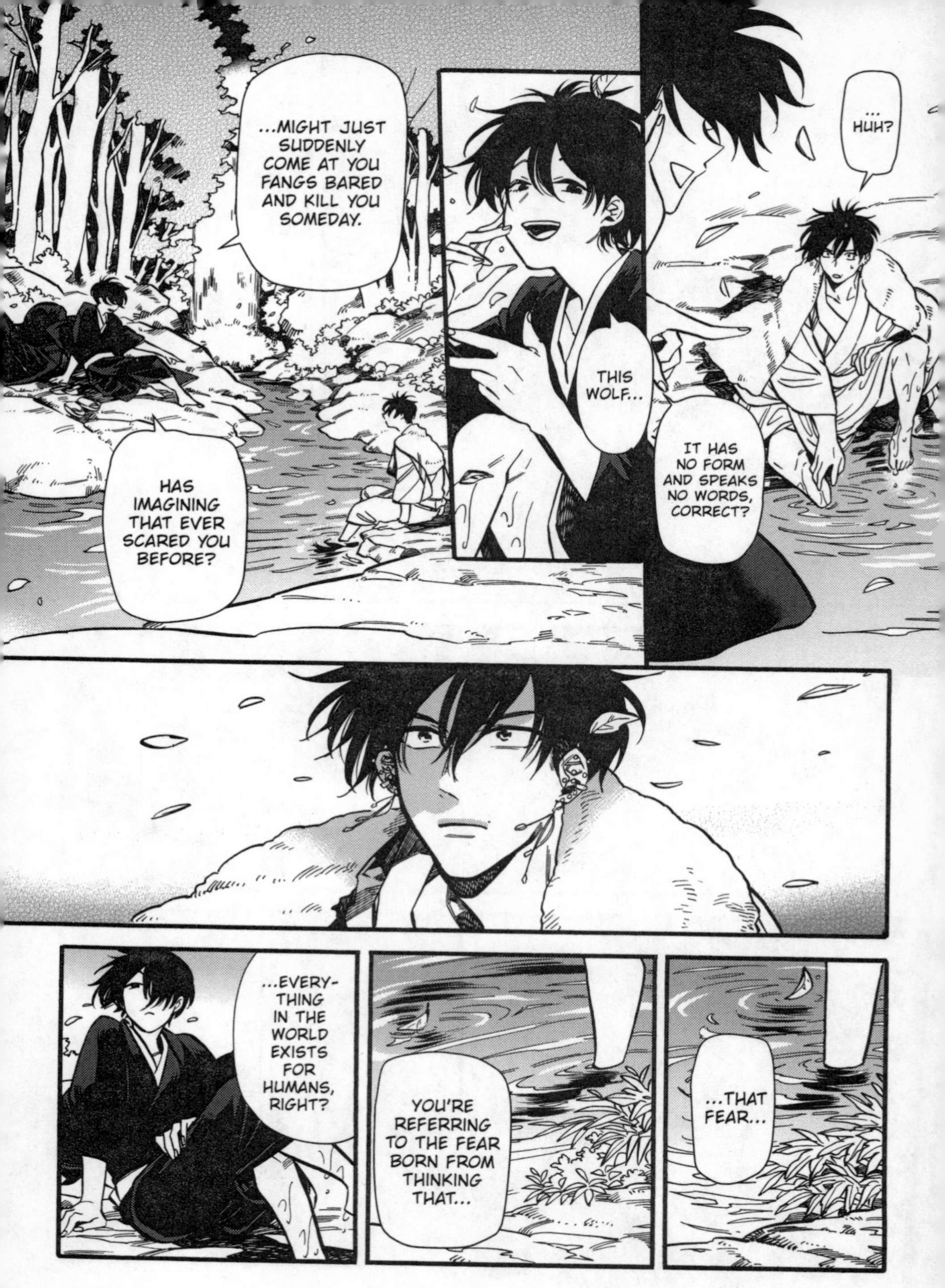
...HUH?
THIS WOLF...
IT HAS NO FORM AND SPEAKS NO WORDS, CORRECT?
...MIGHT JUST SUDDENLY COME AT YOU FANGS BARED AND KILL YOU SOMEDAY.
HAS IMAGINING THAT EVER SCARED YOU BEFORE?
...THAT FEAR...
YOU'RE REFERRING TO THE FEAR BORN FROM THINKING THAT...
...EVERY-THING IN THE WORLD EXISTS FOR HUMANS, RIGHT?

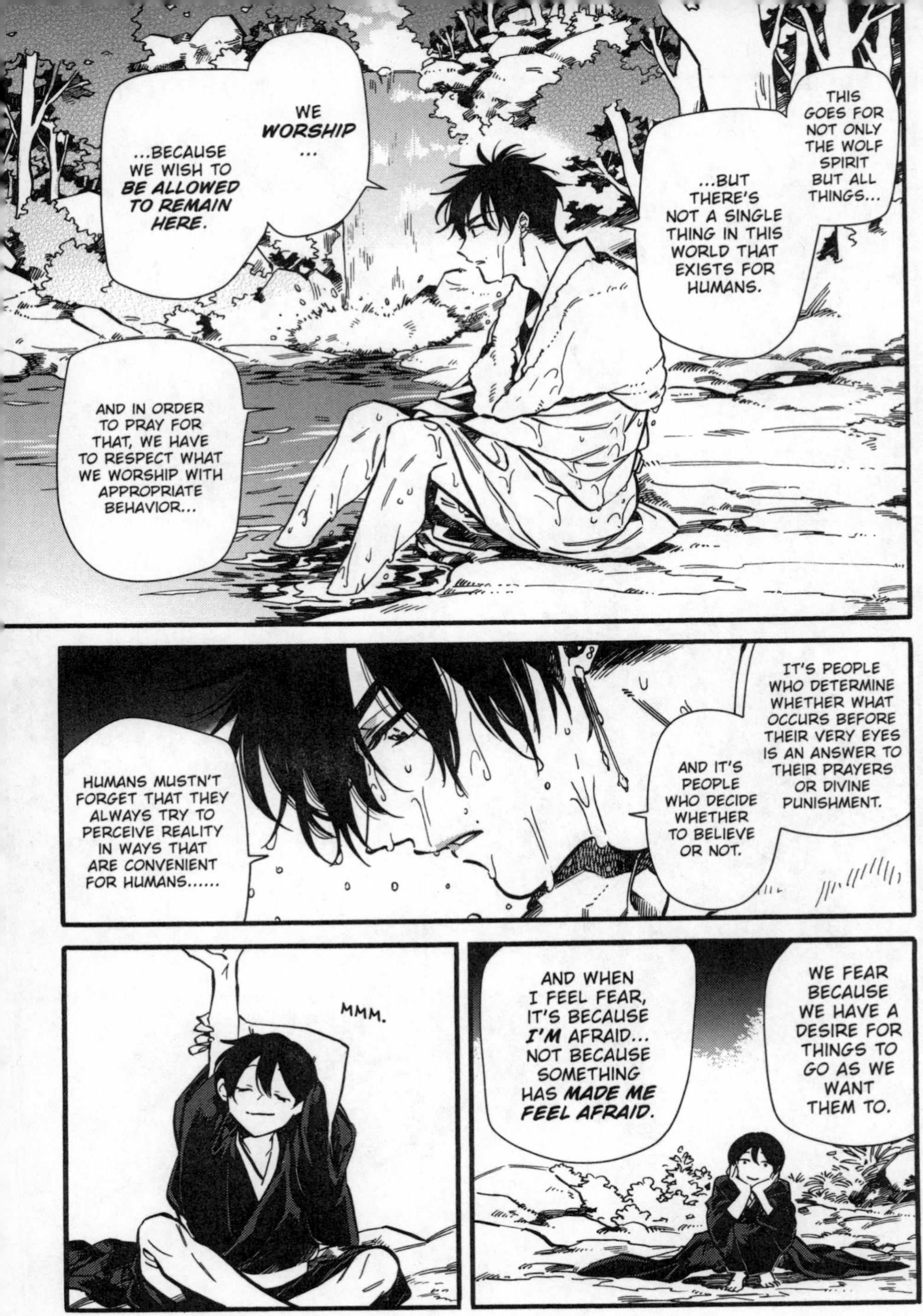

THIS GOES FOR NOT ONLY THE WOLF SPIRIT BUT ALL THINGS...
...BUT THERE'S NOT A SINGLE THING IN THIS WORLD THAT EXISTS FOR HUMANS.
WE **WORSHIP** ...
...BECAUSE WE WISH TO **BE ALLOWED TO REMAIN HERE.**
AND IN ORDER TO PRAY FOR THAT, WE HAVE TO RESPECT WHAT WE WORSHIP WITH APPROPRIATE BEHAVIOR...
IT'S PEOPLE WHO DETERMINE WHETHER WHAT OCCURS BEFORE THEIR VERY EYES IS AN ANSWER TO THEIR PRAYERS OR DIVINE PUNISHMENT.
AND IT'S PEOPLE WHO DECIDE WHETHER TO BELIEVE OR NOT.
HUMANS MUSTN'T FORGET THAT THEY ALWAYS TRY TO PERCEIVE REALITY IN WAYS THAT ARE CONVENIENT FOR HUMANS......
WE FEAR BECAUSE WE HAVE A DESIRE FOR THINGS TO GO AS WE WANT THEM TO.
AND WHEN I FEEL FEAR, IT'S BECAUSE ***I'M*** AFRAID... NOT BECAUSE SOMETHING HAS ***MADE ME FEEL AFRAID.***
MMM.

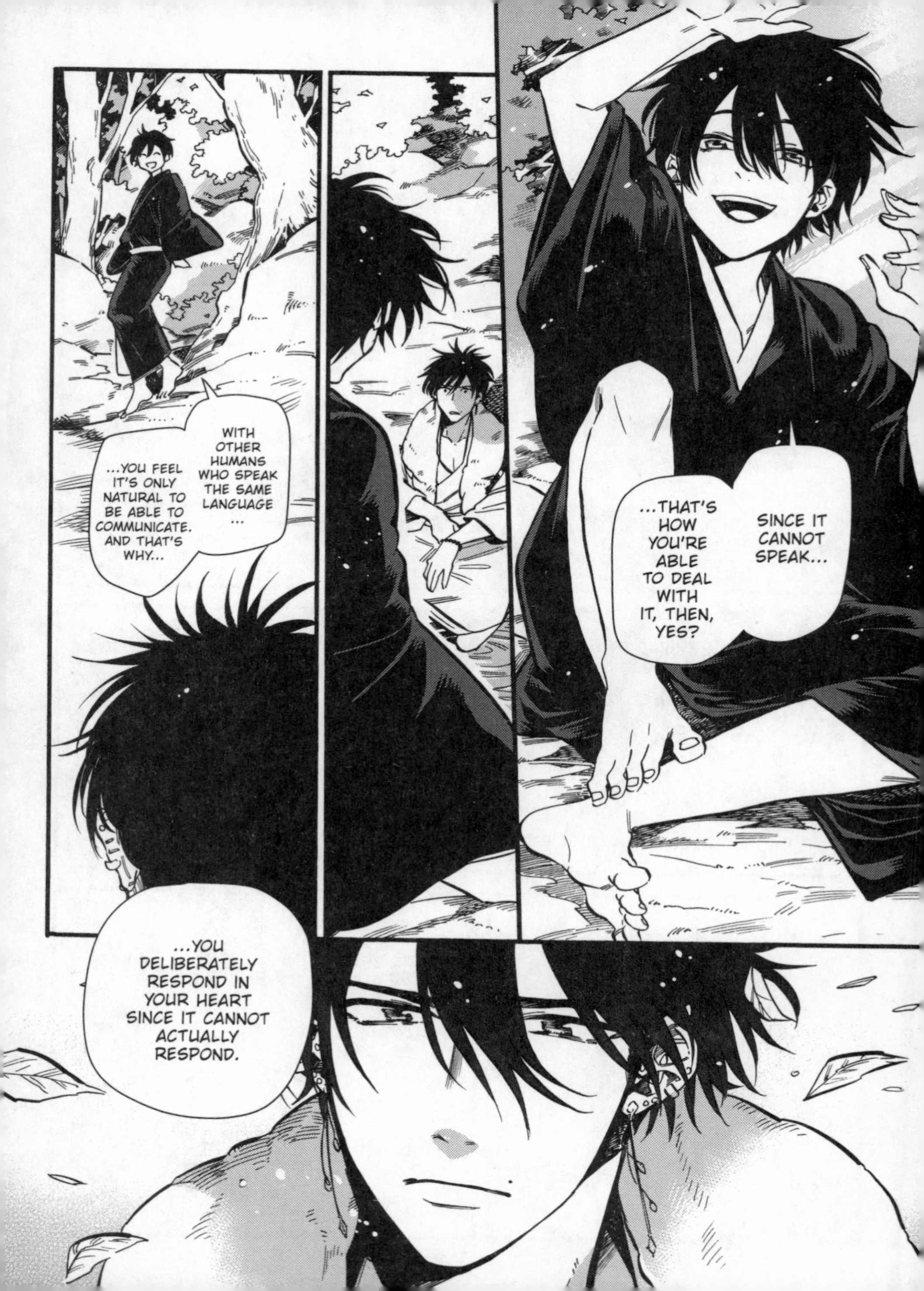
SINCE IT CANNOT SPEAK...
...THAT'S HOW YOU'RE ABLE TO DEAL WITH IT, THEN, YES?
.....
WITH OTHER HUMANS WHO SPEAK THE SAME LANGUAGE...
...YOU FEEL IT'S ONLY NATURAL TO BE ABLE TO COMMUNICATE. AND THAT'S WHY...
...YOU DELIBERATELY RESPOND IN YOUR HEART SINCE IT CANNOT ACTUALLY RESPOND.

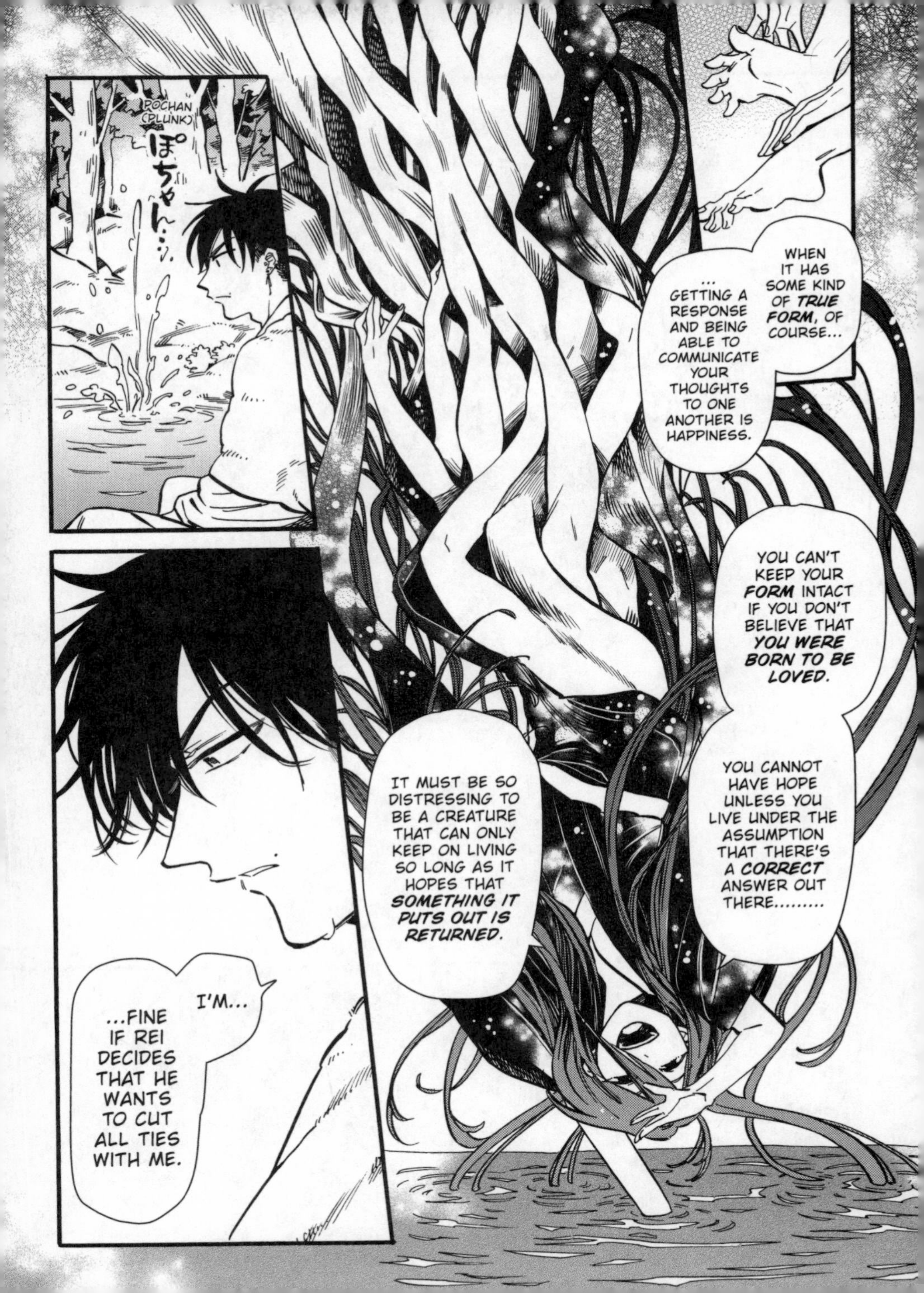
WHEN IT HAS SOME KIND OF **TRUE FORM**, OF COURSE...
...GETTING A RESPONSE AND BEING ABLE TO COMMUNICATE YOUR THOUGHTS TO ONE ANOTHER IS HAPPINESS.
YOU CAN'T KEEP YOUR **FORM** INTACT IF YOU DON'T BELIEVE THAT **YOU WERE BORN TO BE LOVED**.
YOU CANNOT HAVE HOPE UNLESS YOU LIVE UNDER THE ASSUMPTION THAT THERE'S A **CORRECT** ANSWER OUT THERE.........
IT MUST BE SO DISTRESSING TO BE A CREATURE THAT CAN ONLY KEEP ON LIVING SO LONG AS IT HOPES THAT **SOMETHING IT PUTS OUT IS RETURNED**.
POCHAN (PLUNK)
ぽちゃん…
I'M...
...FINE IF REI DECIDES THAT HE WANTS TO CUT ALL TIES WITH ME.

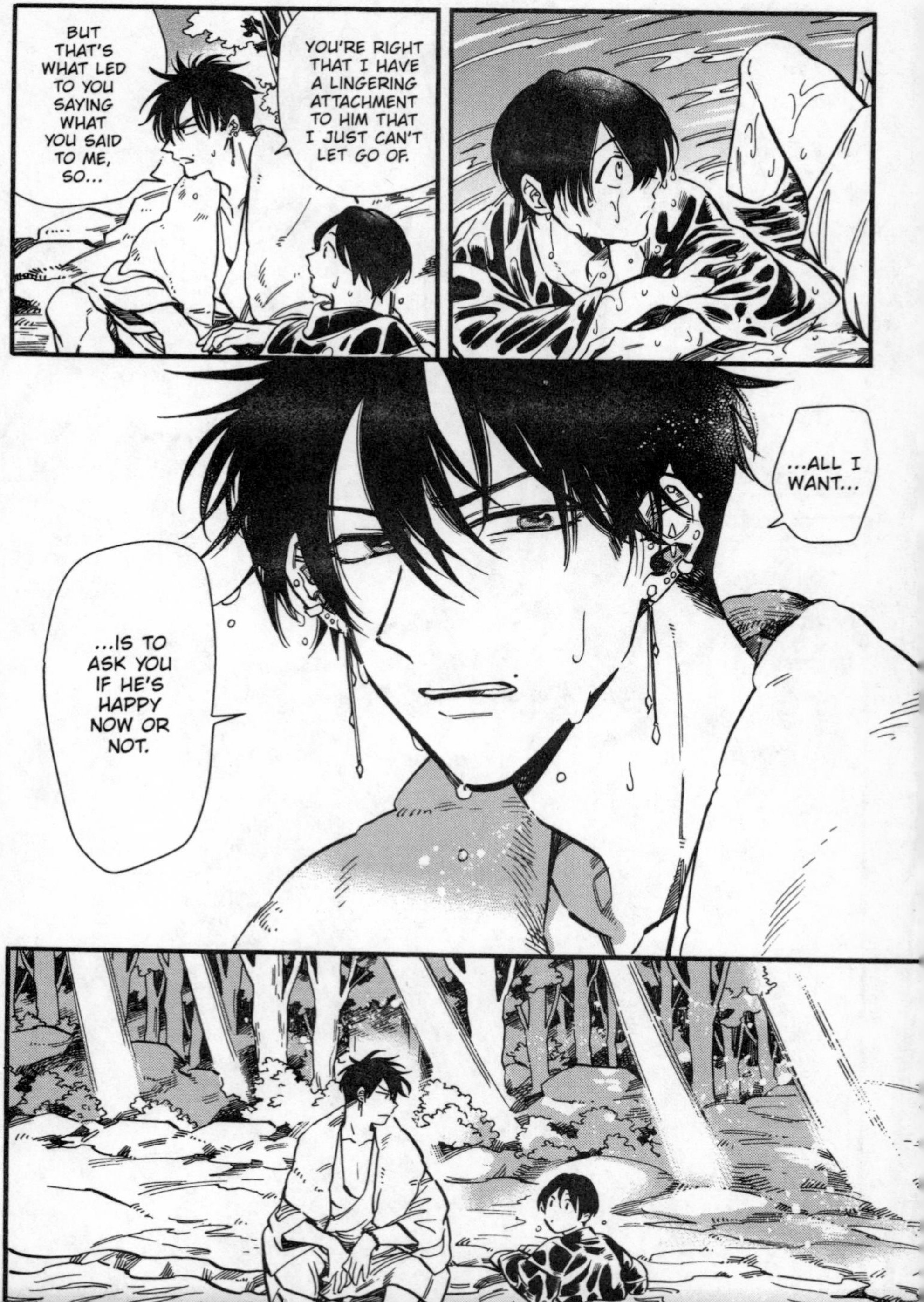
YOU'RE RIGHT THAT I HAVE A LINGERING ATTACHMENT TO HIM THAT I JUST CAN'T LET GO OF.
BUT THAT'S WHAT LED TO YOU SAYING WHAT YOU SAID TO ME, SO...
...ALL I WANT...
...IS TO ASK YOU IF HE'S HAPPY NOW OR NOT.

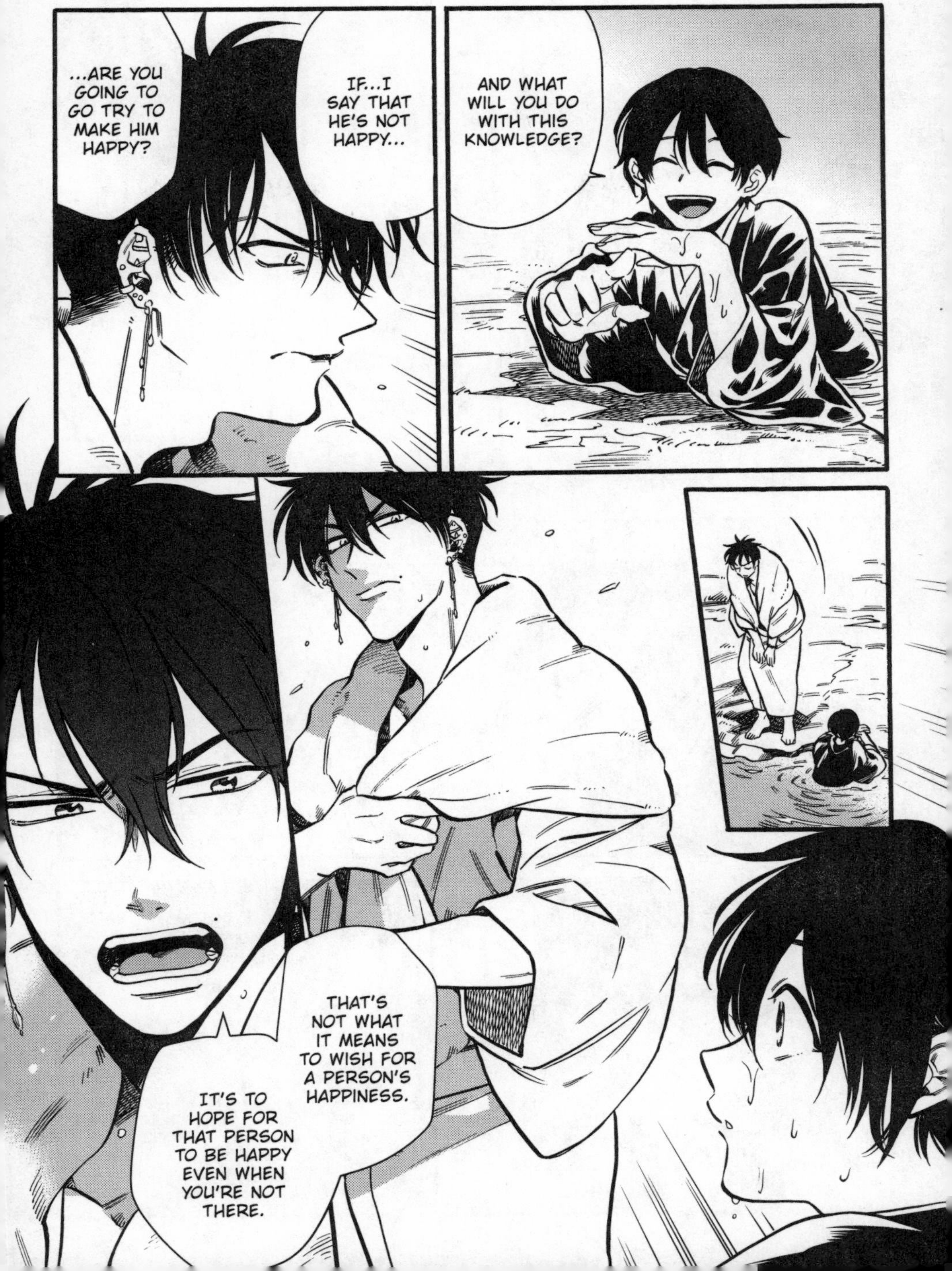
AND WHAT WILL YOU DO WITH THIS KNOWLEDGE?
IF...I SAY THAT HE'S NOT HAPPY...
...ARE YOU GOING TO GO TRY TO MAKE HIM HAPPY?
THAT'S NOT WHAT IT MEANS TO WISH FOR A PERSON'S HAPPINESS.
IT'S TO HOPE FOR THAT PERSON TO BE HAPPY EVEN WHEN YOU'RE NOT THERE.

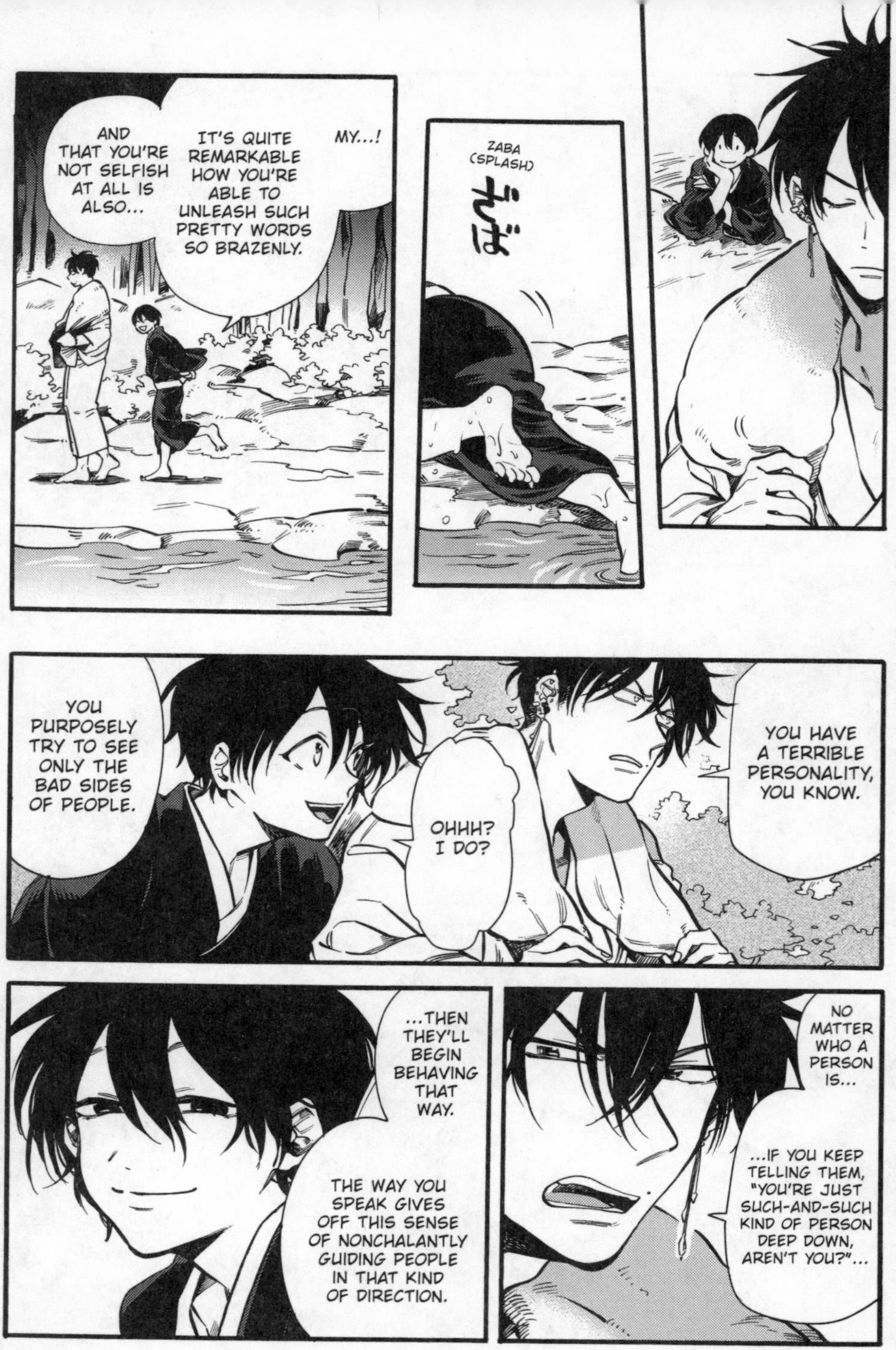
ZABA (SPLASH)
ざば
MY...!
IT'S QUITE REMARKABLE HOW YOU'RE ABLE TO UNLEASH SUCH PRETTY WORDS SO BRAZENLY.
AND THAT YOU'RE NOT SELFISH AT ALL IS ALSO...
YOU HAVE A TERRIBLE PERSONALITY, YOU KNOW.
OHHH? I DO?
YOU PURPOSELY TRY TO SEE ONLY THE BAD SIDES OF PEOPLE.
NO MATTER WHO A PERSON IS...
...IF YOU KEEP TELLING THEM, "YOU'RE JUST SUCH-AND-SUCH KIND OF PERSON DEEP DOWN, AREN'T YOU?"...
...THEN THEY'LL BEGIN BEHAVING THAT WAY.
THE WAY YOU SPEAK GIVES OFF THIS SENSE OF NONCHALANTLY GUIDING PEOPLE IN THAT KIND OF DIRECTION.

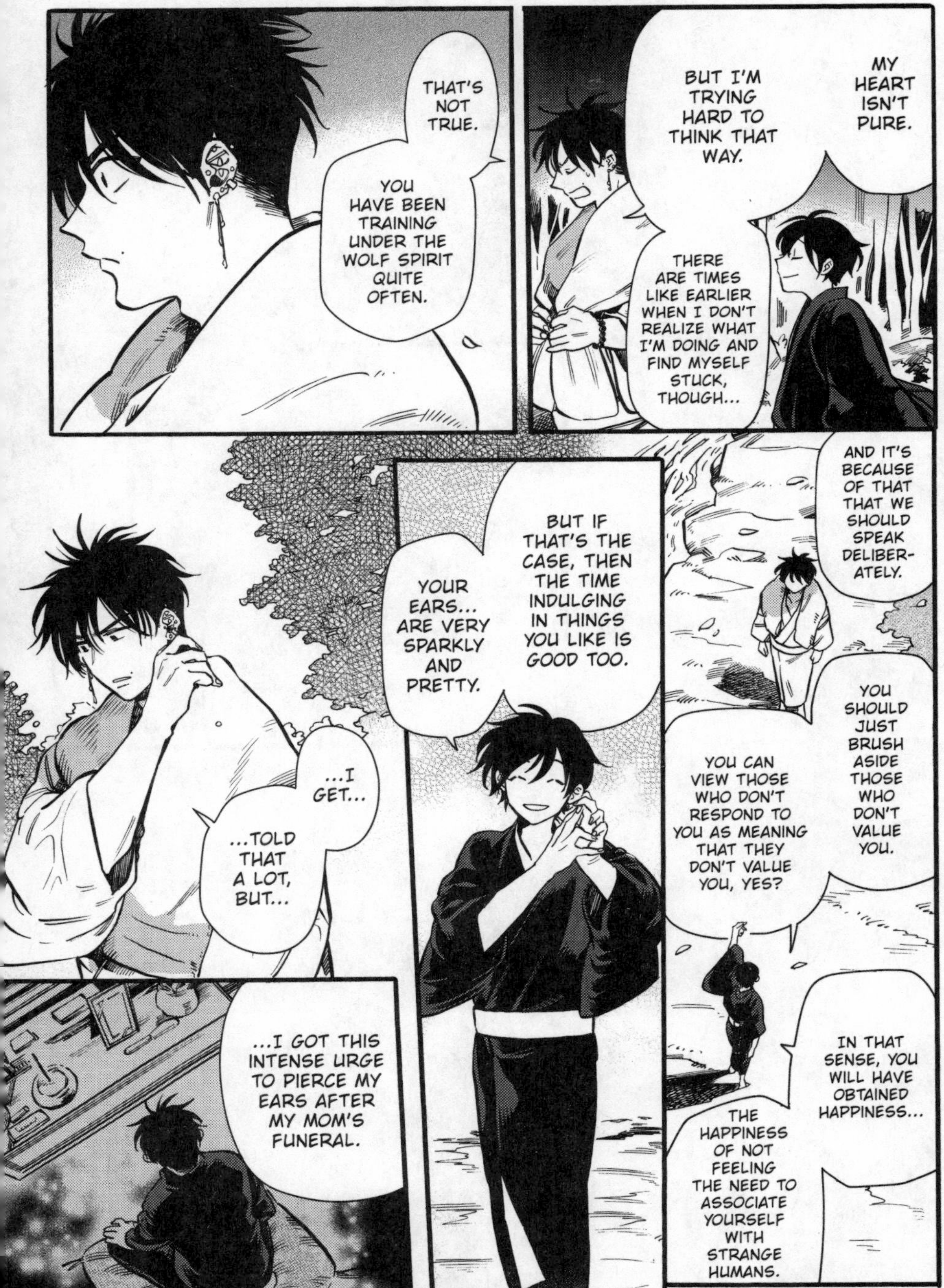
MY HEART ISN'T PURE.
BUT I'M TRYING HARD TO THINK THAT WAY.
THERE ARE TIMES LIKE EARLIER WHEN I DON'T REALIZE WHAT I'M DOING AND FIND MYSELF STUCK, THOUGH...
THAT'S NOT TRUE.
YOU HAVE BEEN TRAINING UNDER THE WOLF SPIRIT QUITE OFTEN.
AND IT'S BECAUSE OF THAT THAT WE SHOULD SPEAK DELIBER-ATELY.
YOU SHOULD JUST BRUSH ASIDE THOSE WHO DON'T VALUE YOU.
YOU CAN VIEW THOSE WHO DON'T RESPOND TO YOU AS MEANING THAT THEY DON'T VALUE YOU, YES?
IN THAT SENSE, YOU WILL HAVE OBTAINED HAPPINESS...
THE HAPPINESS OF NOT FEELING THE NEED TO ASSOCIATE YOURSELF WITH STRANGE HUMANS.
BUT IF THAT'S THE CASE, THEN THE TIME INDULGING IN THINGS YOU LIKE IS GOOD TOO.
YOUR EARS... ARE VERY SPARKLY AND PRETTY.
...I GET...
...TOLD THAT A LOT, BUT...
...I GOT THIS INTENSE URGE TO PIERCE MY EARS AFTER MY MOM'S FUNERAL.

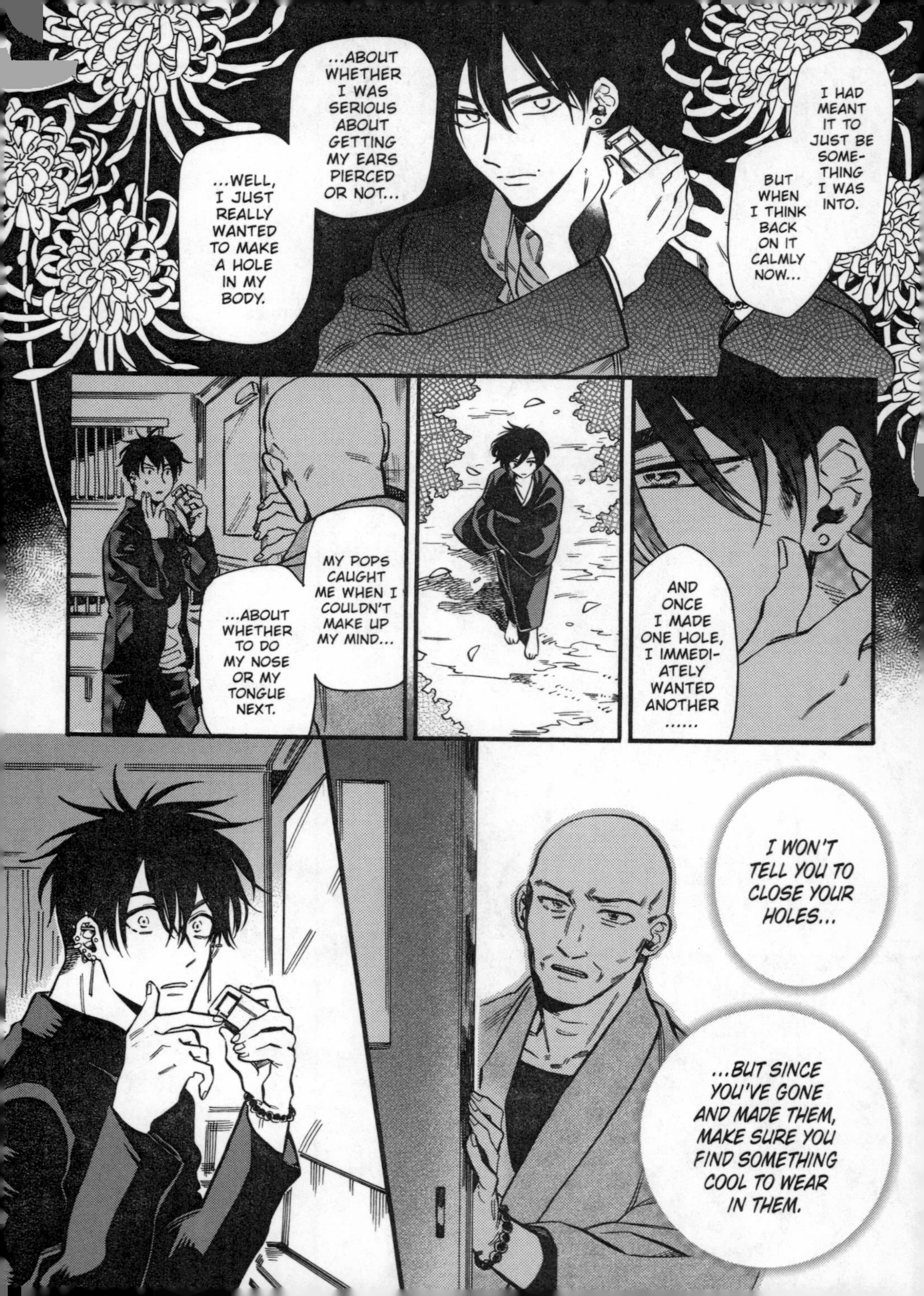

I HAD MEANT IT TO JUST BE SOMETHING I WAS INTO.
BUT WHEN I THINK BACK ON IT CALMLY NOW...
...ABOUT WHETHER I WAS SERIOUS ABOUT GETTING MY EARS PIERCED OR NOT...
...WELL, I JUST REALLY WANTED TO MAKE A HOLE IN MY BODY.
AND ONCE I MADE ONE HOLE, I IMMEDIATELY WANTED ANOTHER ......
MY POPS CAUGHT ME WHEN I COULDN'T MAKE UP MY MIND...
...ABOUT WHETHER TO DO MY NOSE OR MY TONGUE NEXT.
I WON'T TELL YOU TO CLOSE YOUR HOLES...
...BUT SINCE YOU'VE GONE AND MADE THEM, MAKE SURE YOU FIND SOMETHING COOL TO WEAR IN THEM.

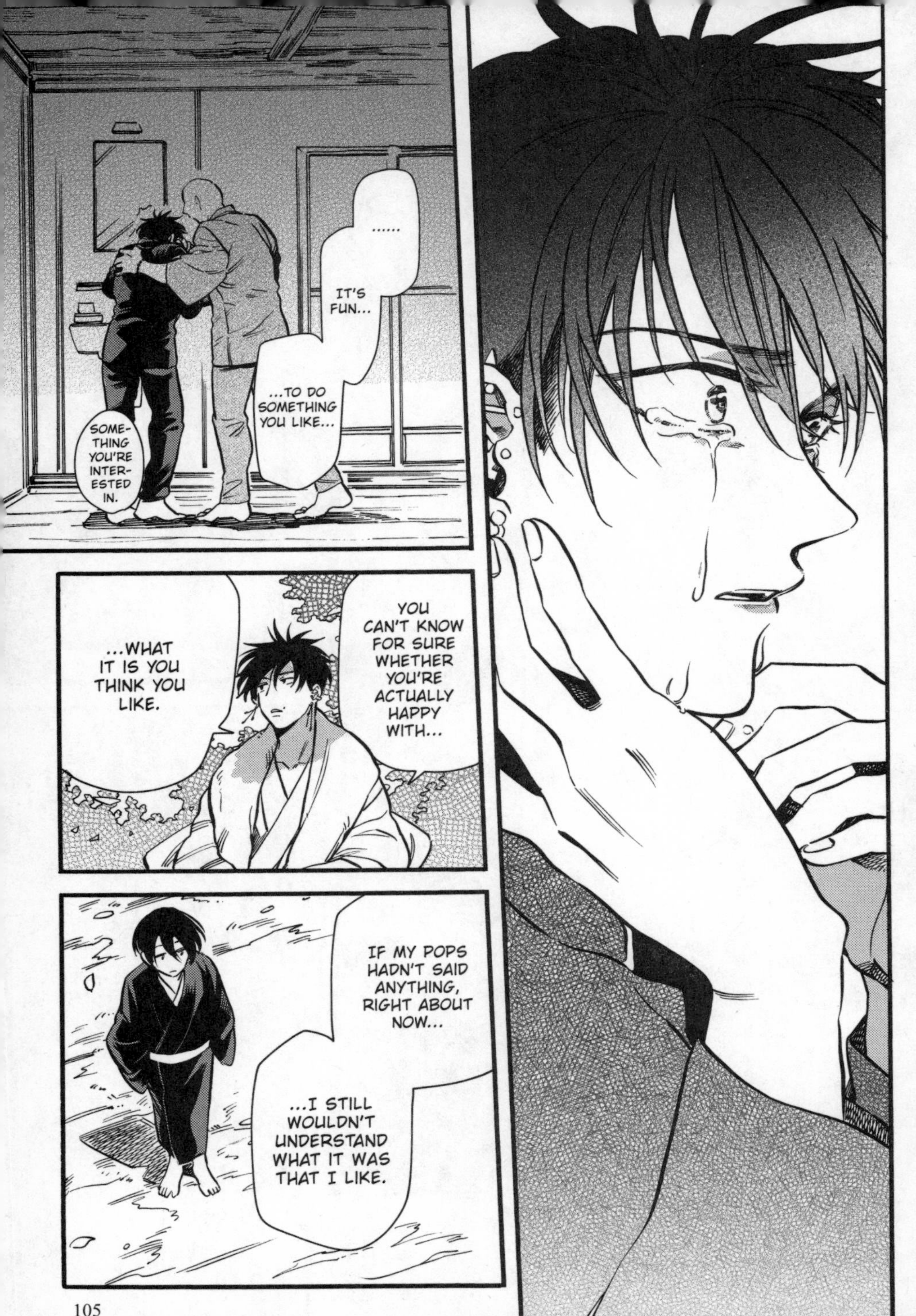
......
IT'S FUN...
...TO DO SOMETHING YOU LIKE...
SOMETHING YOU'RE INTERESTED IN.
YOU CAN'T KNOW FOR SURE WHETHER YOU'RE ACTUALLY HAPPY WITH...
...WHAT IT IS YOU THINK YOU LIKE.
IF MY POPS HADN'T SAID ANYTHING, RIGHT ABOUT NOW...
...I STILL WOULDN'T UNDERSTAND WHAT IT WAS THAT I LIKE.

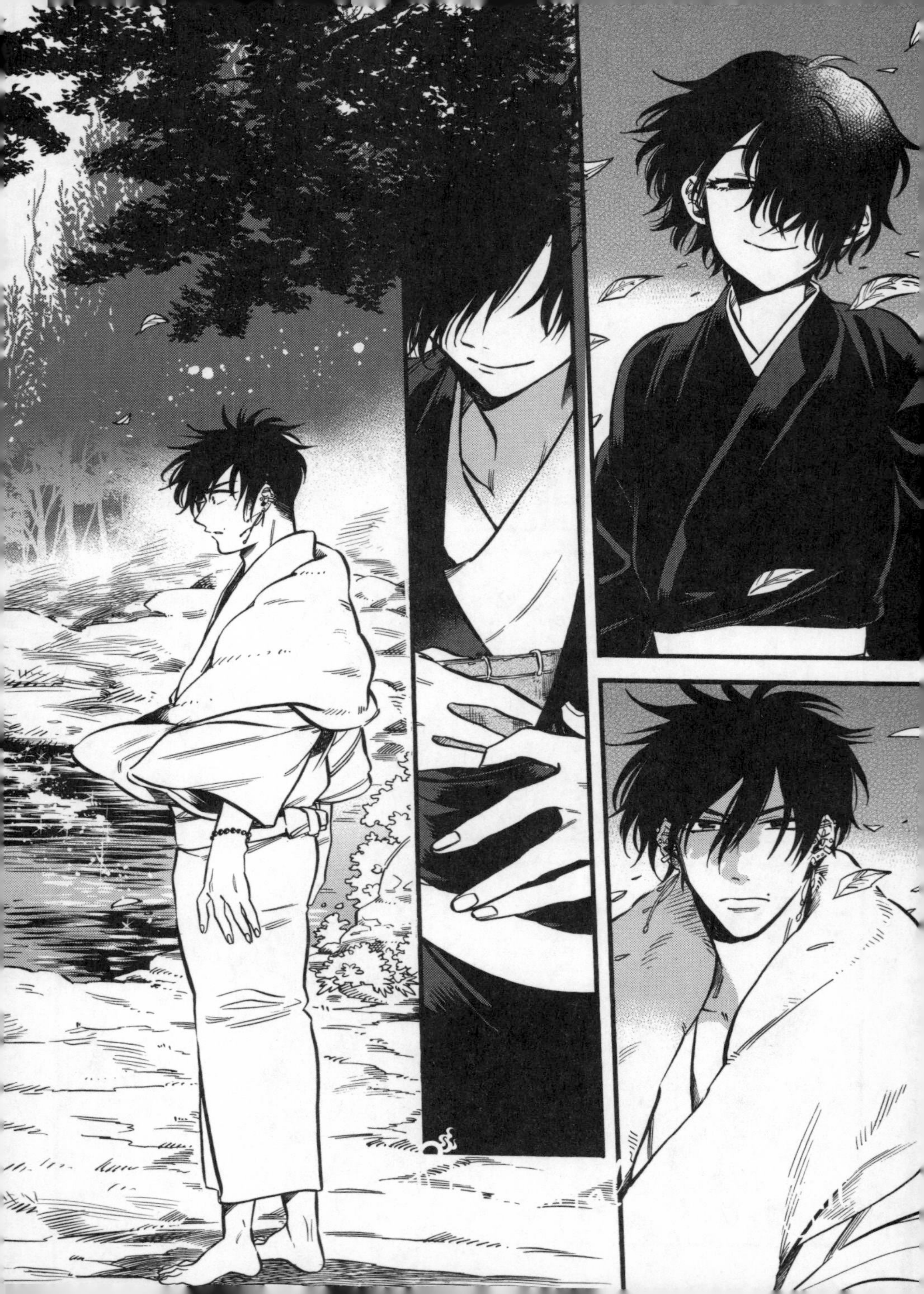

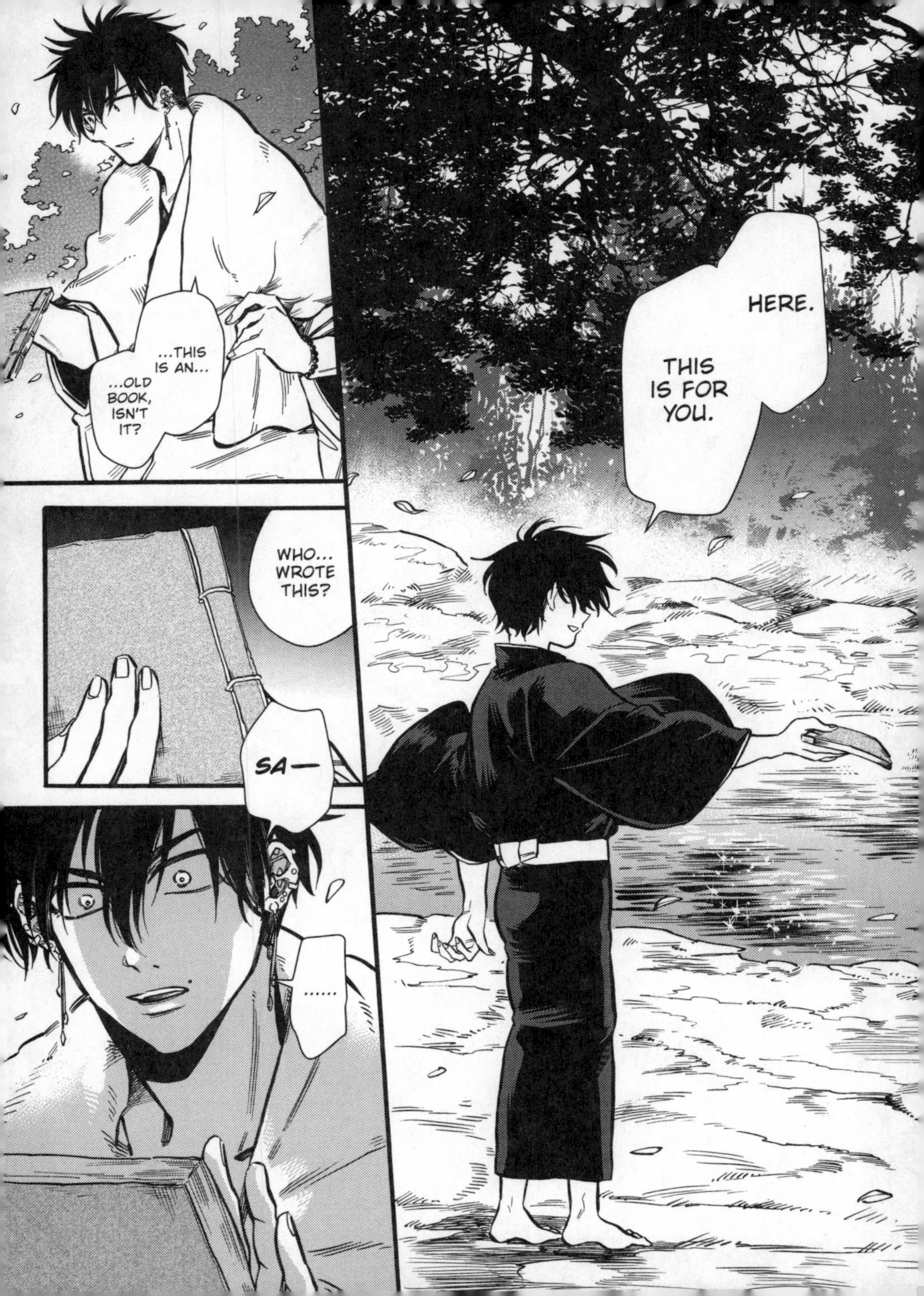
HERE.
THIS IS FOR YOU.
...THIS IS AN...
...OLD BOOK, ISN'T IT?
WHO... WROTE THIS?
SA—
......

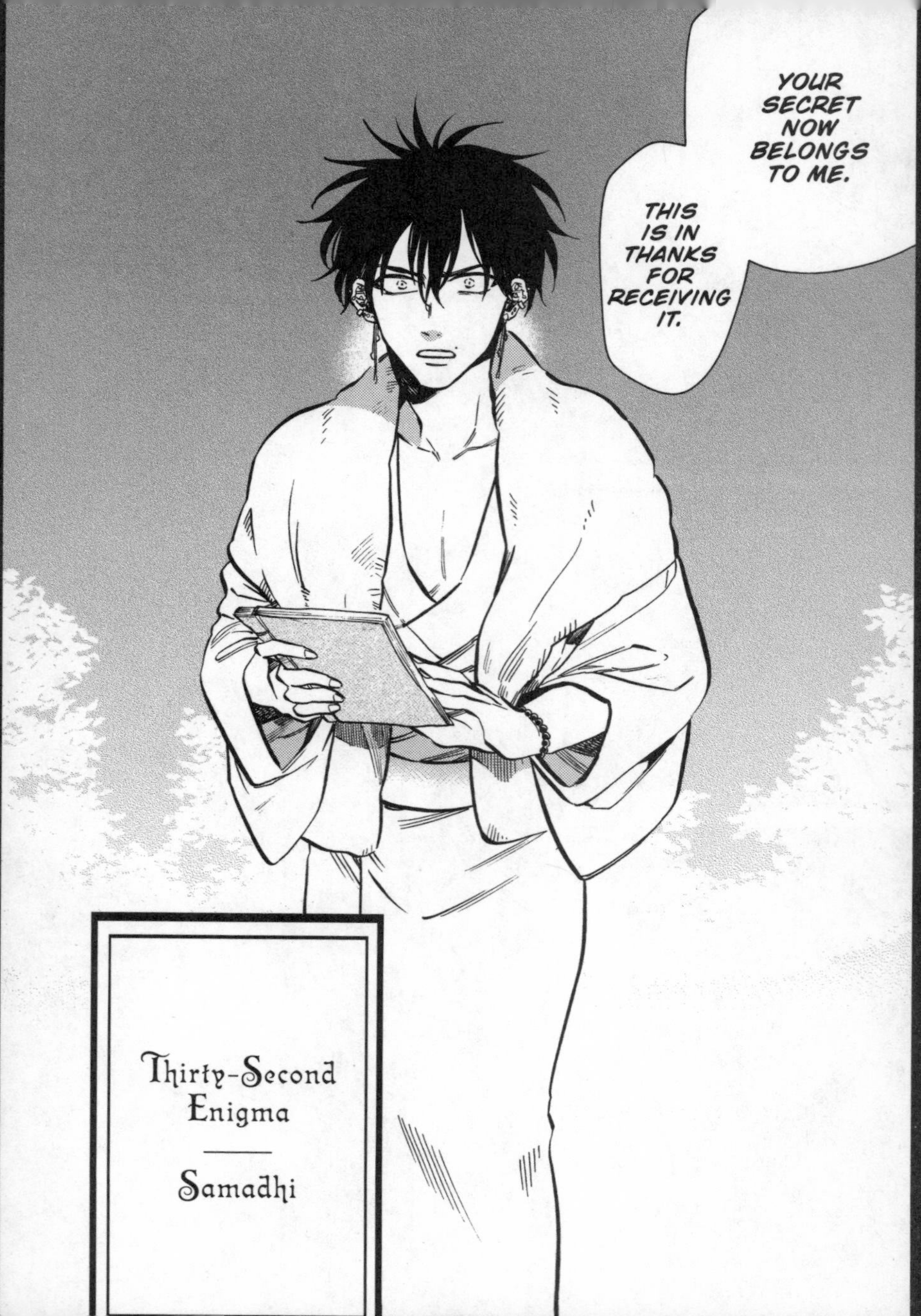
YOUR SECRET NOW BELONGS TO ME.
THIS IS IN THANKS FOR RECEIVING IT.

Thirty-Second Enigma

Samadhi

Phantom Tales of the Night

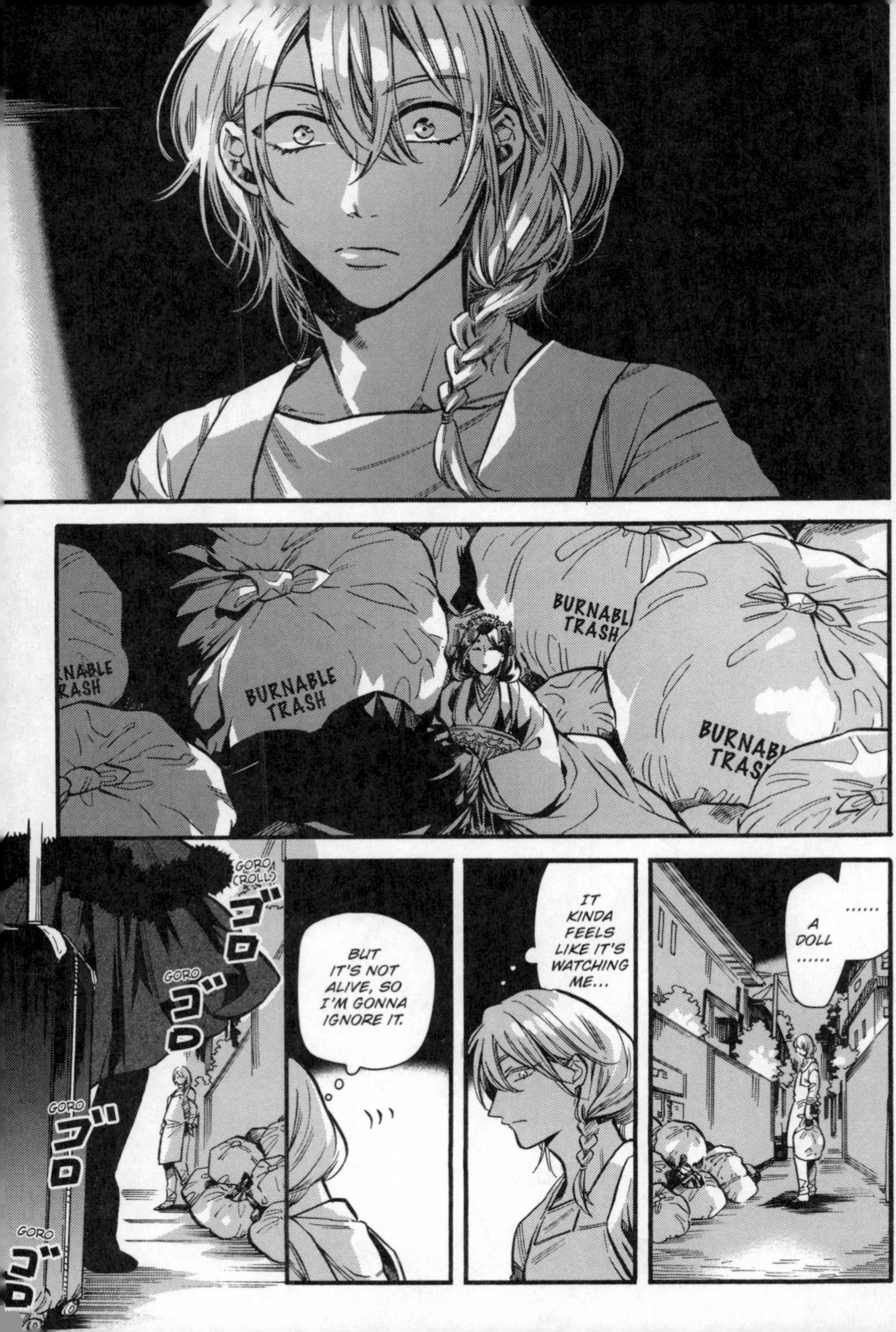
BURNABL TRASH
BURNABL TRAS
BURNABLE TRASH
NABLE RASH
...... A DOLL ......
IT KINDA FEELS LIKE IT'S WATCHING ME...
BUT IT'S NOT ALIVE, SO I'M GONNA IGNORE IT.
GORO (ROLL) ゴロ
GORO ゴロ
GORO ゴロ
GORO ゴロ

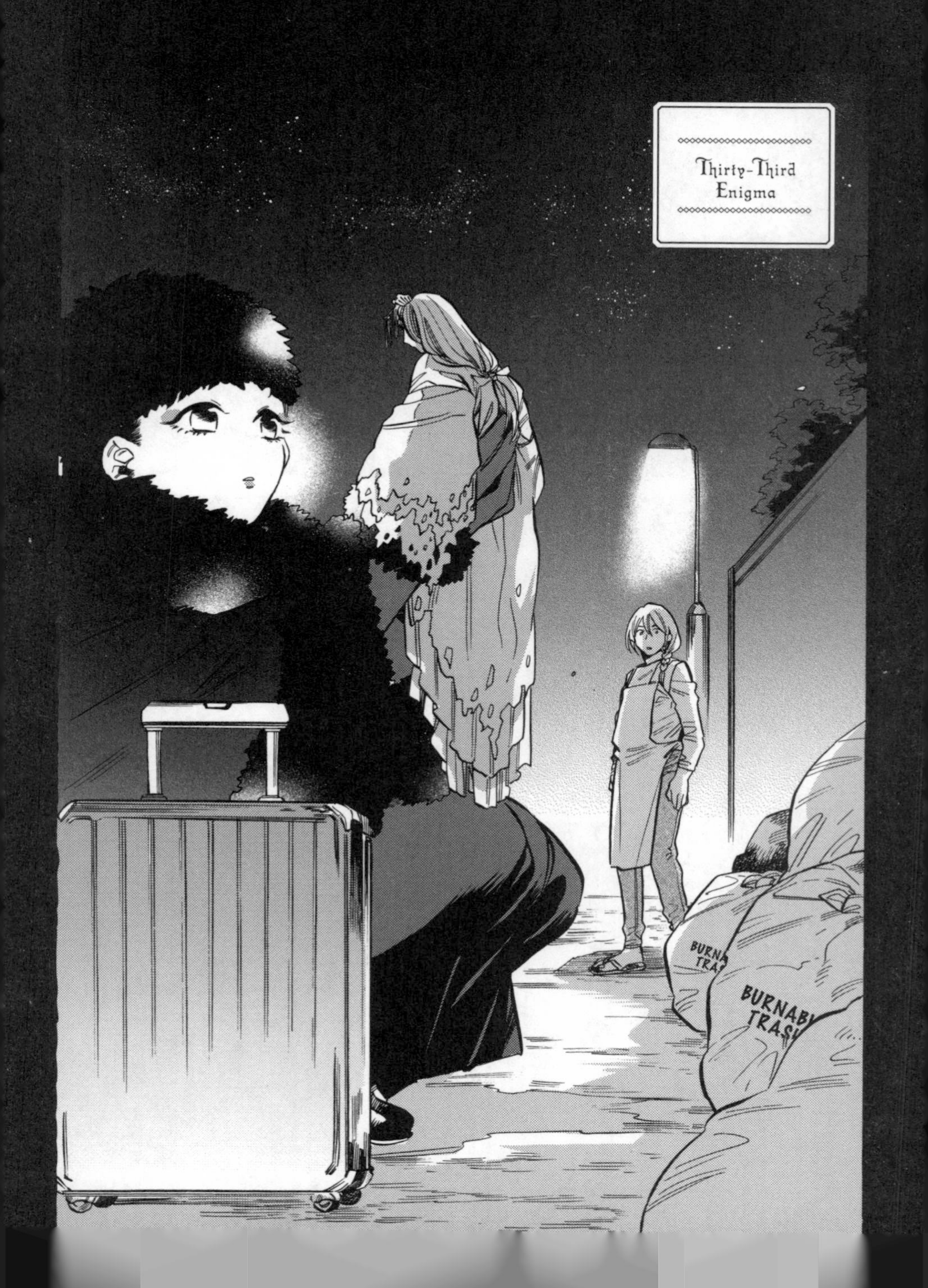
Thirty-Third Enigma
BURNA TRAS
BURNAB TRAS

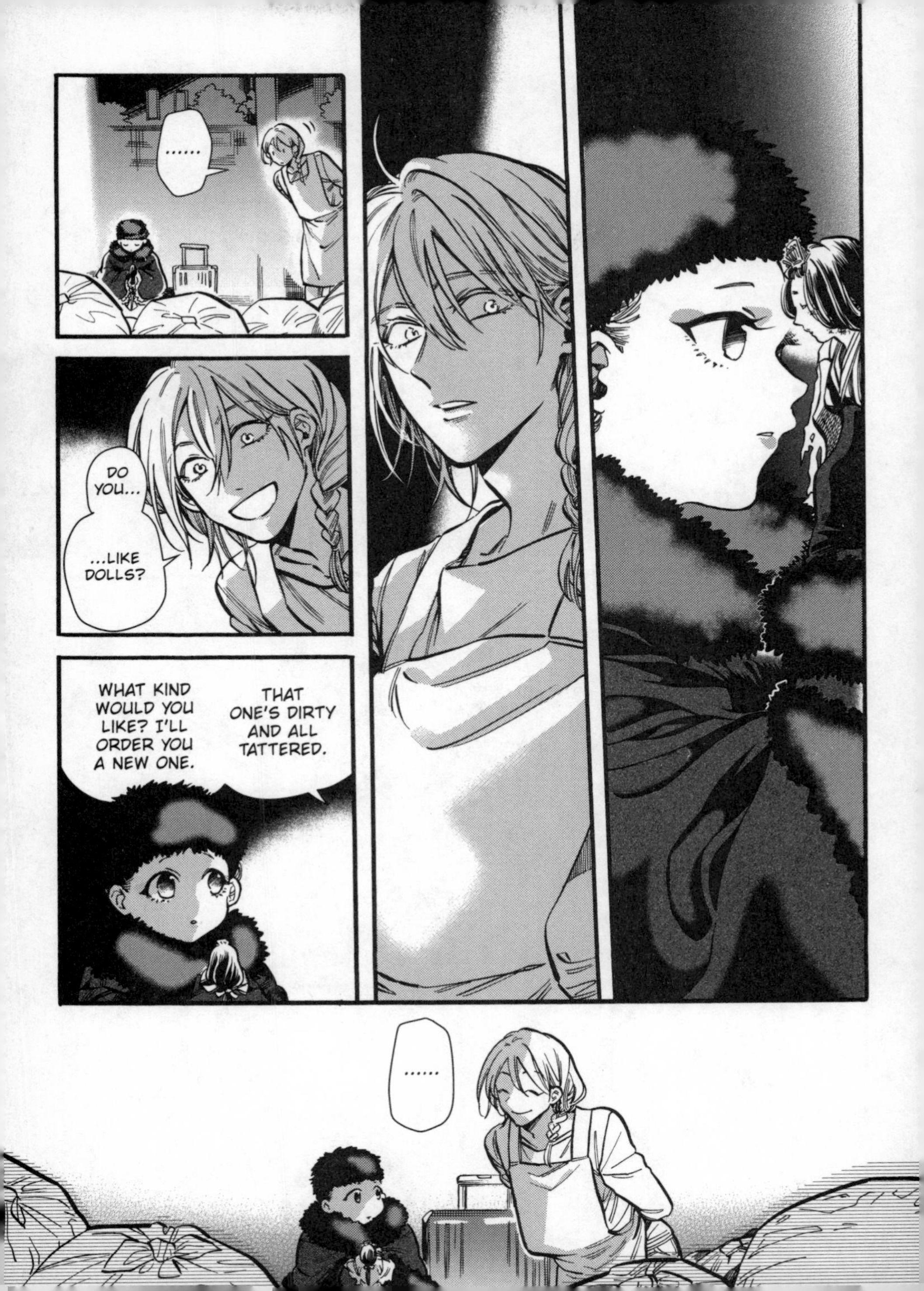
......
DO YOU...
...LIKE DOLLS?
THAT ONE'S DIRTY AND ALL TATTERED.
WHAT KIND WOULD YOU LIKE? I'LL ORDER YOU A NEW ONE.
......

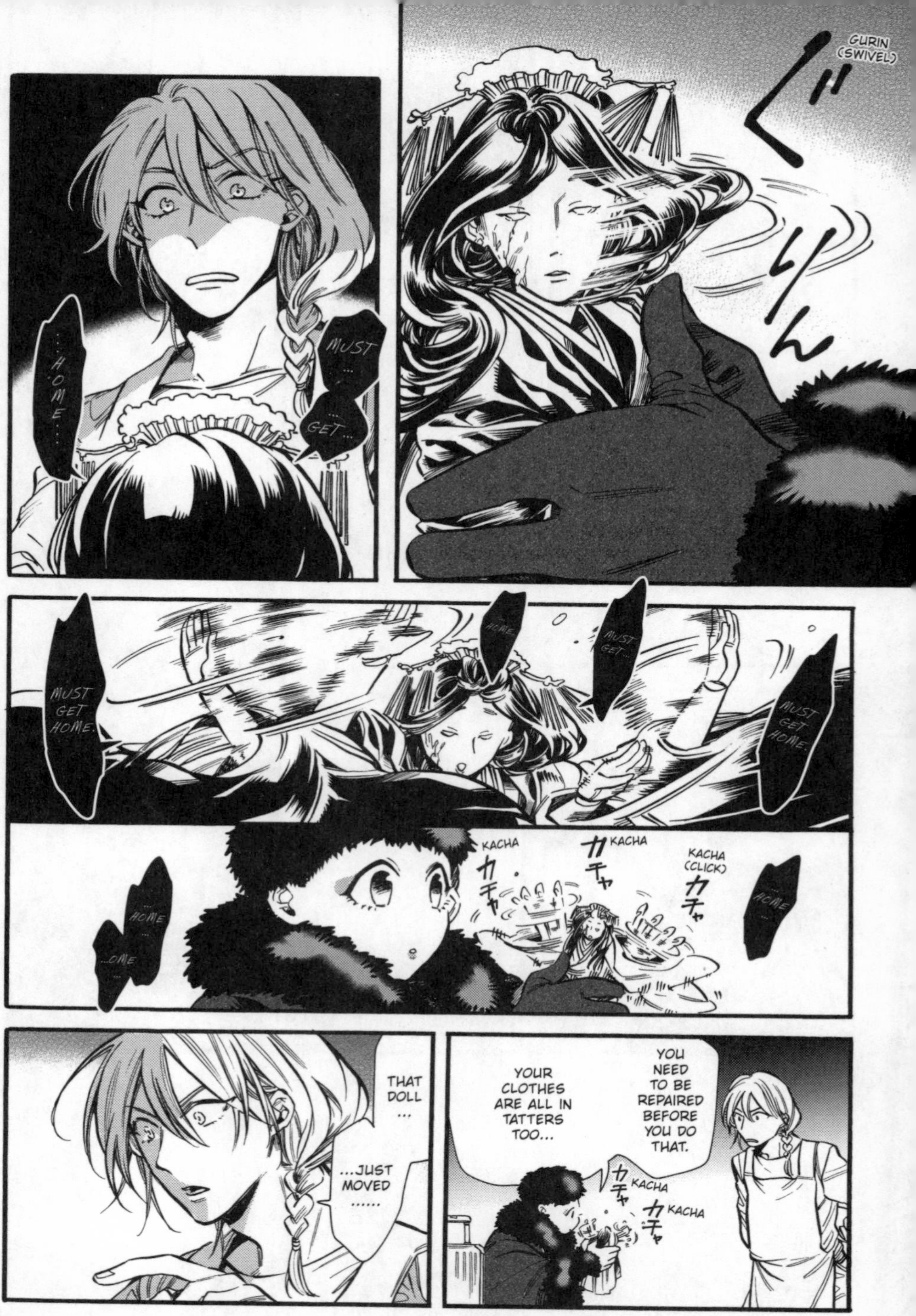

ぐりん
GURIN (SWIVEL)
MUST ... GET ...
...HOME...
MUST GET HOME.
MUST GET...
HOME
MUST GET HOME.
...HOME...
カチャ
KACHA (CLICK)
カチャ
KACHA
カチャ
KACHA
...HOME ... ...OME ...
YOU NEED TO BE REPAIRED BEFORE YOU DO THAT.
YOUR CLOTHES ARE ALL IN TATTERS TOO...
カチャ
KACHA
カチャ
KACHA
THAT DOLL ...
...JUST MOVED ......

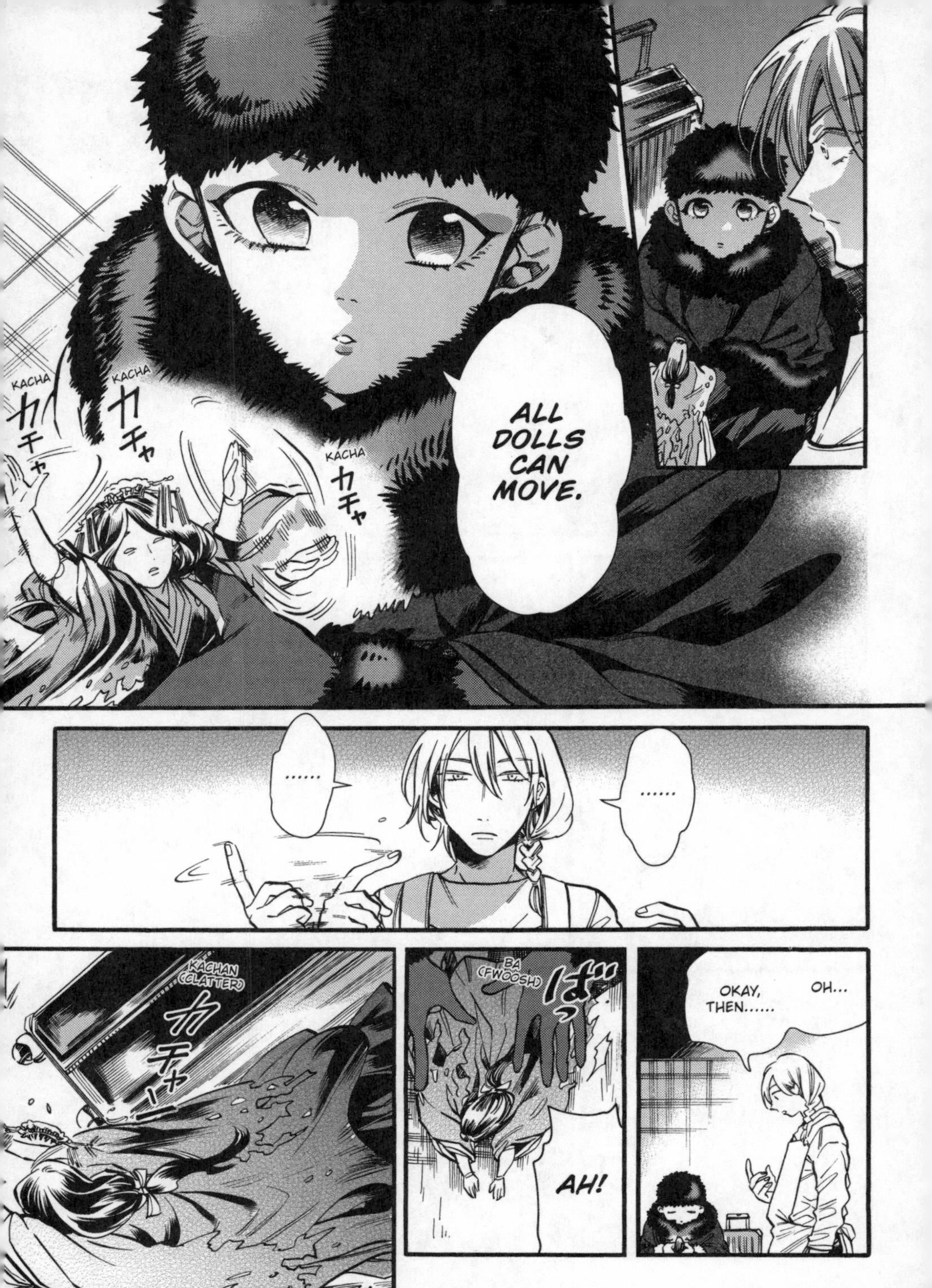
ALL DOLLS CAN MOVE.
KACHA
カチャ
KACHA
カチャ
KACHA
カチャ
......
......
OH...
OKAY, THEN......
BA (FWOOSH)
ばっ
AH!
KACHAN (CLATTER)
カチャー

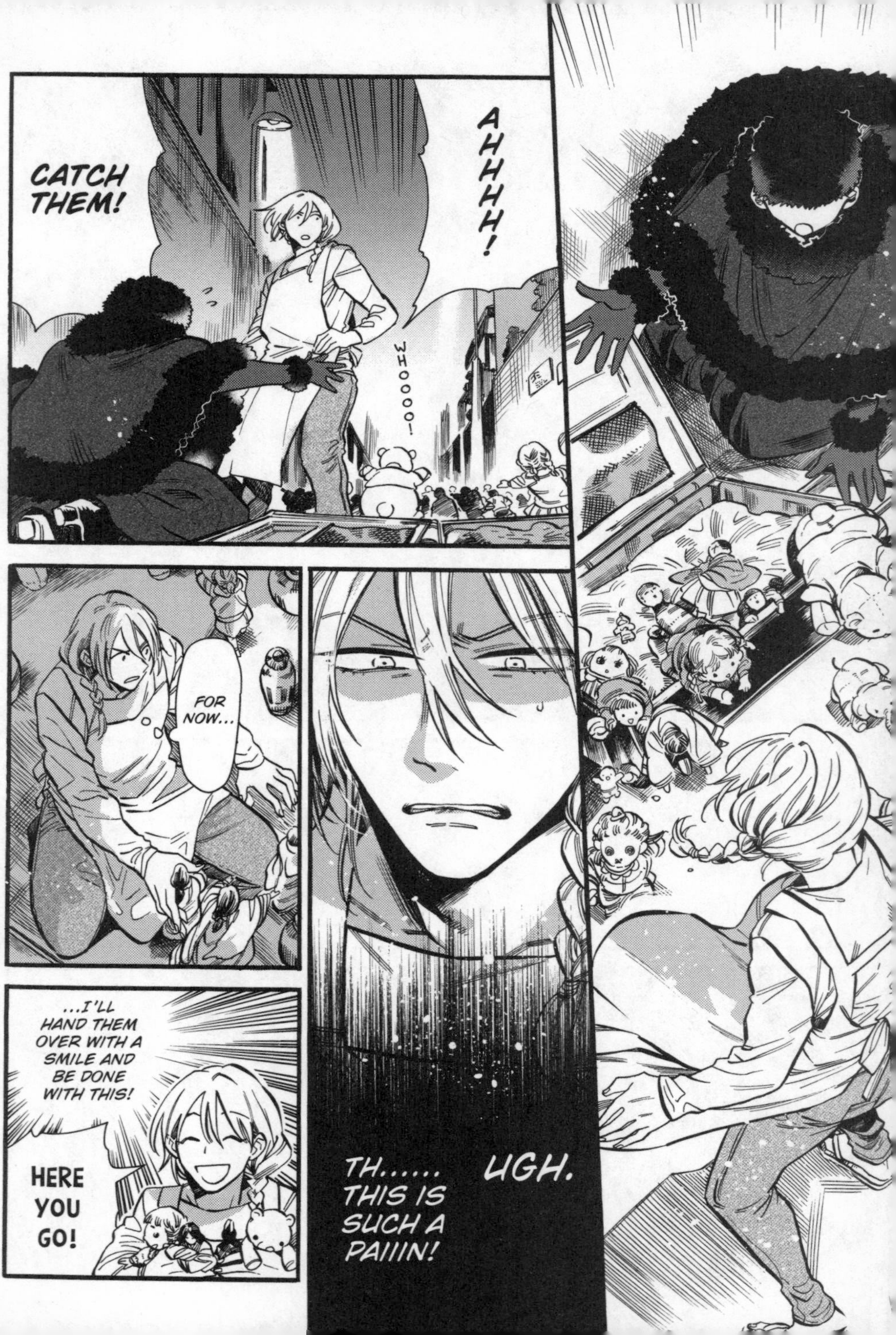
AHHHH!
WHOOOO!
CATCH THEM!
UGH.
TH...... THIS IS SUCH A PAIIIN!
FOR NOW...
...I'LL HAND THEM OVER WITH A SMILE AND BE DONE WITH THIS!
HERE YOU GO!

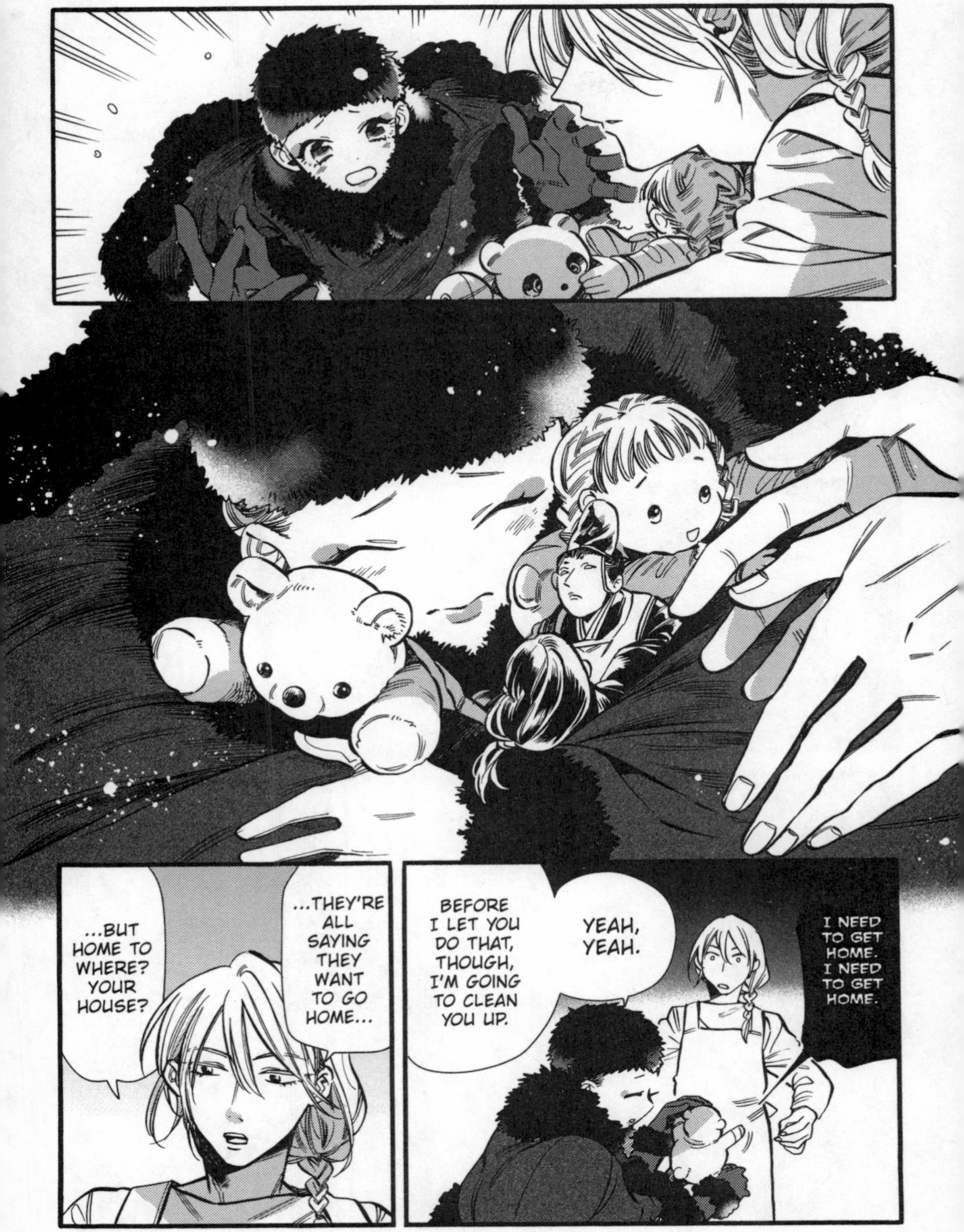
I NEED TO GET HOME. I NEED TO GET HOME.
YEAH, YEAH.
BEFORE I LET YOU DO THAT, THOUGH, I'M GOING TO CLEAN YOU UP.
...THEY'RE ALL SAYING THEY WANT TO GO HOME...
...BUT HOME TO WHERE? YOUR HOUSE?

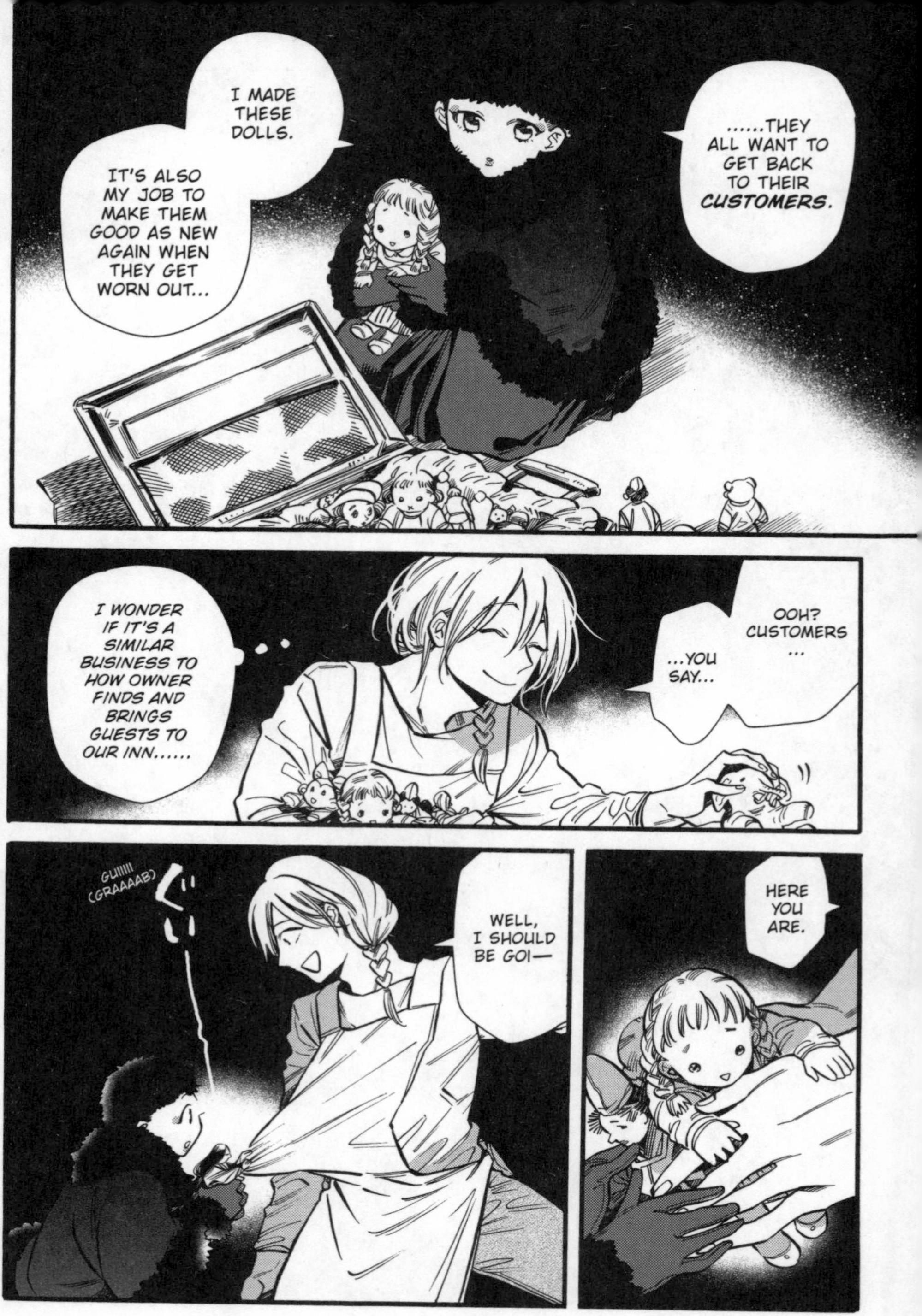
I MADE THESE DOLLS.
IT'S ALSO MY JOB TO MAKE THEM GOOD AS NEW AGAIN WHEN THEY GET WORN OUT...
......THEY ALL WANT TO GET BACK TO THEIR CUSTOMERS.
OOH? CUSTOMERS ...
...YOU SAY...
I WONDER IF IT'S A SIMILAR BUSINESS TO HOW OWNER FINDS AND BRINGS GUESTS TO OUR INN......
HERE YOU ARE.
WELL, I SHOULD BE GOI—
GUIIIII (GRAAAAB)

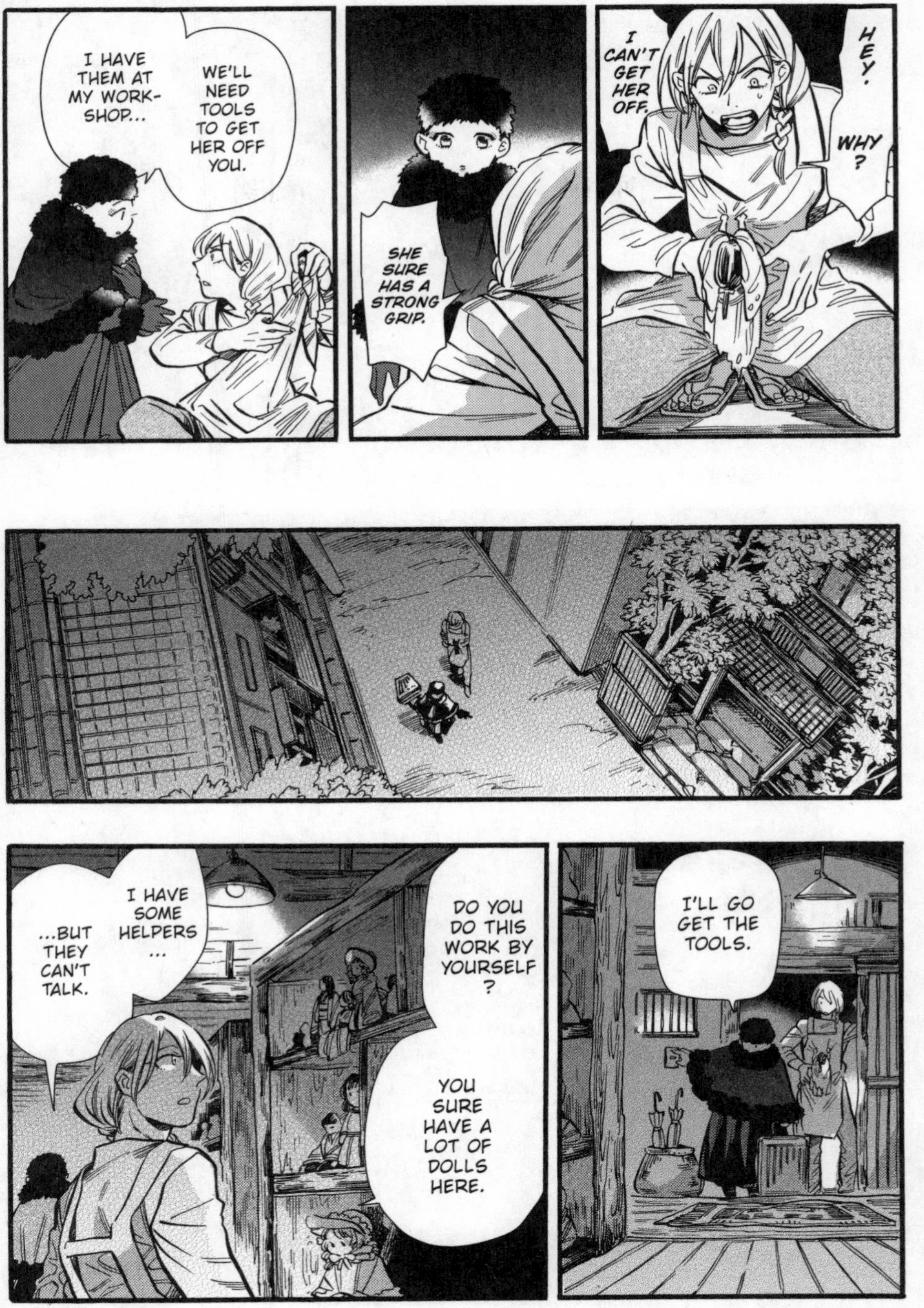
HEY.
I CAN'T GET HER OFF.
WHY?
SHE SURE HAS A STRONG GRIP.
WE'LL NEED TOOLS TO GET HER OFF YOU.
I HAVE THEM AT MY WORK-SHOP...
I'LL GO GET THE TOOLS.
DO YOU DO THIS WORK BY YOURSELF?
I HAVE SOME HELPERS...
...BUT THEY CAN'T TALK.
YOU SURE HAVE A LOT OF DOLLS HERE.

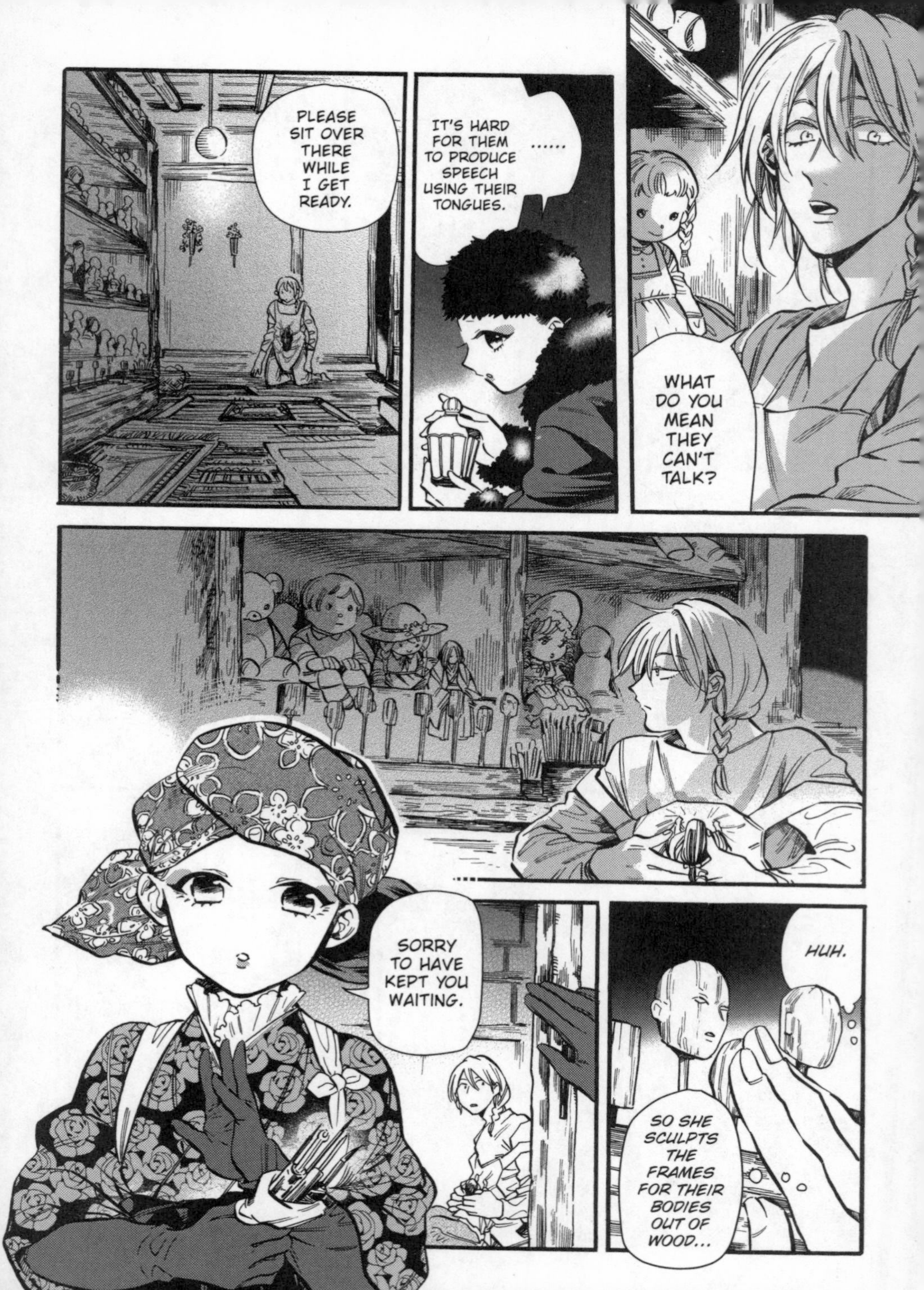
WHAT DO YOU MEAN THEY CAN'T TALK?
......
IT'S HARD FOR THEM TO PRODUCE SPEECH USING THEIR TONGUES.
PLEASE SIT OVER THERE WHILE I GET READY.
HUH.
SO SHE SCULPTS THE FRAMES FOR THEIR BODIES OUT OF WOOD...
SORRY TO HAVE KEPT YOU WAITING.

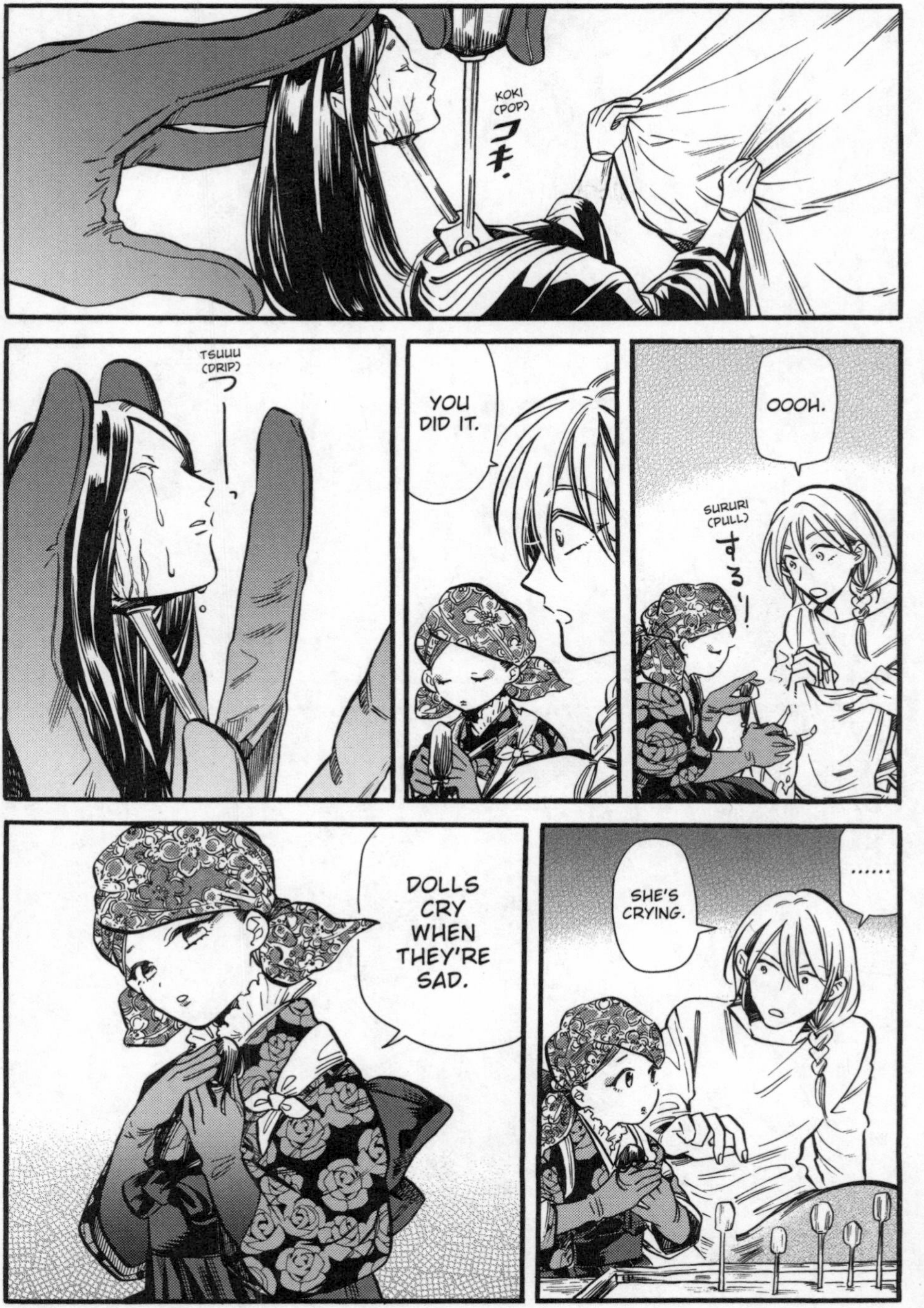
KOKI (POP)
コキ.
OOOH.
SURURI (PULL)
するー!
YOU DID IT.
TSUUU (DRIP)
つー
......
SHE'S CRYING.
DOLLS CRY WHEN THEY'RE SAD.

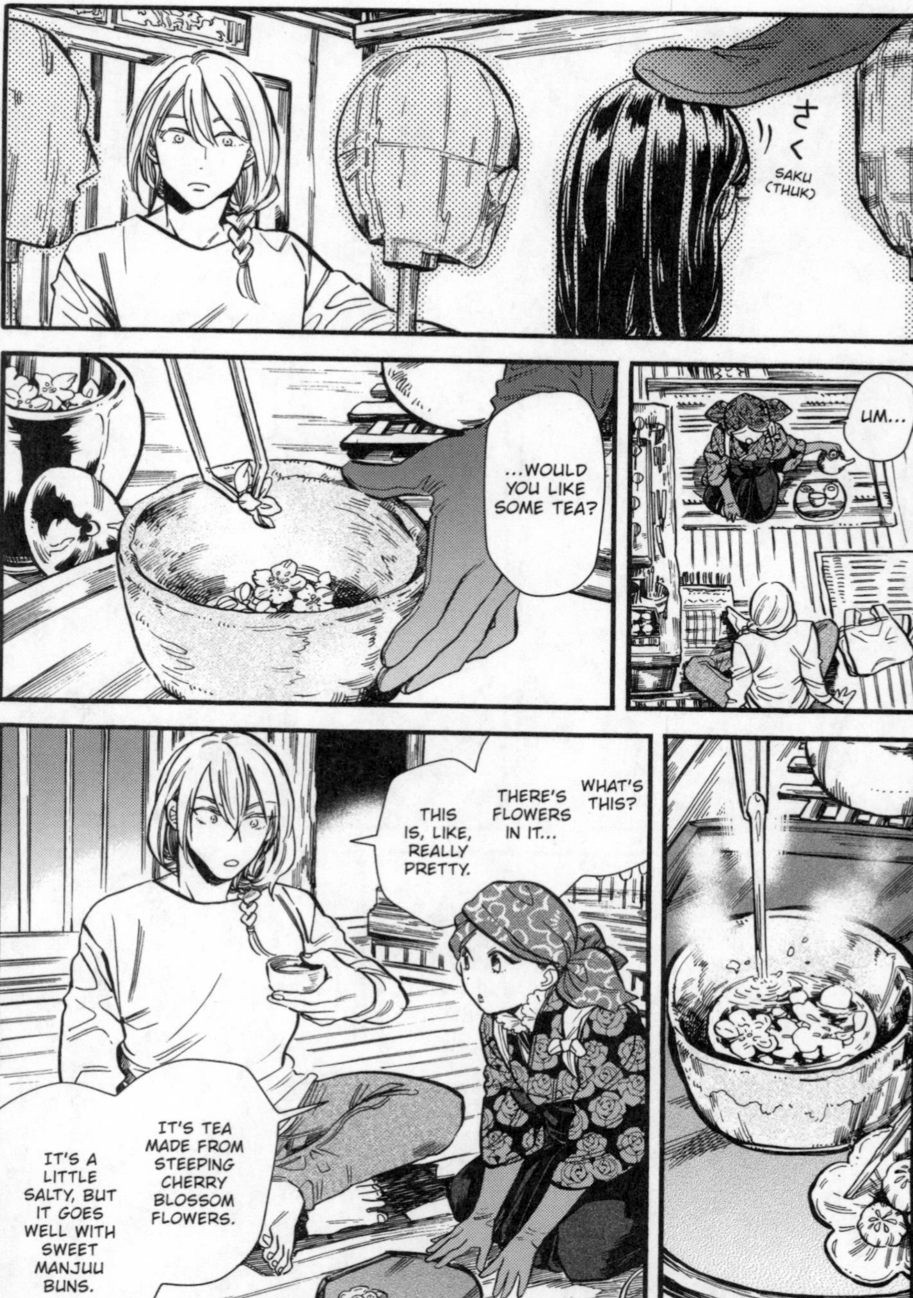
さくり
SAKU (THUK)
UM...
...WOULD YOU LIKE SOME TEA?
WHAT'S THIS?
THERE'S FLOWERS IN IT...
THIS IS, LIKE, REALLY PRETTY.
IT'S TEA MADE FROM STEEPING CHERRY BLOSSOM FLOWERS.
IT'S A LITTLE SALTY, BUT IT GOES WELL WITH SWEET MANJUU BUNS.

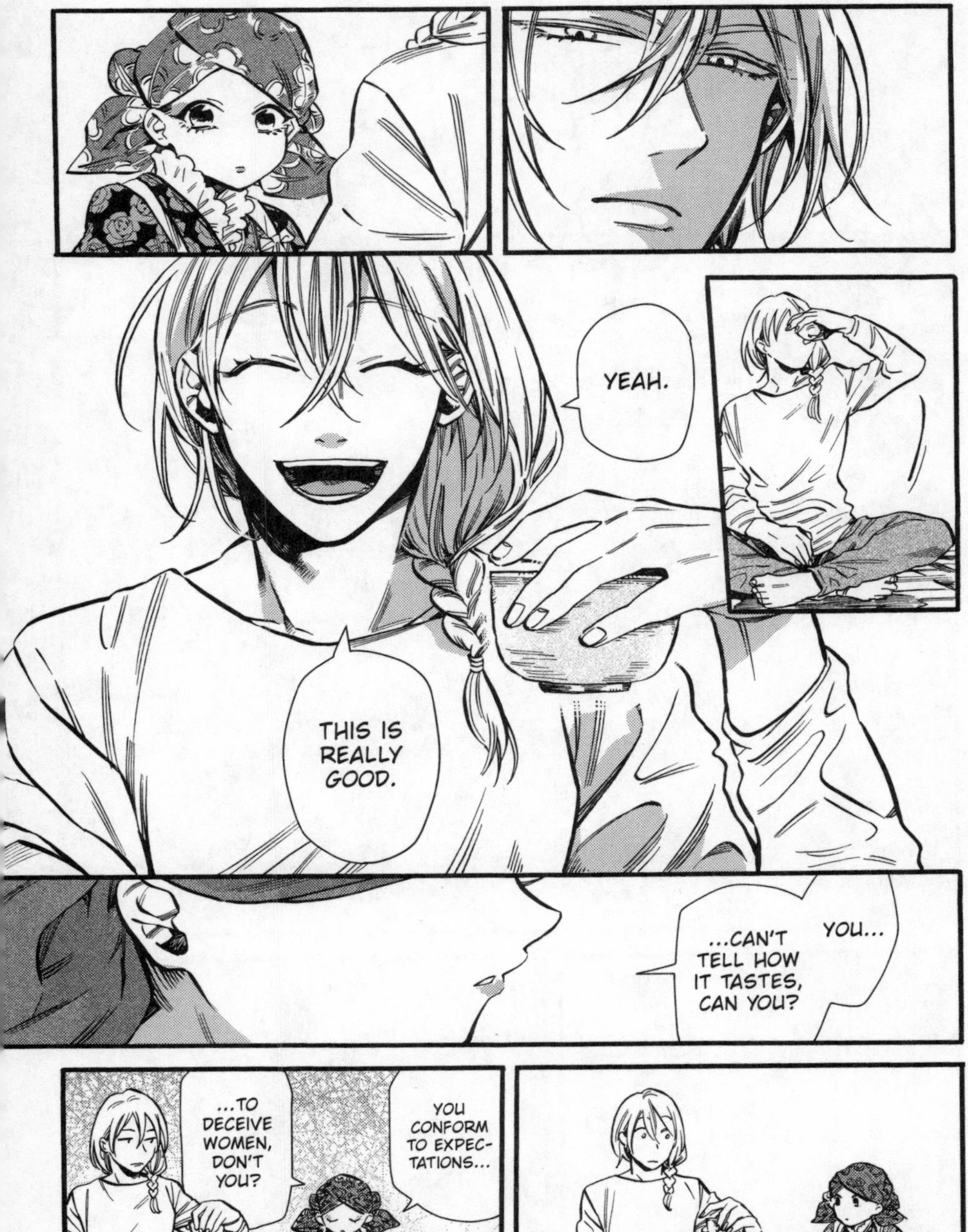
YEAH.
THIS IS REALLY GOOD.
YOU...
...CAN'T TELL HOW IT TASTES, CAN YOU?
YOU CONFORM TO EXPEC-TATIONS...
...TO DECEIVE WOMEN, DON'T YOU?

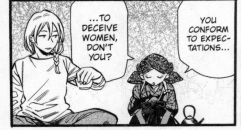

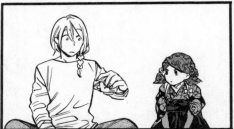

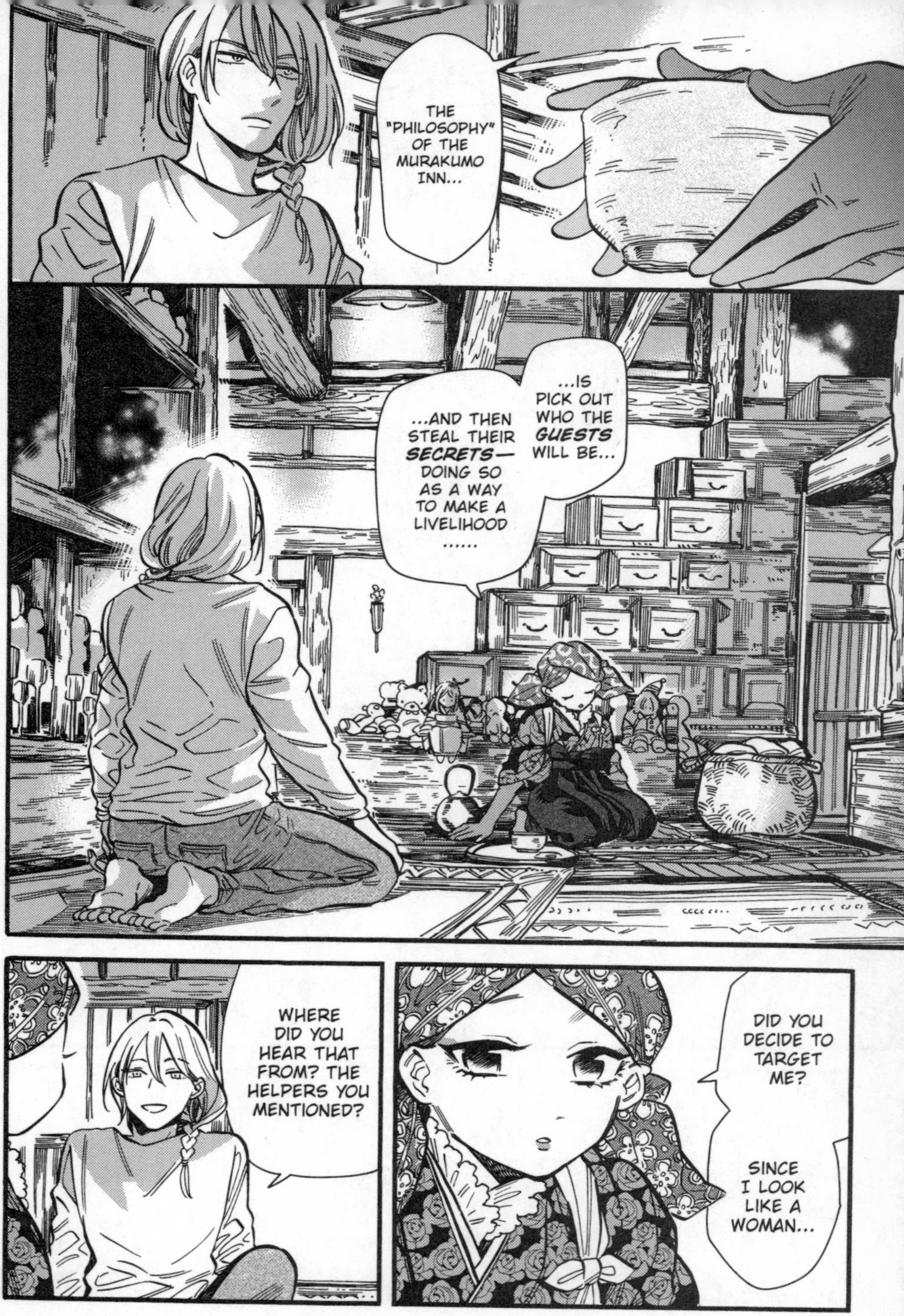
THE "PHILOSOPHY" OF THE MURAKUMO INN...
...IS PICK OUT WHO THE GUESTS WILL BE...
...AND THEN STEAL THEIR SECRETS— DOING SO AS A WAY TO MAKE A LIVELIHOOD ......
DID YOU DECIDE TO TARGET ME?
SINCE I LOOK LIKE A WOMAN...
WHERE DID YOU HEAR THAT FROM? THE HELPERS YOU MENTIONED?

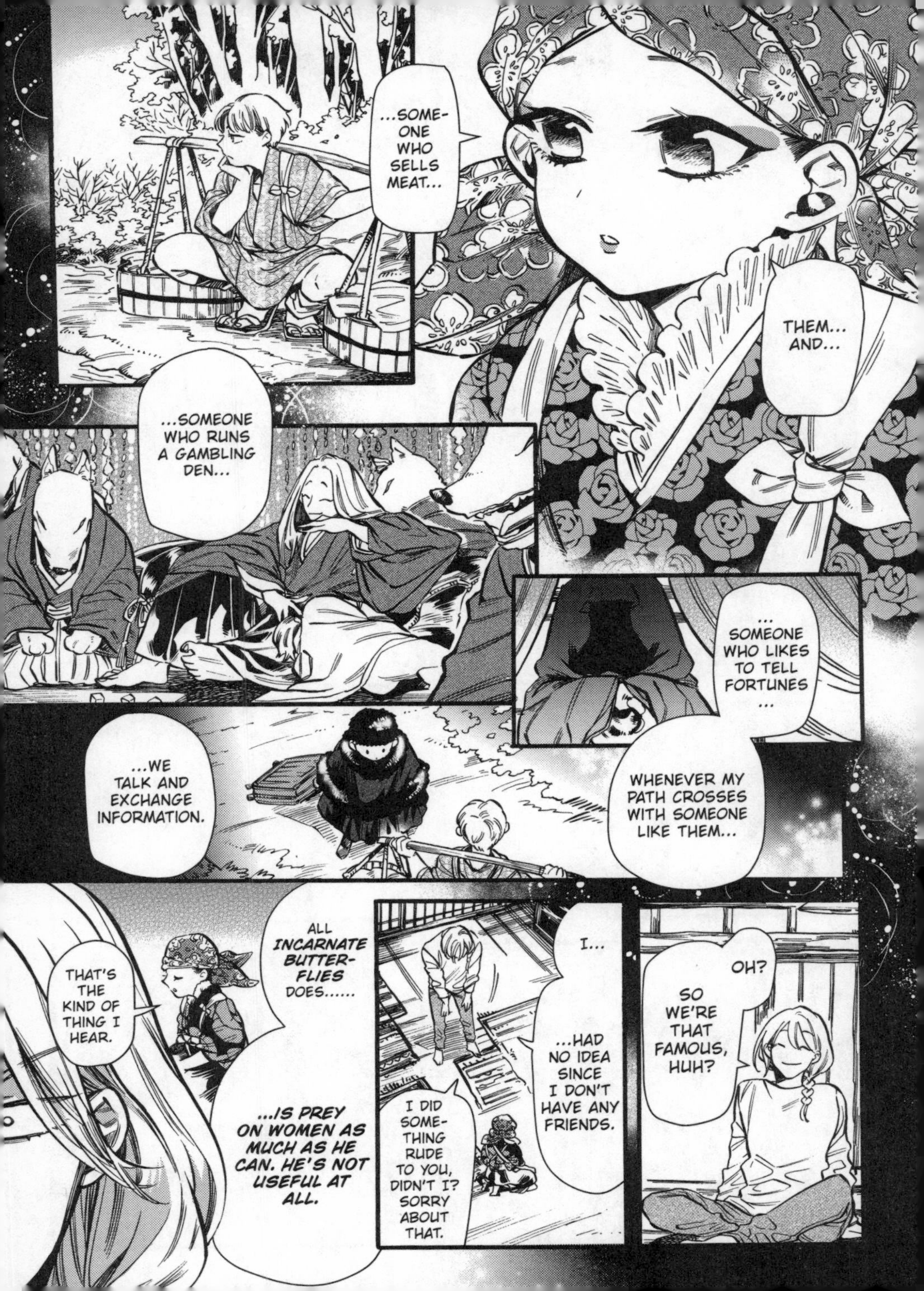
THEM... AND...
...SOME-ONE WHO SELLS MEAT...
...SOMEONE WHO RUNS A GAMBLING DEN...
...SOMEONE WHO LIKES TO TELL FORTUNES...
WHENEVER MY PATH CROSSES WITH SOMEONE LIKE THEM...
...WE TALK AND EXCHANGE INFORMATION.
OH?
SO WE'RE THAT FAMOUS, HUH?
I...
...HAD NO IDEA SINCE I DON'T HAVE ANY FRIENDS.
I DID SOME-THING RUDE TO YOU, DIDN'T I? SORRY ABOUT THAT.
ALL *INCARNATE BUTTER-FLIES* DOES......
...IS PREY ON WOMEN AS MUCH AS HE CAN. HE'S NOT USEFUL AT ALL.
THAT'S THE KIND OF THING I HEAR.

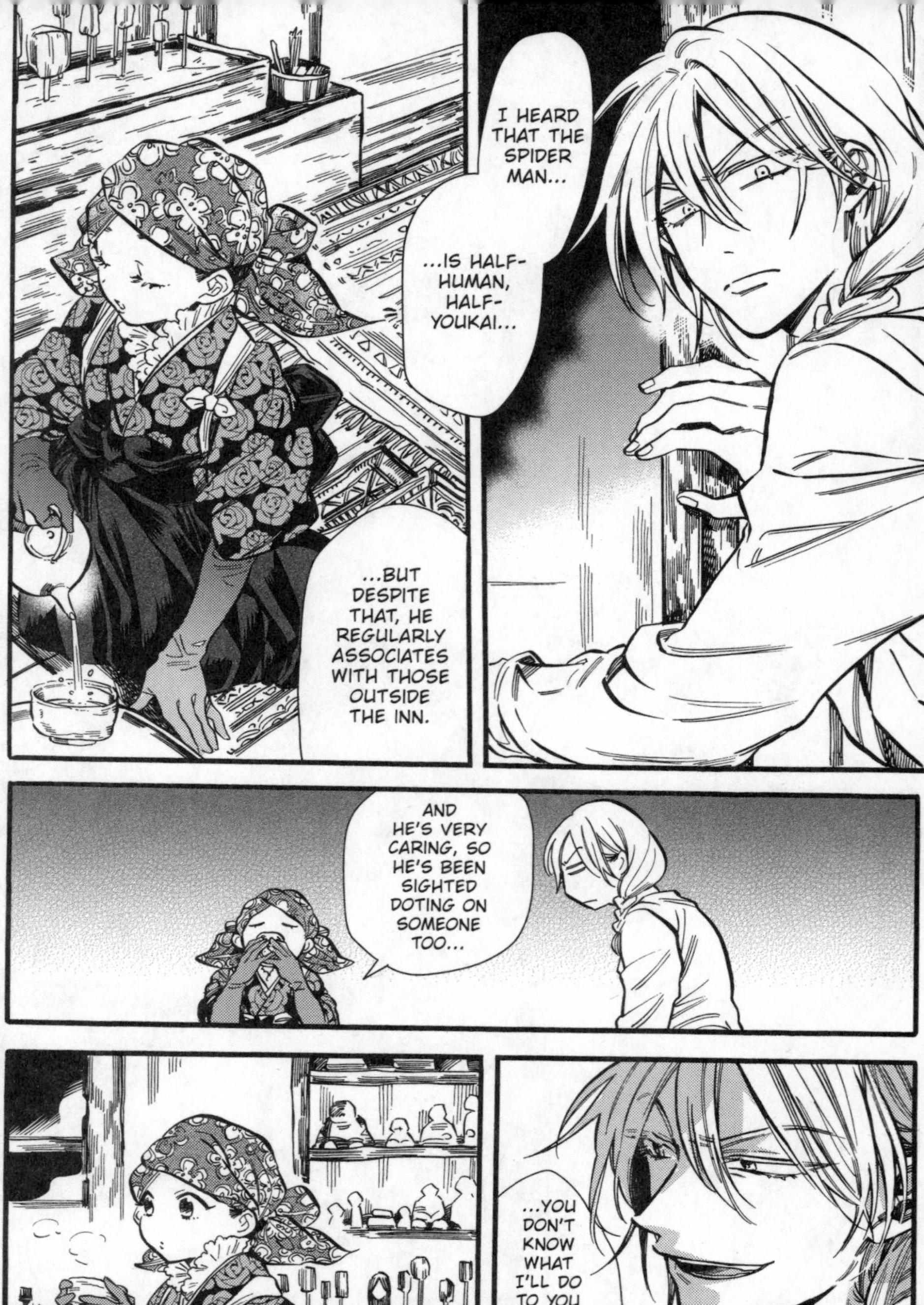
I HEARD THAT THE SPIDER MAN...
...IS HALF-HUMAN, HALF-YOUKAI...
...BUT DESPITE THAT, HE REGULARLY ASSOCIATES WITH THOSE OUTSIDE THE INN.
AND HE'S VERY CARING, SO HE'S BEEN SIGHTED DOTING ON SOMEONE TOO...
...YOU DON'T KNOW WHAT I'LL DO TO YOU AFTER BEING TOLD THAT.

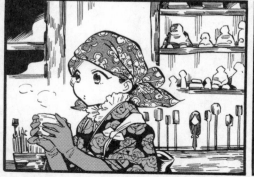

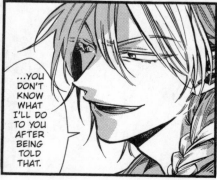

SIGN: LOOKING FOR TENANT

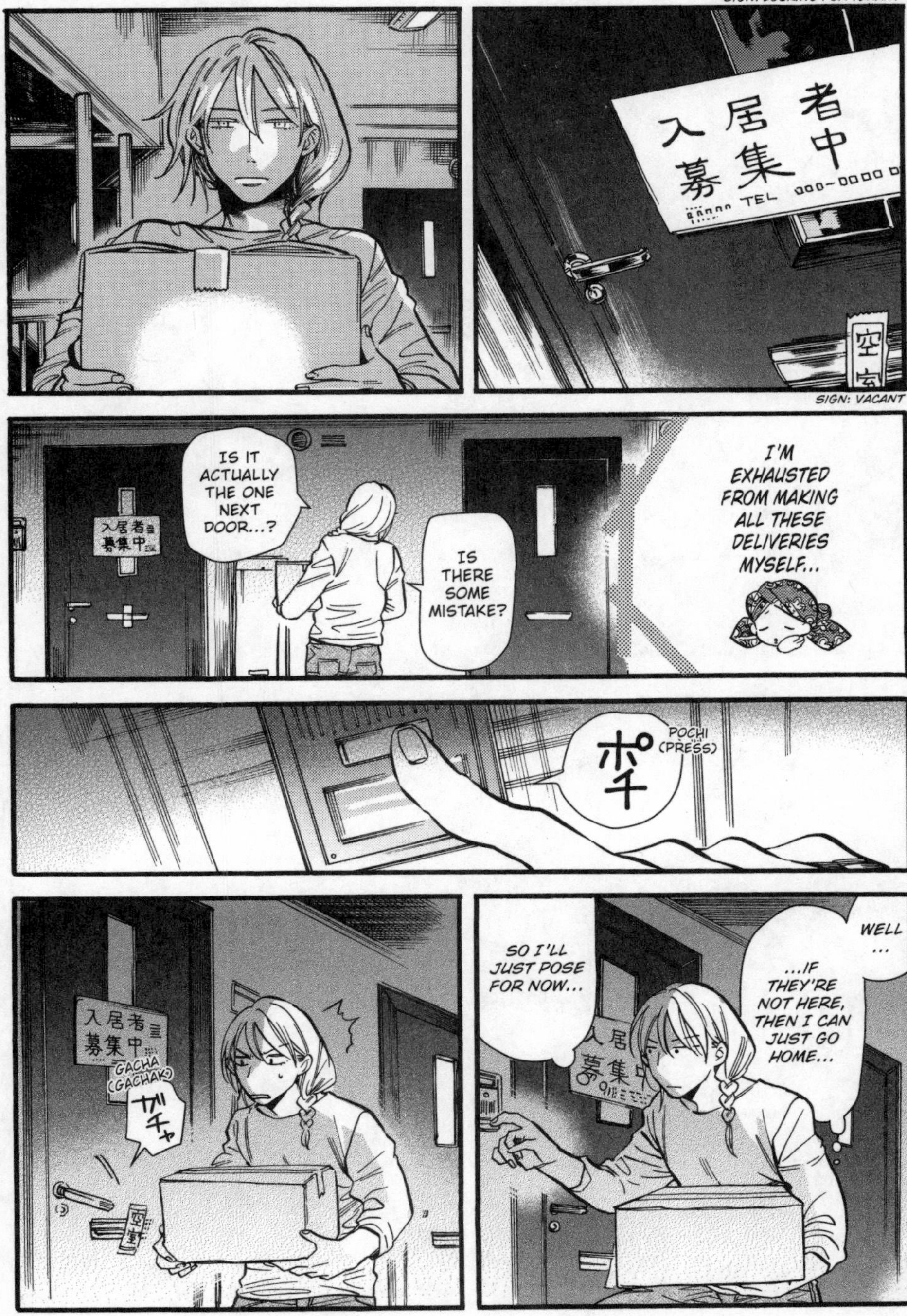
入居者募集中
TEL
空室
IS IT ACTUALLY THE ONE NEXT DOOR...?
IS THERE SOME MISTAKE?
I'M EXHAUSTED FROM MAKING ALL THESE DELIVERIES MYSELF...
ポチ
POCHI (PRESS)
WELL...
...IF THEY'RE NOT HERE, THEN I CAN JUST GO HOME...
SO I'LL JUST POSE FOR NOW...
ガチャ
GACHA (GACHAK)

SIGN: VACANT

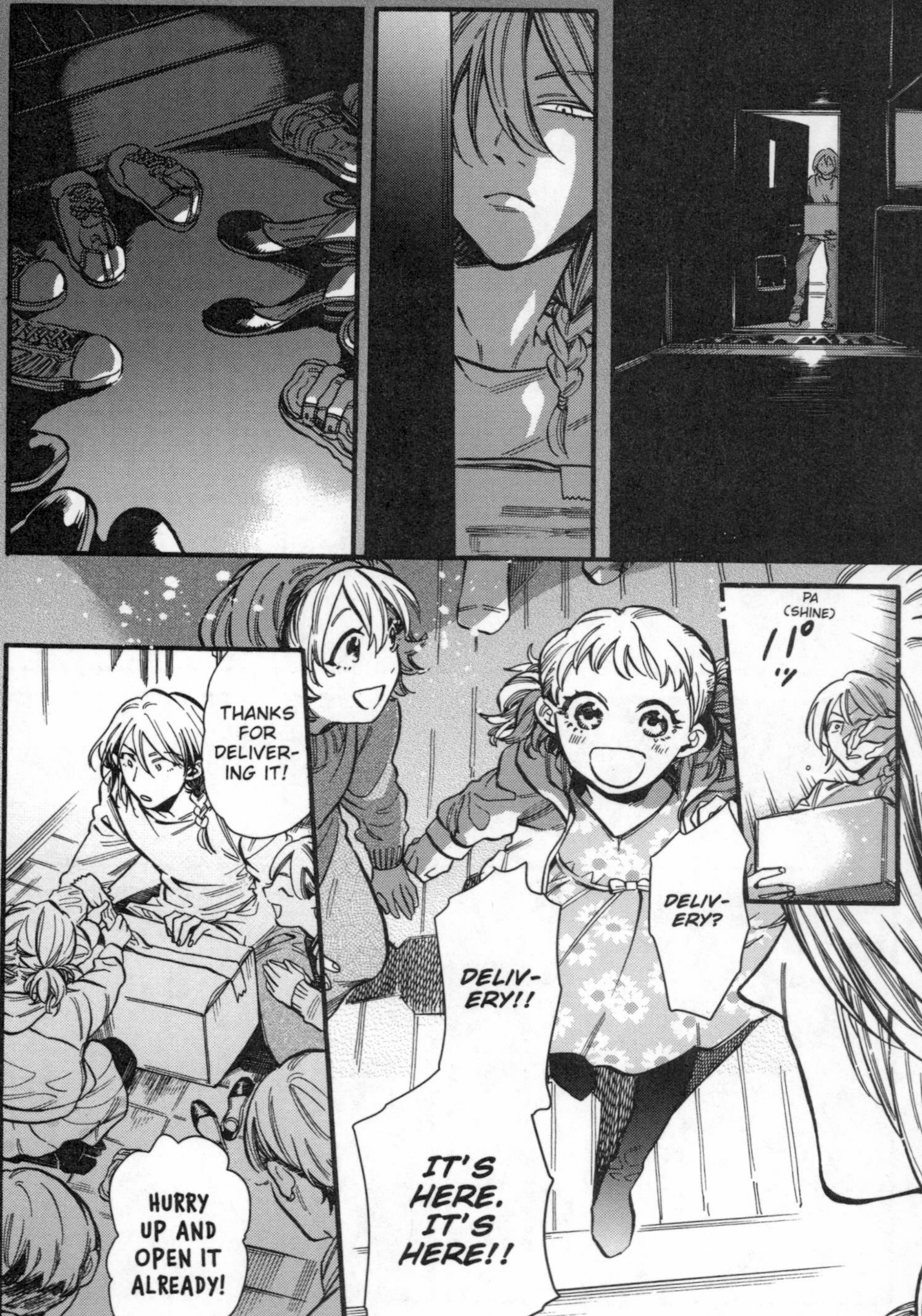
PA (SHINE)
パッ
DELIV-ERY?
DELIV-ERY!!
IT'S HERE. IT'S HERE!!
THANKS FOR DELIVER-ING IT!
HURRY UP AND OPEN IT ALREADY!

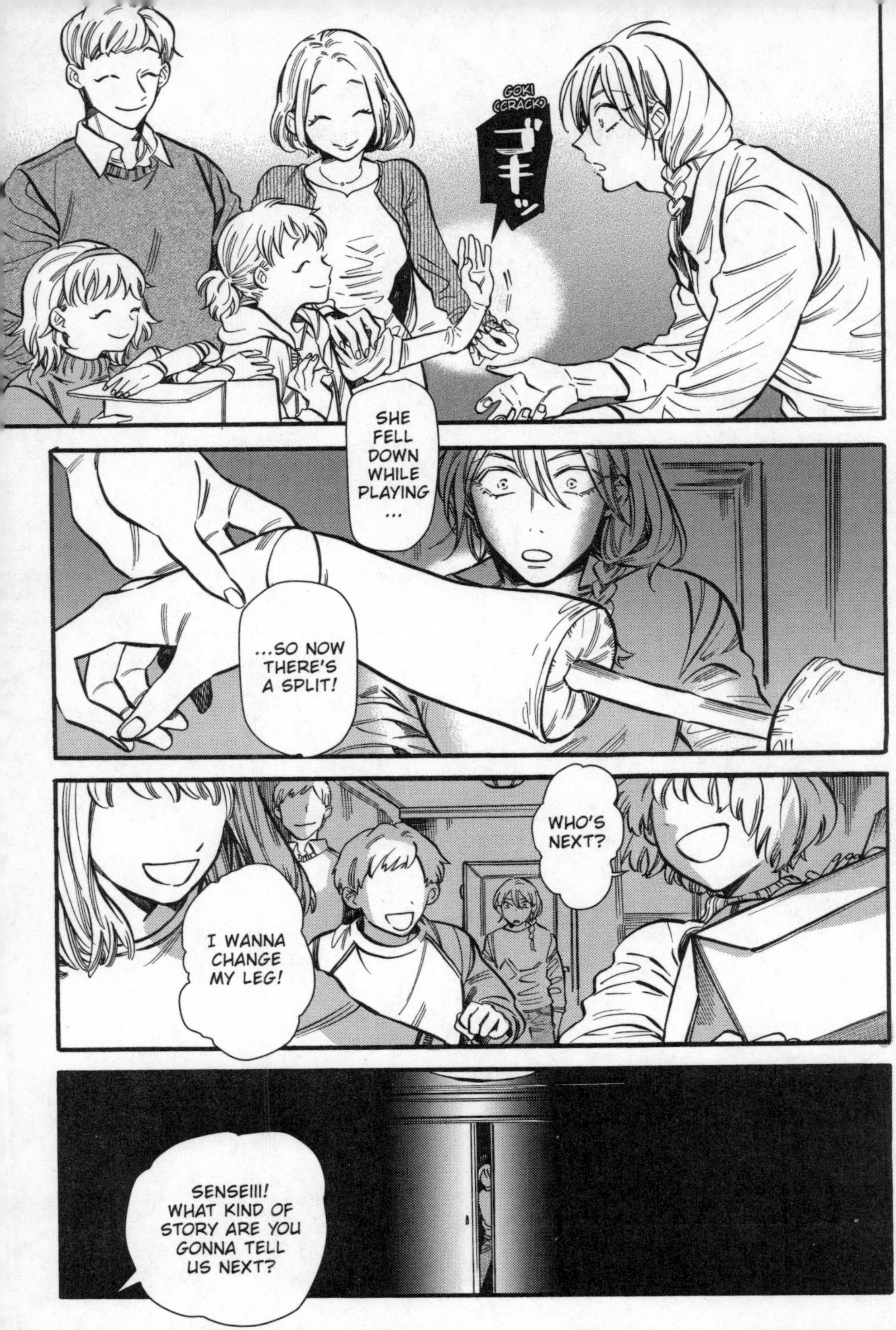
GOKI (CRACK)
ゴキッ
SHE FELL DOWN WHILE PLAYING...
...SO NOW THERE'S A SPLIT!
WHO'S NEXT?
I WANNA CHANGE MY LEG!
SENSEIII! WHAT KIND OF STORY ARE YOU GONNA TELL US NEXT?

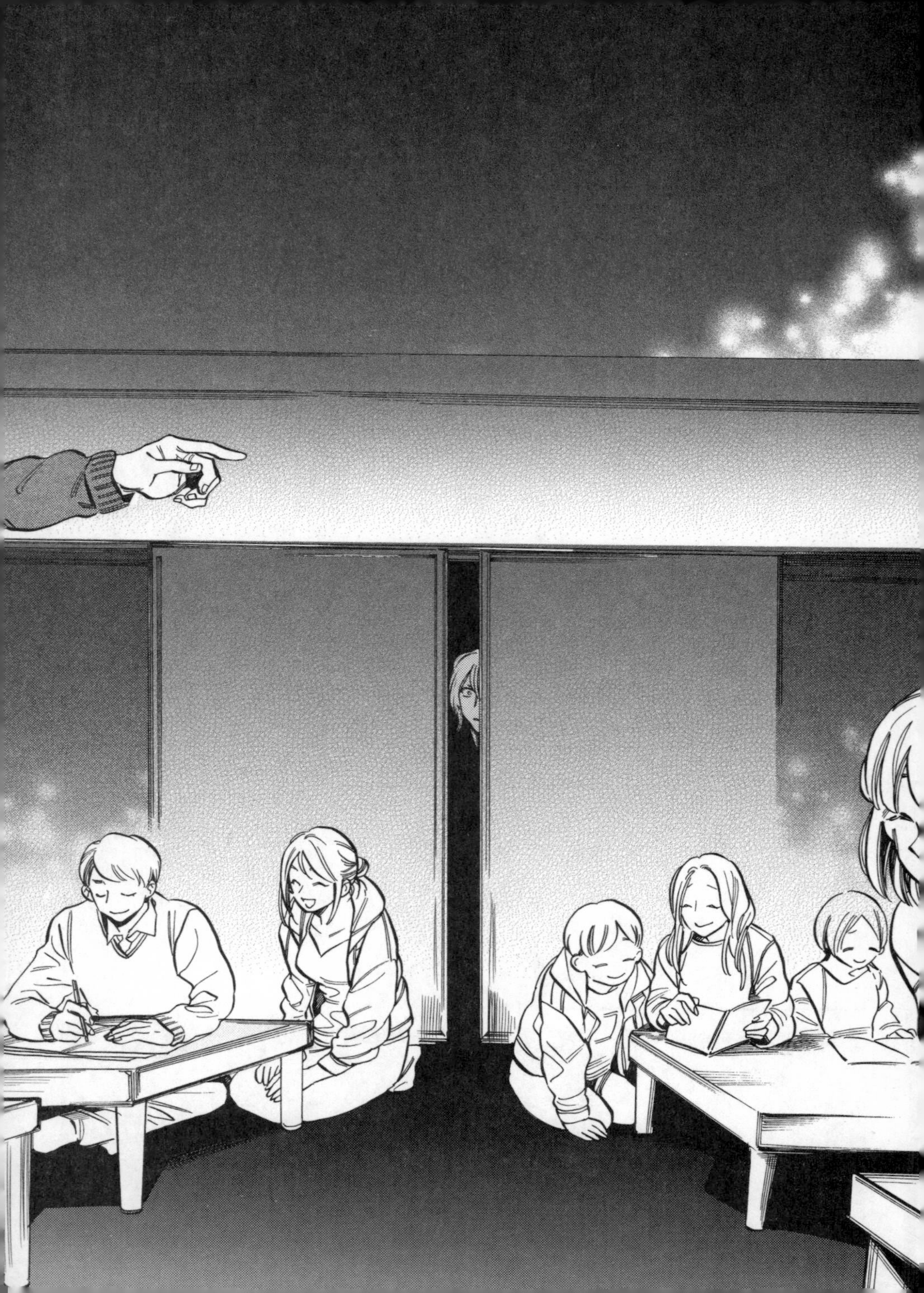

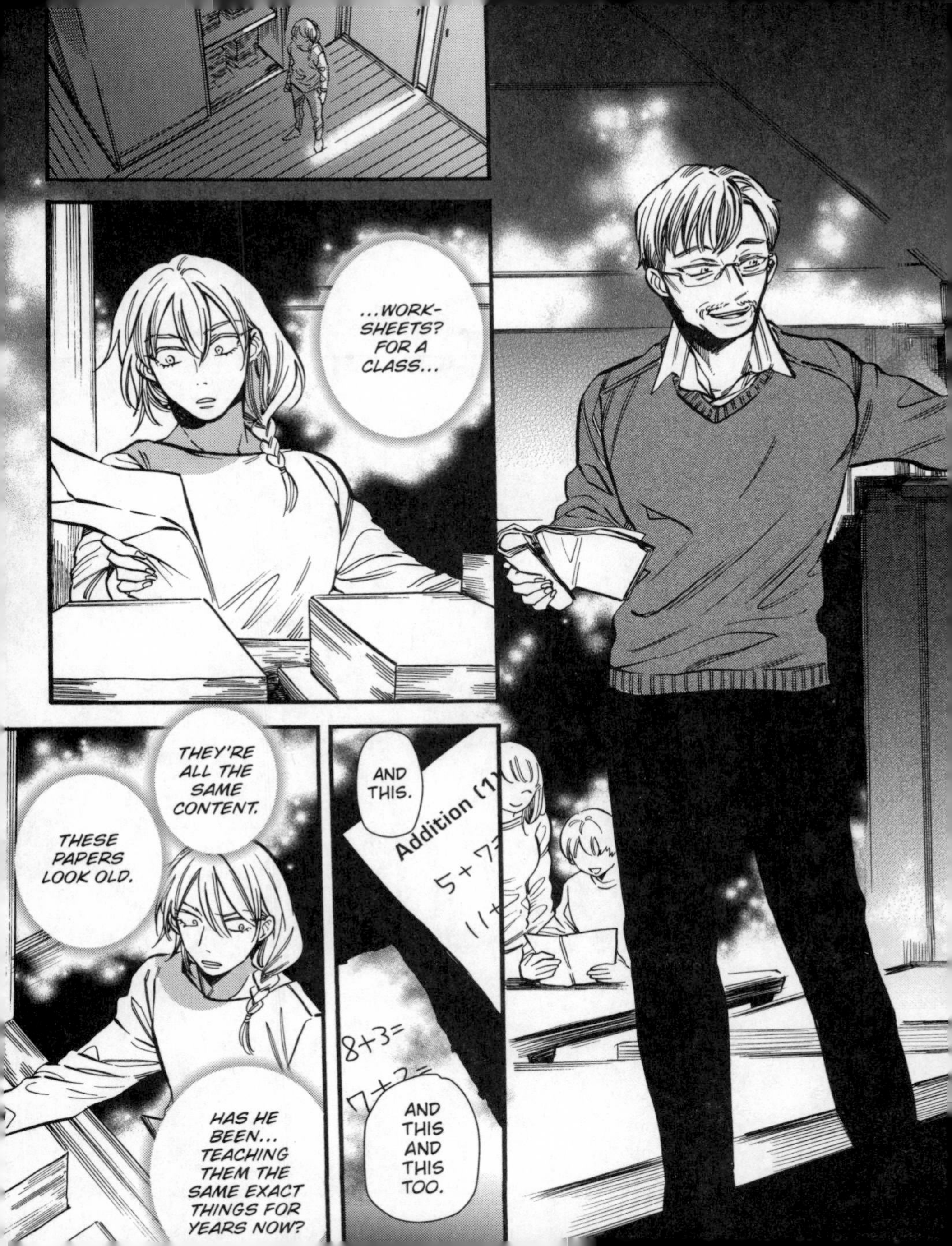
...WORK-SHEETS? FOR A CLASS...
AND THIS.
Addition (1
5 + 7=
8+3=
AND THIS AND THIS TOO.
THEY'RE ALL THE SAME CONTENT.
THESE PAPERS LOOK OLD.
HAS HE BEEN... TEACHING THEM THE SAME EXACT THINGS FOR YEARS NOW?

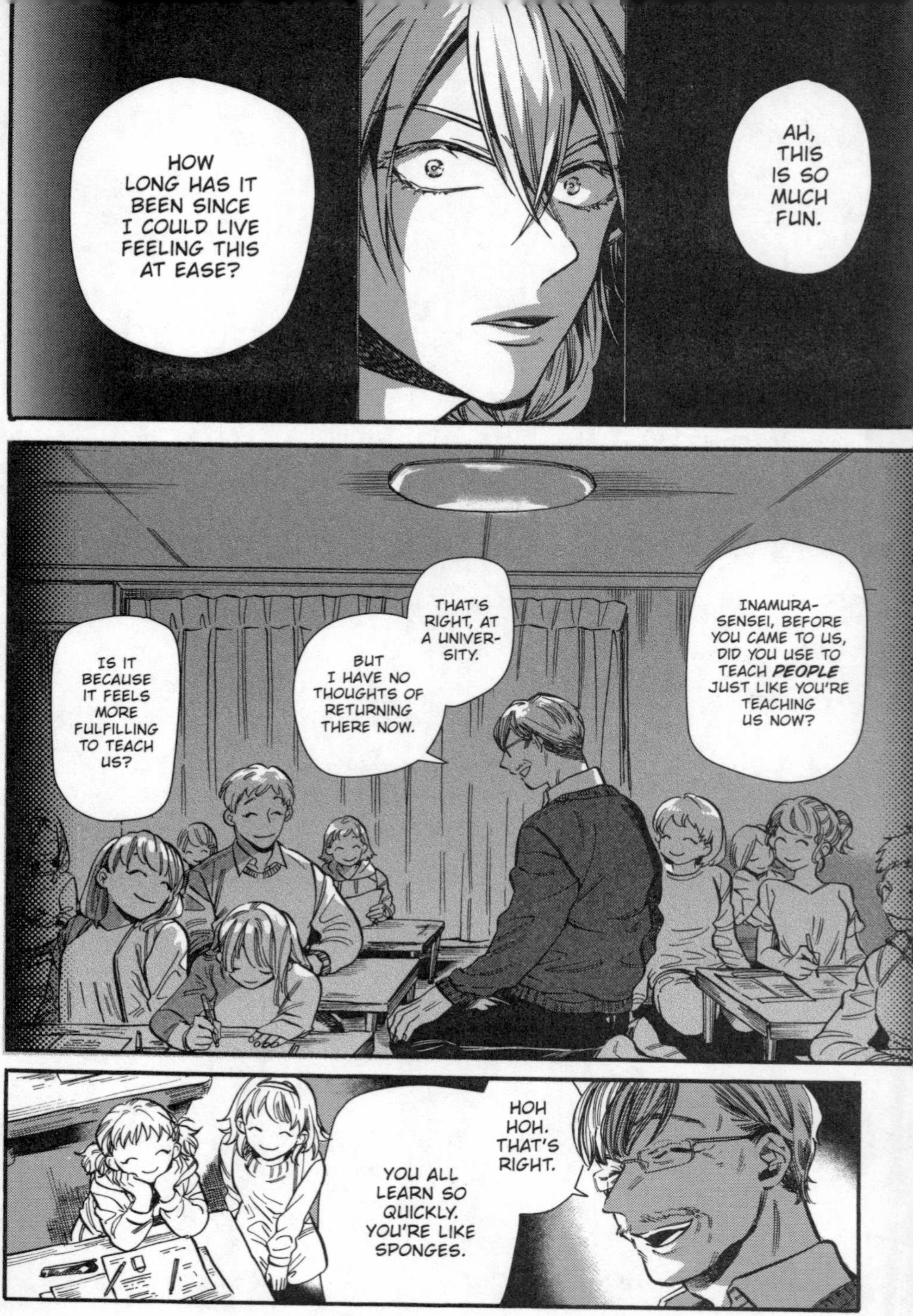
AH, THIS IS SO MUCH FUN.
HOW LONG HAS IT BEEN SINCE I COULD LIVE FEELING THIS AT EASE?
INAMURA-SENSEI, BEFORE YOU CAME TO US, DID YOU USE TO TEACH ***PEOPLE*** JUST LIKE YOU'RE TEACHING US NOW?
THAT'S RIGHT, AT A UNIVERSITY.
BUT I HAVE NO THOUGHTS OF RETURNING THERE NOW.
IS IT BECAUSE IT FEELS MORE FULFILLING TO TEACH US?
HOH HOH. THAT'S RIGHT.
YOU ALL LEARN SO QUICKLY. YOU'RE LIKE SPONGES.

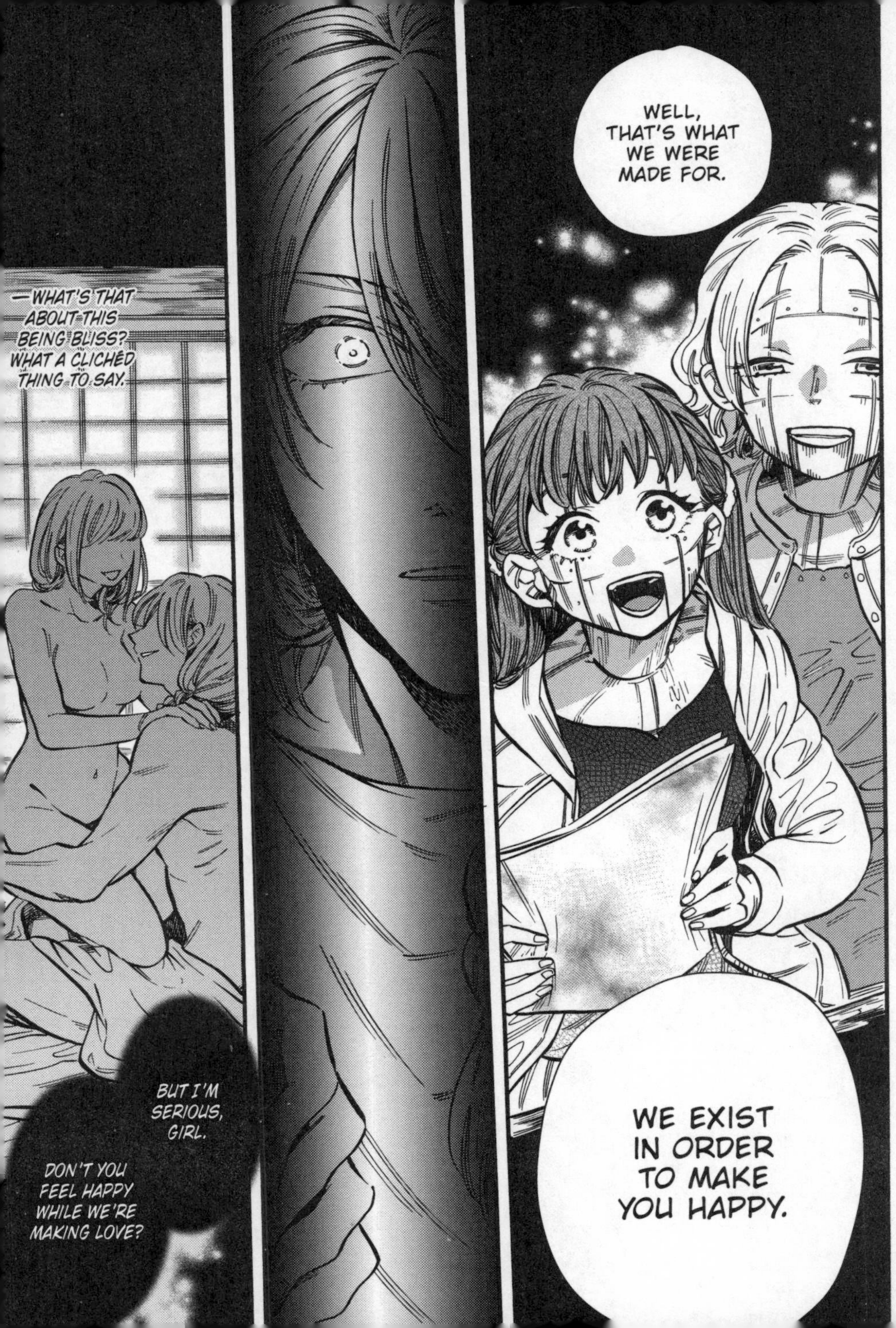
WELL, THAT'S WHAT WE WERE MADE FOR.
WE EXIST IN ORDER TO MAKE YOU HAPPY.
—WHAT'S THAT ABOUT THIS BEING BLISS? WHAT A CLICHED THING TO SAY.
BUT I'M SERIOUS, GIRL.
DON'T YOU FEEL HAPPY WHILE WE'RE MAKING LOVE?

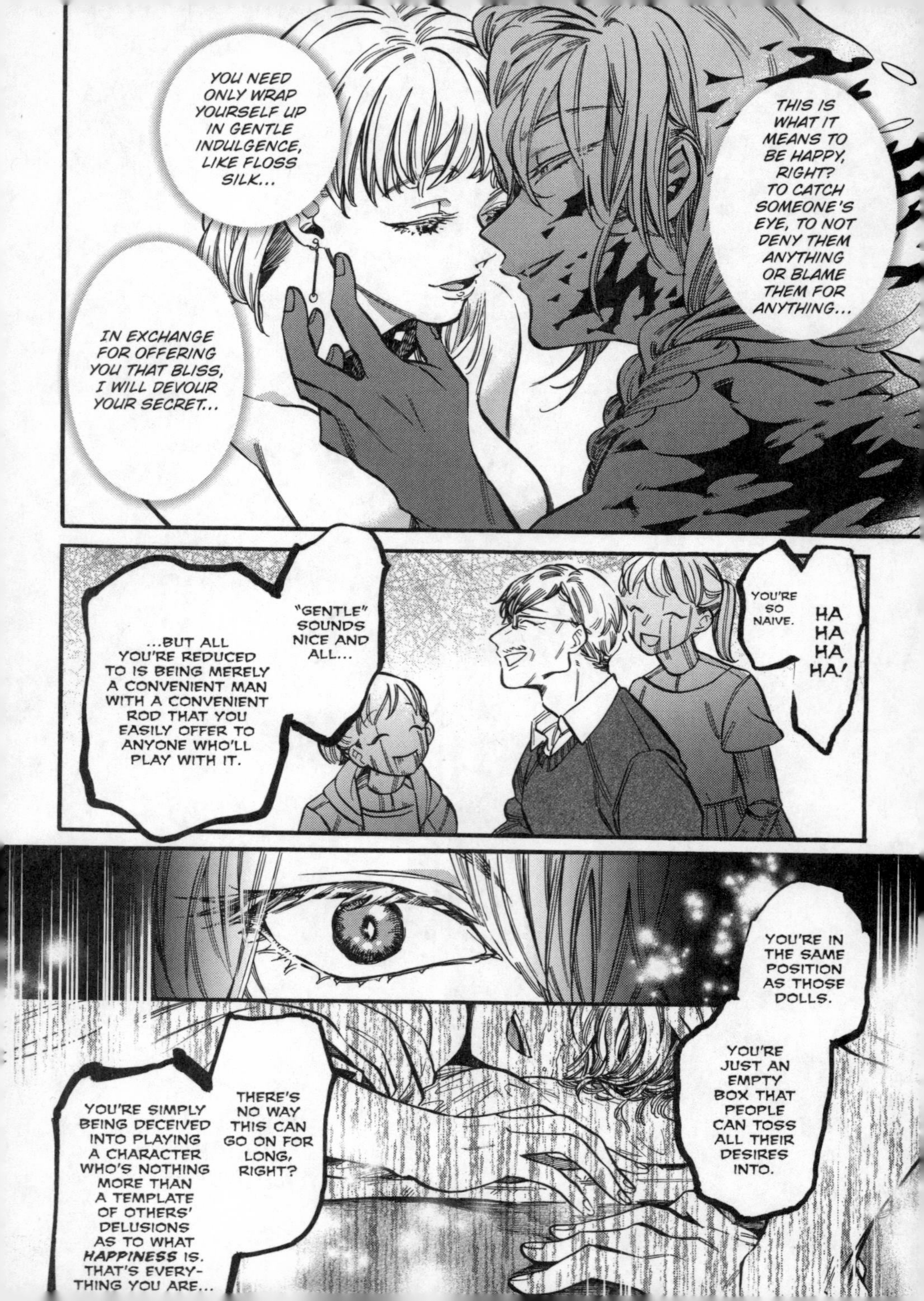
THIS IS WHAT IT MEANS TO BE HAPPY, RIGHT? TO CATCH SOMEONE'S EYE, TO NOT DENY THEM ANYTHING OR BLAME THEM FOR ANYTHING...
YOU NEED ONLY WRAP YOURSELF UP IN GENTLE INDULGENCE, LIKE FLOSS SILK...
IN EXCHANGE FOR OFFERING YOU THAT BLISS, I WILL DEVOUR YOUR SECRET...
YOU'RE SO NAIVE.
HA HA HA HA!
"GENTLE" SOUNDS NICE AND ALL...
...BUT ALL YOU'RE REDUCED TO IS BEING MERELY A CONVENIENT MAN WITH A CONVENIENT ROD THAT YOU EASILY OFFER TO ANYONE WHO'LL PLAY WITH IT.
YOU'RE IN THE SAME POSITION AS THOSE DOLLS.
YOU'RE JUST AN EMPTY BOX THAT PEOPLE CAN TOSS ALL THEIR DESIRES INTO.
THERE'S NO WAY THIS CAN GO ON FOR LONG, RIGHT?
YOU'RE SIMPLY BEING DECEIVED INTO PLAYING A CHARACTER WHO'S NOTHING MORE THAN A TEMPLATE OF OTHERS' DELUSIONS AS TO WHAT ***HAPPINESS*** IS. THAT'S EVERYTHING YOU ARE...

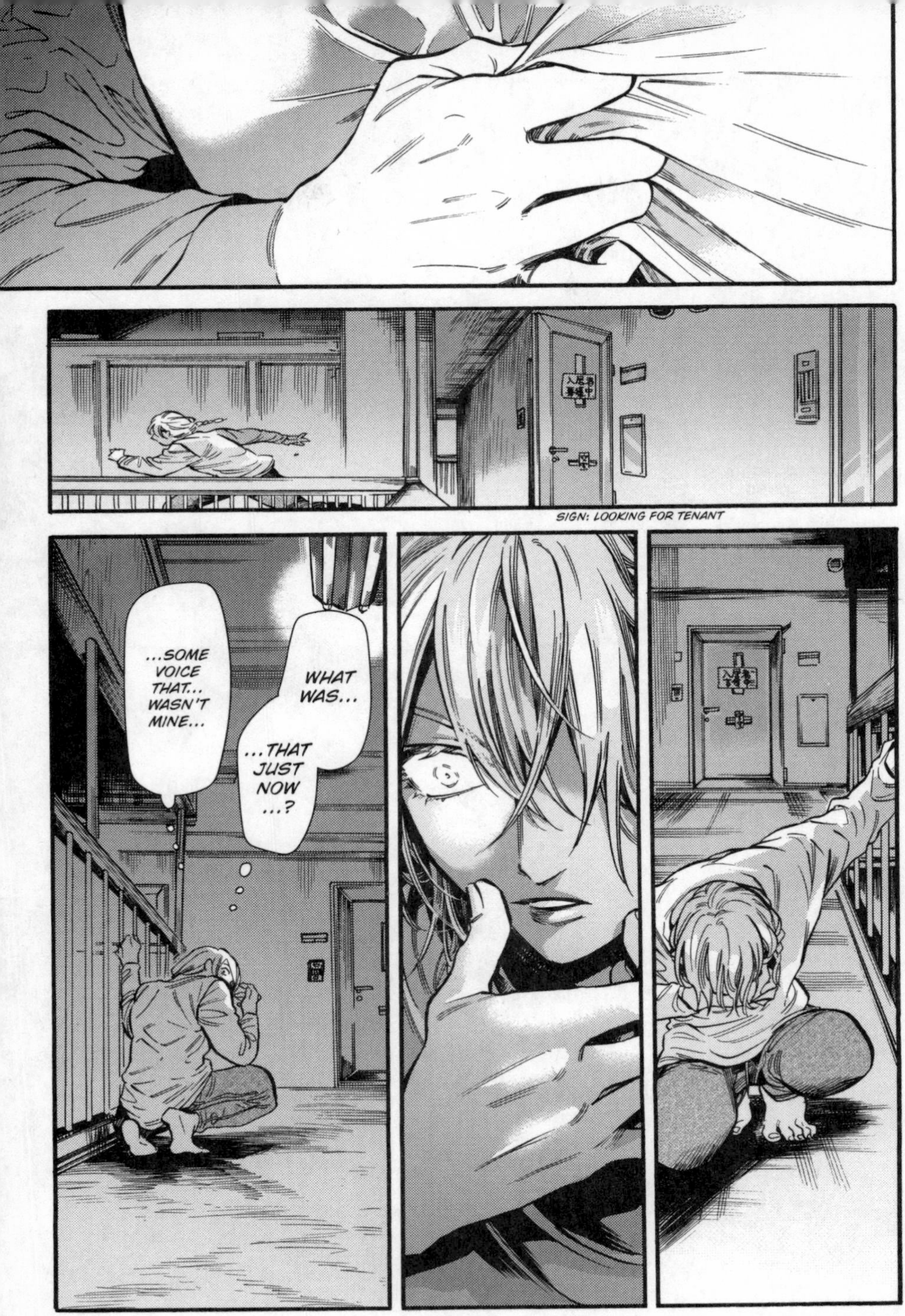
SIGN: LOOKING FOR TENANT
WHAT WAS...
...THAT JUST NOW ...?
...SOME VOICE THAT... WASN'T MINE...

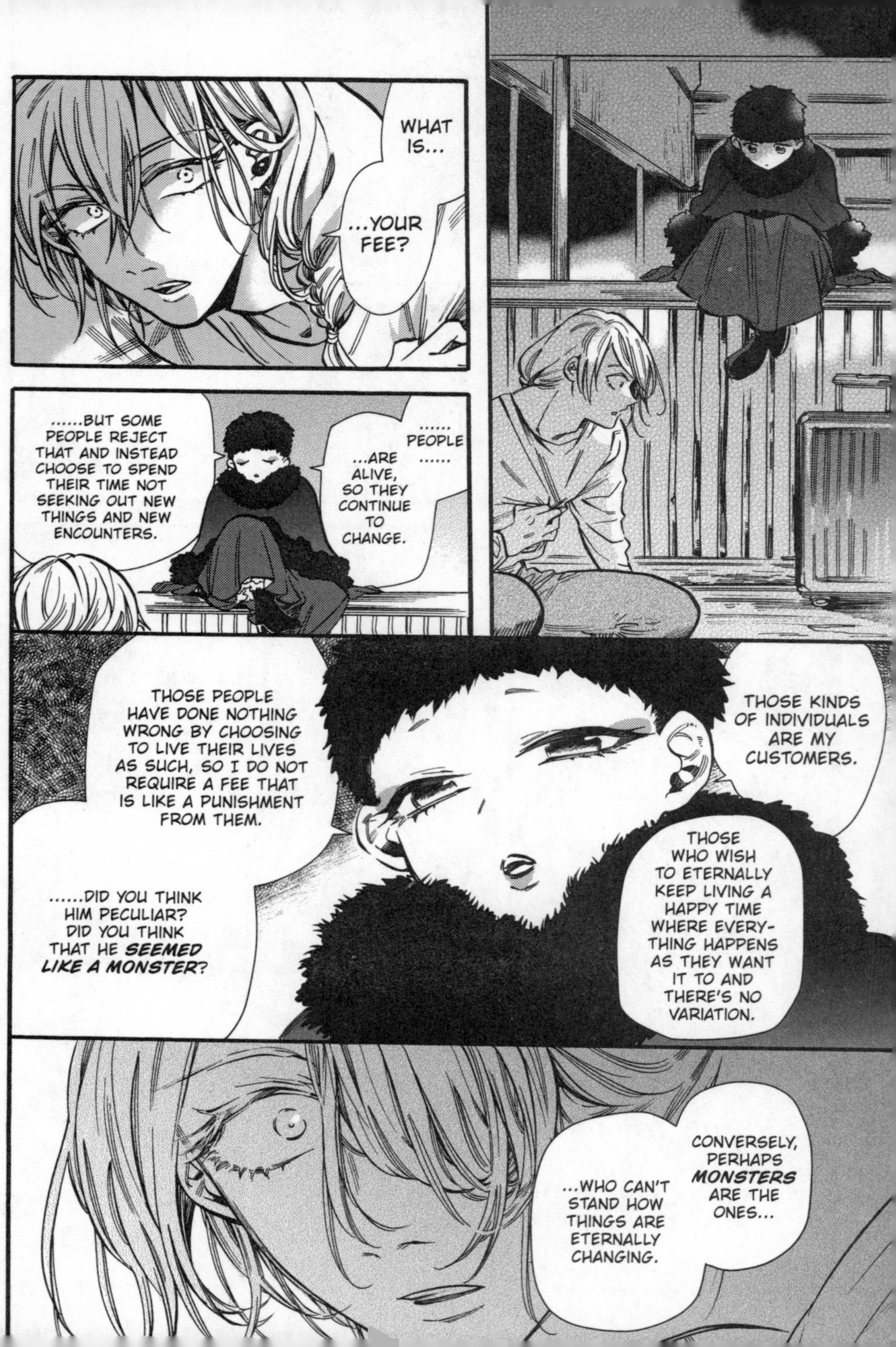

WHAT IS...
...YOUR FEE?
...... PEOPLE ....ARE ALIVE, SO THEY CONTINUE TO CHANGE.
......BUT SOME PEOPLE REJECT THAT AND INSTEAD CHOOSE TO SPEND THEIR TIME NOT SEEKING OUT NEW THINGS AND NEW ENCOUNTERS.
THOSE KINDS OF INDIVIDUALS ARE MY CUSTOMERS.
THOSE WHO WISH TO ETERNALLY KEEP LIVING A HAPPY TIME WHERE EVERY-THING HAPPENS AS THEY WANT IT TO AND THERE'S NO VARIATION.
THOSE PEOPLE HAVE DONE NOTHING WRONG BY CHOOSING TO LIVE THEIR LIVES AS SUCH, SO I DO NOT REQUIRE A FEE THAT IS LIKE A PUNISHMENT FROM THEM.
......DID YOU THINK HIM PECULIAR? DID YOU THINK THAT HE ***SEEMED LIKE A MONSTER***?
CONVERSELY, PERHAPS **MONSTERS** ARE THE ONES...
...WHO CAN'T STAND HOW THINGS ARE ETERNALLY CHANGING.

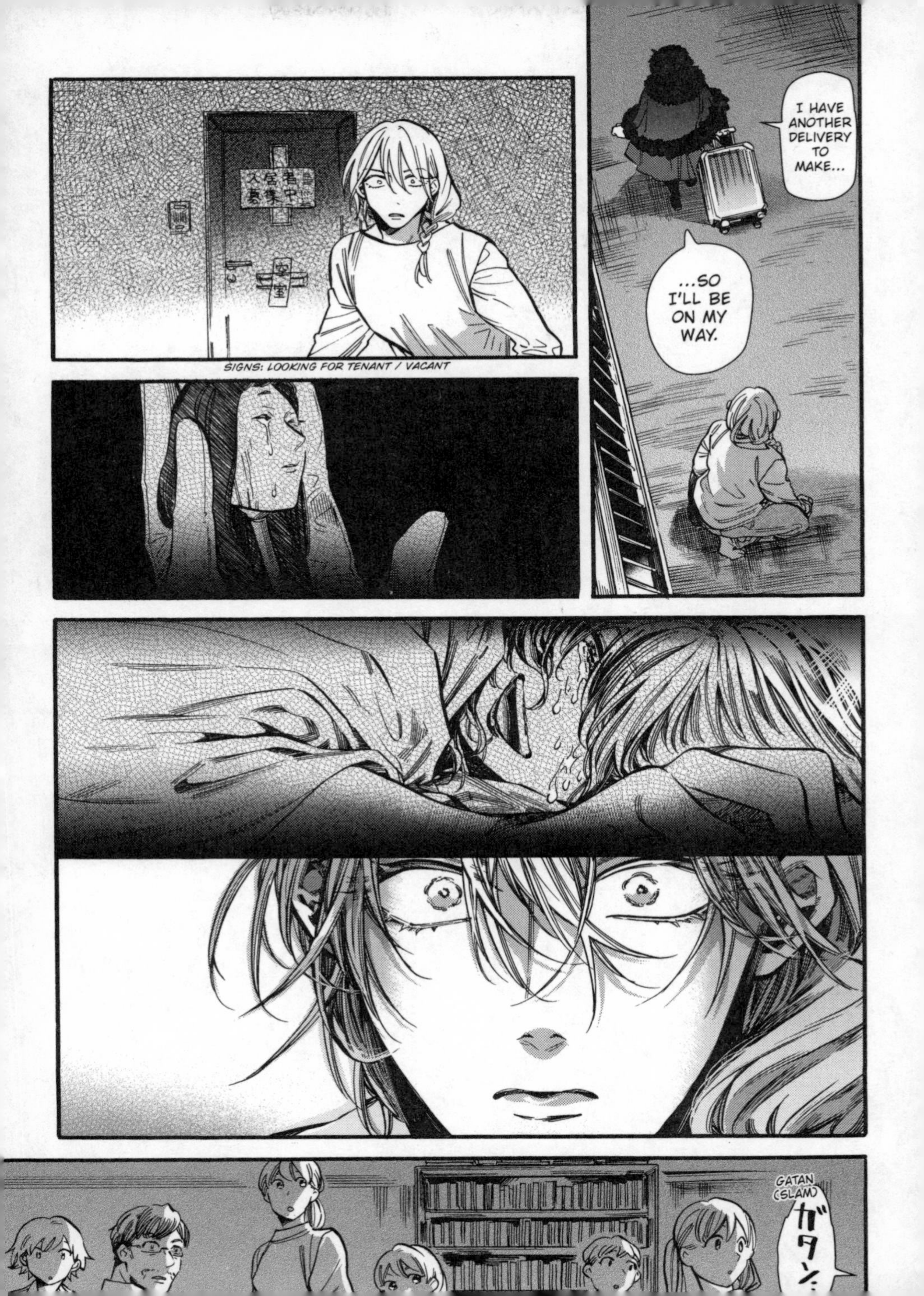
I HAVE ANOTHER DELIVERY TO MAKE...
...SO I'LL BE ON MY WAY.
SIGNS: LOOKING FOR TENANT / VACANT
GATAN (SLAM)
ガタン！

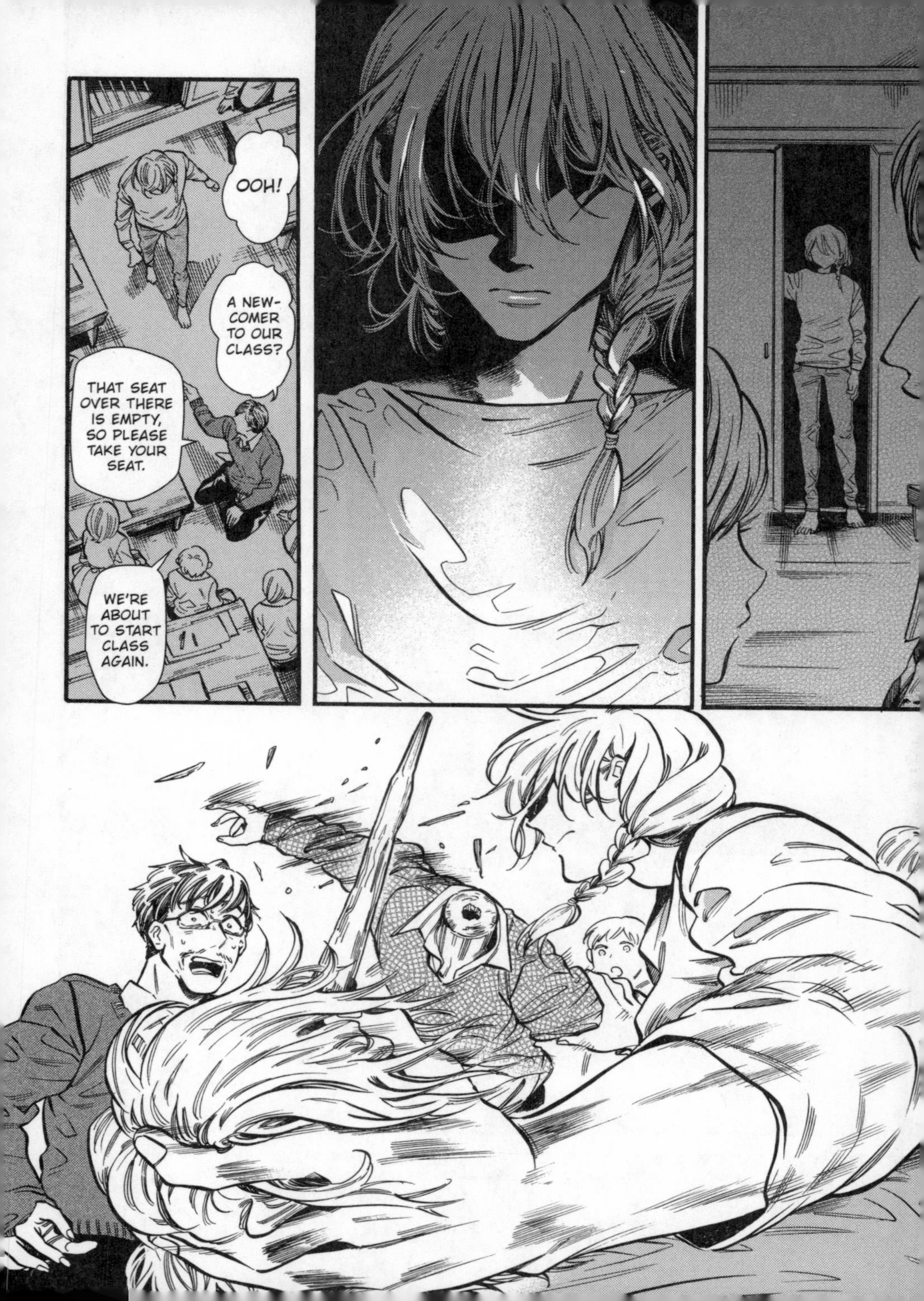
OOH!
A NEW-COMER TO OUR CLASS?
THAT SEAT OVER THERE IS EMPTY, SO PLEASE TAKE YOUR SEAT.
WE'RE ABOUT TO START CLASS AGAIN.

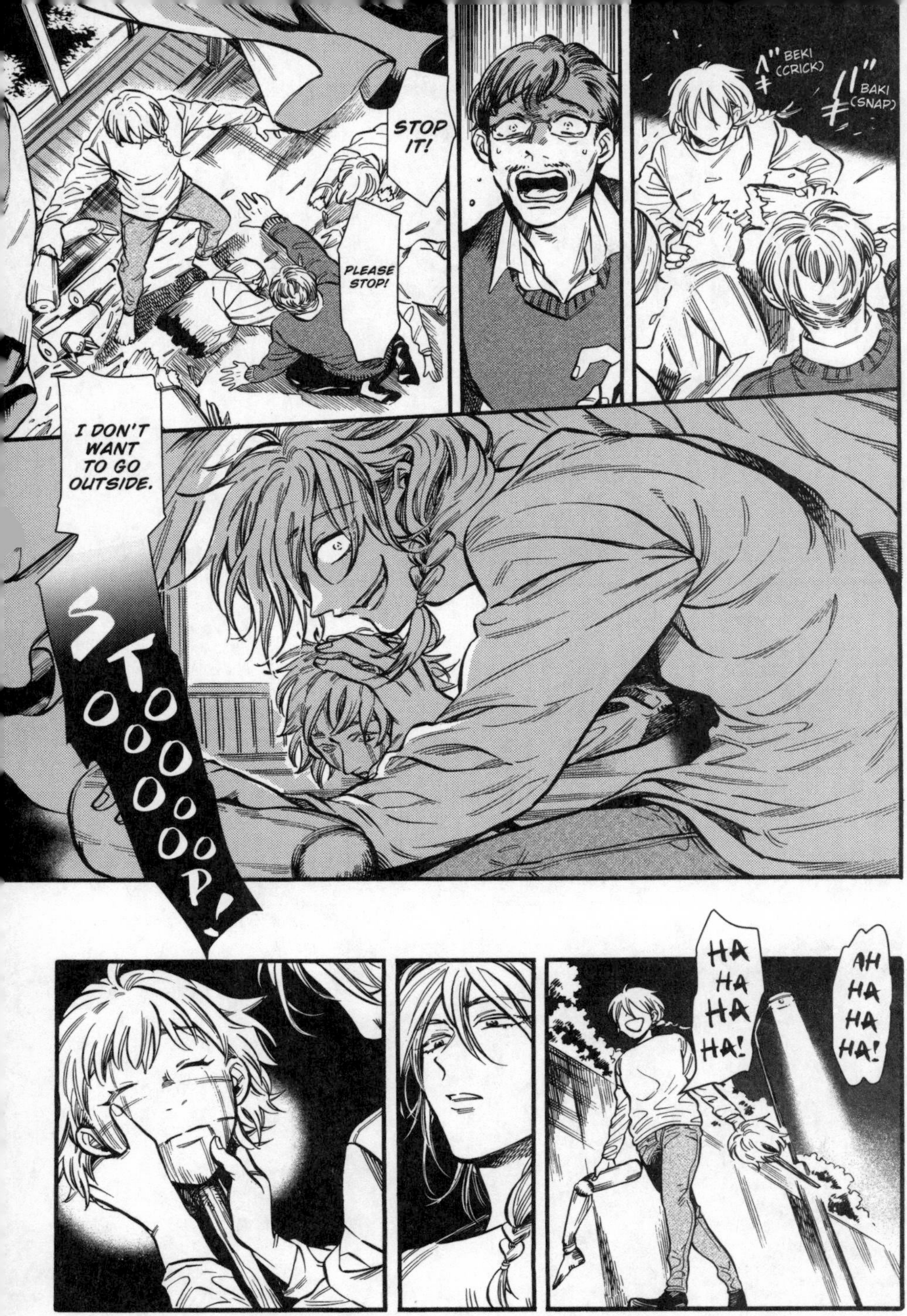
BEKI (CRICK)
BAKI (SNAP)
STOP IT!
PLEASE STOP!
I DON'T WANT TO GO OUTSIDE.
STOOOOOOOOOP!
AH HA HA HA HA!
HA HA HA HA!

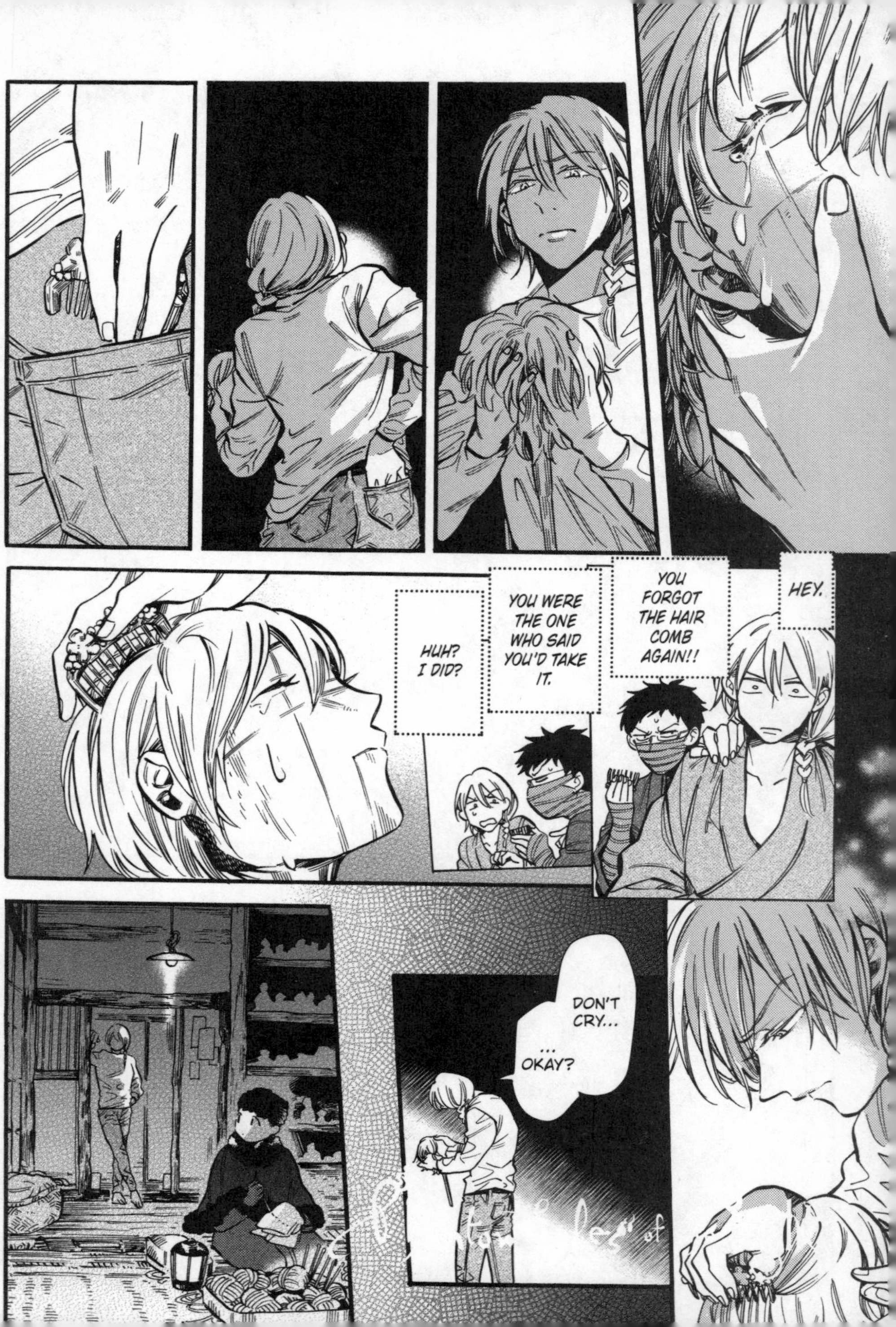
HEY.
YOU FORGOT THE HAIR COMB AGAIN!!
YOU WERE THE ONE WHO SAID YOU'D TAKE IT.
HUH? I DID?
DON'T CRY...
... OKAY?

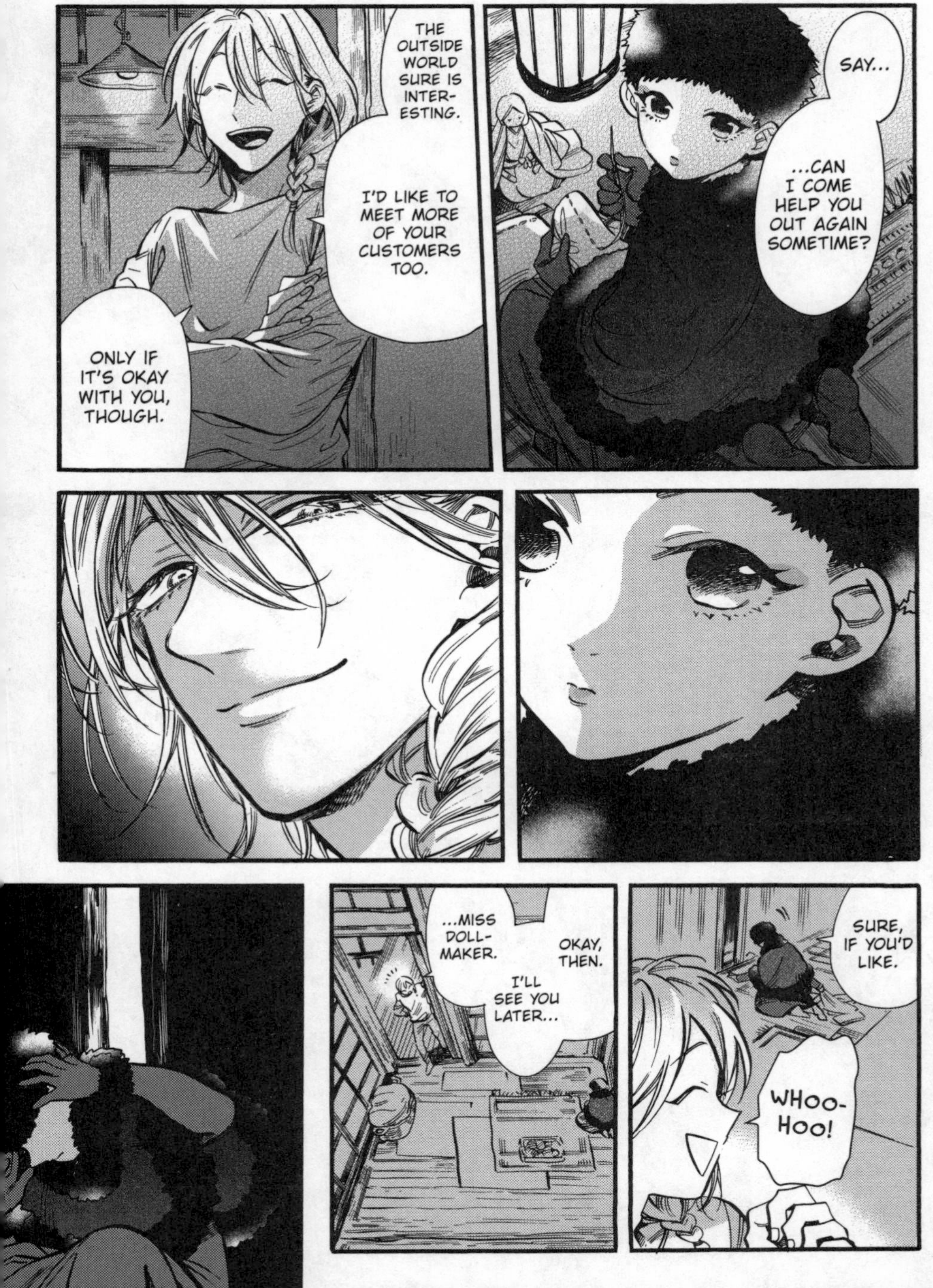
SAY...
...CAN I COME HELP YOU OUT AGAIN SOMETIME?
THE OUTSIDE WORLD SURE IS INTER-ESTING.
I'D LIKE TO MEET MORE OF YOUR CUSTOMERS TOO.
ONLY IF IT'S OKAY WITH YOU, THOUGH.
SURE, IF YOU'D LIKE.
WHOO-HOO!
...MISS DOLL-MAKER.
OKAY, THEN.
I'LL SEE YOU LATER...

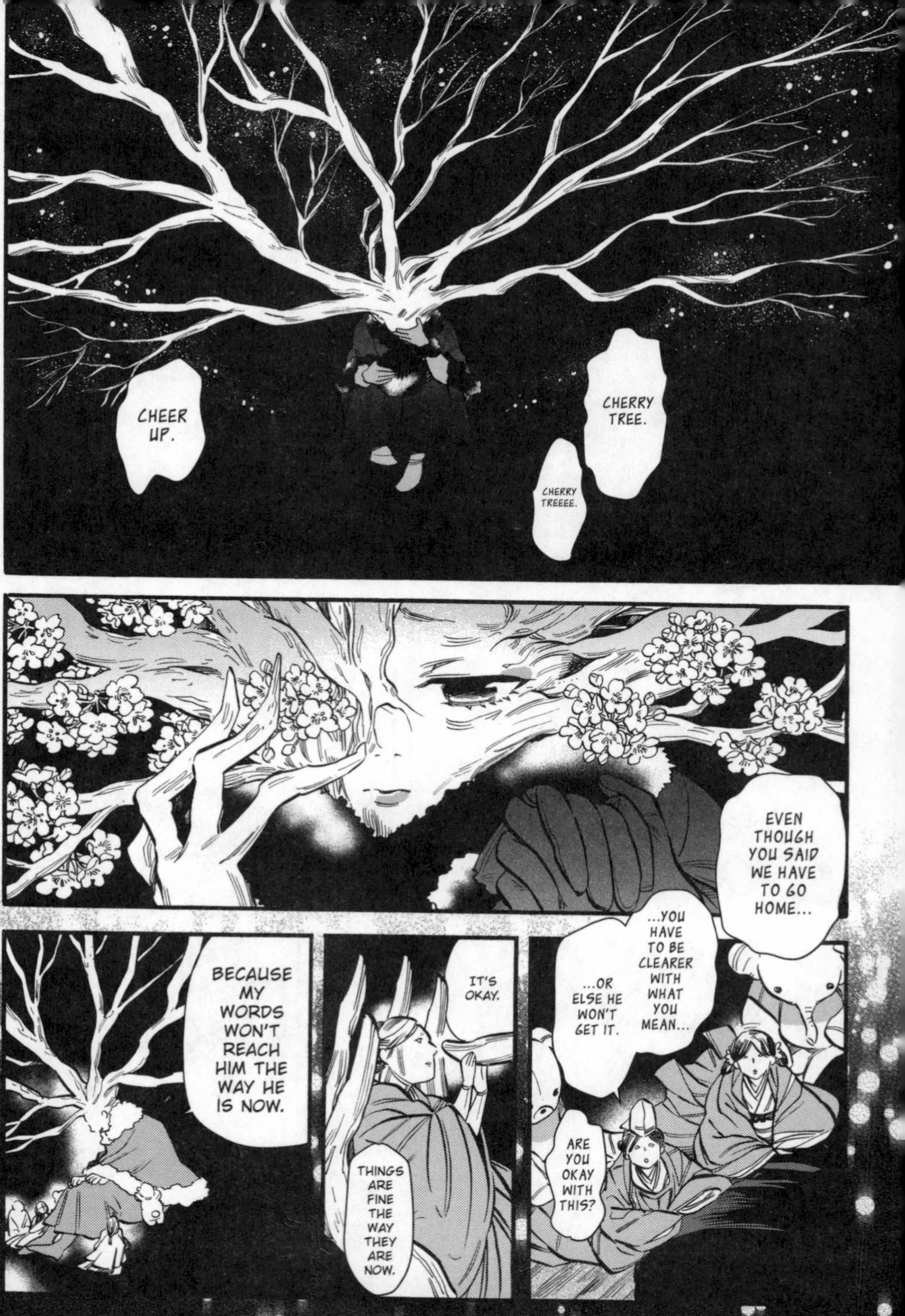
CHERRY TREE.
CHERRY TREEEE.
CHEER UP.
EVEN THOUGH YOU SAID WE HAVE TO GO HOME...
...YOU HAVE TO BE CLEARER WITH WHAT YOU MEAN...
...OR ELSE HE WON'T GET IT.
ARE YOU OKAY WITH THIS?
IT'S OKAY.
THINGS ARE FINE THE WAY THEY ARE NOW.
BECAUSE MY WORDS WON'T REACH HIM THE WAY HE IS NOW.

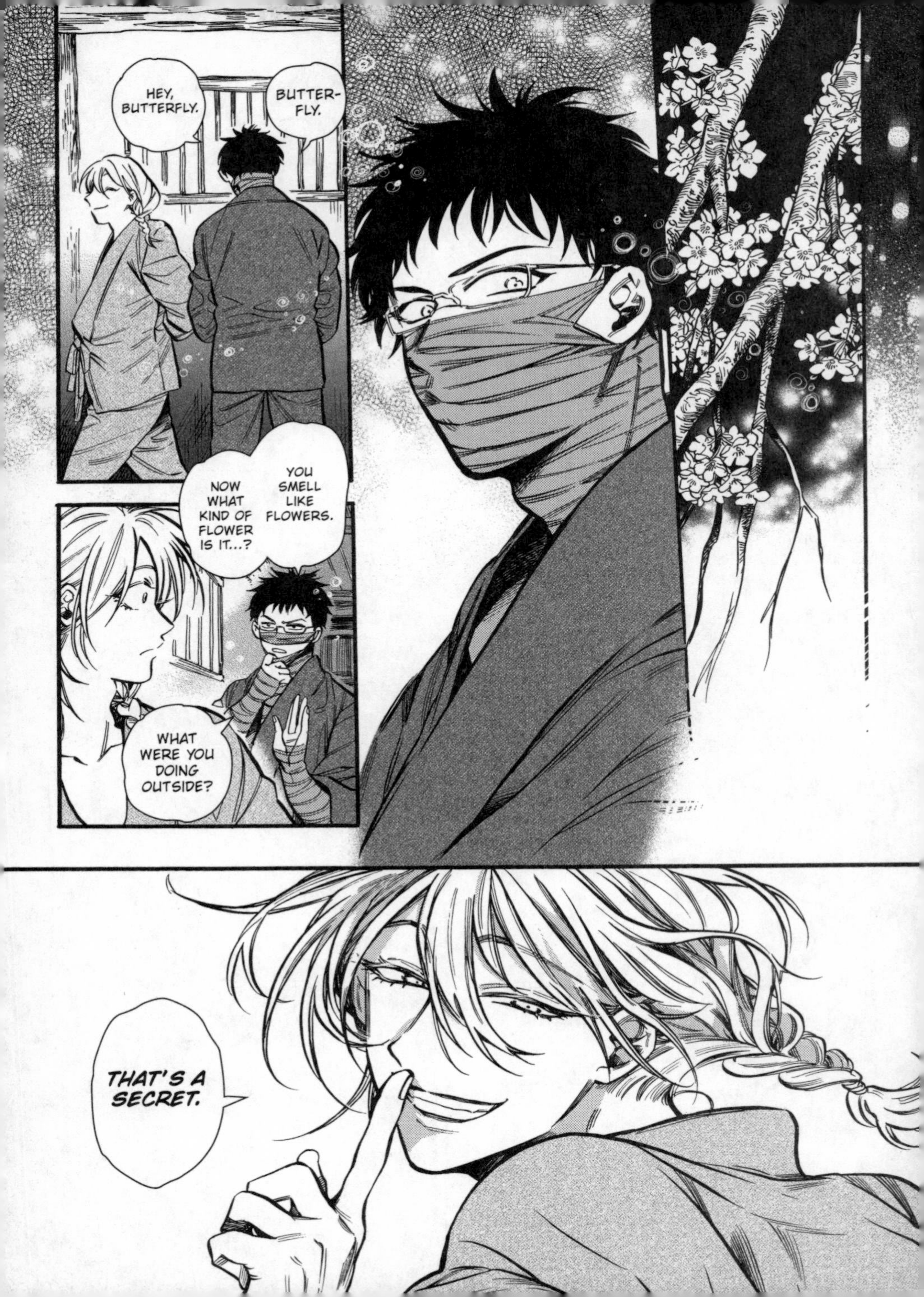
BUTTER-FLY.
HEY, BUTTERFLY.
YOU SMELL LIKE FLOWERS.
NOW WHAT KIND OF FLOWER IS IT...?
WHAT WERE YOU DOING OUTSIDE?
THAT'S A SECRET.

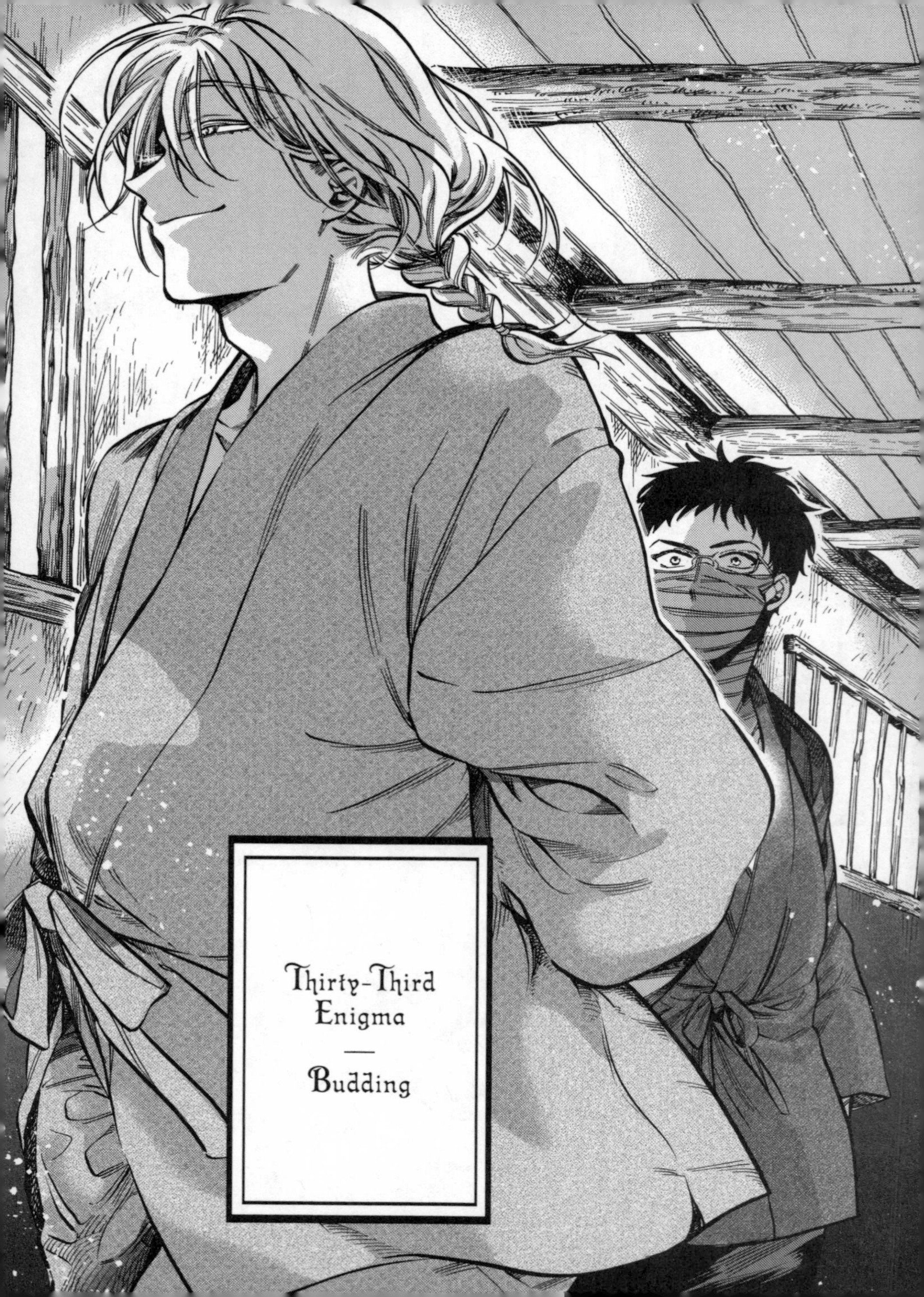
Thirty-Third Enigma
—
Budding

Phantom Tales of the Night

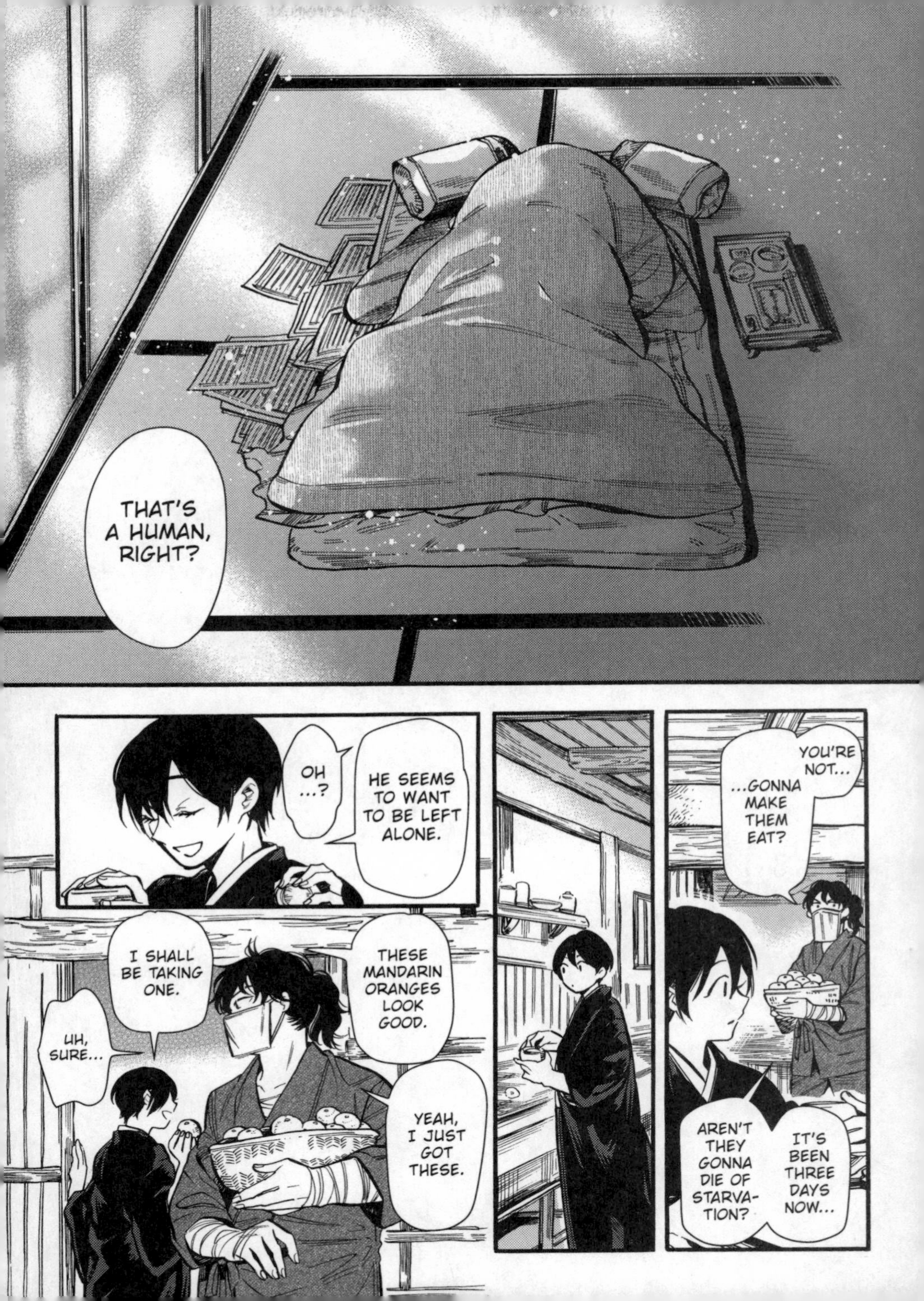
THAT'S A HUMAN, RIGHT?
YOU'RE NOT...
...GONNA MAKE THEM EAT?
IT'S BEEN THREE DAYS NOW...
AREN'T THEY GONNA DIE OF STARVA-TION?
HE SEEMS TO WANT TO BE LEFT ALONE.
OH ...?
THESE MANDARIN ORANGES LOOK GOOD.
I SHALL BE TAKING ONE.
UH, SURE...
YEAH, I JUST GOT THESE.

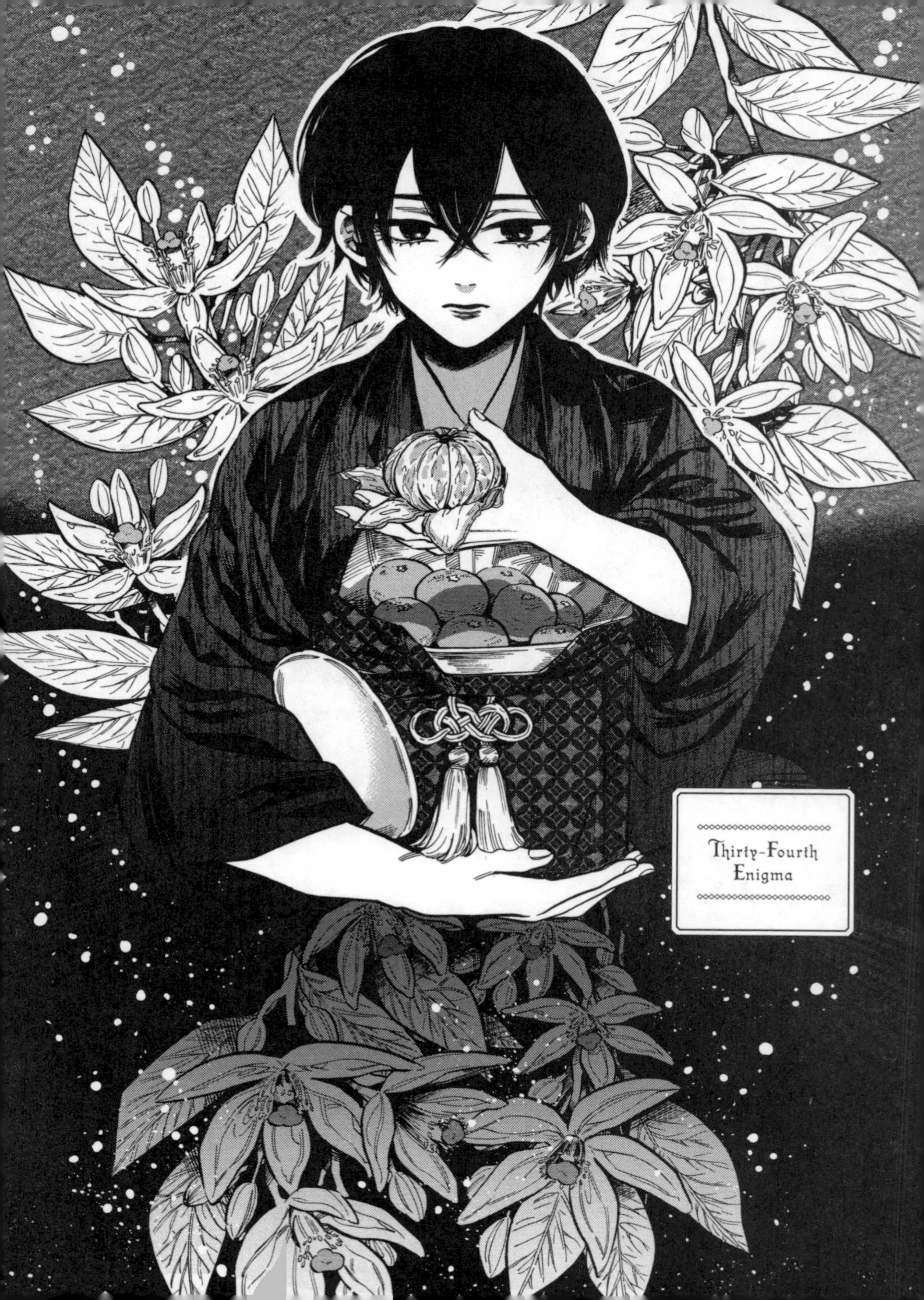
Thirty-Fourth
Enigma

I SHALL COME BY AGAIN TOMORROW MORNING.

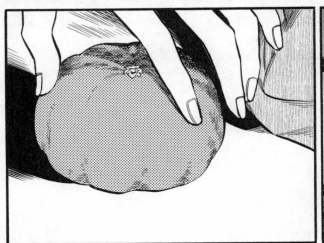

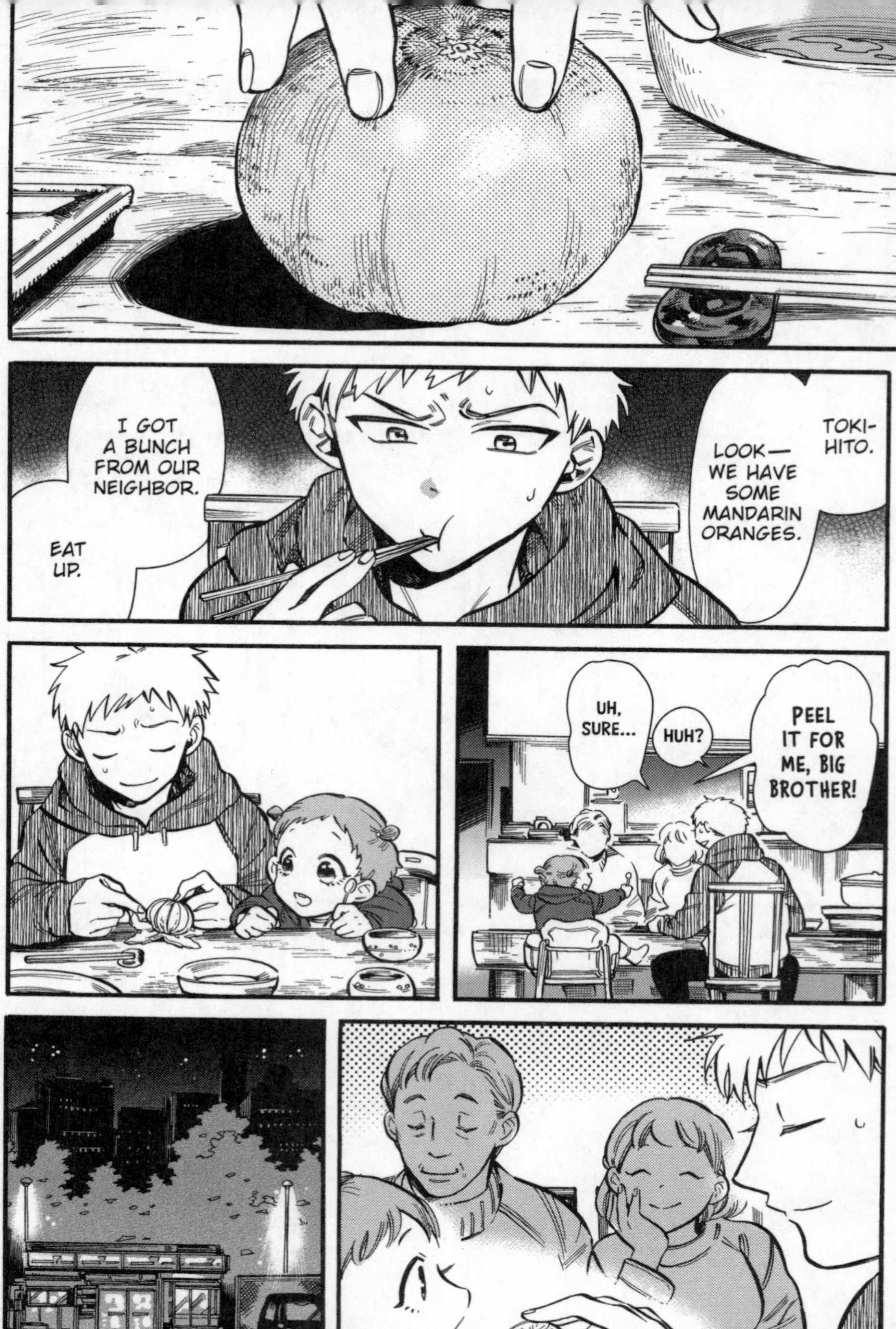
TOKI-HITO.
LOOK— WE HAVE SOME MANDARIN ORANGES.
I GOT A BUNCH FROM OUR NEIGHBOR.
EAT UP.
PEEL IT FOR ME, BIG BROTHER!
HUH?
UH, SURE...

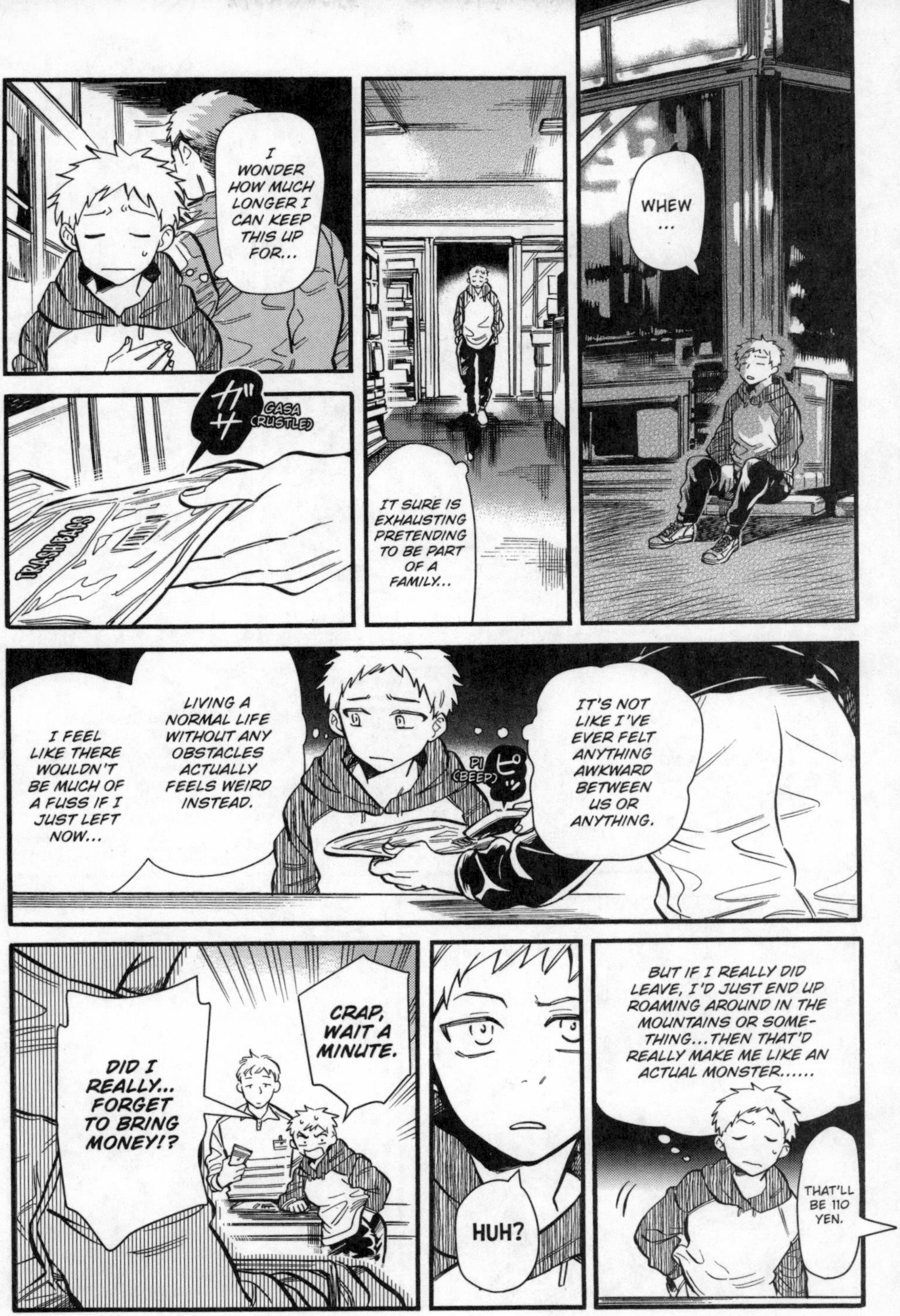
WHEW...
IT SURE IS EXHAUSTING PRETENDING TO BE PART OF A FAMILY...
I WONDER HOW MUCH LONGER I CAN KEEP THIS UP FOR...
ガサ GASA (RUSTLED)
TRASH BAGS
IT'S NOT LIKE I'VE EVER FELT ANYTHING AWKWARD BETWEEN US OR ANYTHING.
ピッ PI (BEEP)
LIVING A NORMAL LIFE WITHOUT ANY OBSTACLES ACTUALLY FEELS WEIRD INSTEAD.
I FEEL LIKE THERE WOULDN'T BE MUCH OF A FUSS IF I JUST LEFT NOW...
BUT IF I REALLY DID LEAVE, I'D JUST END UP ROAMING AROUND IN THE MOUNTAINS OR SOMETHING...THEN THAT'D REALLY MAKE ME LIKE AN ACTUAL MONSTER......
THAT'LL BE 110 YEN.
HUH?
CRAP, WAIT A MINUTE.
DID I REALLY... FORGET TO BRING MONEY!?

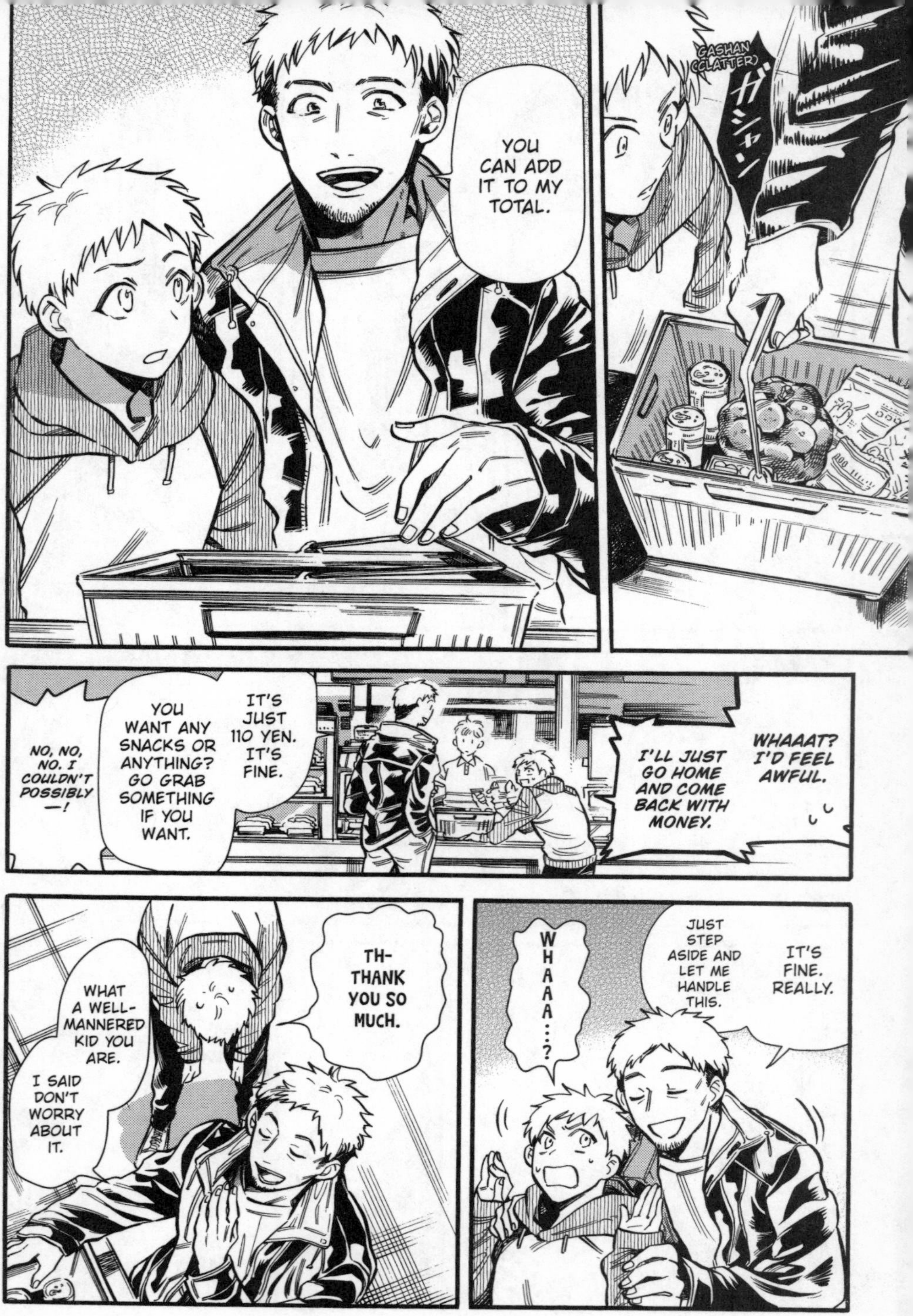
GASHAN (CLATTER)
YOU CAN ADD IT TO MY TOTAL.
WHAAAT? I'D FEEL AWFUL.
I'LL JUST GO HOME AND COME BACK WITH MONEY.
IT'S JUST 110 YEN. IT'S FINE.
YOU WANT ANY SNACKS OR ANYTHING? GO GRAB SOMETHING IF YOU WANT.
NO, NO, NO. I COULDN'T POSSIBLY—!
IT'S FINE. REALLY.
JUST STEP ASIDE AND LET ME HANDLE THIS.
WHAAAA...?
TH-THANK YOU SO MUCH.
WHAT A WELL-MANNERED KID YOU ARE.
I SAID DON'T WORRY ABOUT IT.

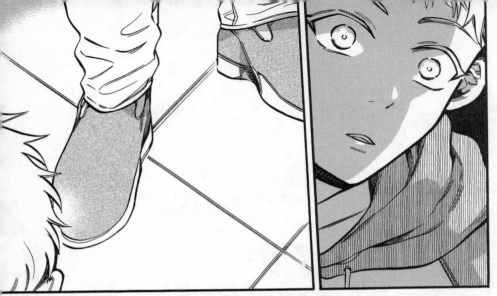

WHAT
NUMBER
?

UHHH
...

OH, I'D
LIKE SOME
CIGARETTES
TOO.

......

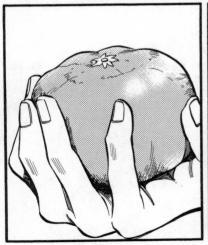

WANT
ONE?

......

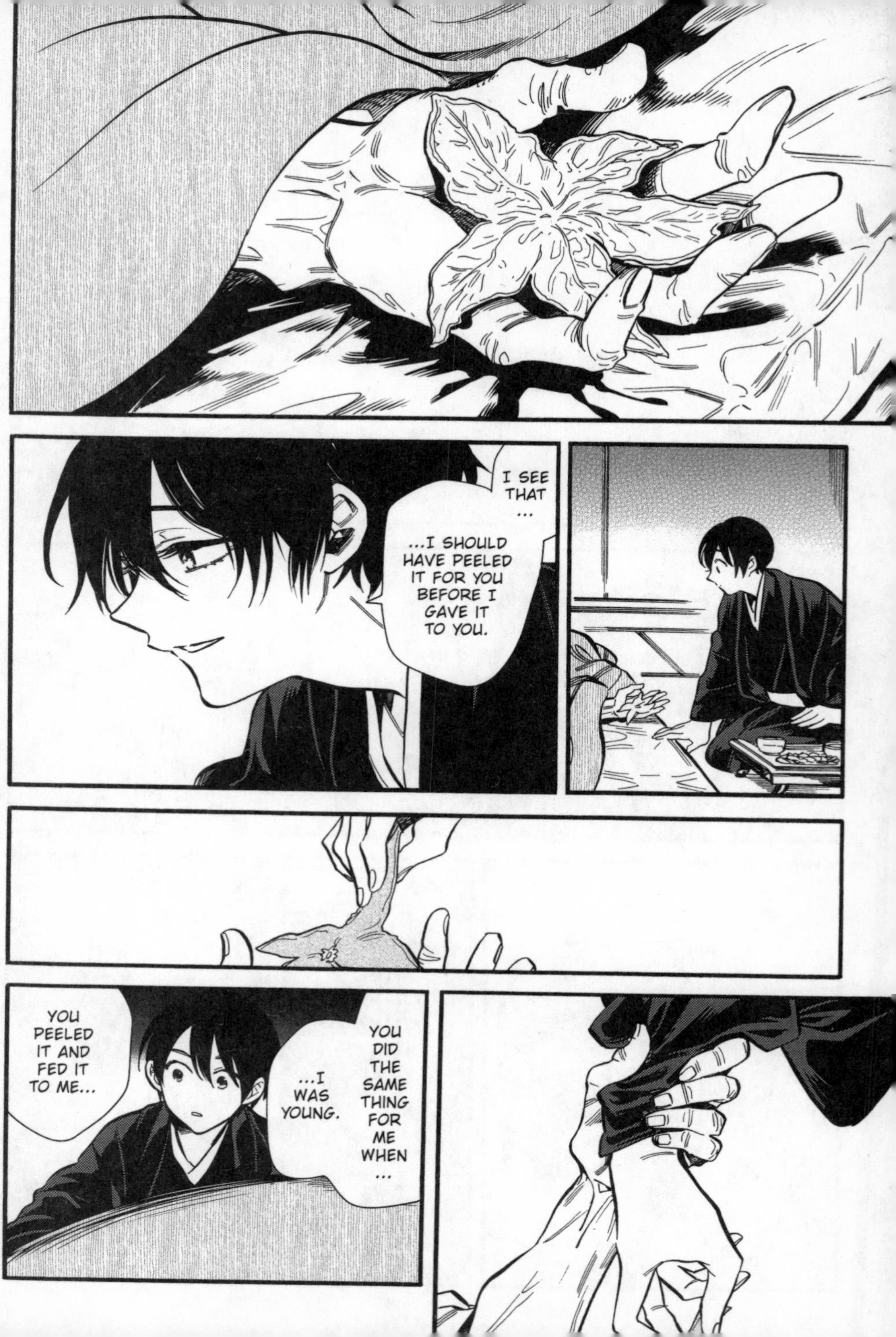
I SEE THAT ...
...I SHOULD HAVE PEELED IT FOR YOU BEFORE I GAVE IT TO YOU.
YOU DID THE SAME THING FOR ME WHEN ...
...I WAS YOUNG.
YOU PEELED IT AND FED IT TO ME...

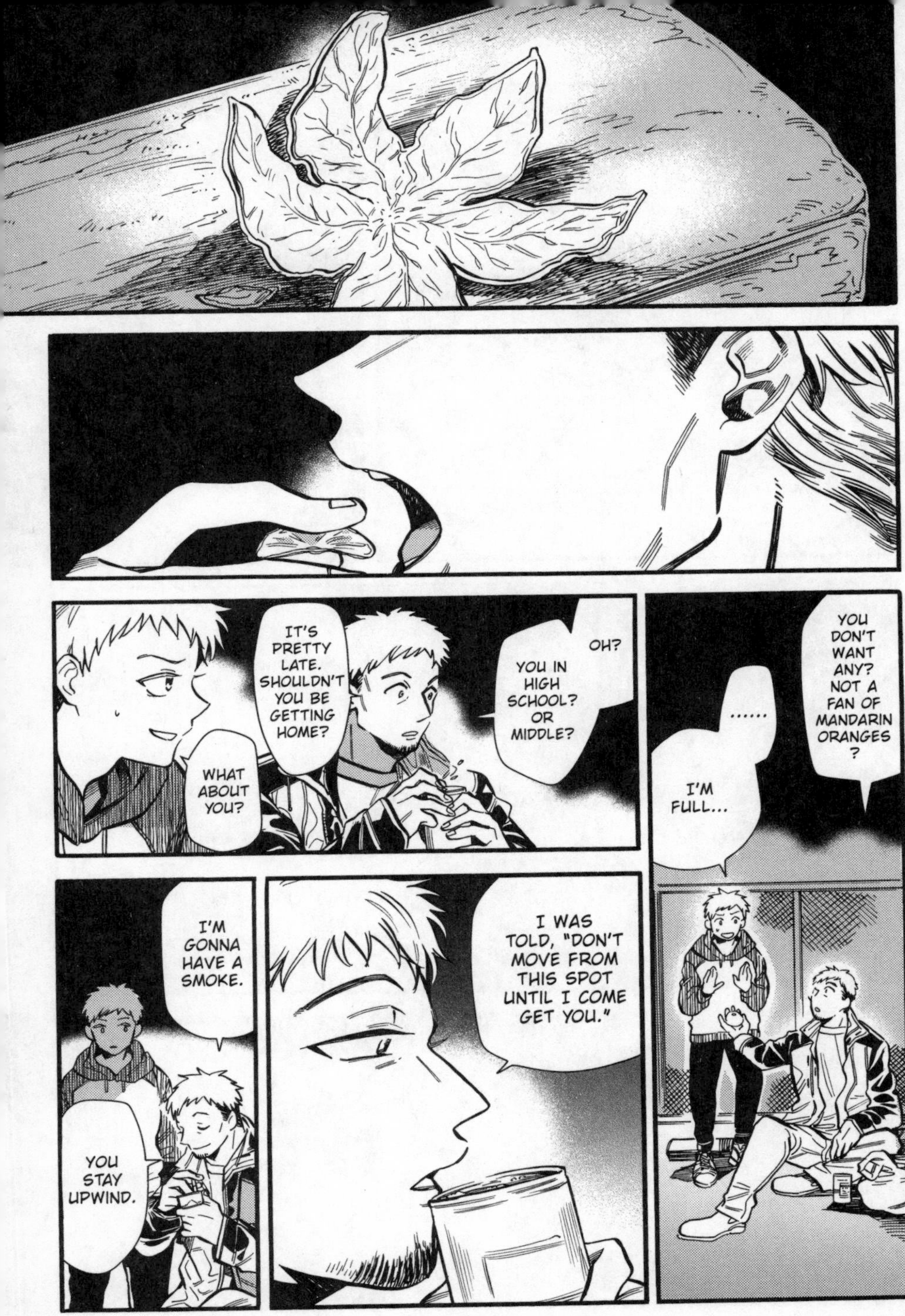
YOU DON'T WANT ANY? NOT A FAN OF MANDARIN ORANGES?
......
I'M FULL...
OH? YOU IN HIGH SCHOOL? OR MIDDLE?
IT'S PRETTY LATE. SHOULDN'T YOU BE GETTING HOME?
WHAT ABOUT YOU?
I WAS TOLD, "DON'T MOVE FROM THIS SPOT UNTIL I COME GET YOU."
I'M GONNA HAVE A SMOKE.
YOU STAY UPWIND.

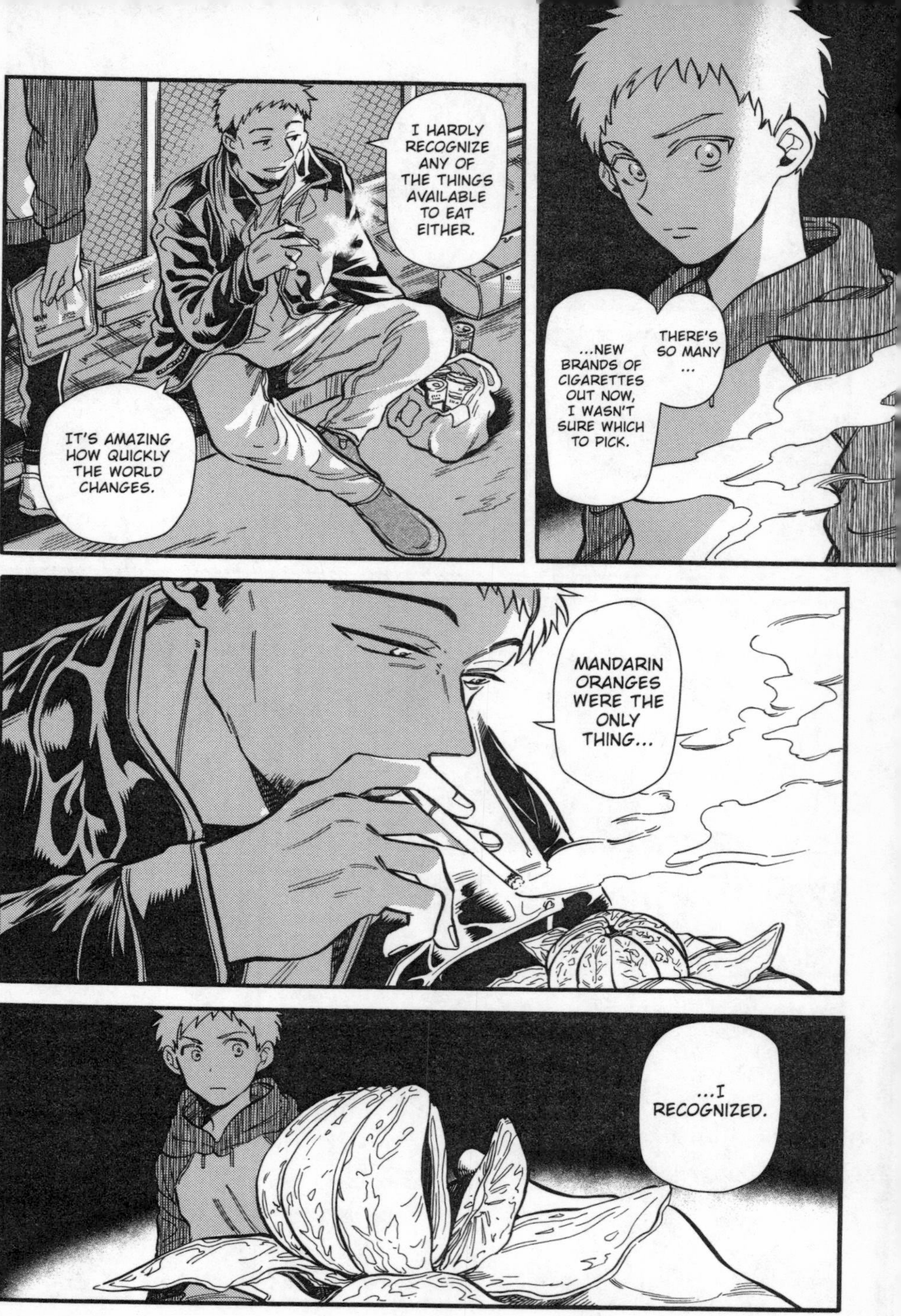
THERE'S SO MANY ...
...NEW BRANDS OF CIGARETTES OUT NOW, I WASN'T SURE WHICH TO PICK.
I HARDLY RECOGNIZE ANY OF THE THINGS AVAILABLE TO EAT EITHER.
IT'S AMAZING HOW QUICKLY THE WORLD CHANGES.
MANDARIN ORANGES WERE THE ONLY THING...
...I RECOGNIZED.

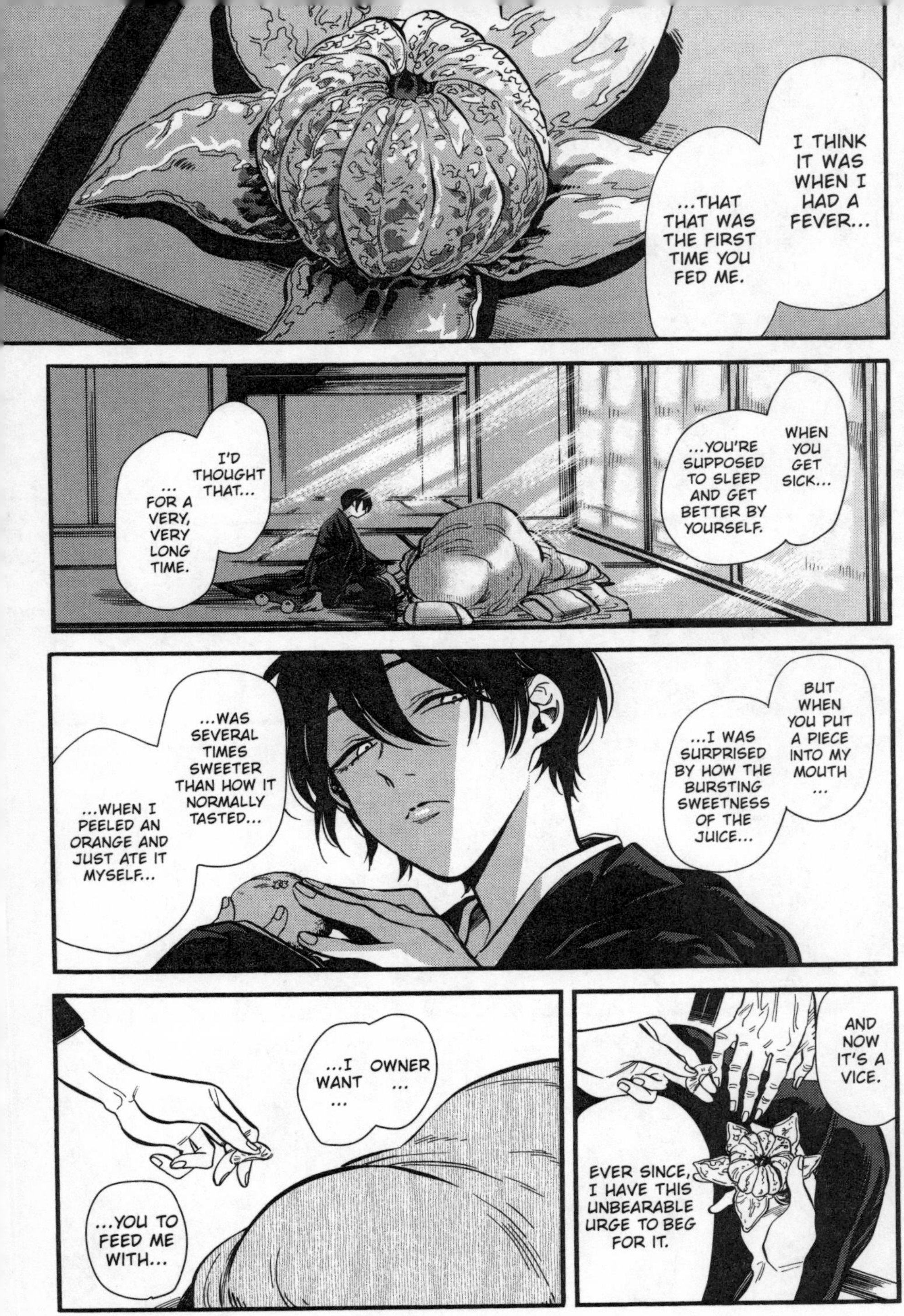
I THINK IT WAS WHEN I HAD A FEVER...
...THAT THAT WAS THE FIRST TIME YOU FED ME.
WHEN YOU GET SICK...
...YOU'RE SUPPOSED TO SLEEP AND GET BETTER BY YOURSELF.
I'D THOUGHT THAT...
... FOR A VERY, VERY LONG TIME.
BUT WHEN YOU PUT A PIECE INTO MY MOUTH ...
...I WAS SURPRISED BY HOW THE BURSTING SWEETNESS OF THE JUICE...
...WAS SEVERAL TIMES SWEETER THAN HOW IT NORMALLY TASTED...
...WHEN I PEELED AN ORANGE AND JUST ATE IT MYSELF...
AND NOW IT'S A VICE.
EVER SINCE, I HAVE THIS UNBEARABLE URGE TO BEG FOR IT.
OWNER ...
...I WANT ...
...YOU TO FEED ME WITH...

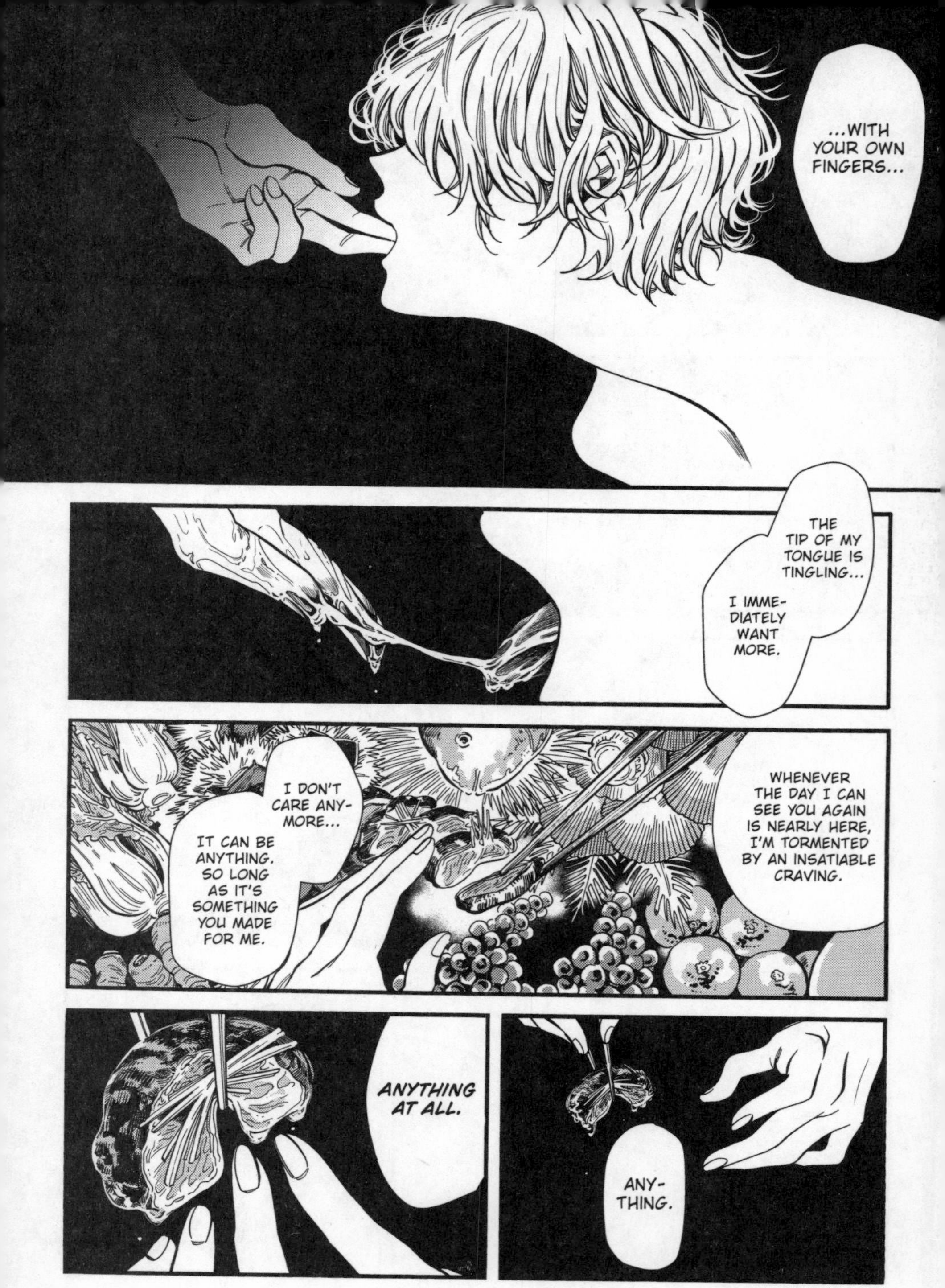
...WITH YOUR OWN FINGERS...
THE TIP OF MY TONGUE IS TINGLING...
I IMMEDIATELY WANT MORE.
WHENEVER THE DAY I CAN SEE YOU AGAIN IS NEARLY HERE, I'M TORMENTED BY AN INSATIABLE CRAVING.
I DON'T CARE ANYMORE...
IT CAN BE ANYTHING. SO LONG AS IT'S SOMETHING YOU MADE FOR ME.
ANY-THING.
ANYTHING AT ALL.

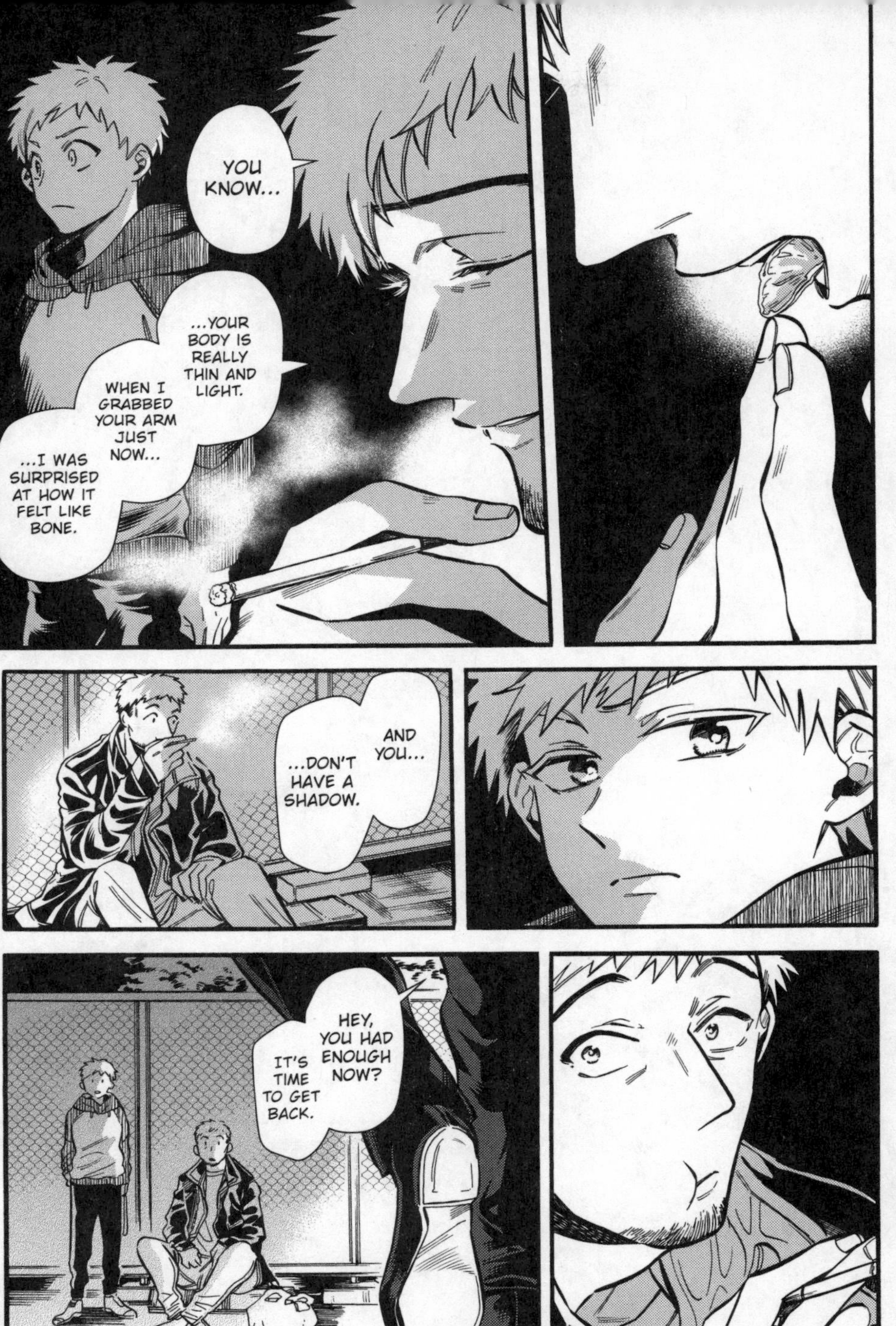
YOU KNOW...
...YOUR BODY IS REALLY THIN AND LIGHT.
WHEN I GRABBED YOUR ARM JUST NOW...
...I WAS SURPRISED AT HOW IT FELT LIKE BONE.
AND YOU...
...DON'T HAVE A SHADOW.
HEY, YOU HAD ENOUGH NOW?
IT'S TIME TO GET BACK.

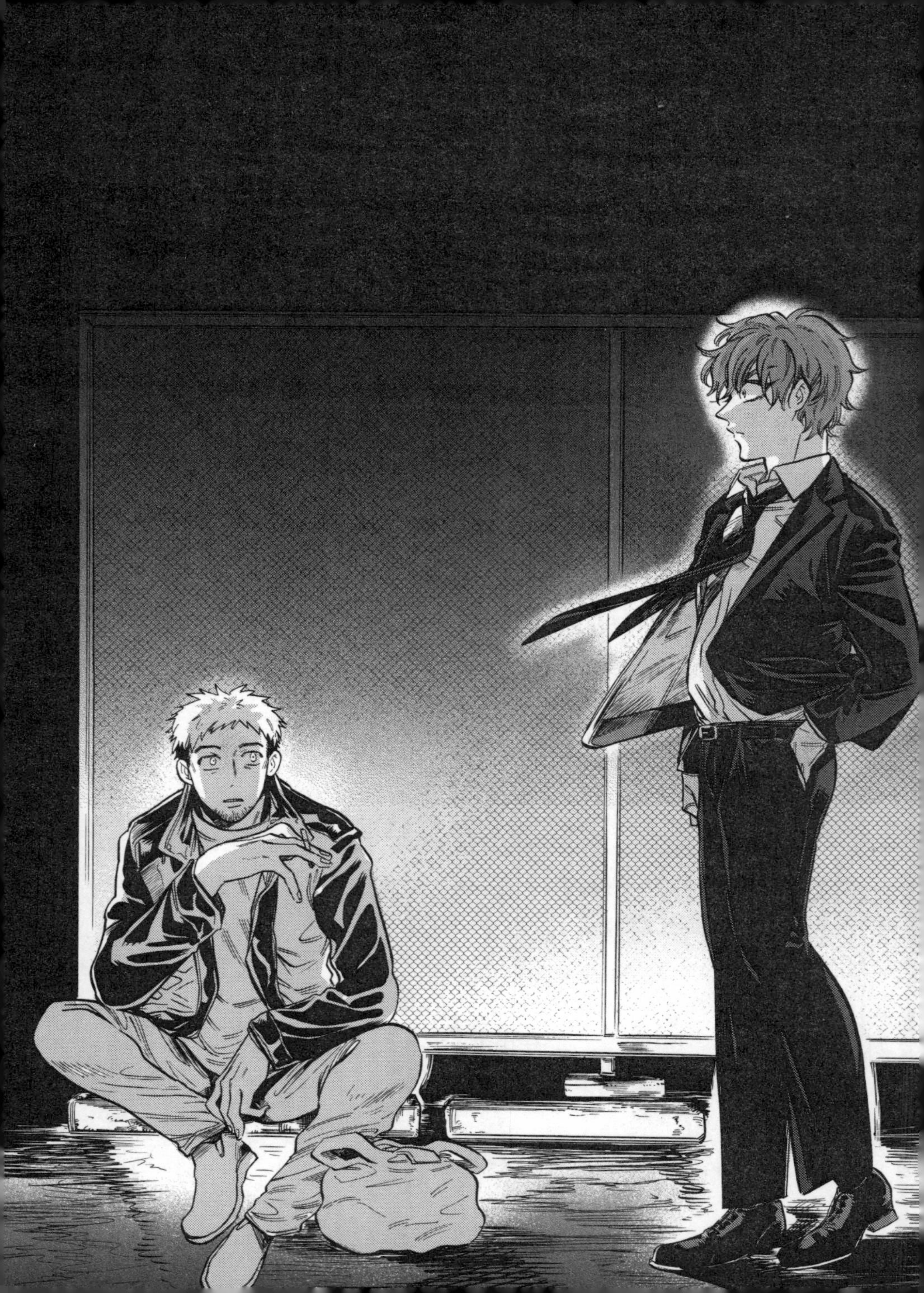

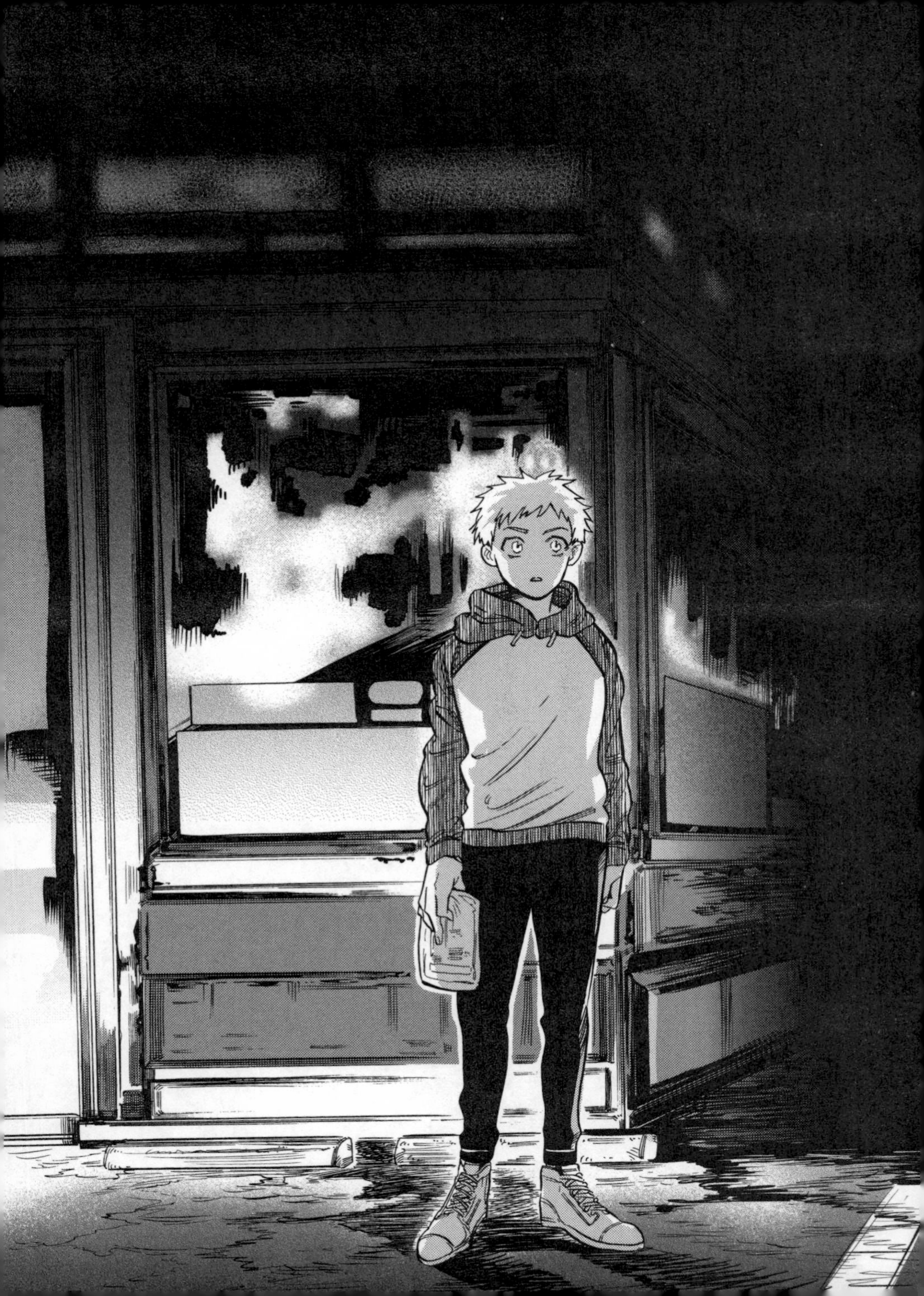

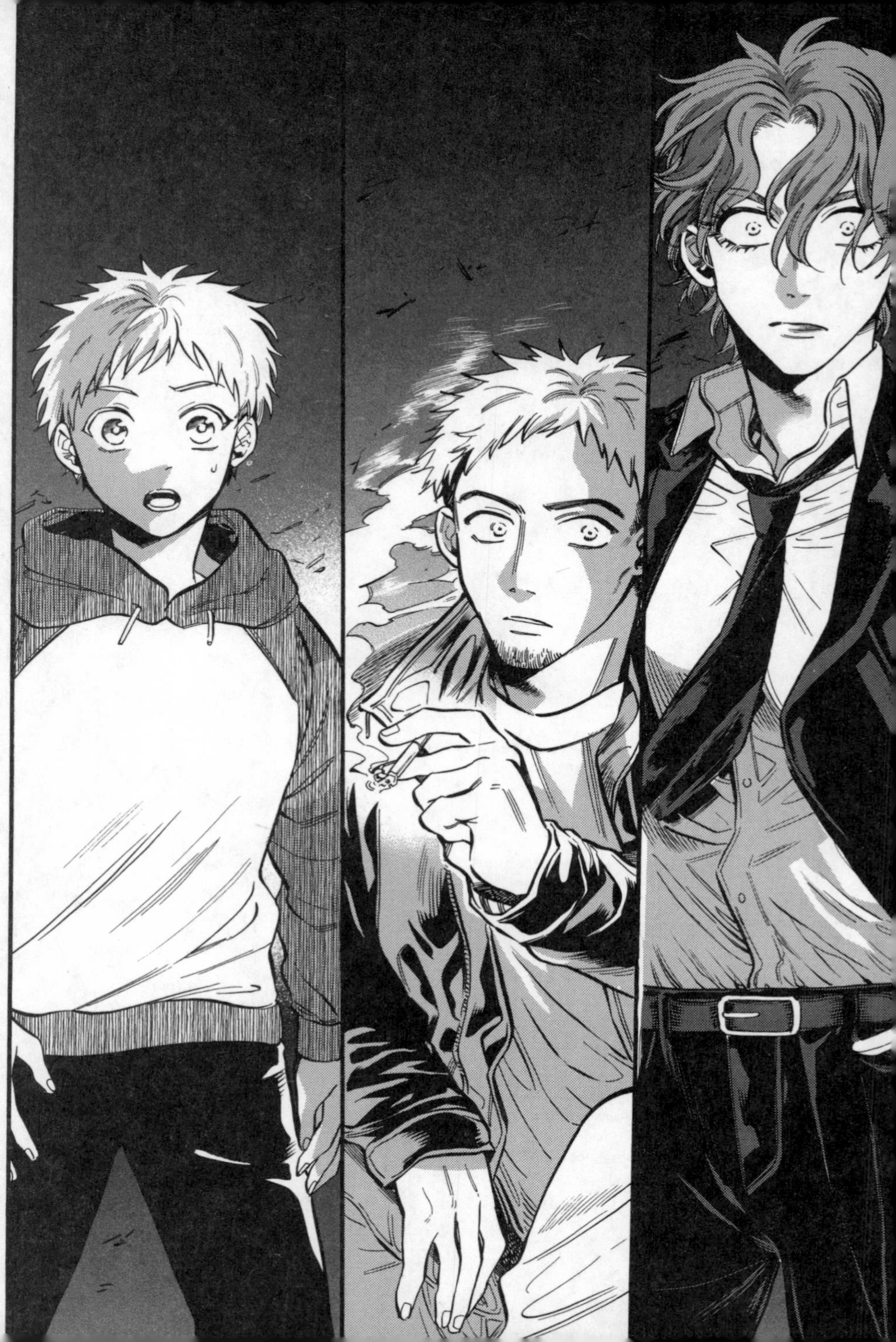

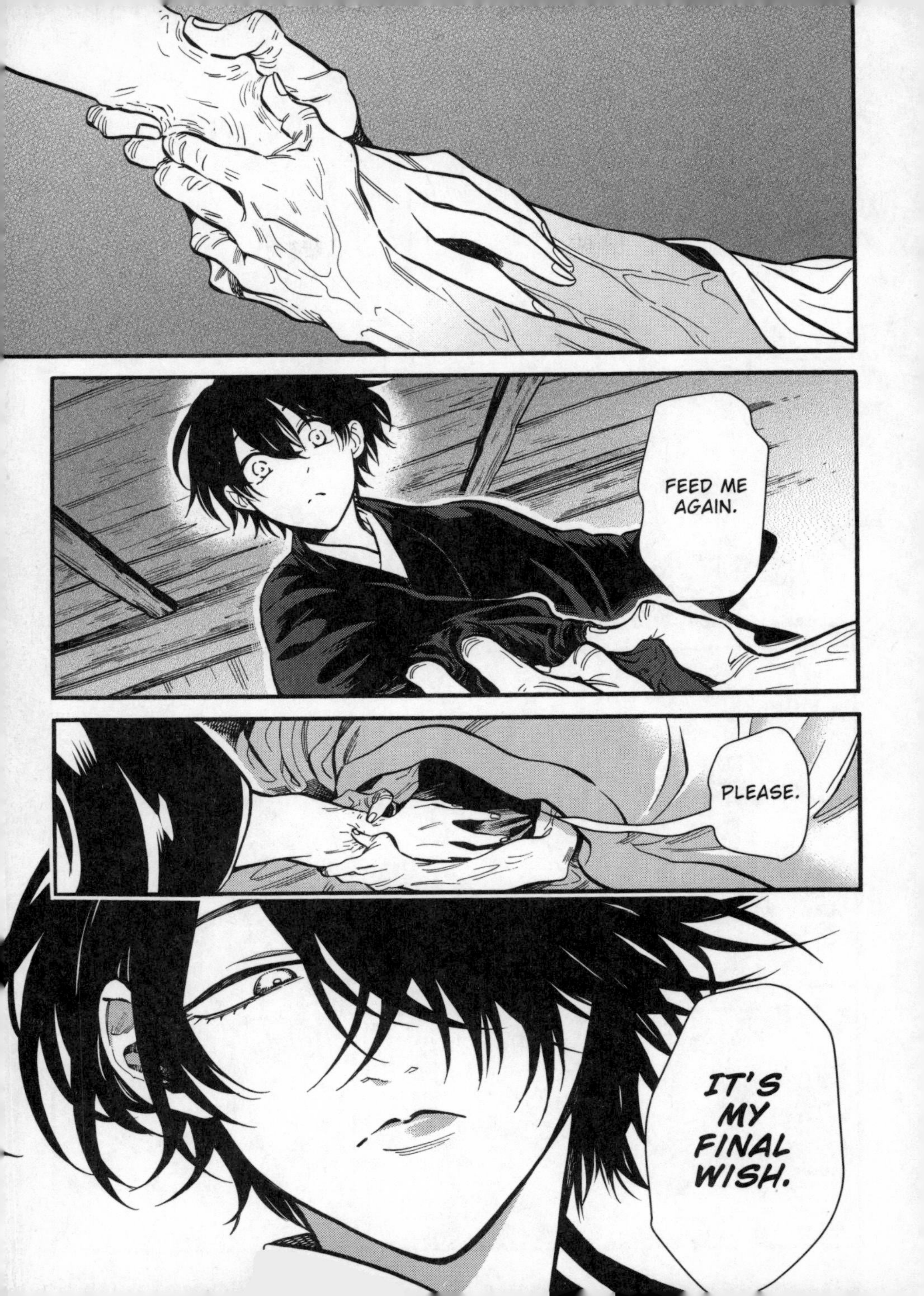
FEED ME AGAIN.
PLEASE.
IT'S MY FINAL WISH.

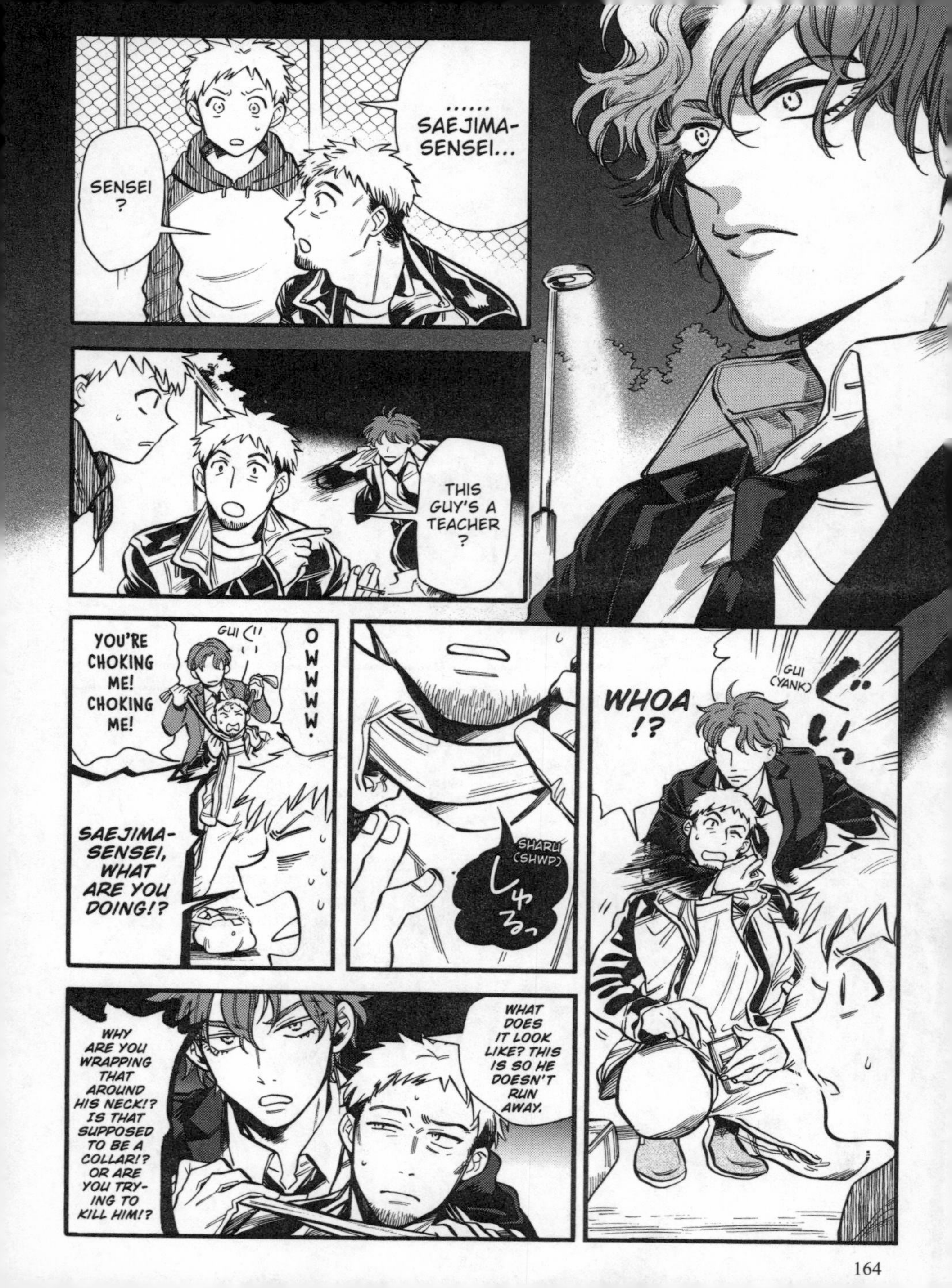

...... SAEJIMA-SENSEI...
SENSEI ?
THIS GUY'S A TEACHER ?
WHOA !?
GUI (YANK)
ぐいっ
SHARU (SHWP)
しゅるっ
OWWWW.
YOU'RE CHOKING ME! CHOKING ME!
GUI ぐい
SAEJIMA-SENSEI, WHAT ARE YOU DOING!?
WHAT DOES IT LOOK LIKE? THIS IS SO HE DOESN'T RUN AWAY.
WHY ARE YOU WRAPPING THAT AROUND HIS NECK!? IS THAT SUPPOSED TO BE A COLLAR!? OR ARE YOU TRY-ING TO KILL HIM!?

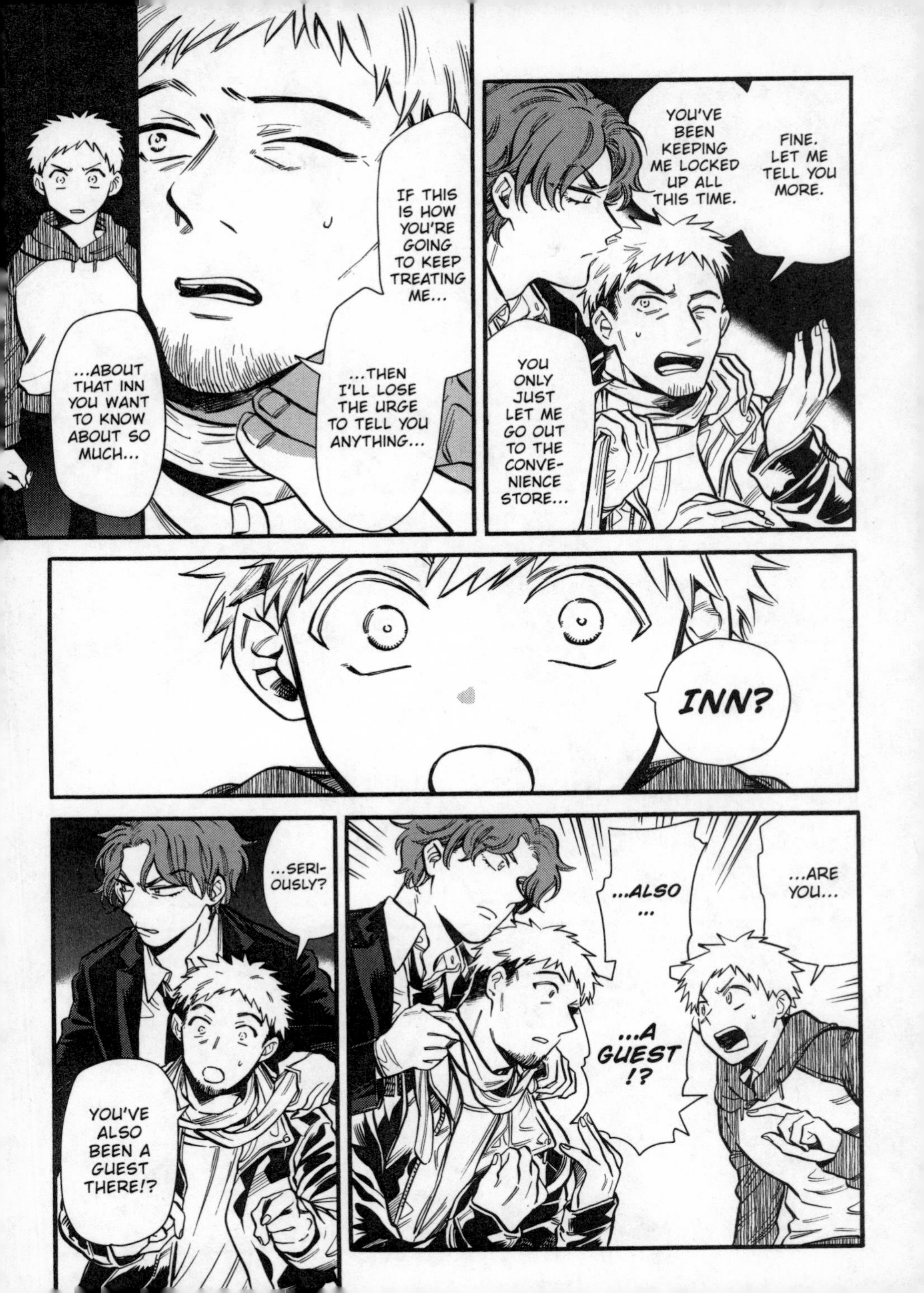
FINE. LET ME TELL YOU MORE.
YOU'VE BEEN KEEPING ME LOCKED UP ALL THIS TIME.
YOU ONLY JUST LET ME GO OUT TO THE CONVENIENCE STORE...
IF THIS IS HOW YOU'RE GOING TO KEEP TREATING ME...
...THEN I'LL LOSE THE URGE TO TELL YOU ANYTHING...
...ABOUT THAT INN YOU WANT TO KNOW ABOUT SO MUCH...
INN?
...ARE YOU...
...ALSO ...
...A GUEST !?
...SERIOUSLY?
YOU'VE ALSO BEEN A GUEST THERE!?

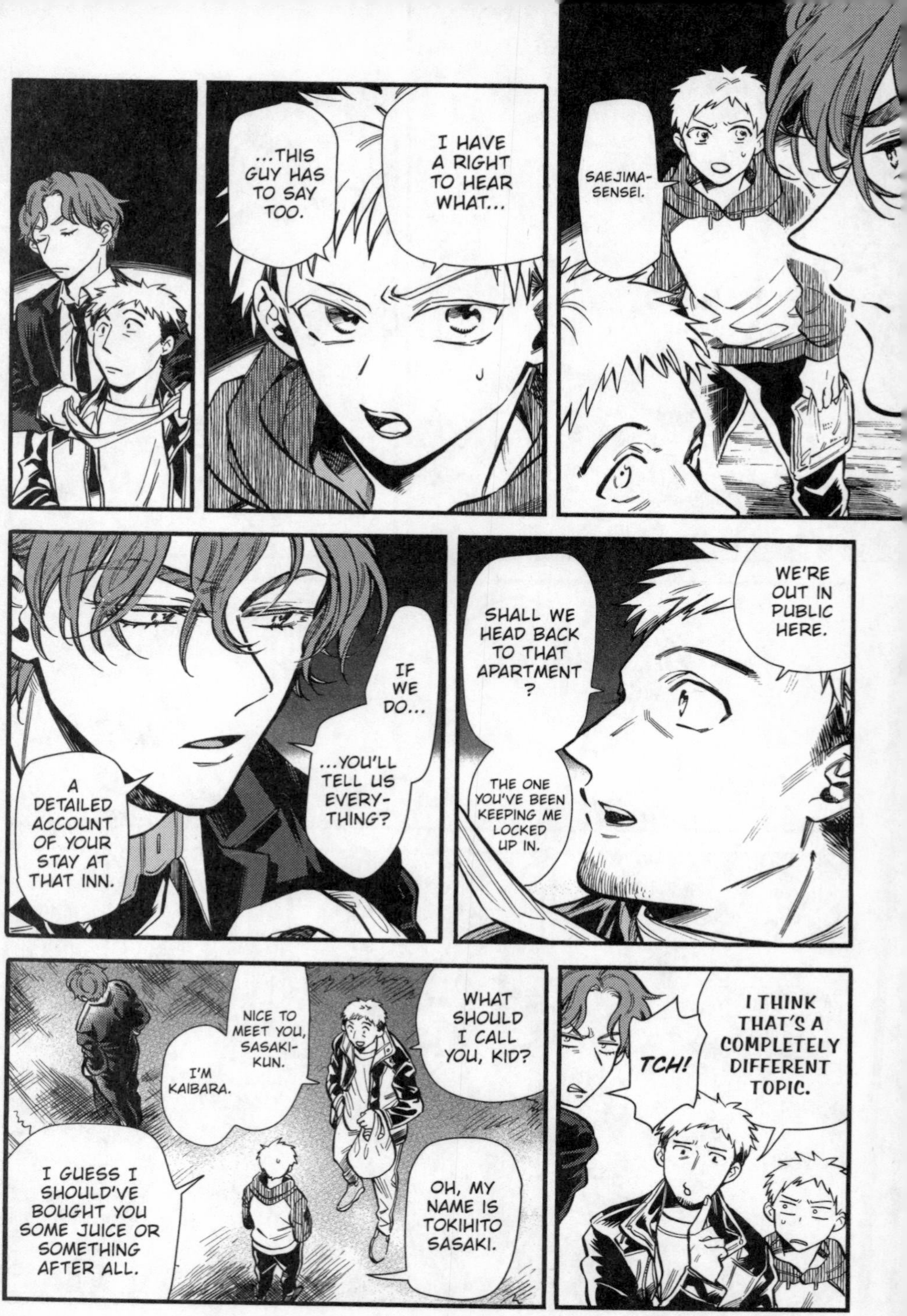
SAEJIMA-SENSEI.
I HAVE A RIGHT TO HEAR WHAT...
...THIS GUY HAS TO SAY TOO.
WE'RE OUT IN PUBLIC HERE.
SHALL WE HEAD BACK TO THAT APARTMENT?
THE ONE YOU'VE BEEN KEEPING ME LOCKED UP IN.
IF WE DO...
...YOU'LL TELL US EVERYTHING?
A DETAILED ACCOUNT OF YOUR STAY AT THAT INN.
I THINK THAT'S A COMPLETELY DIFFERENT TOPIC.
TCH!
WHAT SHOULD I CALL YOU, KID?
OH, MY NAME IS TOKIHITO SASAKI.
NICE TO MEET YOU, SASAKI-KUN.
I'M KAIBARA.
I GUESS I SHOULD'VE BOUGHT YOU SOME JUICE OR SOMETHING AFTER ALL.

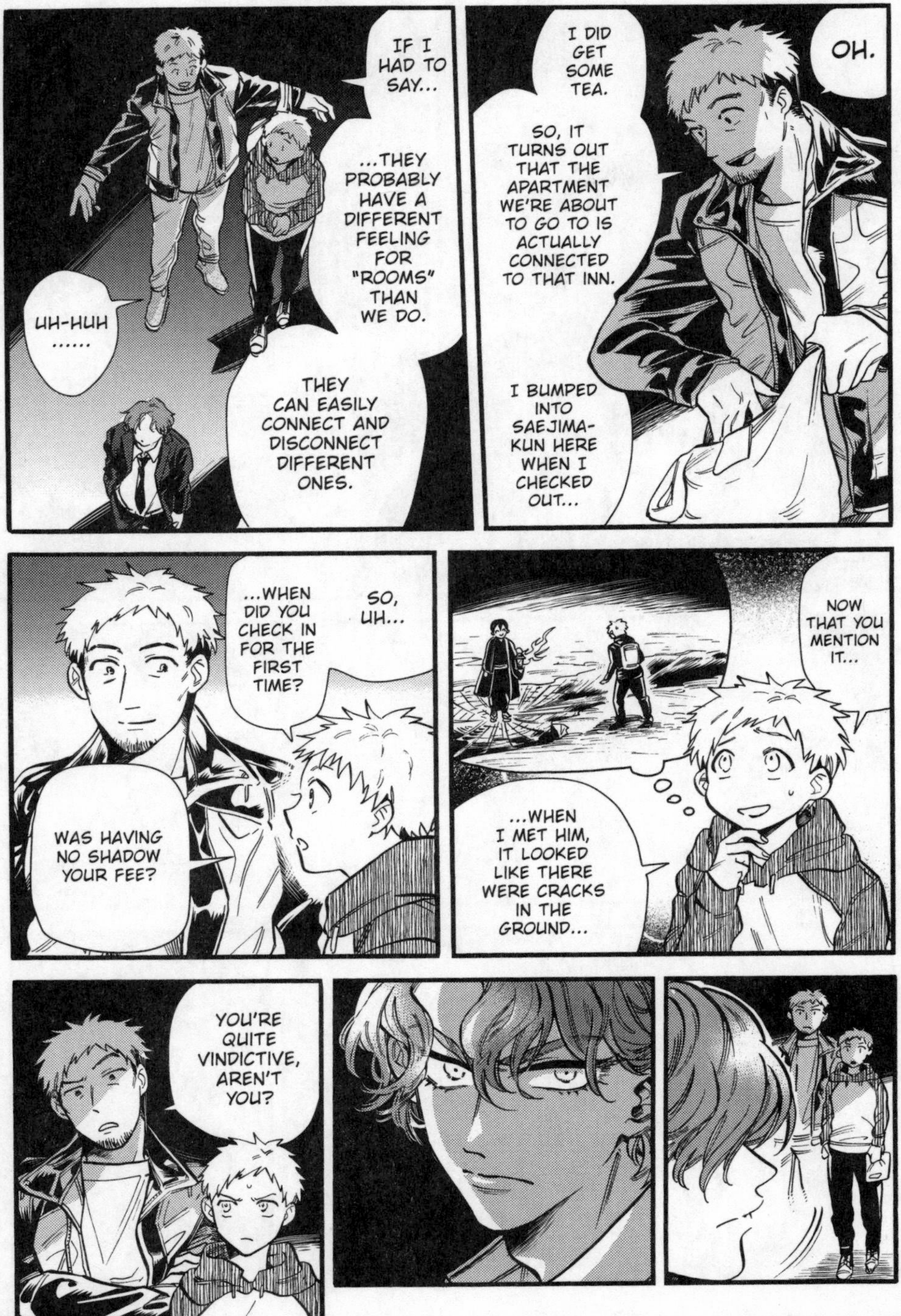
OH.
I DID GET SOME TEA.
SO, IT TURNS OUT THAT THE APARTMENT WE'RE ABOUT TO GO TO IS ACTUALLY CONNECTED TO THAT INN.
I BUMPED INTO SAEJIMA-KUN HERE WHEN I CHECKED OUT...
IF I HAD TO SAY...
...THEY PROBABLY HAVE A DIFFERENT FEELING FOR "ROOMS" THAN WE DO.
UH-HUH ......
THEY CAN EASILY CONNECT AND DISCONNECT DIFFERENT ONES.
NOW THAT YOU MENTION IT...
...WHEN I MET HIM, IT LOOKED LIKE THERE WERE CRACKS IN THE GROUND...
SO, UH...
...WHEN DID YOU CHECK IN FOR THE FIRST TIME?
WAS HAVING NO SHADOW YOUR FEE?
YOU'RE QUITE VINDICTIVE, AREN'T YOU?

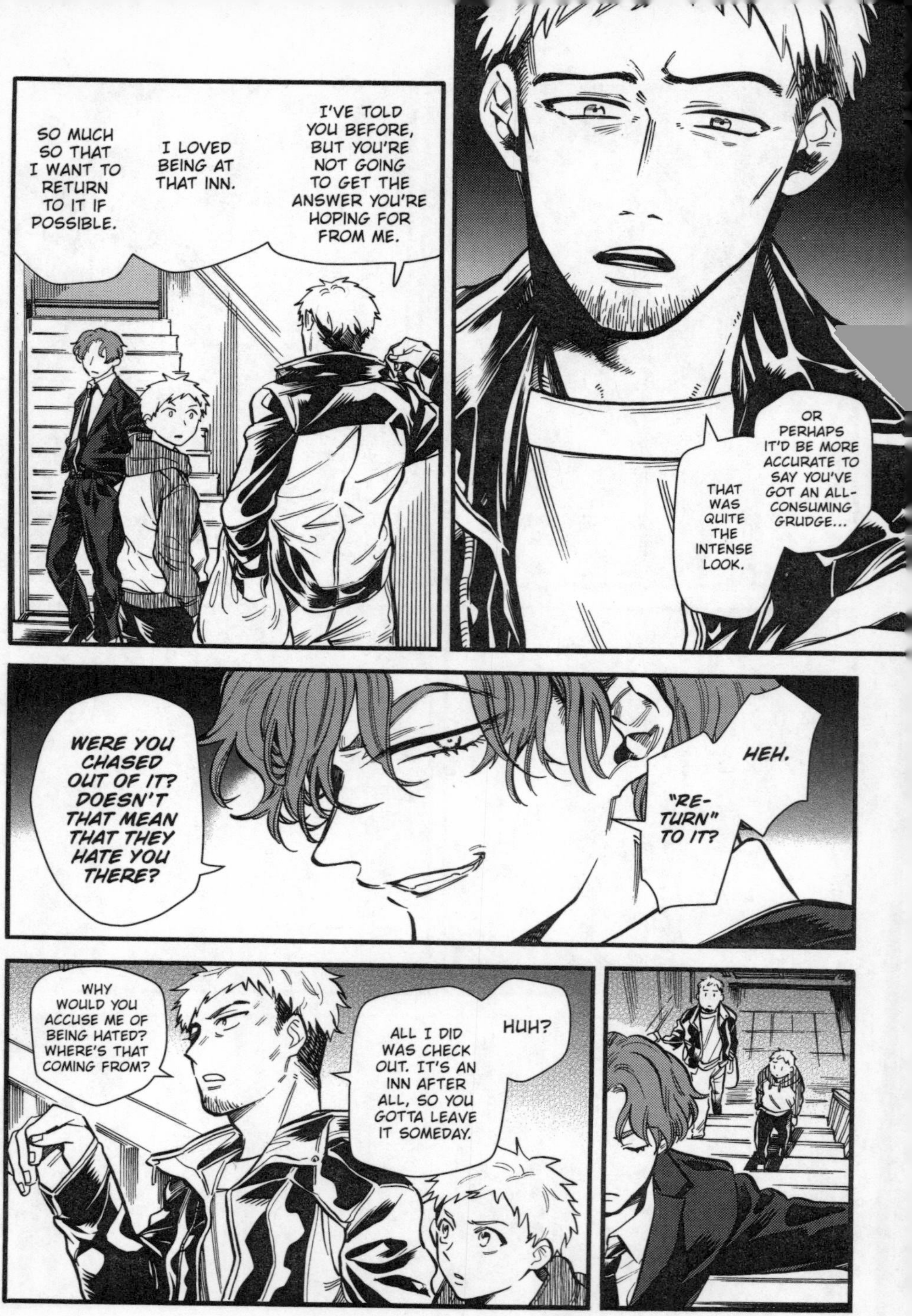
OR PERHAPS IT'D BE MORE ACCURATE TO SAY YOU'VE GOT AN ALL-CONSUMING GRUDGE...
THAT WAS QUITE THE INTENSE LOOK.
I'VE TOLD YOU BEFORE, BUT YOU'RE NOT GOING TO GET THE ANSWER YOU'RE HOPING FOR FROM ME.
I LOVED BEING AT THAT INN.
SO MUCH SO THAT I WANT TO RETURN TO IT IF POSSIBLE.
HEH.
"RE-TURN" TO IT?
WERE YOU CHASED OUT OF IT? DOESN'T THAT MEAN THAT THEY HATE YOU THERE?
HUH?
ALL I DID WAS CHECK OUT. IT'S AN INN AFTER ALL, SO YOU GOTTA LEAVE IT SOMEDAY.
WHY WOULD YOU ACCUSE ME OF BEING HATED? WHERE'S THAT COMING FROM?

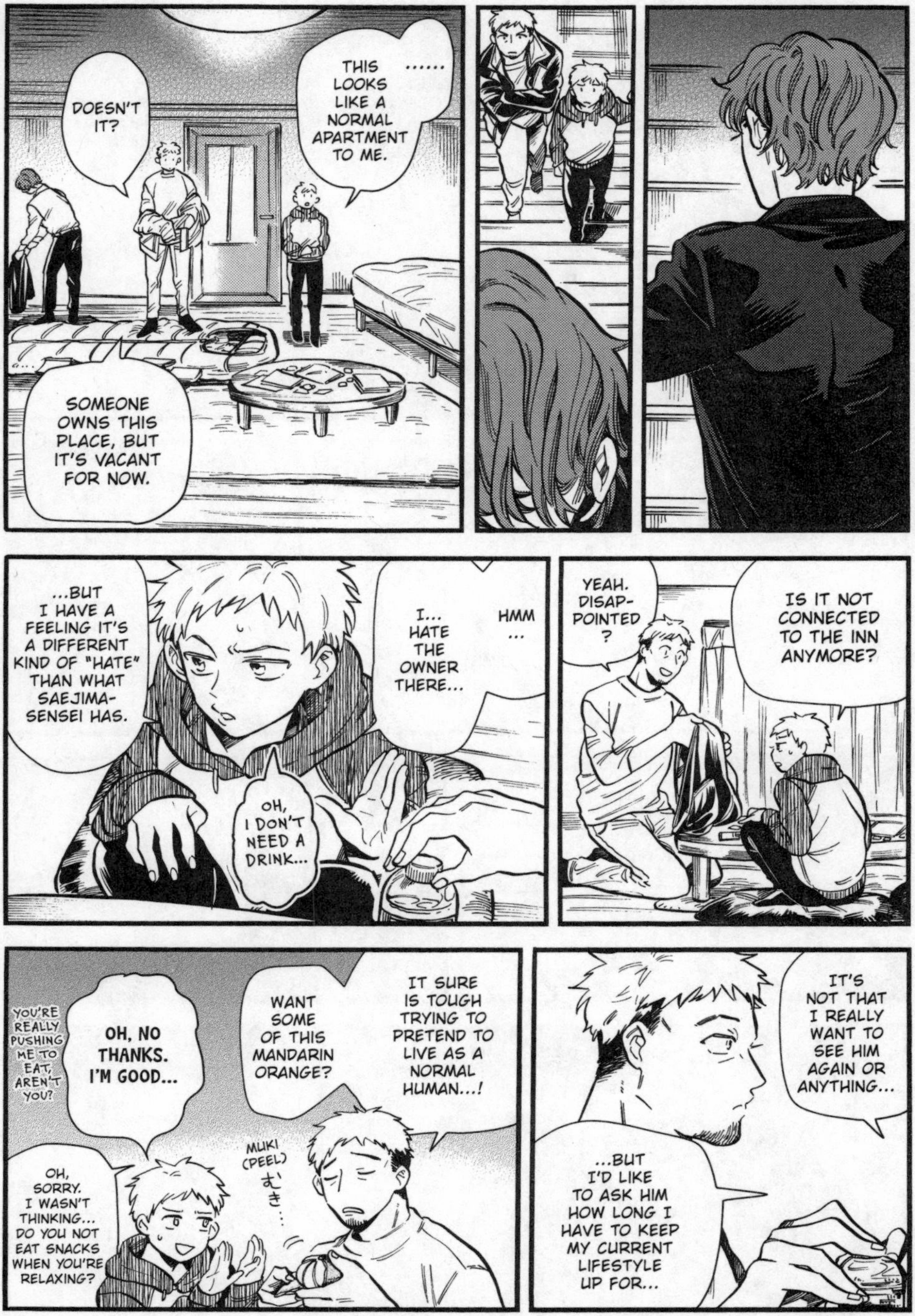
......
THIS LOOKS LIKE A NORMAL APARTMENT TO ME.
DOESN'T IT?
SOMEONE OWNS THIS PLACE, BUT IT'S VACANT FOR NOW.
IS IT NOT CONNECTED TO THE INN ANYMORE?
YEAH. DISAP-POINTED?
HMM ...
I... HATE THE OWNER THERE...
...BUT I HAVE A FEELING IT'S A DIFFERENT KIND OF "HATE" THAN WHAT SAEJIMA-SENSEI HAS.
OH, I DON'T NEED A DRINK...
IT'S NOT THAT I REALLY WANT TO SEE HIM AGAIN OR ANYTHING...
...BUT I'D LIKE TO ASK HIM HOW LONG I HAVE TO KEEP MY CURRENT LIFESTYLE UP FOR...
IT SURE IS TOUGH TRYING TO PRETEND TO LIVE AS A NORMAL HUMAN...!
WANT SOME OF THIS MANDARIN ORANGE?
OH, NO THANKS. I'M GOOD...
YOU'RE REALLY PUSHING ME TO EAT, AREN'T YOU?
MUKI (PEEL) むき…
OH, SORRY. I WASN'T THINKING... DO YOU NOT EAT SNACKS WHEN YOU'RE RELAXING?

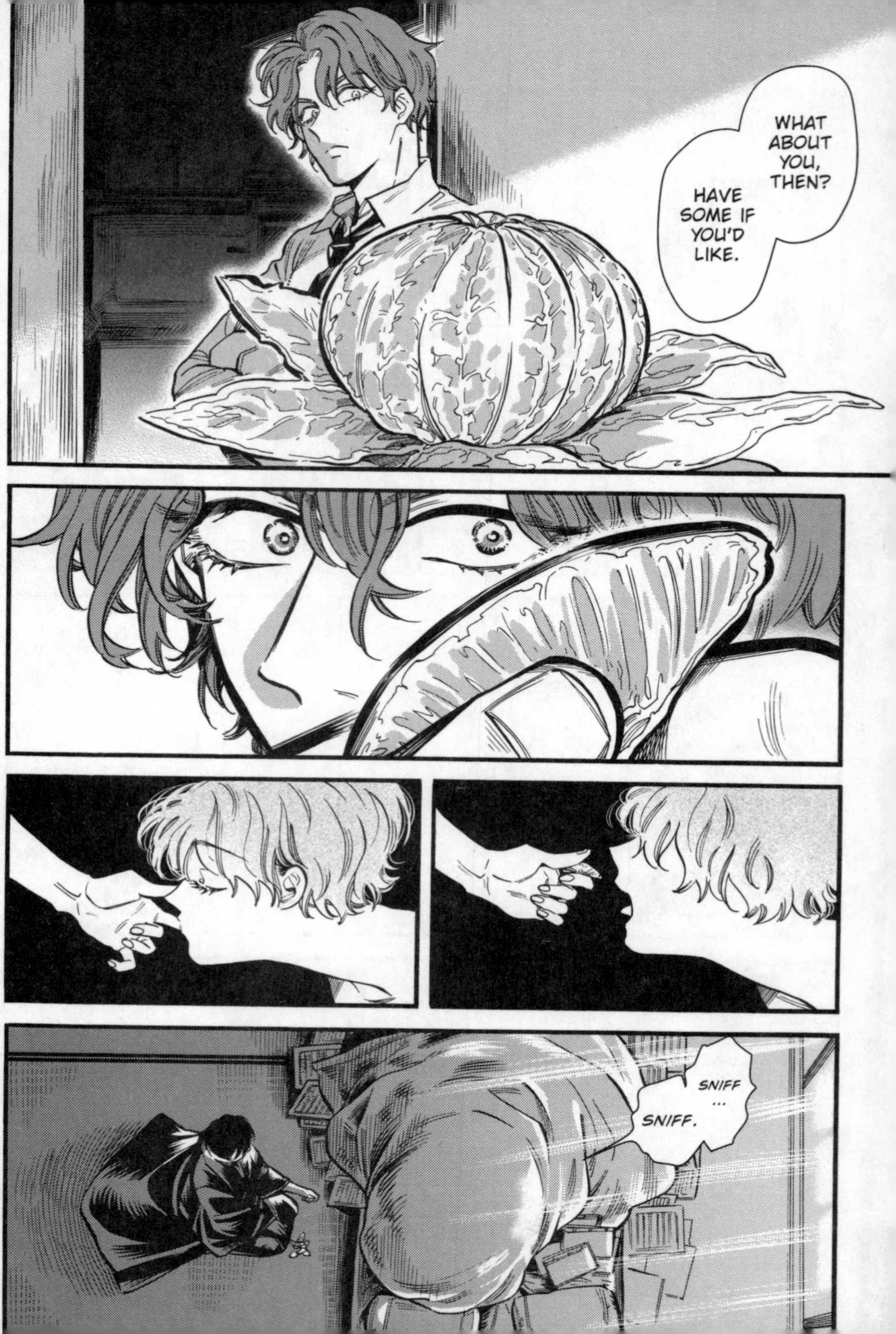
WHAT ABOUT YOU, THEN?
HAVE SOME IF YOU'D LIKE.
SNIFF ... SNIFF.

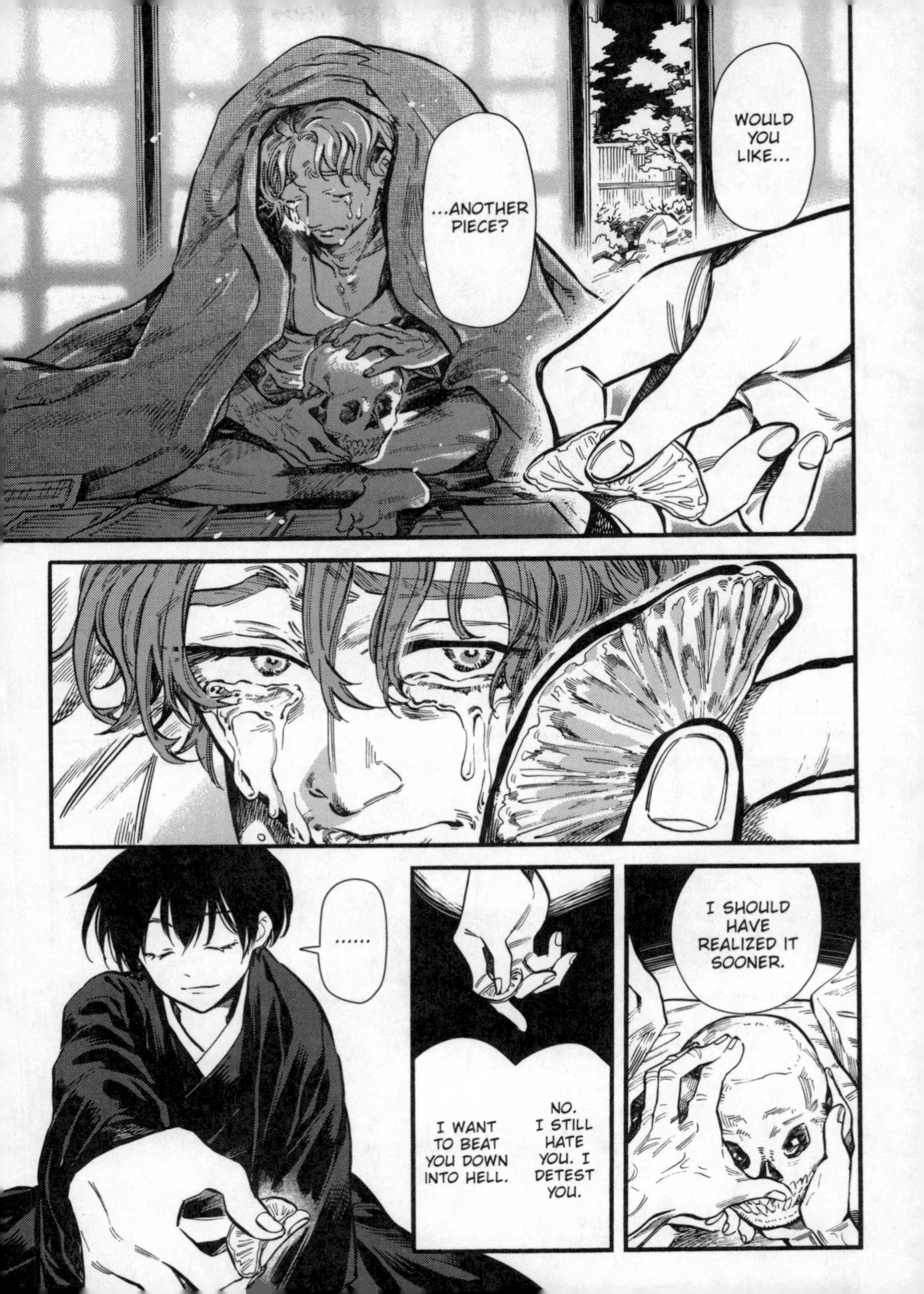
WOULD YOU LIKE...
...ANOTHER PIECE?
I SHOULD HAVE REALIZED IT SOONER.
NO. I STILL HATE YOU. I DETEST YOU.
I WANT TO BEAT YOU DOWN INTO HELL.
......

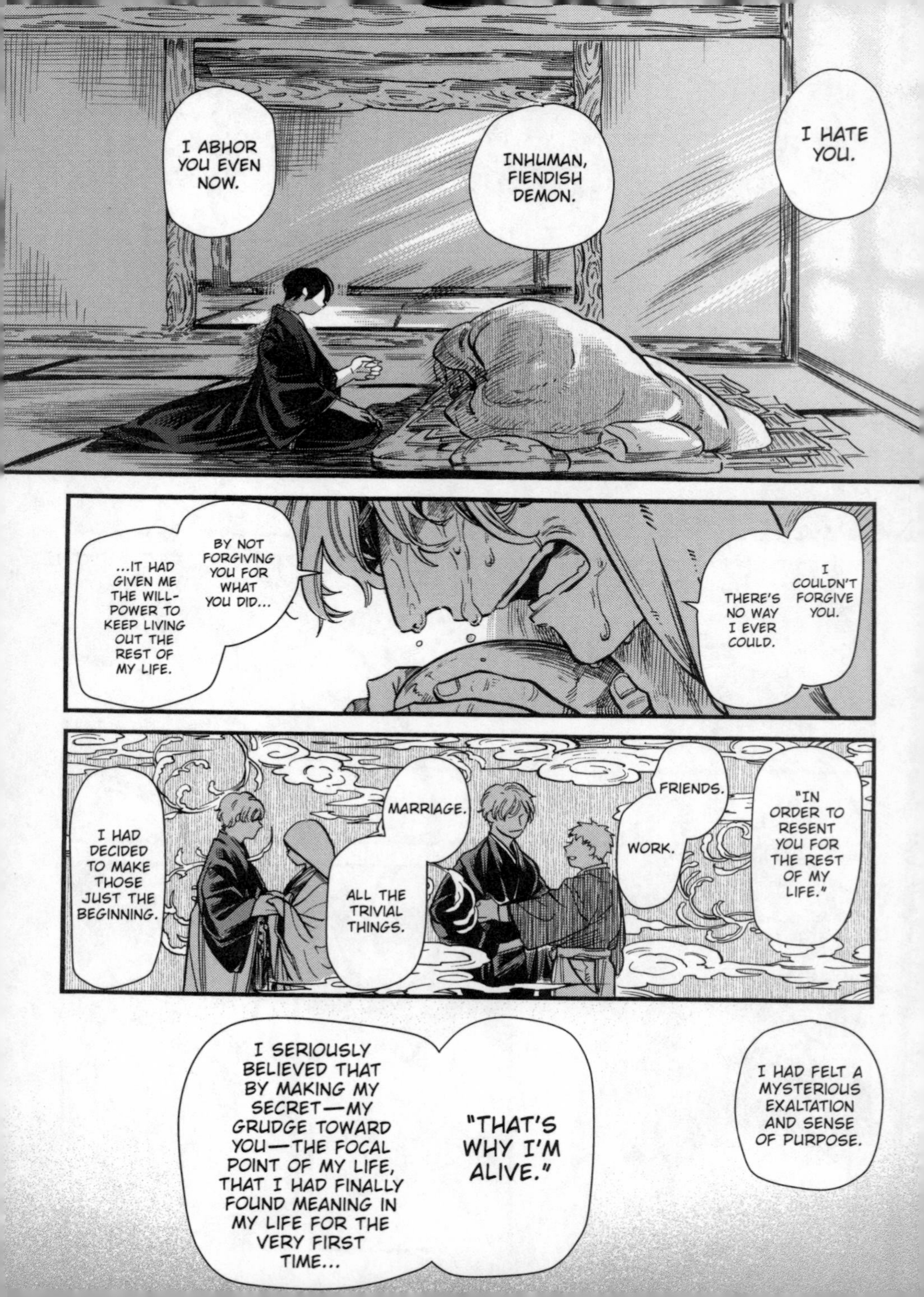
I HATE YOU.
INHUMAN, FIENDISH DEMON.
I ABHOR YOU EVEN NOW.
I COULDN'T FORGIVE YOU.
THERE'S NO WAY I EVER COULD.
BY NOT FORGIVING YOU FOR WHAT YOU DID...
...IT HAD GIVEN ME THE WILL-POWER TO KEEP LIVING OUT THE REST OF MY LIFE.
"IN ORDER TO RESENT YOU FOR THE REST OF MY LIFE."
FRIENDS.
WORK.
MARRIAGE.
ALL THE TRIVIAL THINGS.
I HAD DECIDED TO MAKE THOSE JUST THE BEGINNING.
I HAD FELT A MYSTERIOUS EXALTATION AND SENSE OF PURPOSE.
"THAT'S WHY I'M ALIVE."
I SERIOUSLY BELIEVED THAT BY MAKING MY SECRET—MY GRUDGE TOWARD YOU—THE FOCAL POINT OF MY LIFE, THAT I HAD FINALLY FOUND MEANING IN MY LIFE FOR THE VERY FIRST TIME...

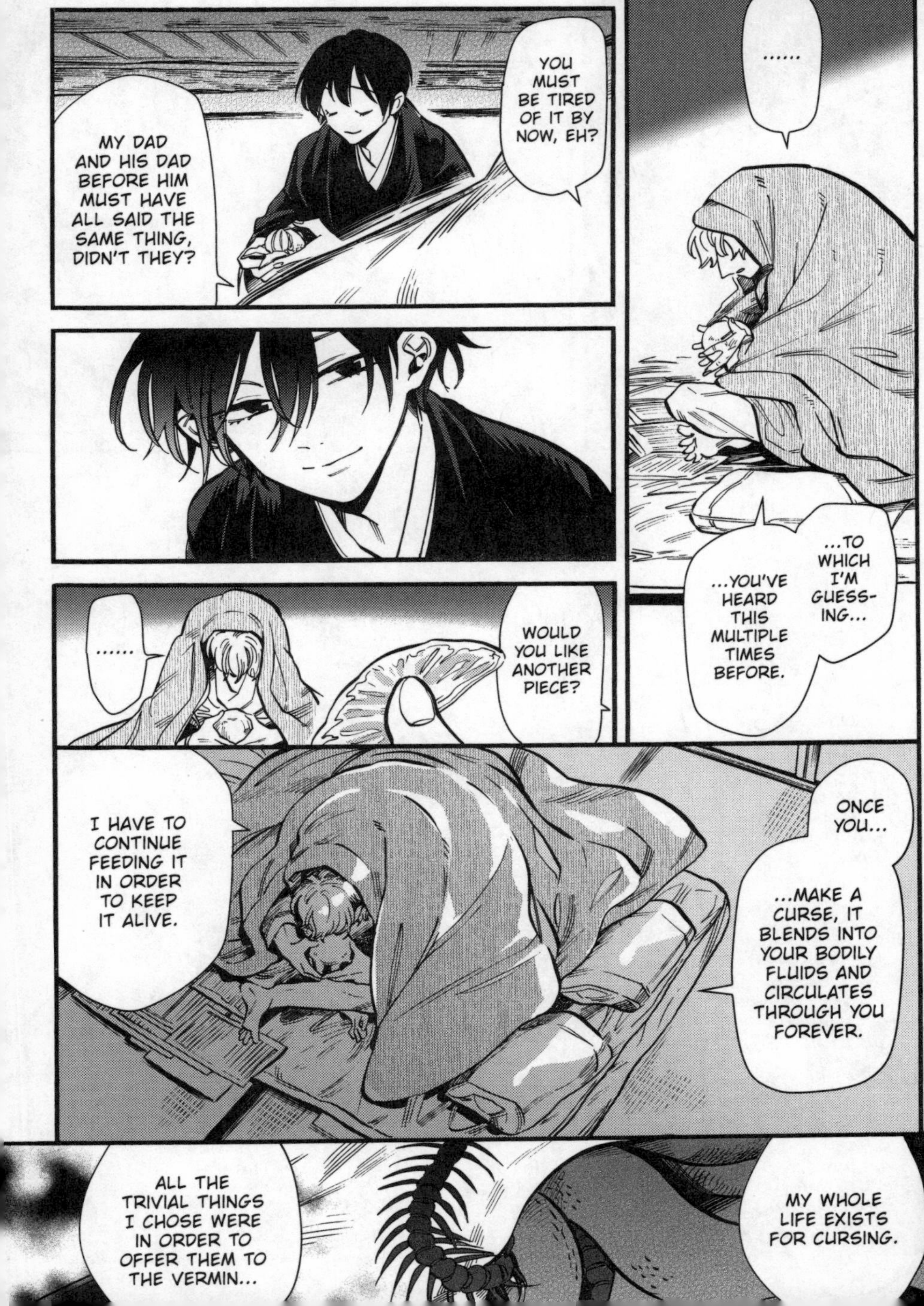
......
...TO WHICH I'M GUESSING...
...YOU'VE HEARD THIS MULTIPLE TIMES BEFORE.
YOU MUST BE TIRED OF IT BY NOW, EH?
MY DAD AND HIS DAD BEFORE HIM MUST HAVE ALL SAID THE SAME THING, DIDN'T THEY?
WOULD YOU LIKE ANOTHER PIECE?
......
ONCE YOU...
...MAKE A CURSE, IT BLENDS INTO YOUR BODILY FLUIDS AND CIRCULATES THROUGH YOU FOREVER.
I HAVE TO CONTINUE FEEDING IT IN ORDER TO KEEP IT ALIVE.
MY WHOLE LIFE EXISTS FOR CURSING.
ALL THE TRIVIAL THINGS I CHOSE WERE IN ORDER TO OFFER THEM TO THE VERMIN...

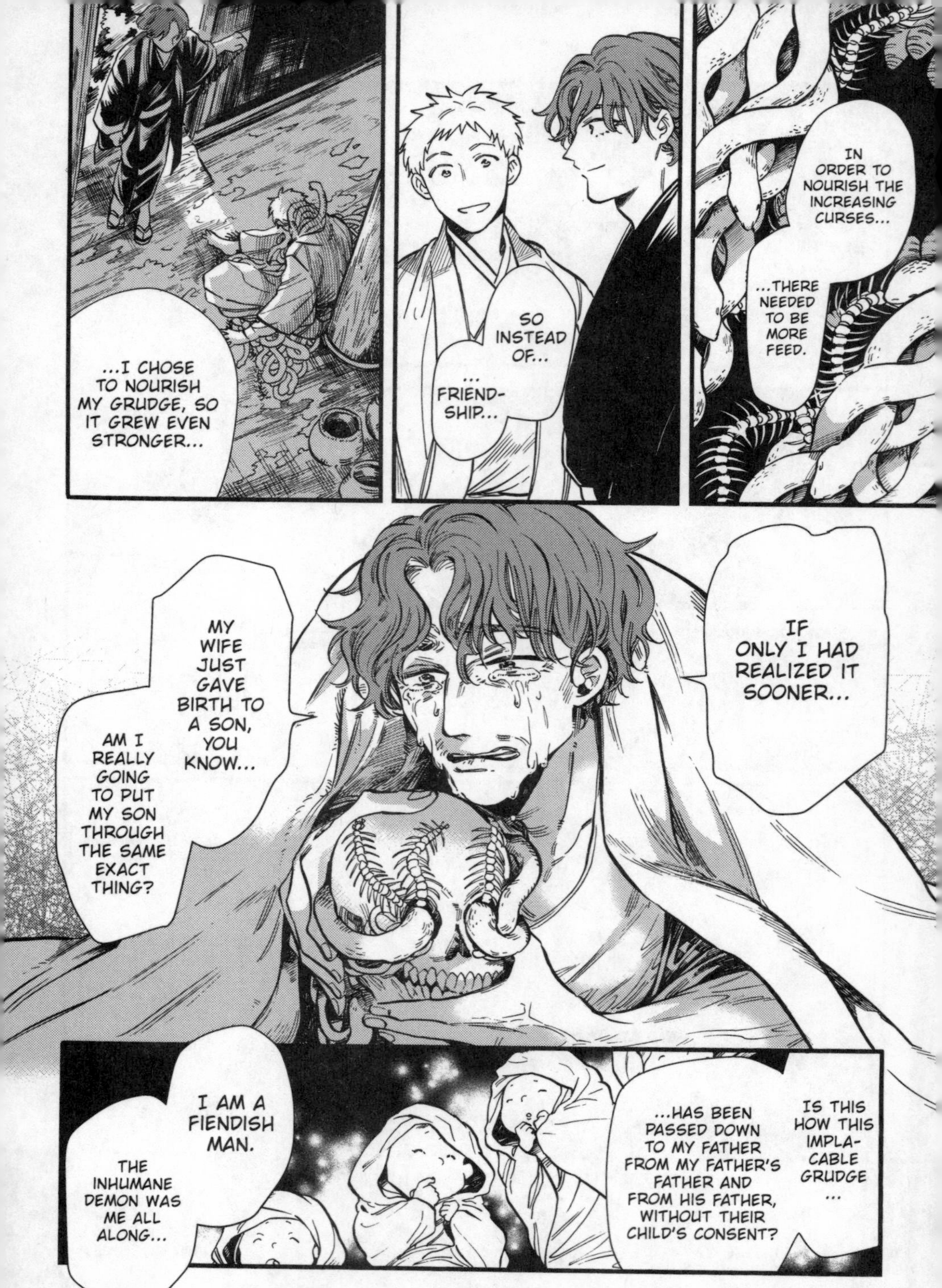
IN ORDER TO NOURISH THE INCREASING CURSES...
...THERE NEEDED TO BE MORE FEED.
SO INSTEAD OF...
...FRIENDSHIP...
...I CHOSE TO NOURISH MY GRUDGE, SO IT GREW EVEN STRONGER...
IF ONLY I HAD REALIZED IT SOONER...
MY WIFE JUST GAVE BIRTH TO A SON, YOU KNOW...
AM I REALLY GOING TO PUT MY SON THROUGH THE SAME EXACT THING?
IS THIS HOW THIS IMPLACABLE GRUDGE...
...HAS BEEN PASSED DOWN TO MY FATHER FROM MY FATHER'S FATHER AND FROM HIS FATHER, WITHOUT THEIR CHILD'S CONSENT?
I AM A FIENDISH MAN.
THE INHUMANE DEMON WAS ME ALL ALONG...

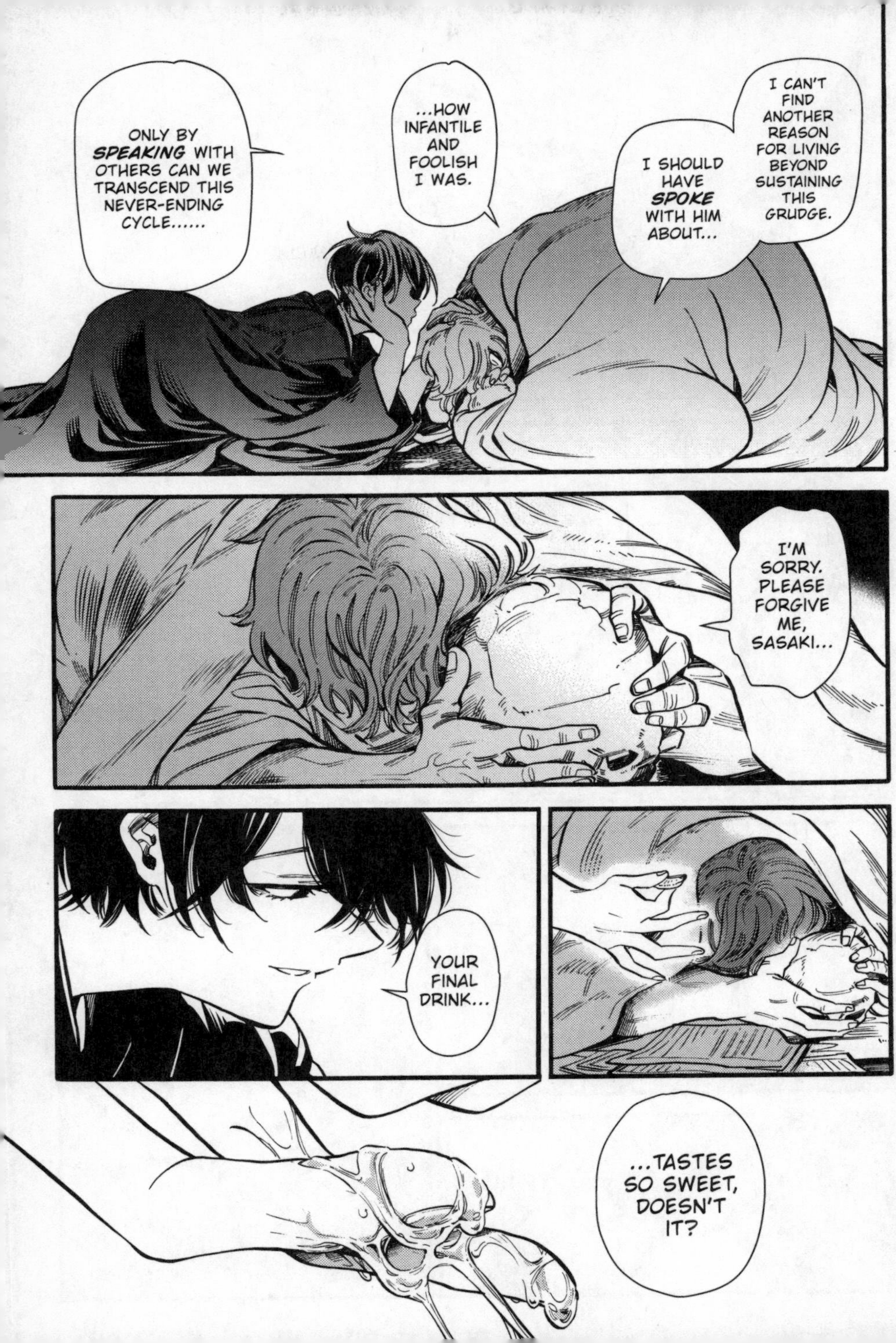
I CAN'T FIND ANOTHER REASON FOR LIVING BEYOND SUSTAINING THIS GRUDGE.
I SHOULD HAVE SPOKE WITH HIM ABOUT...
...HOW INFANTILE AND FOOLISH I WAS.
ONLY BY SPEAKING WITH OTHERS CAN WE TRANSCEND THIS NEVER-ENDING CYCLE......
I'M SORRY. PLEASE FORGIVE ME, SASAKI...
YOUR FINAL DRINK...
...TASTES SO SWEET, DOESN'T IT?

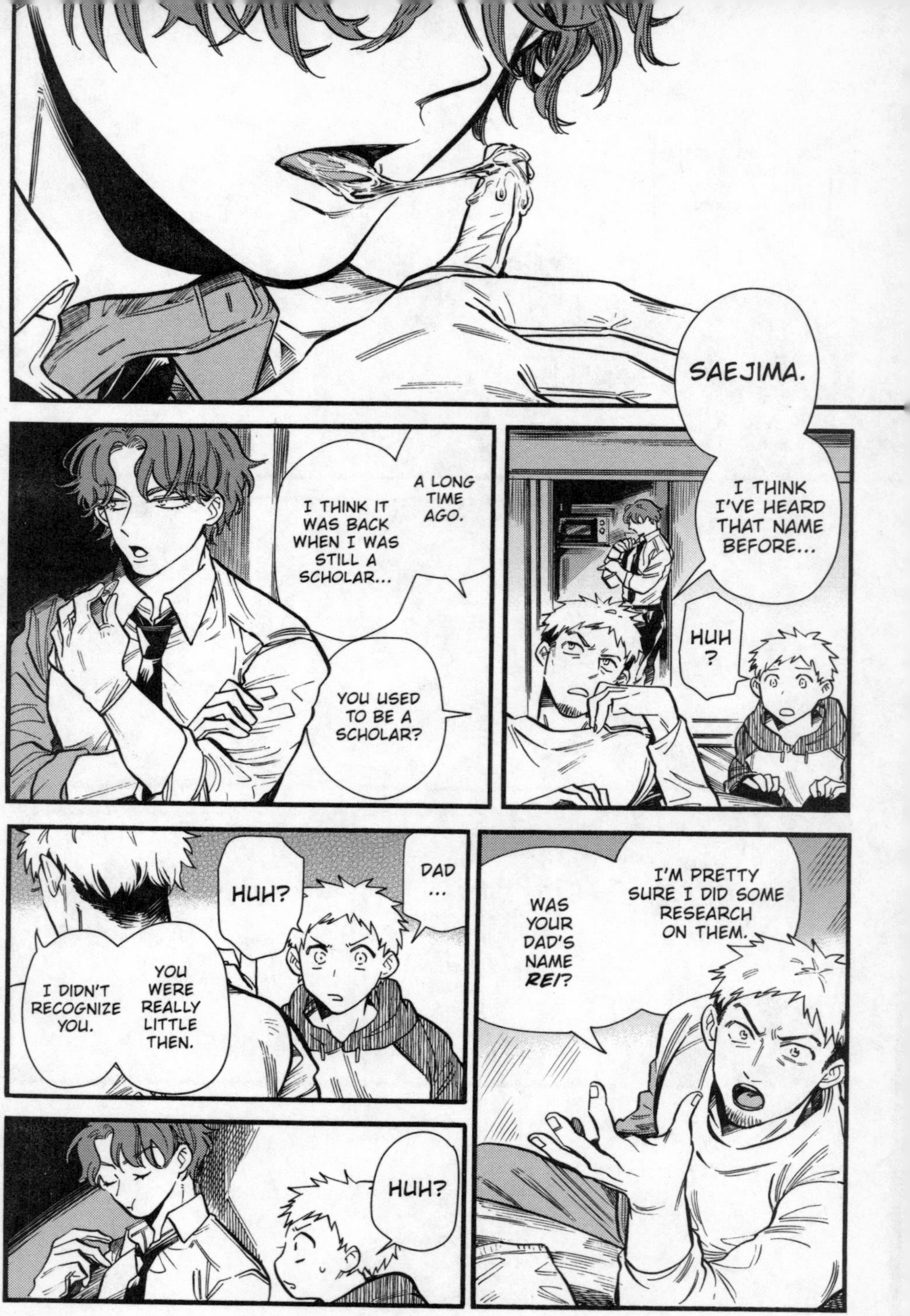
SAEJIMA.
I THINK I'VE HEARD THAT NAME BEFORE...
HUH?
A LONG TIME AGO.
I THINK IT WAS BACK WHEN I WAS STILL A SCHOLAR...
YOU USED TO BE A SCHOLAR?
I'M PRETTY SURE I DID SOME RESEARCH ON THEM.
WAS YOUR DAD'S NAME *REI*?
DAD ...
HUH?
YOU WERE REALLY LITTLE THEN.
I DIDN'T RECOGNIZE YOU.
HUH?

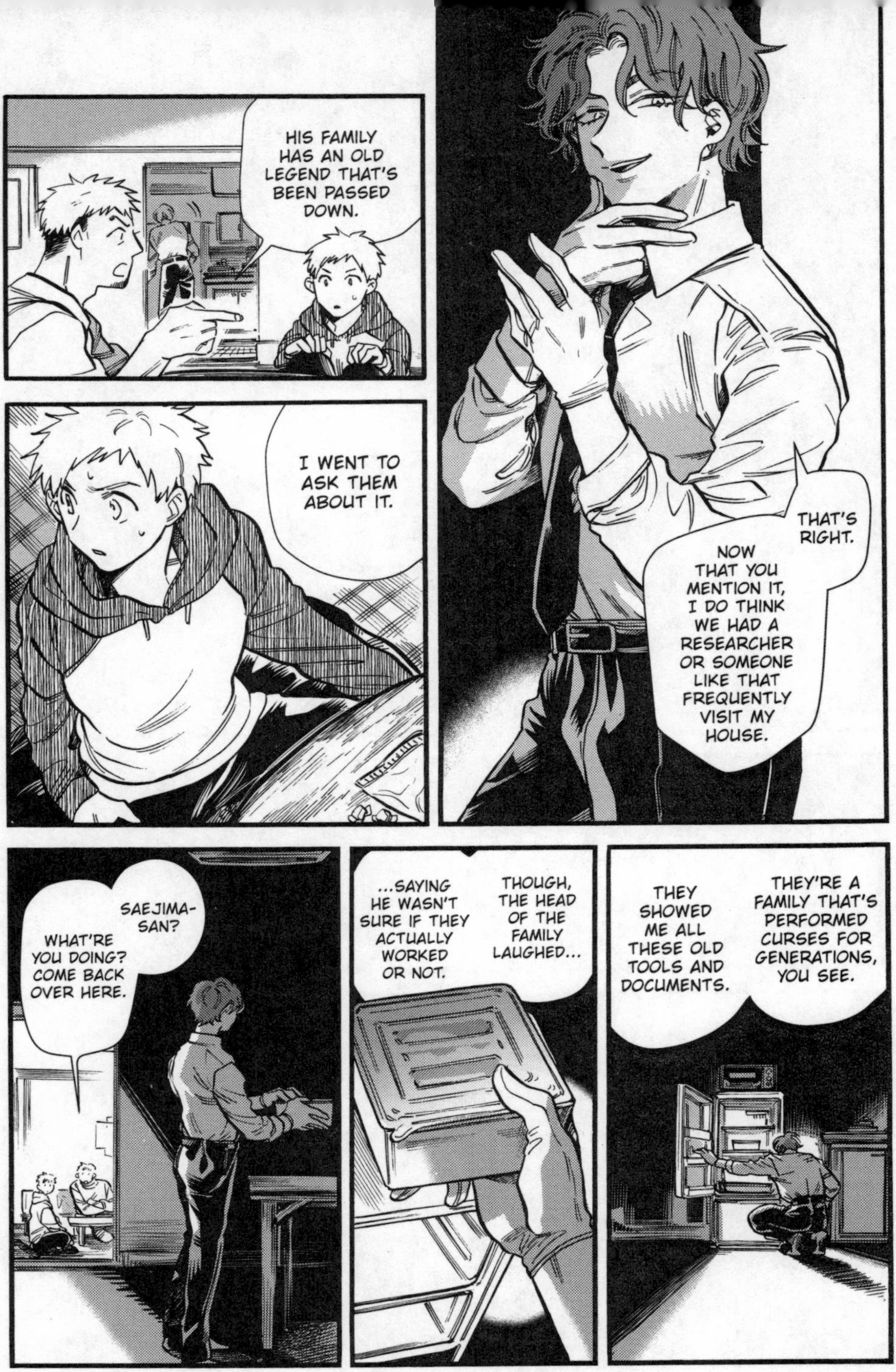
THAT'S RIGHT.
NOW THAT YOU MENTION IT, I DO THINK WE HAD A RESEARCHER OR SOMEONE LIKE THAT FREQUENTLY VISIT MY HOUSE.
HIS FAMILY HAS AN OLD LEGEND THAT'S BEEN PASSED DOWN.
I WENT TO ASK THEM ABOUT IT.
THEY'RE A FAMILY THAT'S PERFORMED CURSES FOR GENERATIONS, YOU SEE.
THEY SHOWED ME ALL THESE OLD TOOLS AND DOCUMENTS.
THOUGH, THE HEAD OF THE FAMILY LAUGHED...
...SAYING HE WASN'T SURE IF THEY ACTUALLY WORKED OR NOT.
SAEJIMA-SAN?
WHAT'RE YOU DOING? COME BACK OVER HERE.

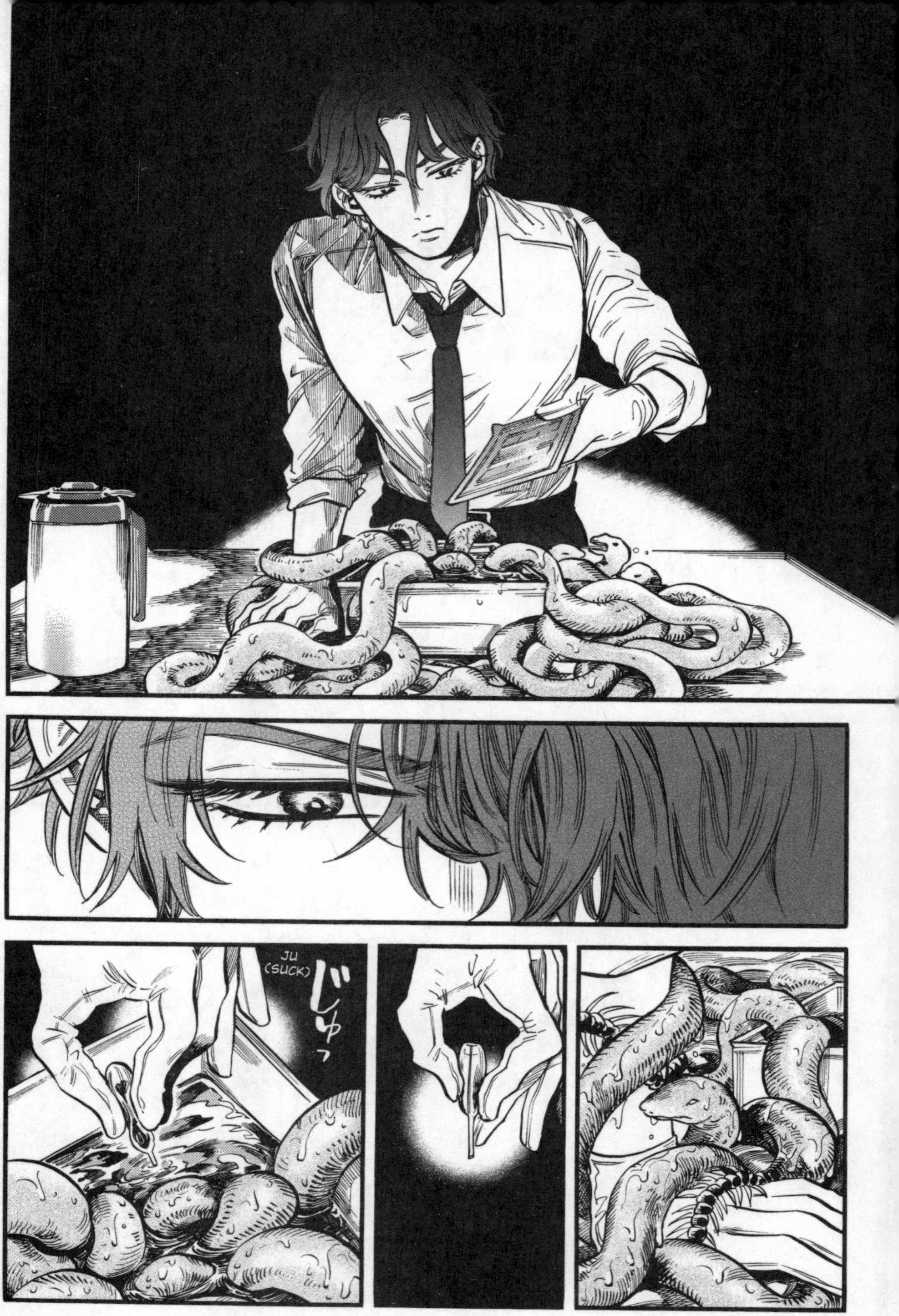
JU (SUCK)
じゅっ

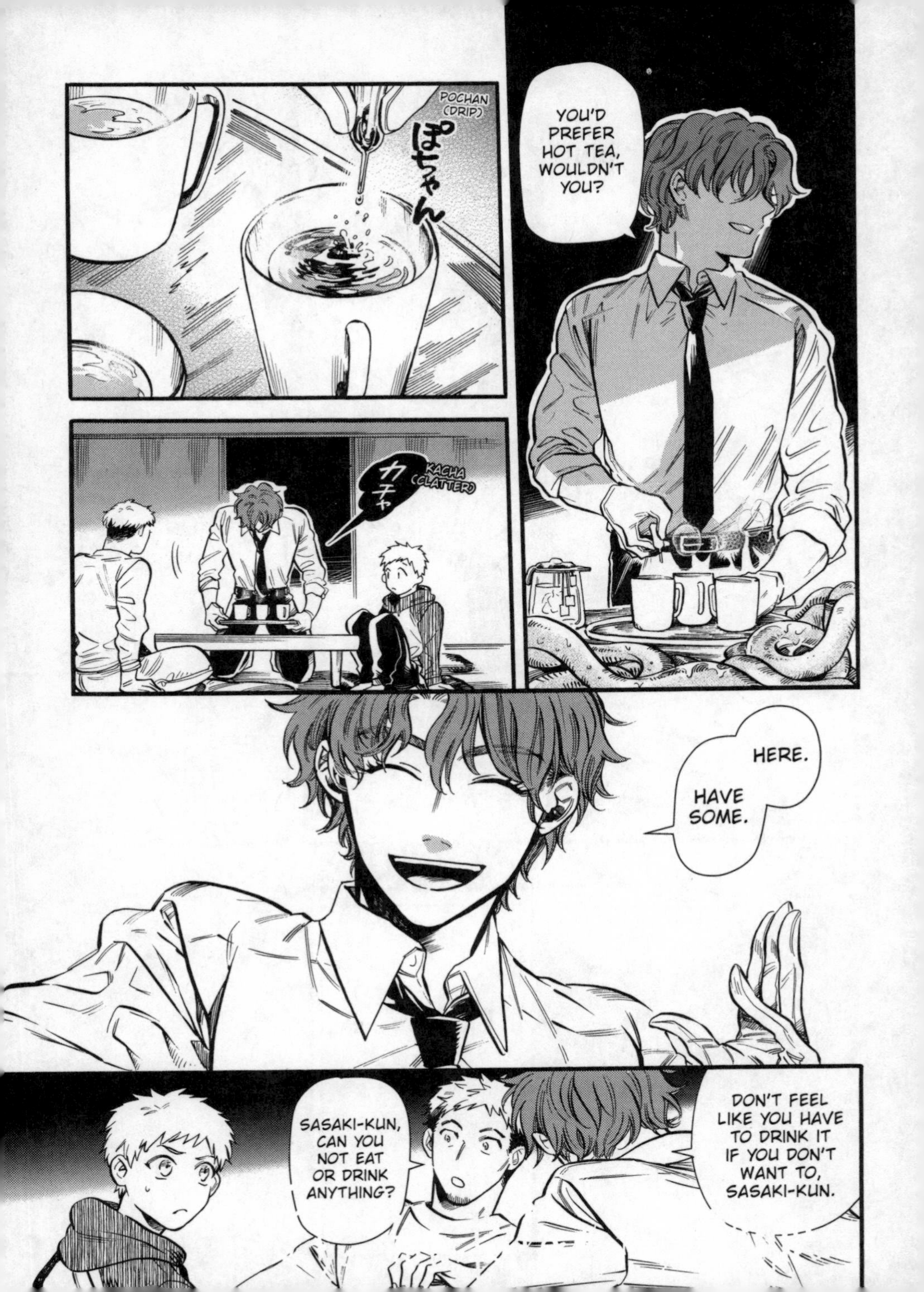
YOU'D PREFER HOT TEA, WOULDN'T YOU?
ぽちゃん
POCHAN (DRIP)
カチャ
KACHA (CLATTER)
HERE.
HAVE SOME.
DON'T FEEL LIKE YOU HAVE TO DRINK IT IF YOU DON'T WANT TO, SASAKI-KUN.
SASAKI-KUN, CAN YOU NOT EAT OR DRINK ANYTHING?

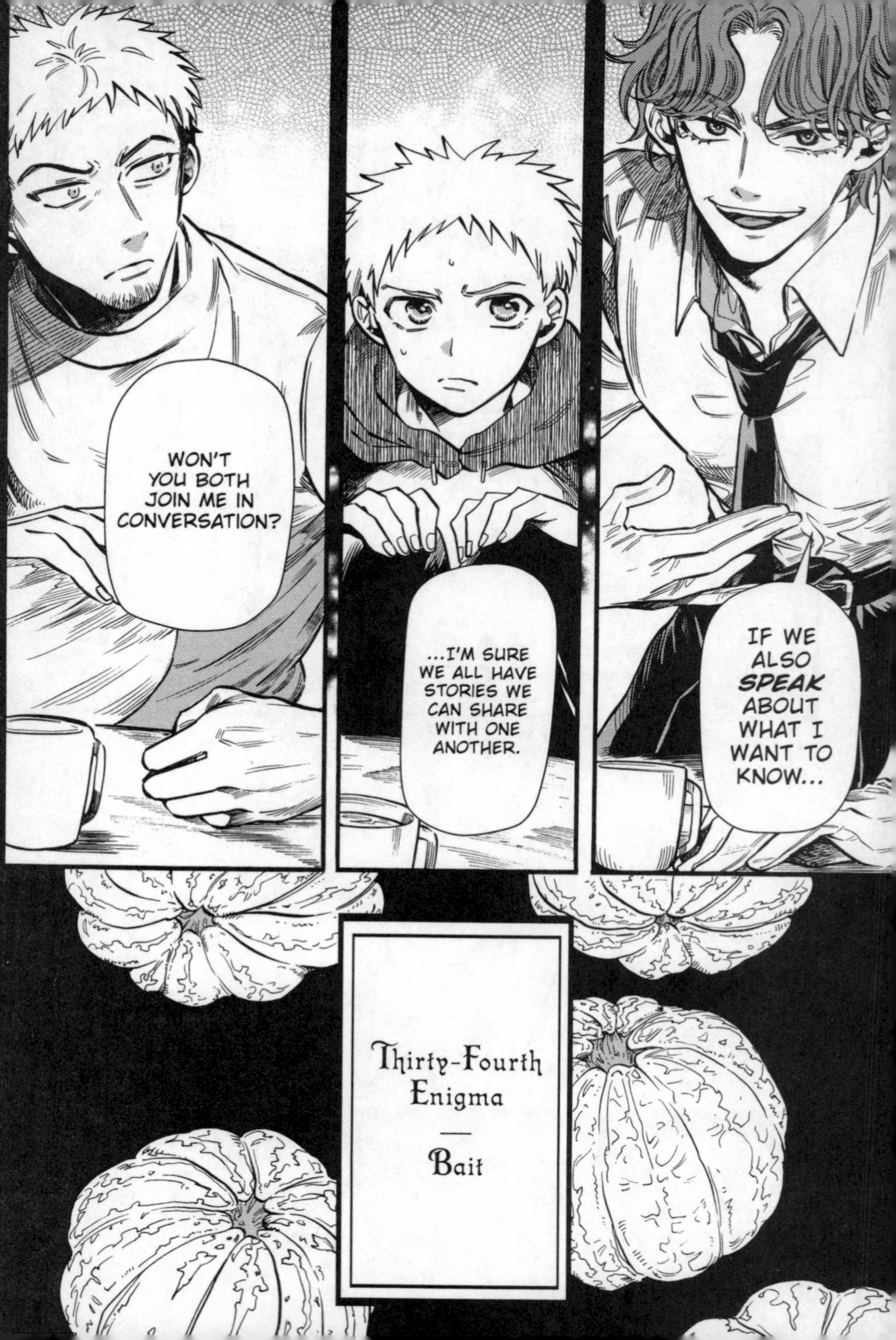
IF WE ALSO **SPEAK** ABOUT WHAT I WANT TO KNOW...
...I'M SURE WE ALL HAVE STORIES WE CAN SHARE WITH ONE ANOTHER.
WON'T YOU BOTH JOIN ME IN CONVERSATION?
Thirty-Fourth Enigma
—
Bait

Phantom Tales of the Night

To be continued in Volume 8

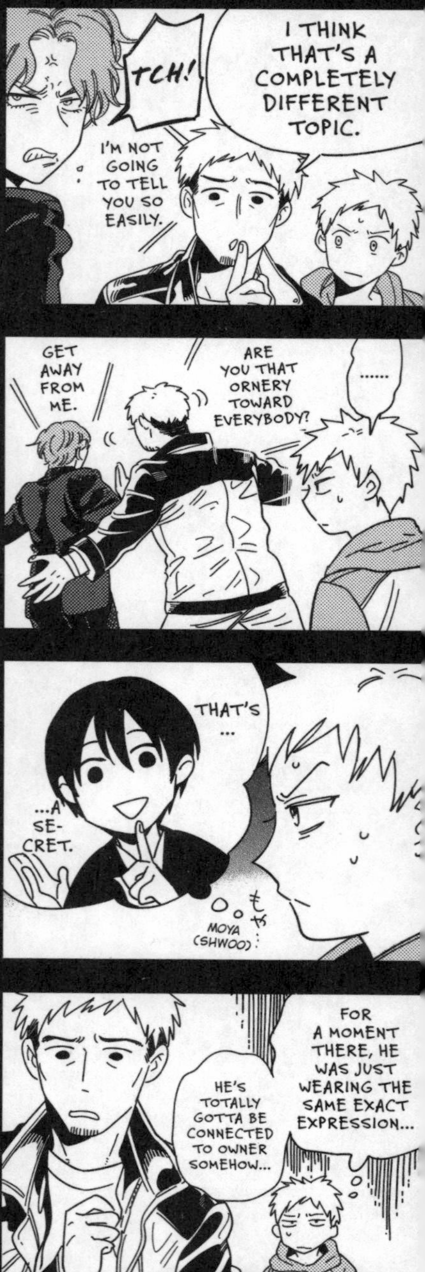
I THINK THAT'S A COMPLETELY DIFFERENT TOPIC.
TCH!
I'M NOT GOING TO TELL YOU SO EASILY.
......
ARE YOU THAT ORNERY TOWARD EVERYBODY?
GET AWAY FROM ME.
THAT'S...
...A SE-CRET.
もや
MOYA (SHWOO)
FOR A MOMENT THERE, HE WAS JUST WEARING THE SAME EXACT EXPRESSION...
HE'S TOTALLY GOTTA BE CONNECTED TO OWNER SOMEHOW...
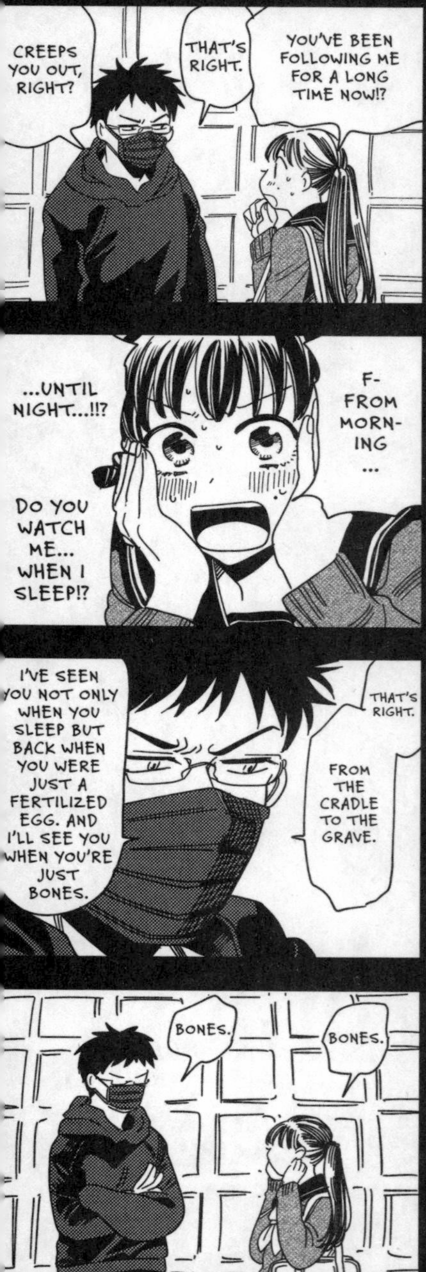
YOU'VE BEEN FOLLOWING ME FOR A LONG TIME NOW!?
THAT'S RIGHT.
CREEPS YOU OUT, RIGHT?
F- FROM MORNING...
...UNTIL NIGHT...!!?
DO YOU WATCH ME... WHEN I SLEEP!?
THAT'S RIGHT.
FROM THE CRADLE TO THE GRAVE.
I'VE SEEN YOU NOT ONLY WHEN YOU SLEEP BUT BACK WHEN YOU WERE JUST A FERTILIZED EGG. AND I'LL SEE YOU WHEN YOU'RE JUST BONES.
BONES.
BONES.

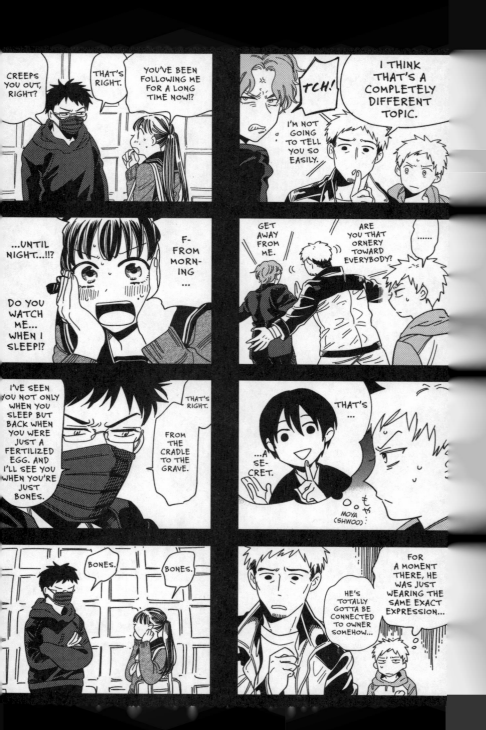

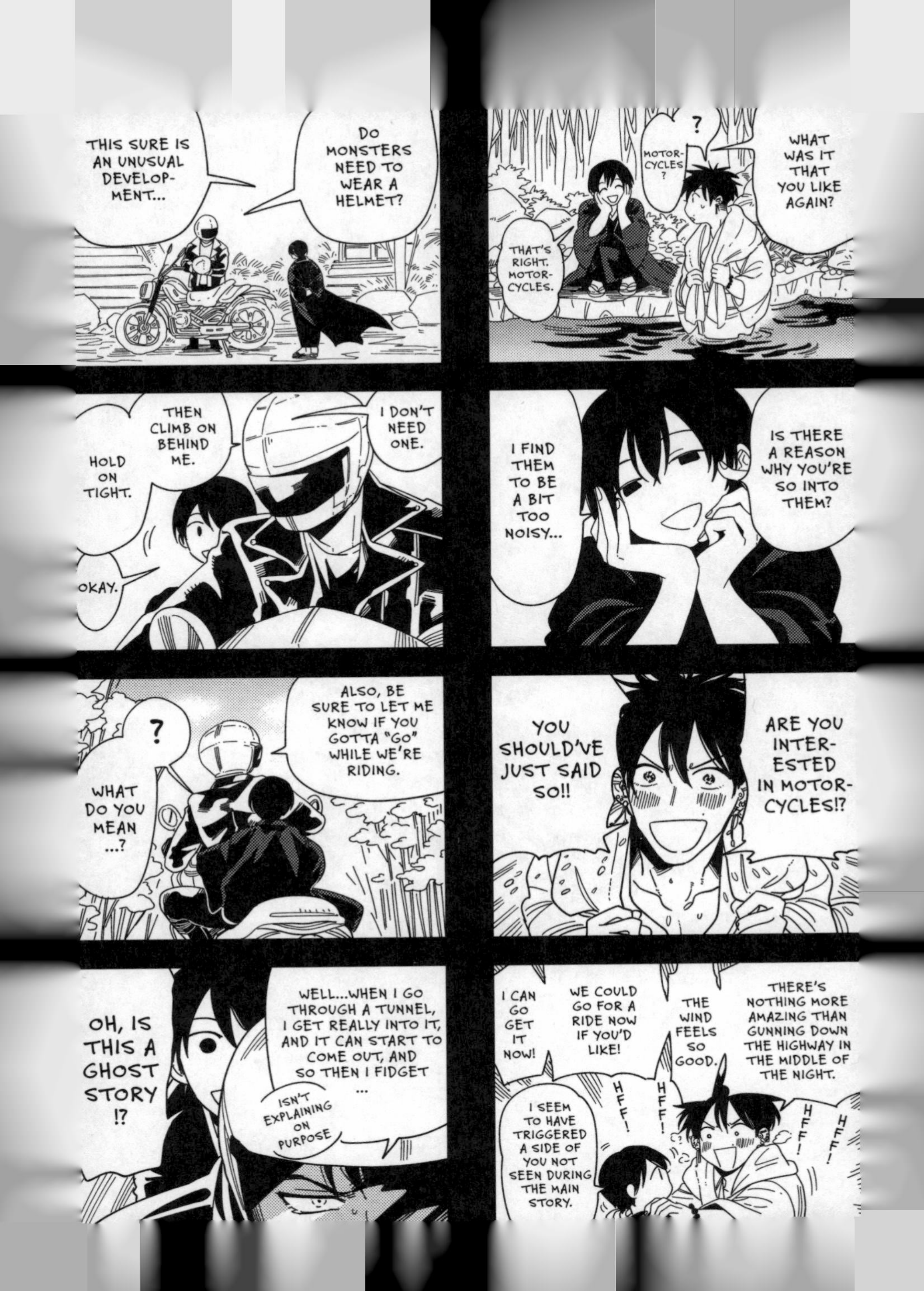
WHAT WAS IT THAT YOU LIKE AGAIN?
?
MOTOR-CYCLES?
THAT'S RIGHT. MOTOR-CYCLES.
DO MONSTERS NEED TO WEAR A HELMET?
THIS SURE IS AN UNUSUAL DEVELOP-MENT...
IS THERE A REASON WHY YOU'RE SO INTO THEM?
I FIND THEM TO BE A BIT TOO NOISY...
I DON'T NEED ONE.
THEN CLIMB ON BEHIND ME.
HOLD ON TIGHT.
OKAY.
ARE YOU INTER-ESTED IN MOTOR-CYCLES!?
YOU SHOULD'VE JUST SAID SO!!
ALSO, BE SURE TO LET ME KNOW IF YOU GOTTA "GO" WHILE WE'RE RIDING.
?
WHAT DO YOU MEAN ...?
THERE'S NOTHING MORE AMAZING THAN GUNNING DOWN THE HIGHWAY IN THE MIDDLE OF THE NIGHT.
THE WIND FEELS SO GOOD.
WE COULD GO FOR A RIDE NOW IF YOU'D LIKE!
I CAN GO GET IT NOW!
HFF! HFF! HFF! HFF!
I SEEM TO HAVE TRIGGERED A SIDE OF YOU NOT SEEN DURING THE MAIN STORY.
WELL...WHEN I GO THROUGH A TUNNEL, I GET REALLY INTO IT, AND IT CAN START TO COME OUT, AND SO THEN I FIDGET ...
ISN'T EXPLAINING ON PURPOSE
OH, IS THIS A GHOST STORY !?

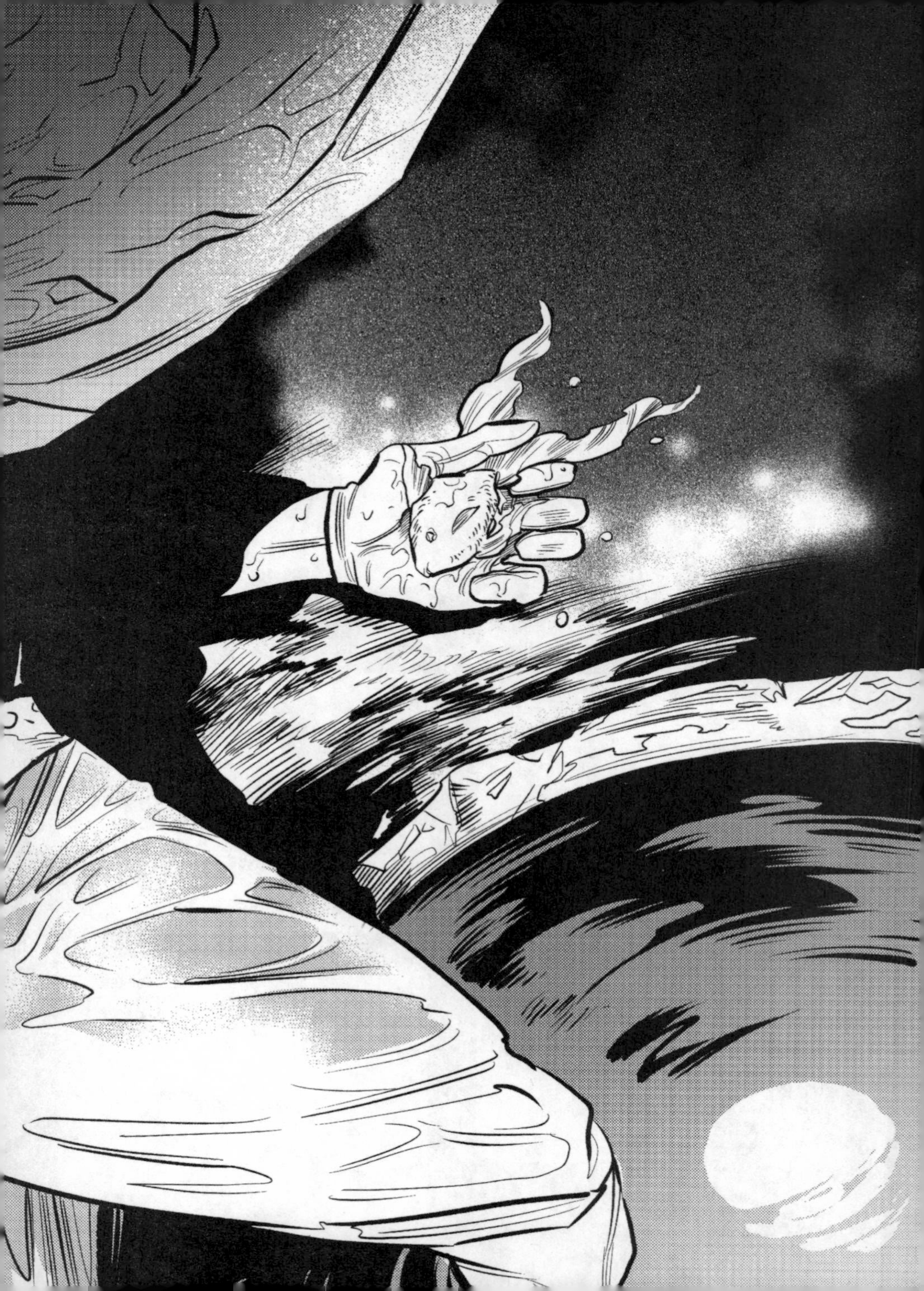

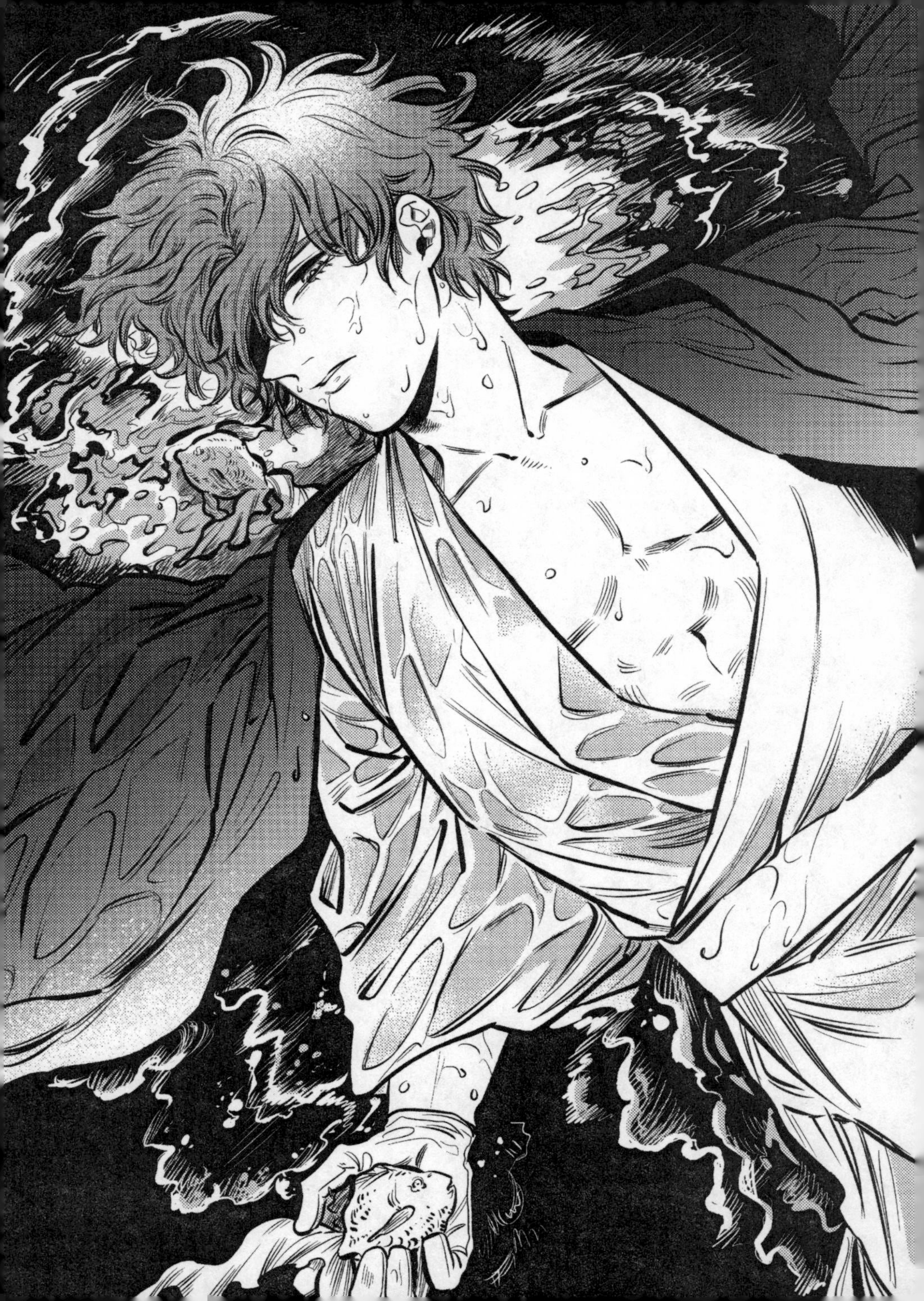

Translation Notes

Common Honorifics

no honorific: Indicates familiarity or closeness; if used without permission or reason, addressing someone in this manner would constitute an insult.

-san: The Japanese equivalent of Mr./Mrs./Miss. If a situation calls for politeness, this is the fail-safe honorific.

-kun: Used most often when referring to boys, this indicates affection or familiarity. Occasionally used by older men among their peers, but it may also be used by anyone referring to a person of lower standing.

-chan: An affectionate honorific indicating familiarity used mostly in reference to girls; also used in reference to cute persons or animals of either gender.

-sensei: A respectful term for teachers, artists, or high-level professionals.

-sama: Conveys great respect; may also indicate that the social status of the speaker is lower than that of the addressee.

(o)nee: Japanese equivalent to "older sister."

(o)nii: Japanese equivalent to "older brother."

General

Youkai are a class of Japanese supernatural being, translated variously in English as "ghosts," "demons," "monsters," etc.

In Japanese, **Owner** is called *Taishou*, a term used to refer to the owners of traditional Japanese restaurants and inns. It generally means "boss" or "chief."

Spider in Japanese is *kumo*, and the character is referred to as such in Japanese. His full name, **Earth Spider**, is a translation of *tsuchigumo*, a youkai spider grown to gigantic size.

Butterfly in Japanese is *chou*, which is also the character's name in Japanese. His full name, **Incarnate Butterflies**, is a translation of *chou keshin*, a youkai consisting of butterflies merged with human souls.

Page 15

Written Japanese consists of three different systems known as **kanji** (Chinese ideograms), **hiragana** (an alphabet) and **katakana** (a different alphabet). In modern Japanese, the distinction among these written symbols is that *kanji* and *hiragana* used mostly for natively Japanese and Chinese words, while *katakana* is used for loanwords. However, this has not always been the case. Japan imported its writing system from China, and inherent differences in the languages made for inconsistencies. *Katakana* was invented by Buddhist monks in the ninth century as a way to read official and formal texts from China, and *hiragana* was originally "women's writing" before it eventually became the standard for written Japanese. Also, while it is common today to see *hiragana* and *katakana* in the same text, even that was once considered rare.

Page 36

The **I-novel** (known as *watakushi shousetsu* or *shishousetsu*) is a genre of literature that emerged in early twentieth century Japan. I-novels are typically semi-autobiographical confessionals or deeply revealing probes about the author's perspective on everyday life, and are often written from the first-person perspective (hence the "I" in I-novel).

Page 76

Equinoctial week occurs twice a year with the spring and autumnal equinoxes falling in the middle of the weeks. During this time, Buddhist memorial services are performed and it is custom for people to visit the graves of their ancestors to pray, tidy up the graves, and leave offerings.

Page 108

In Buddhism, **samadhi** is a state of total contemplation of the Absolute, where one is undisturbed by fear, desire, and other ego-driven emotions. It is the last of eight steps on the path to enlightenment.

Page 111

In Japan, nonrecyclable garbage is separated into two different types for disposal: **burnable trash** (which is sent to be incinerated) and nonburnable trash.

Page 122
Manjuu are a classic Japanese confection consisting of soft wheat bun on the outside and a sweet filling, most typically an *azuki* red bean paste, on the inside.

Page 142
Cherry Tree in Japanese is *sakura*, which refers to both the tree itself and its cherry blossoms. The *youkai*'s full name is *obake-zakura*, previously translated as Spirit Cherry Tree.

Page 175
Saejima's **final drink** is from a custom known as *matsugo-no-mizu* ("water of the last moment") in which relatives moisten a deceased person's lips with water immediately after death. In the old days, they used to do this just before a person was expected to die.

Page 183
Two riders, two number twos was originally a pun based on the fact that the Japanese term for riding double on a bicycle or motorcycle is *niketsu*, which also sounds like "two butts."

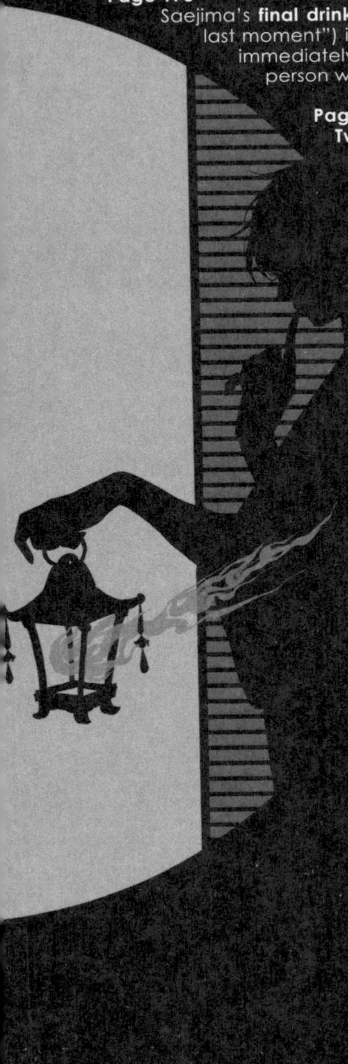

Phantom Tales of the Night

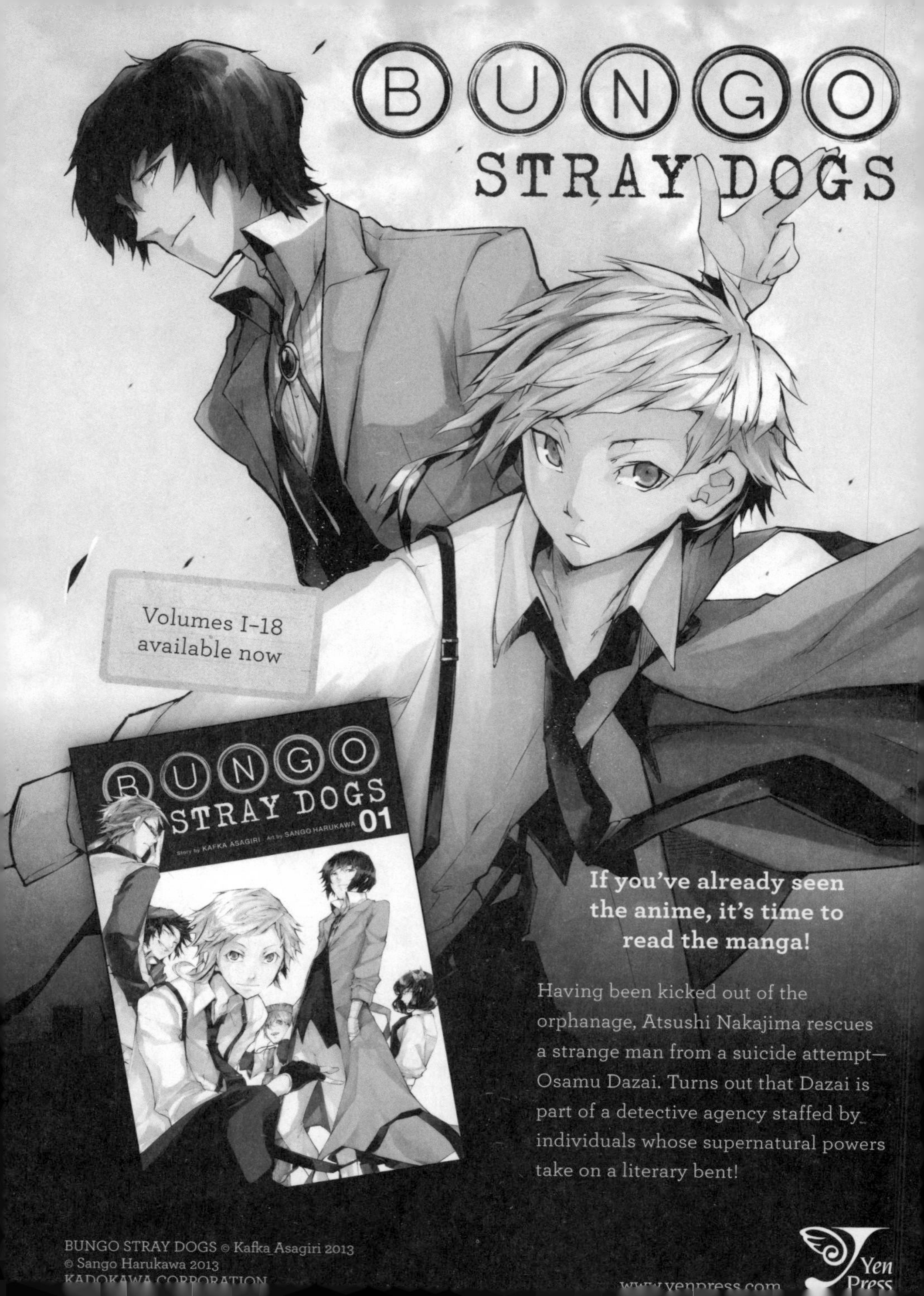
BUNGO STRAY DOGS
Volumes 1–18 available now
BUNGO STRAY DOGS 01
Story by KAFKA ASAGIRI Art by SANGO HARUKAWA
If you've already seen the anime, it's time to read the manga!
Having been kicked out of the orphanage, Atsushi Nakajima rescues a strange man from a suicide attempt—Osamu Dazai. Turns out that Dazai is part of a detective agency staffed by individuals whose supernatural powers take on a literary bent!
BUNGO STRAY DOGS © Kafka Asagiri 2013
© Sango Harukawa 2013
KADOKAWA CORPORATION
www.yenpress.com
Yen Press

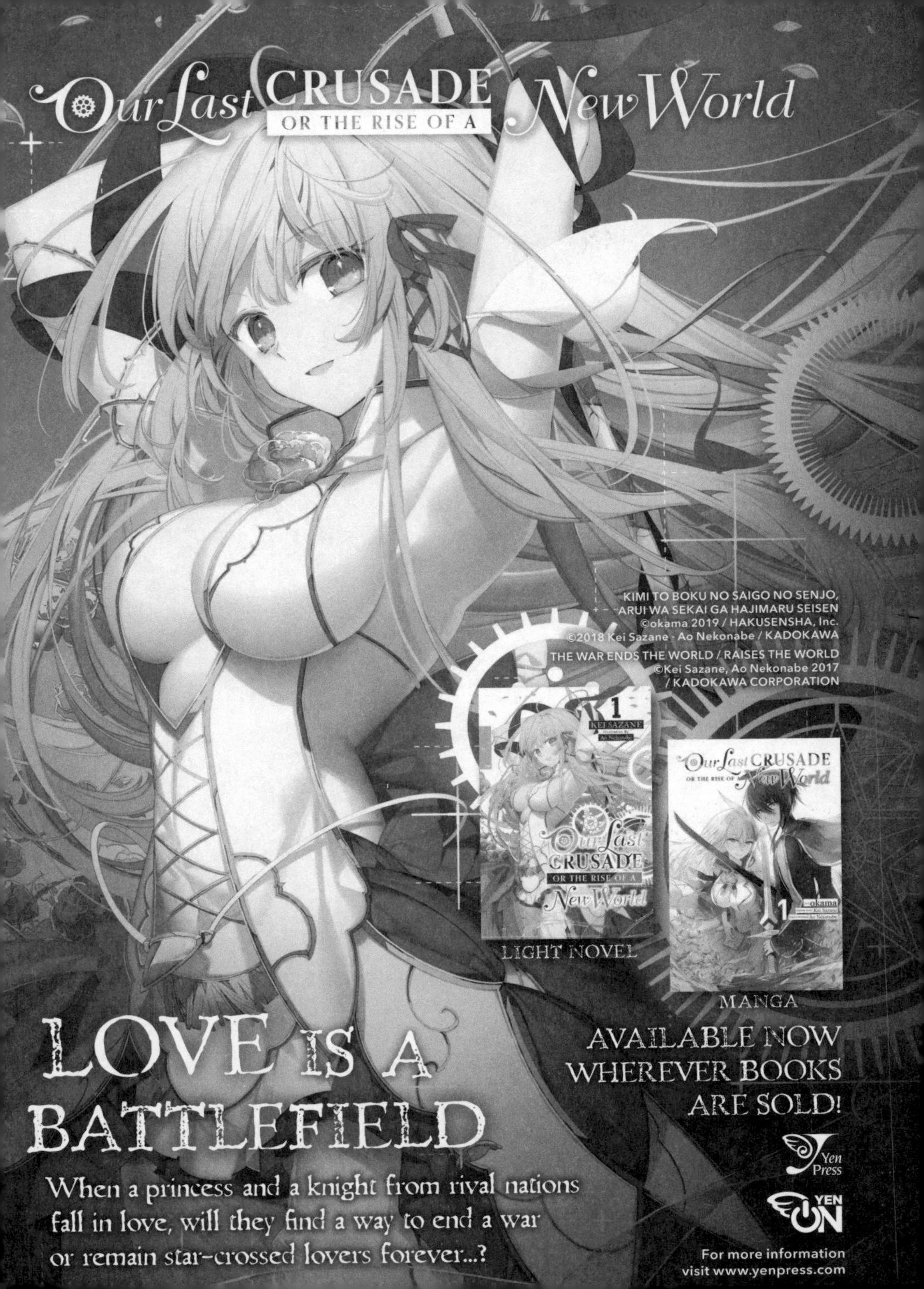
Our Last CRUSADE OR THE RISE OF A New World
KIMI TO BOKU NO SAIGO NO SENJO, ARUI WA SEKAI GA HAJIMARU SEISEN
©okama 2019 / HAKUSENSHA, Inc.
©2018 Kei Sazane · Ao Nekonabe / KADOKAWA
THE WAR ENDS THE WORLD / RAISES THE WORLD
©Kei Sazane, Ao Nekonabe 2017 / KADOKAWA CORPORATION
LIGHT NOVEL
MANGA
LOVE IS A BATTLEFIELD
AVAILABLE NOW WHEREVER BOOKS ARE SOLD!
When a princess and a knight from rival nations fall in love, will they find a way to end a war or remain star-crossed lovers forever...?
Yen Press
YEN ON
For more information visit www.yenpress.com

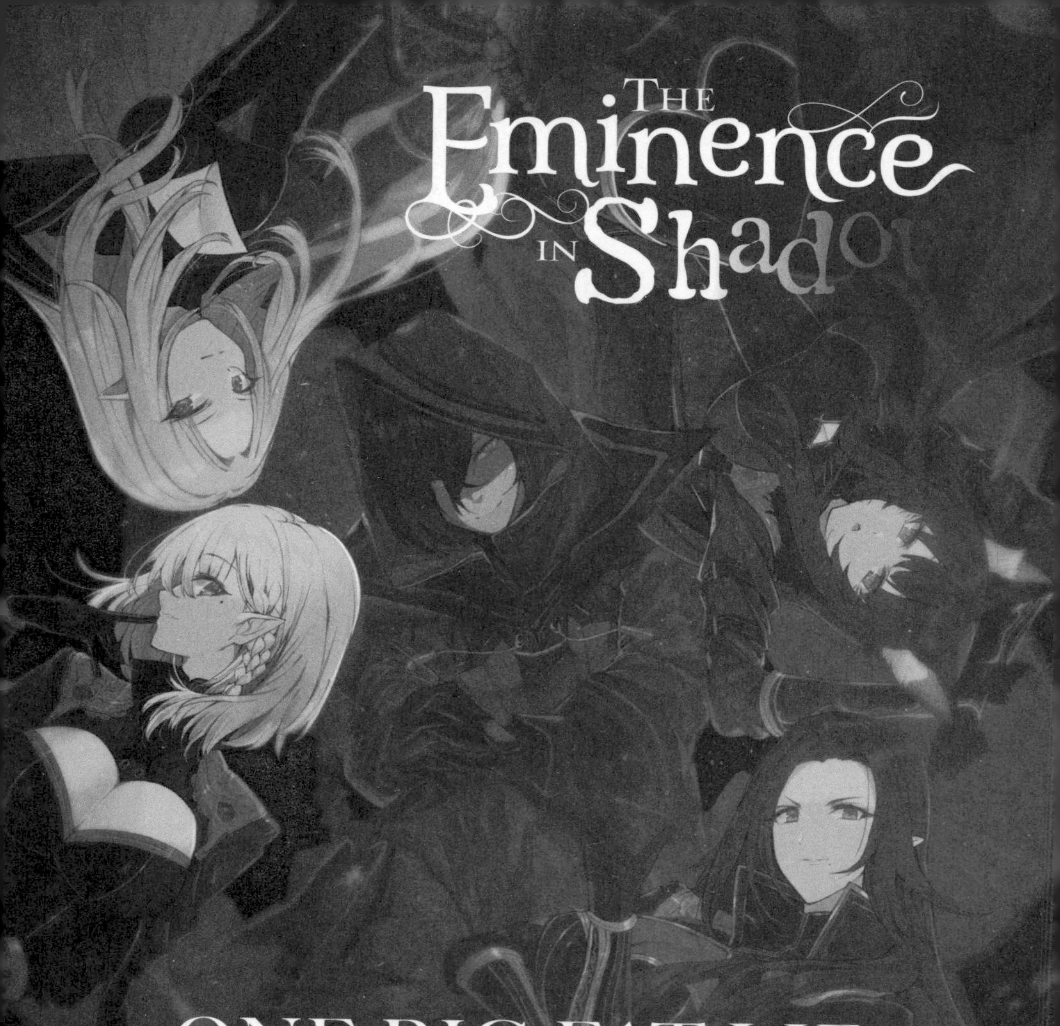
THE
Eminence
IN Shadow

COMBATANTS WILL BE DISPATCHED!

AVAILABLE WHEREVER BOOKS ARE SOLD!

LIGHT NOVEL
VOLUMES 1-5

MANGA
VOLUMES 1-4

Always bring a gun to a sword fight!

With world domination nearly in their grasp, the Supreme Leaders of the Kisaragi Corporation—an underground criminal group turned evil megacorp—have decided to try their hands at interstellar conquest. A quick dice roll nominates their chief operative, Combat Agent Six, to be the one to explore an alien planet...and the first thing he does when he gets there is change the sacred incantation for a holy ritual to the most embarrassing thing he can think of. But evil deeds are business as usual for Kisaragi operatives, so if Six wants a promotion and a raise, he'll have to work much harder than that! For starters, he'll have to do something about the other group of villains on the planet, who are calling themselves the "Demon Lord's Army" or whatever. After all, this world doesn't need two evil organizations!

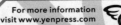

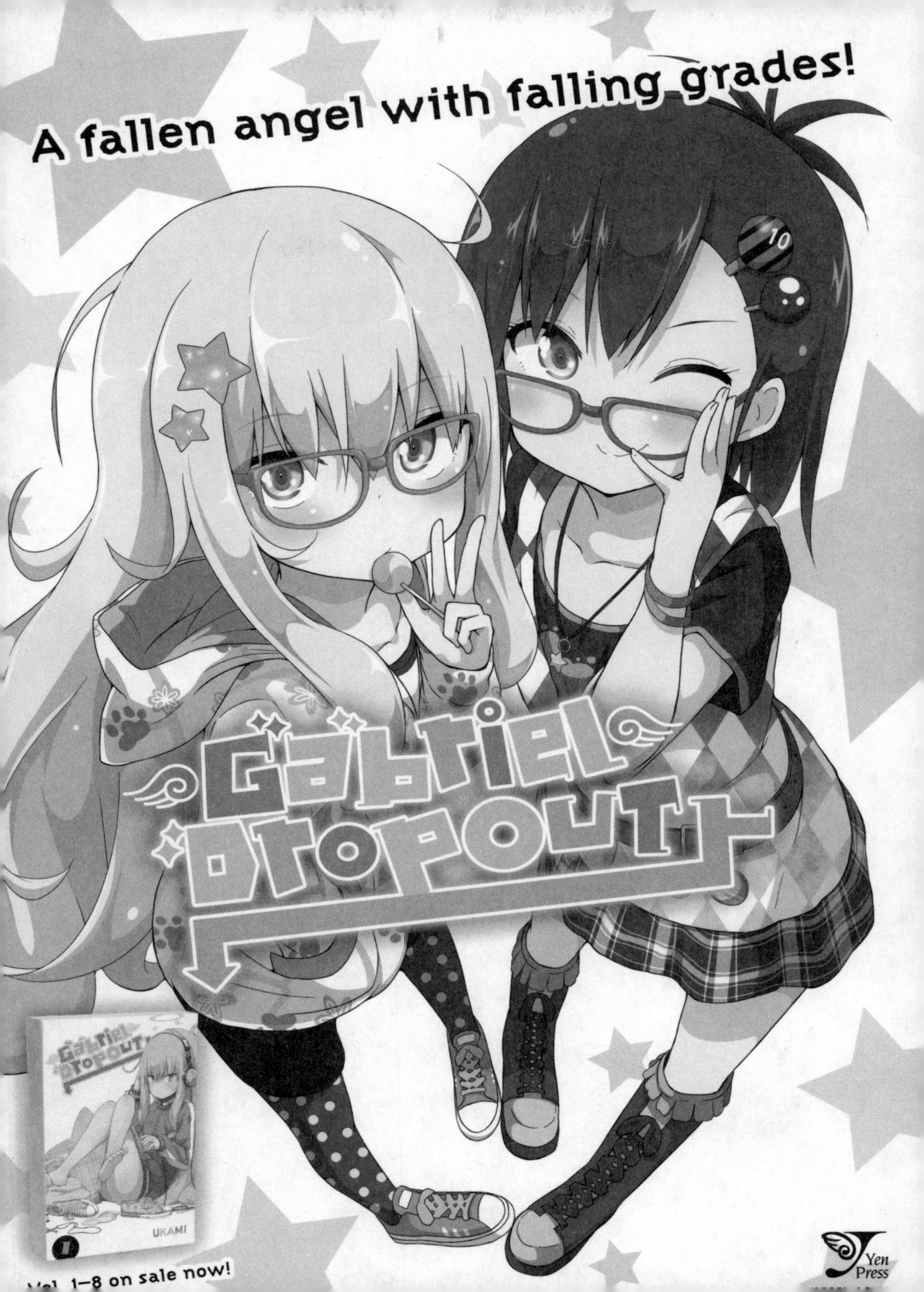
A fallen angel with falling grades!
Gabriel Dropout
UKAMI
Vol. 1–8 on sale now!
Yen Press

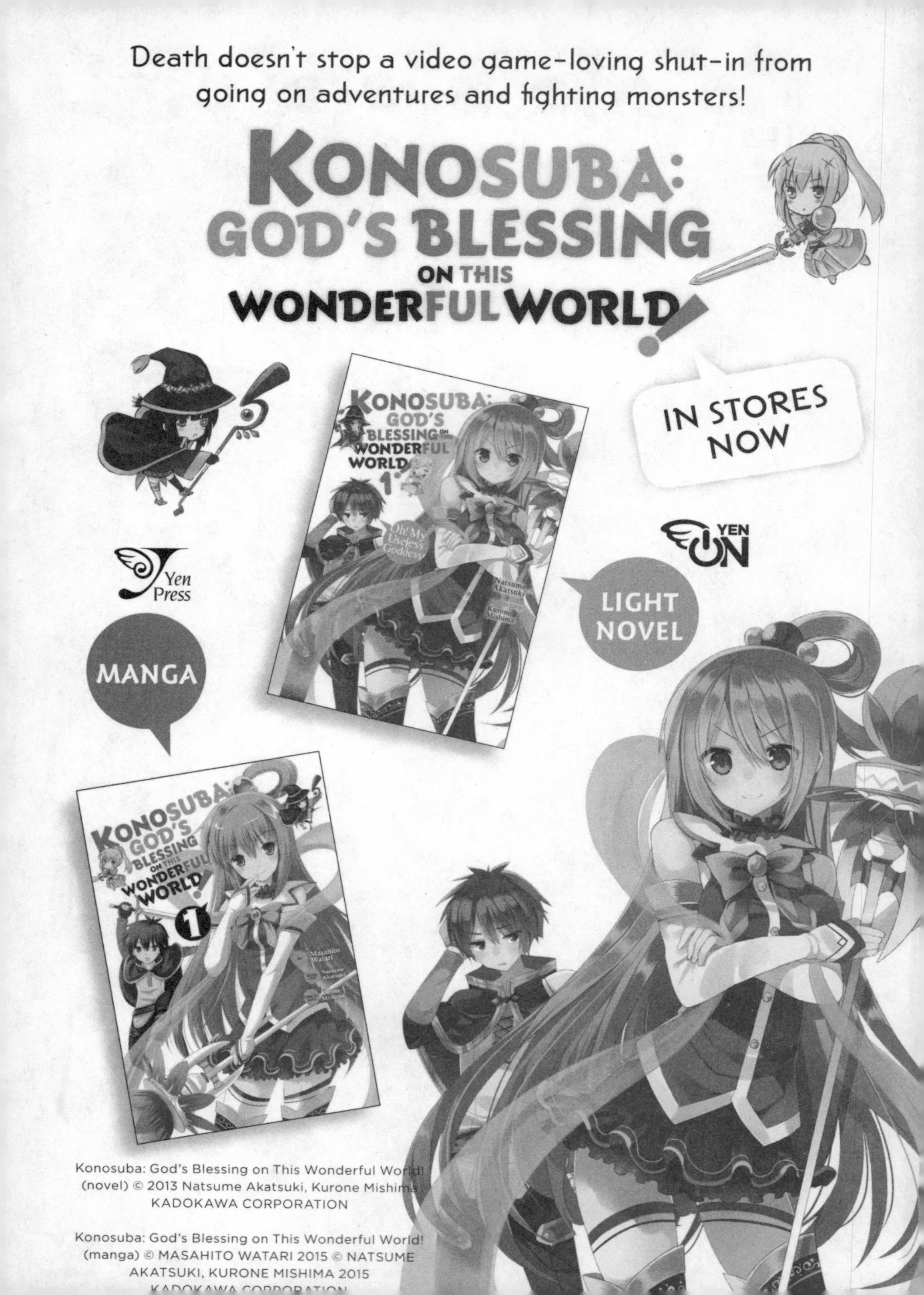
Death doesn't stop a video game-loving shut-in from going on adventures and fighting monsters!
KONOSUBA: GOD'S BLESSING ON THIS WONDERFUL WORLD!
IN STORES NOW
Yen Press
YEN ON
MANGA
LIGHT NOVEL
KONOSUBA: GOD'S BLESSING ON THIS WONDERFUL WORLD! 1
Oh! My Useless Goddess!
Natsume Akatsuki
Kurone Mishima
KONOSUBA: GOD'S BLESSING ON THIS WONDERFUL WORLD! 1
Masahito Watari
Natsume Akatsuki
Kurone Mishima
Konosuba: God's Blessing on This Wonderful World! (novel) © 2013 Natsume Akatsuki, Kurone Mishima KADOKAWA CORPORATION
Konosuba: God's Blessing on This Wonderful World! (manga) © MASAHITO WATARI 2015 © NATSUME AKATSUKI, KURONE MISHIMA 2015 KADOKAWA CORPORATION